Let's Take it From the Top!

Let's Take it From the Top!

a musical life odyssey

PETER JANSEN

LET'S TAKE IT FROM THE TOP
A Musical Life Odyssey

Copyright © Peter Jansen, 2022

All rights reserved. No part of this publication may be reproduced, stored in a retrieval system, or transmitted in any form or by any means, electronic, mechanical, photocopying, recording, or otherwise, without written permission of the author and publisher.

Published by Peter Jansen, Edmonton, Canada

www.peterandmary.net

ISBN:
                Paperback (colour)   978-1-77354-406-9
        Paperback (black & white)   978-1-77354-435-9

Publication assistance by

PageMaster.ca

*For Mary
without whom
most of this book
could never have happened*

Programme

Overture 1
Prologue 3
Act One 5

    EARLY DAYS 7
    THE "CHERRYPIPS" (first Skiffle Group) 21
    THE "TRAVELLERS" (pop/rock) 23
    THE "JAZZ GENTLEMEN" 24
    "COME AGAIN" and "FREE AS AIR" 51

ACT TWO *57*

    "BAND SEVEN" / "MANISH BOYS" 59
    "THE PEEJAY SOUND SYSTEM" 71
    "THE AFTER THREE" 71
    "PETER, JAN, AND JON" 76

ACT THREE *91*

    "THE GIACONDA YEARS" 92
    "WESTMINSTER CITY SOUND" 109
    "PETER & ELISABETH" 111
    "SWINGING LONDON" 123

ACT FOUR *133*

    "THE ZEPHYRS" and GERMANY 134
    "LONDON COUNTRY" 151
    SUE THOMPSON TOUR 152
    VICEROY HOTEL, LONDON 153
    LEE BINDER TRIO 153
    SERPENTINE RESTAURANT, HYDE PARK 160
    PETER JANSEN FOUR 161

ACT FIVE *165*

    THE BERMUDA YEARS 167
    MARY ARRIVES 181

ACT SIX *193*

    "PETER & MARY" – AT LAST! 195
    "MONTE TOLEDO" 195
    ATLANTIC CANADA TOUR 199
    "ALEXANDR PUSHKIN" 211
    REMZI'S 212
        MOLLY'S 226
        THE "ROYAL YORK" 227
    WEST TO THE ROCKIES 229
    COUNTRY MUSIC TOURS – BRITAIN 240

ACT SEVEN *253*

    RESORTS (East & West) 255
        BANFF PARK LODGE 255
        JASPER PARK LODGE 256
        CHATEAU LAKE LOUISE 265
        THE BANFF SPRINGS 271
        FAIRMONT HOT SPRINGS 272
        MINAKI LODGE 274
        THE ALGONQUIN 275
        NEWFOUNDLAND 279
        FREDERICTON 283
        HARRISON HOT SPRINGS 286
        "THE GRENADINES" 290
    THE "LOVE BOAT" 295
    A BERMUDA WEDDING 299
    CANADIAN HUNGER FOUNDATION CONCERTS 303
    "EARTH DAY" FESTIVAL 306
    THE KENYA PROJECT 320

ACT EIGHT ***335***

- SCHOOLS (fun and learning)...337
- SANTA CLAUS PARADES 341
- A "DAY OUT WITH THOMAS"..343
- FESTIVALS, FAIRS, FORT EDMONTON, and more… 349
    - HEADING WEST…...358
    - "KLONDIKE DAYS"..363
    - HERITAGE FESTIVAL..367
    - FORT EDMONTON PARK..368
    - UKRAINIAN CULTURAL HERITAGE VILLAGE...........................375
    - FORT CALGARY..378
    - TELETHONS..379
    - MUTTART CONSERVATORY 387
- VENTRILOQUISM & LAUGHTER...399
- SOUTHERN TOURS: ARIZONA, CALIFORNIA, and LAS VEGAS........403
- FULL CIRCLE..425

EPILOGUE ***429***

- RANDOM THOUGHTS...430
- SELECTED WRITINGS BY PETER..433
- Acknowledgements 447
- Suggested Reading..448
- RECORDINGS 450

*At U.S.A.F.
Chateauroux, France, 1966
Photo: David Ames A.F.N. Radio*

Overture

It is late in January 2018, and we are sitting outside our trailer looking at shadowy patterns on the mountains caused by the rays of an early morning sun. We are parked in Desert Edge, just by Palm Springs, California. This is currently the warmest bit of the whole U.S. and Canada, and Mary, Jenny the dog, and I are clinging on to it for dear life, as are several others. Temperatures reach the 80°s and even 90°s daily, though can drop by as much as 40° at night. We have hummingbirds visiting the orange flowered bushes close by, and even our own personal road runner, who checks on us every few hours in case there is something interesting to eat.

    This is the first actual break we have ever taken from our musical endeavours, where we go to a place for a little while with no set plans, and then move on to one or two others. Every day for so many years has been scheduled with calls, appointments, meetings etc., to say nothing of thousands of performances, that we really wondered for the first few weeks if slowing down was remotely to be a possibility. We have a busy Easter and spring coming up but are starting to get used to the slower pace for now, which seems like a good opportunity to catch up on events so far, as I remember them. This should be explained. When I was younger, say about thirteen, I witnessed a collision between a motorbike and a car, as did ten other people. We all gave slightly different interpretations of the event, yet each one of us was totally convinced of the accuracy of our account. The policeman who interviewed us explained that in all likelihood not one of us saw everything, and how the human brain automatically fills in the gaps between any bits that were actually seen, rather like some computer programmes nowadays. His job was to take all eleven accounts and decide what really took place; a conversation which I never forgot.

So, the outcome is, that if you are being kind enough to read my musings, and think "no, that's not quite how it was", just realize that we all may have slightly different recollections, and possibly yours are too.

So here goes.......

My parents' wedding

My first publicity shot, with sister Anne

Prologue

Everyone has a first memory. I think mine is lying in a pram under the small verandah at the back of our house in Buckinghamshire, England, and somebody, probably my dad, putting his head over the edge and saying "boo!". Then we jump a couple of years to wartime, and me raising the blackout blinds on my bedroom windows, once lights were off, to watch searchlights sweep the skies. I was tiny, and had no idea of what was going on, but I knew the sounds of the aircraft engines, and was aware that some were "different". My dad was on civil defence duty at this time, after a long spell as a pilot, testing the first rotary engine Avros for the Fleet Air Arm, and subsequently Tiger Moths, for the newly formed R.A.F.

If he was called out because of a possible air raid, my mother, sister and myself had to be ensconced safely in "bed" below the huge oak table, which, coincidentally, is where I often read comics or did homework in later years, whilst still young enough to think of it as my "safe" place.

"The Travellers"
Jock Law, me, Sheila Baker, Norman Hoskins

Later line-up
Me, Jock Law, Peter Marriott, Paul Rodriguez,
In front: Trudy Wise

Act One

Early Days

The "Cherrypips"

The "Travellers"
sometimes called the "Mayfair Set" Dance Band

The "Jazz Gentlemen"

"Come Again" and "Free as Air"

Our First T.V. show. Peter Matthews, Me, Terry Winter, Norman Hoskins, Sheila Baker, Paul Rodriguez (behind), Jimmy Strike, Brian Jenner, Brian Millen. Photo: Peter W. Dickenson, Southampton.

At U.S. Naval Air Station, West Malling. Paul Rodriguez, Jock Law, Jimmy Strike, Me, (Sheila behind), Brian Jenner, (Norman Hoskins behind), Johnny Martin, Brian Millen.

Outdoor event: Roy Gill, Paul Rodriguez, Me, Don Mason, Brian Millen, Roger Eley, Jimmy Strike, Brian Weller. Photo: Kent Messenger

*I*t should have been so simple. You're born; there's a few years getting used to the world around you, then school, maybe further education, job, marriage, house, two point four kids, two or three weeks annual vacation, maybe different, maybe the same place. Retire, possibly travel a bit, or stay home. I heard the sound of a different drum, and no, that's not exactly how things went....

EARLY DAYS

*M*y parents were both musical, so I suppose it's genetic with me. They were both pianists, although I cannot remember hearing my mother play. She reached the level of L.R.A.M., (Licentiate of the Royal Academy of Music), for which there were heavy exams, and also ran the local girl guide troop, when not involved in the challenging job of raising me. My dad played by ear, and if he heard a tune he liked on the radio or T.V., he would immediately head to the piano and play it.

His two favourite pieces were Irving Berlin's "Easter Parade", and the signature tune from a popular (and very gentle) T.V. police drama of the time called "Dixon of Dock Green", with Jack Warner. His style of playing was similar to a well-known radio musician called Charlie Kunz – sort of a mixture of ragtime and stride piano.

They were both children of what in the Anglican Church is called a vicar, and the two families were relatively close geographically. My dad's father was vicar of a small parish called Newton Solney, near Burton upon Trent, in Staffordshire, for the amazing tenure of 56 years! Every time the Archbishop of Canterbury suggested moving him to a new "living" (on which matter one didn't really have a choice), the villagers would set up a petition saying in effect "Hands off our vicar!". After this happened a couple of times the archbishop, (who was Geoffrey Fisher at the time and a family friend), got the message.

I remember my grandfather only as a very vague fuzz, but a few weeks back I was given some newspaper tributes from when he passed; I don't think I have ever seen such heartfelt comments regarding a member of any community. He used to spend much time in his study, writing incredibly well-researched letters to the Times, all of which were published, on a multitude of topics, and his opinions were highly respected, regardless of whether one agreed with him or not.

My mother's father I knew better, he was outgoing and popular, and at the time my parents met he was the vicar of Repton, in Derbyshire, where my mum went to school, before he was transferred to Worthing, on the south coast, a while later. Again, there was music in both families: my mother had a sister Rosamund, (Roz), who was an opera singer, and my father had a sister Kathleen, who taught piano and theory until the day she died, with pupils in several parts of the country over the years. At one time she had five students in the National Youth Orchestra, and one of her "star" pupils, Leon Coates, (son or nephew of Eric, composer of the "Dam Busters" March, "London Landmark Suite" and many other pieces) – in addition to being a world-class organist - went on to be "Master of the Queen's Music" for Queen Juliana, in the Netherlands. I remember him well.

A radio personality of the time, and later T.V., was Ted Moult, from "What's my line?". His daughter took weekly lessons from Auntie Kathleen, and Ted always brought the kind gift of a beautiful large authentic Bakewell tart from his home town, which I can still taste as this is being written.

One of the biggest things I think that my two grandfathers had in common was their innate fear of the summer fête in their respective parishes, where they would be called upon to be a part of the judging of a "beautiful baby" contest – an event that would rightly be unthinkable nowadays, although knobbly knees contests are still permissible!

Back to music. When my father was testing the Tiger Moth aircraft during World War II, they were obviously rolling them off the production line as fast as they could, then the test pilots would take them up to see what was wrong with them! The inevitable eventually happened, and one of my father's charges came down in rather a hurry. He was physically O.K., but probably suffered from what we now call P.T.S.D., at any rate, he never flew again. However, at the time Malcolm Sargent, (later to be given a knighthood for his musical endeavours), was in charge of the band on the airbase, in addition to his incredible skills as a classical pianist, and he and my dad got a double act together. First Malcolm would play something – brilliantly – then my father would come on saying "no – no, that's not how it goes," (or words to that effect, I wasn't there), and proceed by ear to reproduce the piece, jazzed up and swung in a Charlie Kunz style. My dad also loved doing musical monologues ("The Lion and Albert", the "11.69", and many more), so I can only imagine the probability of his doing these, with an oh so tasteful piano accompaniment.

So, you see, not going into music was not actually an option.

Life as a separate entity started in hospital at a town called Aylesbury, famous for white ducks, but the first few years were spent in Brook Cottage, with a stream one side, in a peaceful village called Little Kimble – surprisingly, right next to another peaceful village called Great Kimble. I went to playschool/kindergarten close by at the age of four, (to be dealt with later in the story), and my only other vivid memory was of a fifth birthday party at the house, where a game of hide and seek was instigated, probably by my mother. I knew nothing about Charlie Brown at the time, but there was a little red-haired girl at this party too, called Anna Thomas, and we both went together and hid under the huge rhubarb leaves in the back garden for a long time, until we decided we'd better join the party again, or we'd miss out on the jelly, cake and blancmange rabbit!

Three or four days later, my parents left the house forever, and we moved from Buckinghamshire to a town called Maidstone, roughly halfway between London and the south coast. I still recollect clearly pulling in front of the house, where there was a boy of my age on a tiny little light blue bicycle watching us arrive, of whom we will hear more.

The first actual "performance" took place the following Christmas. The boy on the bike had now become a neighbour by the name of Martin, and an inseparable friend. We put a cardboard box on its side, cut a hole in the top, and jiggled around several cut-out figures suspended on lengths of cotton, while an old wind-up gramophone provided the necessary accompaniment. I believe my parents and sister applauded, together with two visiting aunts, but that may be wishful thinking on my part. We did two performances, one in each house, and the seed was sown.

Now there was no stopping!

The next few years were spent doing fairly normal little boy things: school, games, wolf cubs, climbing trees, etc. Martin and I attended the same school, so we walked to and from school together, occasionally climbing over the fence of a truly magical place, called "The Dell", which was an old, discarded quarry, with house nearby, now exploding with trees, wildflowers, ferns and many birds. Sometimes we were chased out, but usually we were furtive enough to avoid being seen and would stay as long as we could.

In wintertime, if we were fortunate enough to have snow, the two of us were to be seen on toboggans, dodging occasional cars, and haring at breakneck speed down the hill of Cornwallis Road, opposite our homes, or down the white slopes of yet another old quarry, which was on the golf course behind.

During this time period, Martin was given a couple of marionettes and a puppet theatre made by his grandfather, who was a talented woodworker, while I was given an amazing box of tricks! That did it, within months we were putting on a variety show, with singing, comedy, magic, and puppets, to parents and anyone else who could be persuaded to listen. There was a fair-sized room on the ground floor of our house that was rapidly converted into a permanent theatre. The aforementioned table, with a couple of extra leaves, became the stage, and we put up no less than three rows of workable old curtains, two rows for drawing as needed, and one as a permanent backdrop. Behind the stage was a bow window, which when closed off made a perfect changing area, and we had a huge flashlight fixed to the picture rail at the far end of the room, with a system of thin ropes and pulleys which meant that the "spotlight" could be manipulated at will from behind the stage. Three levels of seating completed the auditorium, comprising ten seats in all. If there was an unusually full house, extra seats could be borrowed from the dining room. The table was covered with cloth for protection, and also the front of the table, so that it became impossible to see backstage.

To me this room was heaven, and both Martin and I spent many hours and days here, refining our latest productions. Sometimes I would go downstairs during the night to sleep here; yes, there was a mattress under the table again, but fortunately no bombs to disturb the tranquility of this so special place.

By now I had started writing rhyming pieces to introduce or close the shows, spoken together or conversationally, possibly related to my father's monologue pieces, but there was no music to them - yet.

The front of our house had a large hedge growing up it, which was neatly trimmed around the windows, and had wires behind to safely anchor it to the building. But the main delight of this hedge to two small boys was the appearance of a beautiful hedgehog, who came into the garden one spring to make her nest underneath and raise her babies in safety. She would come around onto the back lawn every night and was soon tame. In those days, the milk that appeared on the back step every morning was natural and not pasteurized, and there was always plenty for our resident hedgehog, especially when her two babies were born. We watched them getting bigger in the nest, and probably the ultimate evening of my young life was the first time that she brought the two baby hedgehogs proudly round onto the back lawn in the moonlight to be officially introduced. We had a reasonably large garden, which was pie-shaped, and much bigger in the back, but once the babies were grown, they would all disappear, leaving until the following year, when she would return to start her new family.

Not all of our "productions" were indoors by any means. On one occasion, Martin and I held a "circus" in the back garden, which I still recall fondly as "The circus in one's head!" Martin rode around the edge of the lawn on his little bike, taking his hands off the handlebars at one point. Our family's pet rabbit Patches came onto the grass, and ate a few Brussels sprout leaves, also we did a couple of magic tricks and sang a song, plus I believe I "emceed" as ringmaster. Not much to look at you may think, but in our minds, we were in a huge Big Top, with thousands of people cheering, bright spotlights and a thirty-piece orchestra. The adrenaline was colossal! In fact, our two mothers watched this together, with no idea of the event they were actually witnessing!

One spring we held an "exhibition" in Martin's garage (even to the extent of stopping passers-by in the street to raise money). Out came a toy fort, dinky toys, Patches, Martin's new bike (with a dynamo no less), newts, tadpoles, terrapins, a lithograph of Queen Victoria, some paintings, and the cat, Martin's, who also proudly had a bullet on show, that had been removed from his grandfather's shoulder without anaesthetic during the Great War, and was now a much prized item, while I had the tail plane of an incendiary bomb that had fallen on our house in Buckinghamshire during World War II. Fortunately, although the detonator went off, the bomb did not explode properly, and the resultant fire was easily put out with a few buckets of water, although there was damage to my sister's room. We were away for the weekend, and it must have been a shock to return and find the house had been hit.

We made over two pounds that day, and took the money to the Pilgrim's Way Seniors' lodge at the other end of Bower Mount Road, where we both lived. We were introduced to some of the residents, and I can still remember how much this small gesture meant to them; a humbling experience, of which there would be many more to come.

A bit more on "Patches", who meant so much to my younger life. My sister went to a boarding "farmhouse school", (Mayortorne Manor, in Buckinghamshire), thus learning farming and agriculture, in addition to normal classes, and brought "Patches" home at the end of one term. I'm not sure how old I was, but remember being ill in bed at the time, and the appearance of this little rabbit was the most exciting thing that could possibly be imagined. "Patches" went back with my sister for several of her school years, then later became a permanent resident at our house. She lived in what had once been a hen house outdoors as a nighttime "hutch", and when my dad got up in the morning, the first order of the day was to open "Patches" little door, at which point she would first tear around the garden at great speed, with several leaps in the air. Then she would come indoors, and I would hear the "thump, thump" of back legs on the stairs as she came up to my room, when she would jump onto the bed, and immediately burrow down beside me to the bottom. What a way to start the day for both of us! She was free all the time, mostly outdoors, where we had loads of fruit and vegetables, and she would usually eat the lower leaves of the Brussels sprouts, which were her very favourite. Lettuce was never touched, and I have yet to see a rabbit that likes it. It is thought to have a soporific effect, while cabbage, dandelion leaves, or carrot tops, (as opposed to the carrot itself), are vastly preferred.

In winter, the hen house could just be squeezed in through the kitchen door, where it was nice and warm, and in summer, our French doors would be left open, so that she could come and go at will, never leaving a calling card when she came inside. She had several litters in her younger years, living to the age of 14, and was a huge loss to all when no longer with us. Quite a large rabbit, she made sure the garden was always "cat free", and therefore there were many songbirds in the trees around.

She never went under the front gate, but remained mostly in the back amongst the vegetables, munching clover contentedly on the lawn, or sleeping in the sun under her favourite peach tree, where she rests to this day; never to be forgotten.

Our house was called "Kitscot" after Kits Coty House, an ancient site a few miles away, of the same vintage as Stonehenge, but considerably smaller, which in my childhood days was hidden by trees, and an unbelievably amazing discovery, especially on first encounter. So, the room with the table became "Kitscot Private Theatre" a name which stuck (as KPT Productions) on posters and calling cards for many years and may in fact still be registered with the Board of Trade to this day.

KPT Productions did a total of twenty-five variety shows, with various casts. Some were held in the little theatre at home, some at the Methodist Church Hall, and some at Boughton Monchelsea Hall. We wrote our own sketches, and own rhyming pieces, also Martin and I created a magic act called "The Magicalis", which did one or two guest spots in the area, occasionally with a sub. for Martin while he was away at school. The little theatre showed silent movies and stills, (on a sheet at the back of the stage), plus another school friend, Geoffrey Bond and I created a quiz show called "Quick with the Wits", that went out to occasional local halls, in addition to sometimes having a shortened version in our variety productions.

Geoff's parents moved to London, so he went to a sister school, Emmanuel, but we still got together on school holidays; especially in the summer. Geoff had an aunt, Margaret Hinxman, who wrote and reviewed movies for the magazine "Picturegoer". We were both movie buffs, or thought we were, and would see a new movie nearly every day, sometimes passing on our own review, which on occasion was published. No, we didn't get a by-line, but we didn't care, we were in print!

There was a comedian named Wilfred Pickles, who had a very popular national radio show called, "Have a go!" – with his wife Mabel at the piano. I dutifully showed up at the theatre, along with many other hopefuls, on transmission night, when the show came to our town. I was not picked, but again didn't care, I had experienced my first brush with stardom!

There is definitely an "aside" that needs to slip in at this point in the story. The back garden of my childhood home contained what had once been an old London Hansom cab. Now bereft of wheels, it stood sideways against the garden fence. At some time, a previous resident had skilfully built another seat to face the existing seat, and a back and sides with one door in the middle, Hansom cabs being normally open to the elements, so that the unit could be completely closed in, and waterproof in all weathers. I believe it had been the residence of chickens at some point, as the centre panel of the door could be removed to reveal chicken wire. However, when we moved to this house the coach was immaculate, inside and out, gold with dark blue velvet padding, and a small window behind the original seat. This was the headquarters of many hundreds of outdoor games between Martin and me. It frequently became a stagecoach in the Old West, and for a while we called it "Sparrows Hut," (for the life of me I don't remember why). When there was all the hoopla surrounding the Coronation, it even became Sandringham, which was and is a retreat for the Royals when they need to escape and be a normal family for a while.

But the key game was "The Professor and the Inventor", with yours truly as the former. As with most childhood games, this one also took place "in one's head"; if I said, "I profess" something, then it was so, and if Martin said, "I have invented" an item, then this was so as well, regardless of the plausibility of the item "just invented". Would that life could be so simple, but in the minds of two small children, it was, and we spent countless hours in bliss, with the coach as our house, plus occasionally a bottle of Tizer, and a "Classics Illustrated" or a "Superman" comic, if we needed serious reading. There was great excitement with the appearance of the very first 3-D comic, which I have to this day. On one occasion my sister's army tent was put on the lawn, with U.S. printed on each side, which we naturally assumed to be U.S. army. Then it rained, and we discovered that U.S. meant something else entirely, i.e., UnServiceable.

There are many types of comedy one sees in daily life. I was introduced to situation comedy in a very real way when, at, the age of about 7, our family and a couple of aunts drove off to Tunbridge Wells, where there is a beautiful 17th century arcade called the Pantiles, with an old teahouse, now sadly defunct, called Binn's, who were famous for their delicious and very gooey cream cakes.

Cakes in those days were served by putting large plates full of cakes in the middle of the tables, when customers would pay for what had been consumed, which of course encouraged one to take more, as they were sitting right in front of you. The table wasn't really big enough for all of us, so my dad took one of the plates of cakes and put it on a chair by the next table. At which point, you are now ahead of me, and rightly so. The door opened, and in came two larger ladies, who came over and sat at the adjacent table, completely unaware of what one of them had just done.

When my dad saw what had happened, he almost totally lost it, and we all left Binn's as fast as we could, spluttering in mirth, while my dad somewhat abashedly, stayed back to pay the bill and no doubt offer some restitution regarding cleaning, and possibly a broken plate.

One day in the fall I remember walking home from school in the rain, kicking the leaves as young boys do, and finding a somewhat damp page from a travel magazine showing a picture of Banff, in the Canadian Rockies, with the now famous view looking down Banff Avenue, and a snow-capped Cascade Mountain behind. I kept this page for many years, resolving deep down inside that it would be an unbelievable dream to see this amazing sight. In the distant future, I was to visit so many times, both to perform music in the huge resort hotels, or to relax in the quiet majesty of the Rocky Mountains, yet I would always think of finding that piece of paper, as a small boy.

Martin's home was next to mine, except there was a gap between for a future road, (still never built). My bedroom window faced his landing window, so that one of our more creative endeavours was to have a tin can at each, with a length of thin string from one to the other for instant communication. How much more fun this was than a smart phone, and at no cost to anyone.

One summer, when I was about nine or ten, I was on holiday with my parents, sister, and two aunts, either in Eastbourne or Folkestone, on the south coast. I had gone off and left them on the beach, probably in search of an ice cream. There was a band in the bandshell close by, and I wandered over to have a look. It was maybe a ten-piece, "Johnny O'Rourke and his Orchestra", and was doing show tunes. But more to the point, there was a sign announcing a Children's Talent Contest at that very minute. A lady, who could have been the band's singer, came over and asked if I wanted to enter, so, I took a deep breath, having never been on a stage, just the table, went up and did one of the songs I had done in a "Kitscot Private Theatre" show, backed by some of the band, at the same time messing about, which included unintentionally tying the band leader up in mic. cable, to everyone's amusement. I finished the song and got off the stage, only to find I was being called back up, as I had won, and was given £2, the most money I had ever had in my life, and proudly ran back to show my folks.

The first musical endeavour that I heard "live" apart from this, and "End of the Pier" theatre shows each summer, such as "Twinkle", (Clarkson Rose and Olive Fox), also "Dazzle", (impresario Eric Ross), or the annual Christmas pantomime, all of which I of course enjoyed immensely, was Stanley Dale's National Skiffle contest, based on the music of "rent" parties in Chicago during the depression. I was now twelve, but could still tell that the competing groups during the first half were not so hot; some had instruments that were vaguely in tune from when they had left the shop; some definitely didn't. The second half, however, was on another planet, with a group called "the Vipers" positively blowing the lid off the theatre. The Vipers were originally formed in a London coffee bar known as "The Bread Basket". During one annual Soho fair they were invited to play in the famed 2I's coffee bar, where they were heard one night by a young George Martin, (yes, that one), who produced and recorded several hit singles with them. They also secured a two-week variety run at the Prince of Wales Theatre; to this day, the only amateur group to ever receive such an honour.

Line-up comprised Wally Whyton, Hank Marvin, Johnny Martyn, (guitars and vocals), Jet Harris, (bass), and John Pilgrim (washboard). Wally went on to be a hugely popular Children's T.V. performer, while Hank and Jet became part of the "Drifters", (later renamed "The Shadows"), who were put together to back up newcomer Cliff Richard on records and tours, and subsequently became stars in their own right, as the most successful British instrumental group ever. But I had yet to hear the music of Lonnie Donegan.

I think it fair to say that July 13th, 1954, was the single most pivotal day in the history of British popular music, and to most of us it means nothing. At this time traditional New Orleans jazz was just starting to get recognized in Britain, the trend probably instigated by trumpeter/clarinettist Humphrey Lyttleton, closely followed by trumpeter Ken Colyer and trombonist Chris Barber, who worked together for some time before each having their own bands. The British music scene was, at its best, a little sleepy, with ballad singers such as Dickie Valentine and David Whitfield topping the charts, or the ladies represented by Ruby Murray, Anne Shelton, or the effervescent Alma Cogan, my favourite, who was Britain's number 1 singer for several years.

All fine artists, but what the youth of the country needed was way more energy than that, so it is hardly surprising that the jazz scene or "Trad" as it came to be called, exploded in the minds of young people in the way that it did. At some point of each evening, both Ken and Chris would come forward with a guitar, (or in Chris's case, a double bass), maybe another guitar, a washboard, or other kitchen utensils, as in the case of the City Ramblers, and perform American folk songs written by Leadbelly or Woody Guthrie, but still in the style of New Orleans Jazz. In the case of Chris Barber, his folk or "skiffle" group was fronted by the band's tenor banjo player, Lonnie Donegan, and this part of the show grew more and more popular.

On the aforementioned date in 1954, Chris, Lonnie, and washboard virtuoso, (yes, it is possible!) Beryl Bryden went into a London studio and put down a version of "Rock Island Line", starting the song very slowly and building to a frenzy by the end. That did it, popular music was never the same again.

Lonnie became huge, as big in Britain as the Beatles would be later; in fact, the Beatles, Elton John, and pretty well all the stars to follow, say they would never have started in music, had they not heard Lonnie. I saw him perform several times, initially with Micky Ashman, (bassist from the Barber band), then Peter Huggett. J. Nick Nicholls was on drums, (who had a spring from a car seat on his hi-hat – our drummer in later years could hardly close it), and Denny Wright, Jimmy Currie, and Les Bennetts on lead guitar at different times.

I first saw Lonnie at the Granada Theatre in Maidstone, where I was blown away by the band's energy, then went with a friend to the "New Musical Express" Poll-winner's concert at Wembley – a great performance, which also included the final set from 21-year-old Eddie Cochran, who was tragically to die en route to Heathrow airport a few weeks later.

But the ultimate performance was to a packed house at London's Royal Albert Hall, where I was three seats from front and centre, and had never seen anything like it, such incredible energy pouring off the stage, and all over the thousands who were lucky enough to be there.

I still have an L.P. of his, which, while not his best, has Elton John, Albert Lee, Ringo Starr, Brian May, Leo Sayer, Michele Phillips, Rory Gallagher, Zoot Money, Ronnie Wood and many others, all eager for a chance to play with and pay tribute to Lonnie; the album produced by Adam Faith.

A few years later, I had the privilege to share a few cups of tea and a quiet chat with Lonnie in the musicians' coffee bar "La Giaconda" in Denmark Street, London, a memory which I will always treasure.

Like so many musicians in the U.K., the first time I heard Lonnie, I had to have a guitar as soon as possible, and one Christmas, following my thirteenth birthday, there was an acoustic guitar waiting for me at the breakfast table. There was no truss rod, and the playing action was a bit high, but I practiced every day until my fingers would let me play no more – yes, of course, with the songs of Leadbelly, Woody Guthrie, Cisco Houston and others.

THE "CHERRYPIPS" (FIRST SKIFFLE GROUP)

Within a short time, I had a skiffle group together, called the "Cherrypips". Martin had gone away to a boarding school at Sevenoaks, while I was at Sutton Valence, nearer to home. A close friend of mine from primary school, Philip Charlton, had for a short while a girlfriend named Cherry, hence the two names were put together, and Philip became our first-ever tea-chest bassist, with the obligatory broom handle on one corner and a thin rope to the centre, for a very satisfying, if not incredibly tuneful, thump! Or another friend would play washboard, the back padded with cotton batten, plus a couple of tin cans and a small frying pan fixed to the top, with a handful of thimbles, but nothing in public – so far!

There was a Methodist church on the corner, and they kindly allowed me to use the hall when not needed. I joined the vibrant youth club, and various school friends or members of the club would play tea-chest bass or washboard, along with an occasional extra guitar whenever possible. The main line-up, apart from me, was by now Peter Matthews (guitar),

Philip Williams or Geoffrey Bond (tea-chest bass), and Paul Clarke or Julian Holt (washboard), but a few other names crept in from time to time, also Margaret Savill and Ann Spawls would help out on vocals. Eventually we got quite a few songs together, of which probably ten were vaguely listenable, so we were ready for the big time, and maybe even paid gigs!

Apart from practicing in the Church Hall, the "Cherrypips" only did seven legitimate performances, the first four at Church halls, then a private party for a girl named Jennifer. I still have a list of venues played over several years, together with songs and keys, which has been so helpful in the writing of this book.

After the private party, it became necessary to raise one's profile a little. The main ballroom in Maidstone was at the Royal Star Hotel, in the town centre. There was a top-quality house band of up to ten musicians with two singers. Just after my sixteenth birthday, a tad nervously, I went in to see hotel manager Bob Harvey, to tell him that he really needed the "Cherrypips". He very kindly asked us to come in and play for the intermission in an upcoming Saturday evening dance, and even paid us £2.10s. The four of us went onstage in the crowded ballroom, and started to play our very high energy, not very good, brand of skiffle. Immediately there was a huge crowd around the stage, with a few dancers behind, and the response was phenomenal. To be fair, I do not think that the appreciation was so much for our musicianship as for our energy, (learned from Lonnie), and the fact that we were still young.

There was only one other "Cherrypips" performance before the name and lineup was changed to the "Travellers". This was at the village hall in Boughton Monchelsea, where Martin Sharp and I had previously appeared as "The Magicalis" on a variety bill a little while before he went off to boarding school. With Geoffrey Bond on tea-chest bass and Paul Clarke on washboard, we had a never to be forgotten show, with no knowledge of what was to come.

THE "TRAVELLERS" (POP/ROCK)

I have never wanted to be a solo musician, although sometimes there have been house jobs in restaurants or hotels in order to keep body and soul together. (The Serpentine in Hyde Park, Shore House in Shoeburyness, Essex, and the Viceroy Hotel in Lancaster Gate, London, come to mind), all three with amazingly supportive management. So, you can imagine how excited I was to receive a letter from a guitarist in Canterbury – David Gentle. A bit older than me, he had played in a dance band, providing chords or melody as required, and was going ballistic over the lack of opportunity for self-expression, now that Skiffle and Rock 'n' Roll had arrived. We got together, (Canterbury was a long way in those days), and immediately hit it off; the first musician with whom I had ever played. He would come over from Canterbury, and we would practice at least once a week, with me assimilating some of the disciplines I needed so badly, and him picking up on the energy from our sessions together.

As if this was not enough, I had a new friend at school in the class below me – Paul Rodriguez, at some time of a French ancestry, so not pronounced in the Spanish way. He was learning French horn, with which I was incredibly impressed, and went on to become the most versatile musician with whom I have ever shared a stage, producing just about any instrument on a week's notice.

So, the "Travellers," (marketed as "Britain's Brightest Beat"), were born. Two guitars, one French horn, (to give us class!), plus Peter Matthews now had a string bass, and Julian Holt, a basic drum kit.

Back to the Royal Star Hotel for several gigs, all the while honing our craft, plus now including the first basic compositions from yours truly.

We started to get calls, one of which was from the community hall in nearby Shepway, where Maidstone's number one rocker, Bill Kent, had a weekly gig with his band, The Kentish Men. Bill already had a hit record and toured on the other side of the Atlantic, so was in a different league to the rest of us, but he welcomed this novice group, and often his bass player Doug Cirie, (the first bass guitarist I had ever seen), and drummer Roger Cable would sit in with us, which meant Julian Holt could leave the drum kit and pick up his clarinet, which was what he really wanted to play. One night, we met a trumpet player, Brian Jenner, and yet another seed was sown....

THE "JAZZ GENTLEMEN"

The first performance of what was later to become "The Jazz Gentlemen", on 16th September 1959, took place pretty much one year after the first performance of "The Cherrypips". With Brian on trumpet, Julian and another school friend, David O'Brien, on clarinets, Paul playing valve trombone parts on French Horn, and Roger Cable on drums, we went into this Rock 'n' Roll venue for a half-hour set and blew the lid off the place. Three days later, we did another show for the Methodist Youth Club, and a few days after that, were back at the Rock 'n' Roll venue of the previous week, by which time Bill Kent's bass player, Doug, had practiced sufficiently to play with us on tunes in Bb, Eb, and Dm, as well as the normal 'pop' keys, which was a huge effort on his part.

Within a month, we had found an excellent trombonist, (or he had found us), by the name of Brian Millen. Brian played a silver trombone, which had a smoother tone than some, and blended beautifully with the French horn. Plus, I had found a 1930's vintage tenor banjo, and the "Jazz Gentlemen" were born. We practiced in the venerable St. Peter's Church Hall whenever possible and did our first proper "set" as a band at my school, before the Saturday night movie in mid-December.

So followed several years of amazing music, with the "Jazz Gentlemen", and the "Travellers" (which was basically the rhythm section on its own); plus, we also occasionally went out as a dance band, ("The Mayfair Set Dance Band," – where we got a few calls because it was a good name!). There was by now a waiting list of musicians who wanted to play with the "Jazz Gentlemen". Julian on clarinet had moved on, (he got the "Times" award for best new poet, among other accolades), and his place was first taken by Roy Gill, (who played a superbly warm mostly low register tone in the style of Johnny Dodds), and then by Jimmy Strike, who unusually had an Albert system clarinet, with completely different fingering to the usual Boehm, and thus gave the band a unique sound. On occasions where Brian Millen was unavailable, we were so fortunate to have a blind trombonist by the name of Robert Pringle eager to step in. The sound of his playing will stay in my head forever. He had a trombone with a huge bore and played in an incredibly gruff tailgate style, which went through one's entire being; my whole back is tingling as I write this.

When Brian Jenner went off to Cambridge University, his place was taken by Tony Swift, who played in a very light, lyrical style, often muted, in contrast to Brian's more "straight-ahead" style, (with sometimes a flugelhorn). Basically, if there was ever a change in our four-piece front line, even for an evening, it sounded like a different band, since each musician would automatically adapt to blend in with the new player, except that the rhythm section remained constant.

My absolute favourite visiting band at the time was out of Copenhagen, "Papa Bue's Viking Jazz Band", fronted by another incredibly gruff trombonist, Arne Bue Jensen (no relation). They always closed their evening with a beautiful rendition of "Brahms' Lullaby", of which I have their single, but you needed to hear it live.

One night, the "Papa Bue" band was playing at the Star, and the banjo player, Bjarne Peterson, was sitting on the drum riser as he always did, so that the two of them were in perfect sync. At one point, Bjarne's chair fell backwards off the riser and the band stopped in horror, as he could have been badly hurt. Then there was a "chink, chink, chink" of a banjo, wafting from the back of the stage. Bjarne was lying on his back, still in his chair, on the floor a couple of feet or so below and hadn't missed a beat. A true musician!

Incidentally, I think it was Bjarne who told me of their bus, which had a toilet, very impressive at the time. The catch was that this toilet was only to be used in emergency on the open road, when nobody was following behind.

One of the greatest gifts of my life, of which I was unaware at the time, related to the age range of the various musicians in the band, who were of course my best friends. The youngest, Julian Holt, was 15 when he moved to clarinet, while of our three pianists, Fred Longhurst was 62 -although there was seldom a remotely in tune piano at the venues where we played. One pianist, Evelyn Ray, played flute, and stepped into the front line when confronted with an unusable piano, possibly the first time this had ever happened in New Orleans jazz, the second being with our clarinet player Jim Lewis, a short while later. Most of us, when at school, draw friends from our own class or grade, often not knowing anyone from the grade above or below. I was so fortunate to miss out on this mindset, and it has remained that way for my entire life.

Attending a private school, (called a "public" school in the U.K.), had its plusses and its challenges for me. Academically, I was good at some subjects and less good at others, like most of us, but when it came to sports, especially team sports involving a ball, I was useless, preferring the solitude of a cross-country run. A few months ago, I had cataract surgery on both eyes. Imagine my amazement after the second operation when the eye shield was removed, and I had depth perception for the very first time in my life, apart from seeing a 3-D movie or comic. My entire life had been like a photograph to this point; perspective fine, but depth perception was something of which I was totally unaware. I did not miss it, because I never knew it existed, but felt very inadequate for much of my school career, until able to get a few "brownie" points from my peers, when they first heard the "Jazz Gentlemen".

On the way home from the eye surgeon, I stopped in a supermarket, where there was an aisle of vegetables running the full length of the building. I stood amazed at the varying depths I was seeing for the first time, especially some containers of brightly coloured red, green, and yellow peppers, every single one of them in a fractionally different location to the next. I stood there in awe for what seemed a long time.

We did two concerts for the school, both before a Saturday night movie, and I recall the entire staff was seated in the balcony at the rear of the hall on each occasion. By now, we had Brian Millen on trombone in the band, so it was a six-piece line up, including Julian Holt, also from the school, on clarinet. If there had ever been any doubt in my mind, (which there wasn't), about what I should do with my life, this clinched it, although I had briefly considered going into the painting of theatrical scenery for a T.V. station. There were ten numbers, closing with "Mamma Don't Allow", which of course contains a solo from everybody, ending with the drummer, (Terry Winter), and the building positively erupted that night, quite the best of my life to date.

The second concert, some four months later, of course had to top the first. We opened with "Battle Hymn of the Republic", using four treble voices from my "house" at school, "Founder's", as a slow acapella opening, then the band exploded onto the stage at full bore. Roy Gill was now on clarinet, with his beautiful low-register tones, while Alan

Noah, brilliant pianist from the school and a good friend, guested for this set. To this day, Alan is the only musician I have known who could hand you the sheet for an improvised solo immediately it was finished. We again did ten numbers, including of course "The Charleston", and using "The Jazz Band Ball", a powerful minor key piece, for a "false tabs". (I was learning fast). Closing was the ever-popular "Saints". We did the first verse and chorus onstage, then the doors at the rear of the hall opened, and both aisles had a full band marching towards the stage, one fronted by Stewart White, trumpeter for the school jazz band, who subsequently joined the National Youth Orchestra, and the other by Philip Charlton, my friend of so many years, also on trumpet, who had been the original tea chest-bass player in the "Cherrypips". We ended up with a full 15-piece orchestra onstage, including two drummers with full kit, Brian Weller on sousaphone, and the first appearance of Jimmy Strike on clarinet, who was to join the "Jazz Gentlemen" as a regular some three weeks later. There were by now many events coming our way, but I did no more school concerts, as I knew this one could never be topped!

The "Jazz Gentlemen", sometimes known as "The Jazz Gentlemen Ragtyme Players," were by now getting to a pretty high standard with constant playing together, and it was of course my responsibility to come up with regular gigs. Sometimes this was easy, and sometimes there could be a dearth, so I took out an ad. in the "The Times" personal column, announcing that "Owing to the pressure of bookings, the "Jazz Gentlemen" would be unable to accept further engagements in the near future, except in the event of a cancellation". Immediately we started to get calls from debutante dances or "coming out" parties, mostly in London, which were held to honour a "society" daughter's 18th birthday; thus rectifying the situation.

Jimmy Strike had to relocate to Canterbury for his work, but we were so fortunate to have a brilliant clarinettist/flautist by the name of Jim Lewis come on board, which kept the standard of the band very high. I learned one huge thing off Jim; apart from being a great friend, he went one Thursday to the local jazz club at Highfield House, and saw the regular Thursday band of Owen Bryce, which blew him away. The Saturday bands varied, Chris Barber, Kenny Ball, Mick Mulligan, Ken Colyer, Cy Laurie and many more, including us. Local people sadly were a bit blasé about Owen Bryce, because he was there every week, and it took a fresh set of ears to realize that this too was a really good band. I resolved then never to over-expose in any area, unless there was a residency, where the clientele was constantly changing.

Talking of Highfield House, there is one occasional visiting band that absolutely needs mentioning, namely that of Eric Allandale and the New Orleans Knights. Eric, originally from the Dominican Republic, played a fine trombone, covering many genres, and was first heard on the British music scene when working as a surveyor in Hammersmith, where he joined the Hammersmith Borough Brass Band on trumpet. He shortly afterwards moved full-time as a trombonist into Jazz, and worked with Terry Lightfoot, Alex Welsh, and even Edmundo Ros' big Latin dance orchestra at Hammersmith Palais, before starting a touring band of his own, which included Will Hastie on clarinet, whom I was to meet some years later when on an Isle of Wight season, and Will was with the "Temperance Seven".

Eric played a huge variety of music, from "Trad" into some rare Ellington works, plus modern arrangements by Kenny Graham, and was possibly more suited for the concert stage than clubs, but there was one never to be forgotten part of his evening where he would borrow a single large tom-tom from the drummer, bring it forward, and proceed to totally mesmerize everyone in the room. I don't know where he took us all, possibly to his homeland, or to some part of Central Africa. Maybe it was different for each one of us, but I do know that this was one of the absolute highlights of the "Trad" years, that will always stay with me.

In the late 60s, Eric went into a new pop group called the "Foundations", playing until their demise in 1970 on many hits, including two million sellers. Then he moved to Zambia to play with a soul band for Independence celebrations, staying there and in Kenya to immerse himself in African Jazz for another four years. He lived variously between London and Paris, composing, producing, and performing for the remainder of his life, and made a significant contribution to the era, even though his name may sadly not be known to as many as it should.

Jim Lewis retired from his work a while back and got a basset horn for a retirement present. How I wish we could have had that amazing sound, coupled with his awesome playing, on some of our tunes all those years ago. We did many things, indoors and out. Sometimes we played at Richard Hearne's (Mr. Pastry's), Manor house. He was the biggest children's performer at the time, with a weekly T.V. show, and several movies to his credit. He would often bring in disadvantaged kids, or those who had been in hospital, for a big party, which would include us whenever possible. We were outdoors for these events, and always included Brian Weller, who played a very satisfactory sousaphone, which carried all over the grounds.

I remember on one occasion being stuck at an intersection in Maidstone, with a fully loaded car of musicians and instruments, and Brian Weller's sousaphone sticking out of the sunshine roof. There was a policeman directing traffic with his back to us, so after a couple of minutes Brian gave him an ever so gentle raspberry on the sousaphone to remind him that we were still there – to great laughter all around, including the policeman.

Whilst on the subject of transit to gigs, there are a couple of other items that bear mentioning. On one dark evening we had reached an intersection with a red traffic light. We dutifully drove over the strip to change the light, which did nothing, so we reversed and tried it again. The light steadfastly refused to change, so after a little while

Brian Millen got out of the car and started jumping on the strip, to the amusement of yet another policeman, who came over, said "it must be faulty", or words to that effect, and waved us across, so we could get to the venue on time.

On another occasion, we had to drive to Gravesend, near London. We had 2 vehicles, fortunately with no double bass or sousaphone, and one of the cars decided it was not going anywhere on this particular evening. We managed to get everything in the other vehicle with the front passengers nursing a bass drum, so that it would be necessary to slightly open the passenger door for any gear changes. No problem, except that 2 of us were not even in the car yet. Fortunately, there were running boards, so I think it was Paul and myself that each stood on a running board and held on over the top of the car. We arrived pretty cold, but managed to warm up enough, probably with sufficient coffee, to play the evening.

Sometimes we would perform at Leeds Castle, for one of Lady Baillie's spectacular house parties, playing in Henry VIII's banqueting hall, and sleeping over on occasion to entertain the golfers the next day. We would usually see Princess Marina (cousin of Prince Philip), and sometimes Princess Margaret, with Tony Armstrong-Jones. This had not been mentioned yet in the press, and we of course promised to "keep mum". Jimmy Strike, Brian Millen, Brian Weller and I also played there once with the "Downtown Jazzmen", of which they were part, (along with Brian Welcome, Johnny Martin, and Alyn Dare), who had earlier been based at St. Peter's Church, but rarely performed as a unit anymore.

There was originally a "Manor" at Leeds, (meaning a unit of land), with records of the site going back as far as the year 855. It was donated by Edward the Confessor to the house, or family, of Godwin, whose most famous son Harold was killed at the Battle of Hastings in 1066. The Domesday book entry of 20 years later says that the property comprised vineyards, 8 acres of meadow or woodland, and 5 mills. In 1119, construction of the castle began, and, after various changes, not all of them peaceful, it was purchased in 1278 by the Spanish-born Queen Eleanor of Castile, beloved wife of Edward Ist, and began its association with no less than six Queens of England. The banqueting hall was created especially for a visit by Henry VIII in May 1520, en route to a meeting with Francis Ist of France; the site now known as the "Field of the Cloth of Gold". Henry travelled with an entourage of 3,997 and his Queen, Catherine of Aragon, with a personal retinue of 1,175 people, all resplendent in their finery, no doubt with Francis putting on a similar show.

In recent times, Leeds Castle has been considerably renovated – in period style - by Lady Baillie and is considered to be one of the world's most beautiful, with the Henry VIII banqueting hall as the largest room, but appearing smaller, because of the huge proportions of ceiling beams, fireplace, doors, and some pictures, making guests look like Lilliputians when there.

On the subject of Royalty, I should mention one time when we were driving from Maidstone at age 7 or 8 to my aunts' house in Derby, for Christmas, which was a big treat every other year. While driving through London, my dad's car came to a sudden stop outside the Royal Albert Hall, to be instantly met by a policeman who asked what was wrong. I believe, but could be mistaken, that we had run out of gas. There was a Rolls with the Royal arms on it waiting to come out, and our car was instantly surrounded by policemen, who swiftly moved us to one side, as the other car's occupant was Queen Mary, who had just been attending a concert. My dad had the car for a total of 28 years, and I think that day was the fastest that it ever moved.

One time, the "Jazz Gentlemen" played an event on the south coast, partially through the auspices of an aunt on my mother's side, Alys, whose passion in life was to raise money for the Royal National Lifeboat

Institute, a U.K. charity of over 40,000 volunteers. This operates lifeboat stations all around the coast, with brave men and women who will tackle all weathers, 24/7, in rescue efforts. At the time of writing, they have saved over 140,000 people from a watery demise since the organization was founded in 1824; Alys raised literally millions to help them.

Back to the event. At some point of the evening, a naval officer came up to the stage and introduced himself as my uncle Bernard, who had been married to another of my mother's sisters, Ruth, and spent much of his career as a Commander in the Royal Navy stationed in Malta and was my godfather whom I hadn't met for many years. I was so very pleased to see him and was able to thank him in person for the fact that he had never missed communicating for a birthday or Christmas in my entire life. In my mind, he was a hero, and to him I was important. Would that all young boys could have a role model like that!

We had an annual "Variety Challenge Week" in Maidstone, to find the "top town" in the area. For five consecutive nights, our town would compete in a fun competition, with a draw to see who went on first. Maidstone's company was called "The Country Towners" and of course included the "Jazz Gentlemen". The show was called "On Parade" – opened by the Freda Boorman dancers, who did a short Rockettes/Tillers style number, also called "On Parade" written by yours truly. I don't think we won that year, but the five variety nights raised a huge amount of money to provide much needed winter coal for impoverished seniors, and all participants had such a great time; I wish that communities still did more things like this.

We were so lucky to have a pool of musicians, some very talented, to be standing in the wings waiting for a chance to play. Apart from the two trumpeters already mentioned, we also had Roger Eley, a little more mainstream, rather like Humphrey Lyttleton in style, plus at least three clarinets from which to draw, and the brilliant Robert Pringle as backup trombonist. In all the many gigs we did as a band, we were only stuck for one of the three lead instruments twice, once for a twenty-minute cabaret spot, and once for a T.V. show, about which we will hear shortly.

At this point, I must mention Norman Hoskins and vocalist Sheila Baker, who joined the "Travellers" in 1960, having been a part of the Sharp's Kreemy Works skiffle group for a while, where Norman was employed. (Maidstone rocker Bill Kent also worked for Sharp's Toffee before taking up music full time). "The Travellers", with the new line up, did a first performance at the beginning of July, which was also the last with David Gentle, who wanted to work more in his home town of Canterbury, (no motorways in those days). A great evening and a smooth transition to the new lineup, which was kept busy for the next year. That Christmas, we did our first residency, at The Edinburgh Hotel in Hastings, both as a dance band and cabaret, for the whole Christmas and New Year's season. This was very successful, and the full ten-piece band went back for the staff party in early '61.

We did many, many events together, Norman and I on guitars, various vocal combinations between us, and usually but not always, drums (Don Mason, Jock Law, or later, Terry Winter). If we did a cabaret spot it was just the three of us, if a dance there would be drums as well, but with the quick changeover of a cabaret this was impractical. So, a very busy year for both bands.

The following May, we went in for a talent competition on Southern Television called "Home Grown" and won our way to the finals with the jazz classic "The World is Waiting for the Sunrise". When we went down to Southampton again for the last show, there was a little girl of 14 or 15 in a white dress with tap shoes, who looked about 10, waiting to go on. Katie Boyle, of "What's my Line" fame, was one of the judges, and I think that Isobel Barnett was the other female judge, so we looked at the little girl, (who hadn't done anything yet), and said to each other, "We'll go for second" – which is exactly how things turned out. Brian Jenner on trumpet had his finals at Cambridge that day, and there was no stand-in available, so Paul Rodriguez took his French horn mouthpiece, stuck it in a trumpet and did his usual amazing job.

While we were doing the initial audition for "Home Grown", John Gledhill from Southern T.V. asked me if I'd mind backing up a couple of hopefuls with guitar, so the judges could get a better idea, which I was happy to do. For the next two seasons John would get in touch, and I would go down to Southampton early one morning by train, (having a huge luxury breakfast courtesy of the T.V. station), accompany singers as needed to the best of my ability, stay over and do a few more the next day, then home. One year there were several female hopefuls in late teens/early 20s, no less than seven of which wanted a show song called "On a Wonderful Day Like Today" – to the amusement of John and Peter Frazer-Jones, the producer, who were out of view killing themselves with laughter. Amazingly, just about nobody brought sheet music with them, unless they had their own pianist, so it was a good job I had a copy with the chords on it. Some years later, I saw that Peter had gone to work for Mary Tyler Moore's company and was directing Ted Knight, Valerie Harper, and others for her.

These trips out from Maidstone were a welcome break from school and later the Insurance company, plus Southern Television looked after me so very well.

There was a good picture of the "Jazz Gentlemen" in the T.V. times the year after we were up for the finals of "Home Grown". Paul and I got several copies of the magazine, cut out the picture, and sent it, (with no letter), to the Mayors or Chambers of Commerce in several towns on the Costa Brava, Spain. Then a few weeks later, we sent a letter "no doubt you have heard of the English Jazz band ------". It worked, and the mayor of a resort town called San Feliu de Guixols volunteered to put a 2 ½ week tour together, which would start the day Paul and I left school. An amazing trip, we arrived at the town by train, (with open bits at the back of each carriage), and they had put the red carpet out to the wrong bit of track, so we of course played a few tunes while this was rectified. One day there was a grass fire, probably from a cigarette, just started by the roadside, so we quickly got out of our vehicle and set to work putting it out. There were pictures in the local press, and this got us huge brownie points for the rest of the tour, especially since there were locals watching us and doing nothing. One night we were at a 5-star resort, Hotel St. Roc, overlooking the Mediterranean, and looking at the huge luxury yachts moored at the marina. There were guards around the property protecting the glitterati inside, of which we were a part for a few hours. The deputy mayor was assigned to be our guide and driver for the whole tour, doing anything we could possibly need.

On the outward journey, we stopped at the Spanish border on the train, where our passports were duly examined. There was a beverage stand on the platform, and Sheila got off to get an orange soda. Immediately she was surrounded by police, with rather large automatic rifles, all yelling simultaneously. (No E.U. yet). Then the train started moving, so Brian J. put his hand out and said, "Come on", pulling her back in the carriage, to even more yelling; we never found out why.

Coming back to England, Paul had a bottle of rum that was too large to be "duty free". He asked the Customs officer what size it should be, removed the top, and drank down to the appointed mark, to the amusement of everyone there, with enthusiastic applause when he eventually stopped, and we helped him board the train. A first ever tour outside the U.K., and a never to be forgotten experience for all of us.

At that time, the gathering place for the late teens/early twenties crowd, was the Delicatessen, in King Street, Maidstone, owned by a Mrs. Syme, who treated us all like family. The ground floor was a typical deli, with imported goods, special cheeses, and other hard to get items, while the next floor up was the most popular coffee bar in town, with homemade cakes and pastries, sandwiches, basically anything you could wish for, even beans on toast!

It was the kind of venue that if Mrs. Syme was busy, and her daughter Kim was not there, one of the "regulars" would go behind the counter and take over. After a couple of years or so, when most of us were a bit older, the basement was set up as a private members' club, with a little bar and soft lighting. (Even at that age, we recognized this to be a plus). Membership was free, on recommendation from two existing members, and all was run, as was the coffee bar, with the more experienced members helping as needed. This was such a haven for all of us, including musicians from various bands in the area, and we were so sad when it eventually closed.

Having now left school, and decided against university, (a hard decision), it was time to seek gainful employment. I was already of the mindset that if one worked for a company, one might as well start in head office, so I joined the ranks of many thousands who commuted to London on a daily basis, having already obtained a job with a big insurance company, reminiscent of trombonist Chris Barber, who was an actuary before taking up music full-time. It was my intent from the beginning to get some qualifications as a 'back up', in case there was a reason in the future where it became physically impossible to play.

I never knew Chris Barber, doyen of the British Traditional Jazz scene, but did become friendly with his clarinettist Monty Sunshine, some time after he had his massive hit with the Sydney Bechet classic "Petite Fleur". Monty eventually formed his own band, along with trumpeter Bob Wallis, and vocalist Val Wiseman, with whom we used to share evenings at the Royal Star. Nobody had ever told Monty that a clarinet was somewhat quieter than a trombone or trumpet, and usually needed a mic., so in his case it wasn't, and he could produce a wall of sound out of his instrument whenever he wished, the only time I have ever seen this, apart from the amazing Doreen Ketchens, who plays with a rhythm section on Jackson Square in New Orleans, with passing "front line" musicians dropping in from time to time, and could certainly have given Monty a run for his money. While mentioning the Barber band, it would however be remiss not to talk of trumpeter Pat Halcox, who was relatively unobtrusive, and occasionally slightly fumbled the ball, of which Chris was of course aware, but would suddenly go into a flight of unbelievable brilliance, which forgave everything, and more.

There were differences between British bands and those in New Orleans, in that in the British bands, the front line always stood, while the New Orleans bands sit, unless marching, only standing to take a solo.

The structure of a "hit" record was usually the same. First would come the tune, with sometimes an (heaven forbid) arrangement, then a vocal, or a couple of solos, followed by a flat out "burn up" to make as big a finish as possible. Hits of the era, apart from "Petite Fleur", included "Whistling Rufus" (Chris), "Midnight in Moscow", and "Samantha", (trumpeter Kenny Ball), "Buona Sera", "Acker Bilk", and "I'm shy, Mary Ellen, I'm shy", by Bob Wallis, which positively rocketed to number one, and still seems to be in my head at some point of every day. But by far the biggest instrumental song of the time was not a jazz tune, it was Acker Bilk's "Stranger on the Shore", originally entitled "Jenny", and composed in the back of the bus after a gig when he was mortified at forgetting a gift for his daughter's birthday.

This was the first ever British number one song in the U.S., and there was also a vocal version (Michael London), on which Acker played the solo. Very clever, and I think the only time this has ever been done.

One or two other members of the band also commuted, but at different times, and on different trains. The commute was a gruelling experience. Nobody spoke, hardly even a "good morning", and if anyone dared to sit in a seat that might be occupied by another "regular" a couple of stops down the line, nothing would be said; the poor unfortunate would just be stared at until he or she moved to another space.

Something had to be done, so with Christmas approaching, 5 of us, plus 2 girlfriends, who very kindly made loads of mince pies, got on what would be the busiest of the open coaches and spread out all over, (with instrument cases, of course). At a pre-arranged signal, the clarinet player bravely got out his clarinet and started to play "God rest ye, merry gentlemen" to be followed rapidly by a trombone from the far end of the carriage, then banjo, trumpet and French horn – playing bass parts - in quick succession, while the 2 girls started walking up the aisle, cake tins full of mince pies, saying "Happy Christmas", (being British), to all and sundry. To give an idea of how well this worked, by the time we pulled into Victoria station, the 2 coaches each side of us were completely empty, while ours was crammed to bursting with the best impromptu Christmas party ever. We played everyone off the platform, then did a few tunes on the main station concourse, so happy that we had brought joy to a few people, before heading off to our respective day's work.

By this time, we had a fairly regular bassist named Mike Thompson, who had a large bass that unfortunately made very little sound, so he would play with his ear on the neck of the bass. When we could, we would mic. him, or none of us would have heard him either.

The "Jazz Gentlemen" had their own club for a short while. Called "The Trad's Retreat", it was situated in some woods close to Maidstone, fortunately with a pub just down the road. Fortunately, because there was no way in which we could have operated a bar as well, and the pub's proximity meant that we could have a colossal audience, in the club, in the pub, and on the road going to and fro. As you can imagine, the publican was overjoyed at our presence every Thursday. We found an old army searchlight that was still operational and sent a vertical beam of light skywards to assist all who wanted to find our music. After a few weeks we got a polite call from the Air Ministry regarding the light, which of course had to be extinguished, but we had run out of the time for which we could get the hall anyway, and the "Trad's Retreat" was possibly the most fun we had ever had as a band.

Mentioning the "Trad's Retreat" is impossible without mentioning David Wigg, entertainments editor for the Kent Messenger, who subsequently went on to the Daily Express, and Peter Mason, his assistant, who later filled his shoes. They wrote brilliantly on the "Trad's Retreat" as well as many other articles on both the "Travellers" and the "Jazz Gentlemen", and without their friendship and support there is no way in which we would have had the following that we did for so long.

Around this time, we also started performances for the United States Navy at their airbase in West Malling, Kent. There were 101 U.S. bases in Britain at the time, unknown to most, and we had an awesome time being introduced to, and immersed in, a so different culture, but very warm and welcoming. Frequently the evening would be broken up with "Travellers" sets as well, and we went on to perform at other bases, such as Brizenorton, Mildenhall and Lakenheath, to name a few.

Sheila and Norman were of course a part of pretty well all of these shows, as well as being an integral part of the "Travellers", but the Sharps Kreemy works group, now called the "Zephyrs", was getting calls too, so they very fairly went with whichever band called first. The "Zephyrs" were doing many performances at the Royal Star Ballroom, and generating a big following of their own, immaculately covering all the latest pops as soon as they came out. It was a very difficult time in the late 50s and early 60s; some big organizations (such as Mecca dancing), insisted on a female singer in the band, others worked on the principle that the girls went to see the boys on the stage, while the boys in the audience went to see the girls in the audience, and a pretty girl on stage was a distraction, so no girls in the band. Some venues would actually pay the female singers extra not to come.

The "Zephyrs" met up with famed record producer Joe Meek and ran afoul of this almost impossible situation. He offered them an ethereal, spacey instrumental piece that he had just written called "Telstar", but the proviso was that the girl singer had to go; Joe's purpose also being that he wanted to produce an instrumental group to compete with "The Shadows". The Zephyrs honourably refused to ditch Sheila, so the tune was given to Billy Fury's backing group, "The Tornadoes", two of whom had been original members of Johnny Kidd's "Pirates", and subsequently moved on to form a new band. Joe originally played much of the tune himself, and "The Tornadoes" became as big, or bigger than the 'star' for whom they had been up to now providing backing.

Especially in the U.S., where "Telstar" was the second number one hit from the U.K., the first, as mentioned, being Acker Bilk's "Stranger on the Shore", the previous year. The "Tornadoes" had other, smaller U.S. hits and it was only the emergence of the Beatles that lessened their huge popularity.

Joe proudly showed me the tiny keyboard, which clipped under the right-hand side of a piano, about 1 ½ octaves, on which he'd first composed "Telstar", but I have since seen a picture of him at a Clavichord, while "Tornadoes" photos are always with the ubiquitous Vox Continental, so beloved by British bands at the time. The drummer, Clem Cattini, subsequently became one of London's top session drummers, and we were always pleased if we ran into each other at "La Giaconda" for a cup of coffee.

So followed a year and a half of commuting to London. I would leave the house at 6:40 AM to catch the 7.12 which arrived in Victoria a little after 8:30 AM. Then to the subway and to the City to arrive at work by

9:15. The "Jazz Gentlemen" and the "Travellers" were still going strong, and in the case of the former I would frequently change clothes in the washroom on the return train journey, to be met by a band member to take me to that evening's gig. Sheila and Norman had moved permanently to the "Zephyrs", while the "Travellers" had a new rhythm player, Peter Marriott, who had large hands, and played a very full clean style that was a delight, with some chords other players could not reach. A reliable bassist was always hard to find, so the redoubtable Paul produced a bass guitar for when he was with the "Travellers" and a euphonium as a bass for the jazz band, a tuba being impractical to transport, also Trudy Wise, (once of the Freda Boorman dancers), came in as an occasional vocalist.

I loved the music of Connie Francis, as did several of us, and one day we were invited to perform at Caxton Hall, London, for Connie's Fan Club. She was going to be there on her first ever U.K. tour and would do a few numbers with us. Great excitement, and we duly arrived at the venue with all our instruments. We met Connie for the first time, and were all ready to go, when one of the Caxton Hall staff came in and said, "Oh, we can't have any music, there's a wedding next door". It was one of those sliding partitions through which one can hear a mouse walking on the other side. So much for that!

I was working as a solo at the Barbarela restaurant/Pub on the Square, St George's, in Bermuda, some years later, and just missed Connie, who went in for lunch one day. A little while ago she was a doing a very rare concert in Indio, California, after which we had a chat about that night, and also the poor lady who ran the fan club, Mildred Maclening, who was so embarrassed, even though it was in no way her fault.

Amazingly, some halls in Britain, especially out in the country, still had direct current for electricity, rather than the normal a/c. Since we only ever played those with the jazz band, it was not too serious.

I had one small Watkins amp with probably a ten-inch speaker, into which a mic could be plugged for the clarinet or vocals, also a guitar for "Travellers" gigs, however it was still a great laugh when the band was blowing up a storm, and the room was suddenly plunged into darkness, to be followed almost immediately by the cry of "has anybody got a shilling?". Not only did these venues have DC, (we carried a transformer), they also had slot machines to pay for the electricity, and there was no way to tell how much money was in the machine before the evening started. I think this only happened on one "Travellers" gig, when the drummer immediately stopped playing and Sheila, Norman and I sang together until the power came back - and we were no longer in total blackness.

The jazz band did about three concerts for the inmates in Maidstone prison, which was a maximum-security operation. The first time we went there, we were advised by several of the "residents" never to put anything down, and never to let anything out of our sight. We took these words seriously; there were a few close calls, but everything came and went smoothly. We did the shows with only one vehicle for seven of us, plus instruments, to the total amazement of security, who could not believe what we could pack in a car, and I think they learned a bit from us.

We had a colossal response, and I like to think that our music would have somehow helped the poor unfortunates for whom we were playing, regardless of their reasons for being there.

A little more on school before that subject is left forever. I am a firm believer that the subjects in which one does best are those where you relate to the teacher as a human being; in my case, with one exception, it certainly was. Art and English literature were undoubtedly the best, and I was able to consistently do fairly well. In the case of art, once I had my "O" level, my art teacher, Derek Simmons, asked me if I would take it again the following term, just for him. My own personal style of painting was a little different to the norm, and he wanted to see how the examiners would respond. The painting was to be (Oh Joy!) a theatrical trunk, with props and costumes everywhere. I did about 80% of the picture in my own style but had what looked like a small slice of pie very carefully drawn and painted in the way the examiners would normally want to see it. I got really good marks, and even a little note from the examiner, which was highly unusual.

I liked history, and the stories involved, but had difficulty remembering dates, in fact some parts of this book may well be out of sync. At carpentry, also taught by Derek Simmons, I was amazingly useless, and it was never going to change. It was all done with hand tools, and after a few terms Derek kindly let me head off to the Art room where I could be more productive. Maybe my total lack of depth perception affected my woodworking skills at the time; I will never know.

Geography was great, the teacher, Robert Coutts, was constantly inserting little jokes and puns, also drawing beautiful maps on the blackboard, to both of which I, of course, related. In my "A" level paper there was one exam related to "man and the environment", called "human geography", which had no syllabus; one had to work out the possibilities. I will always remember the fun I had with these papers, and the amazing 98% that went with it! (It was a one-off; don't get worried).

French was fine, one had to choose between biology and art at one point, so biology had to go, and in any event, there were things I would have simply refused to do.

My housemaster, Edward Craven, taught Chemistry, but, far more to the point, he taught by his own example how to live and how to treat others. He taught me so very much, without a word of instruction, and we kept in touch by mail for the rest of his life. We had an English-Speaking Union exchange student from Boston, Massachusetts, on my first or second year at Sutton Valence. Apart from having the only crew cut I had ever seen in real life, he played very fine organ in the Chapel service that took place every morning but one. His name was Carl Erickson, and he was in an upper form (grade) to me, also in a different "house", so it is unlikely that we ever met in my school years. The junior day-boys, of which I was one, were seated in the organ loft for these services, so we could hear magnificently, and there were maybe three boys who played organ, in addition to the senior music teacher. When Carl played, all the hymns were mighty, and we would always leave Chapel to the sound of Bach's "Tocatta & Fugue", possibly the most powerful piece of music on the planet, at which point not only the earth moved, but also the heavens. I, for one, always left the building a full two inches taller than I had walked in and knowing I could face anything.

Some years later, I was playing in Fredericton, New Brunswick, in Canada, and had received a letter from Edward Craven, telling me that Carl was a professor at the University of New Brunswick, and asking me to make contact on behalf of the school alumni (old boys) association. Which I did, along with my wife, Mary, (whom you have yet to meet), and we had a good visit with Carl and his wife, more especially I was able to thank him for the difference his music had made to the life of a young boy, which meant so much to him.

One day Princess Marina, Philip's cousin, was coming for speech day. I had prepared an exhibit for the geographical society, and the headmaster ushered in the Princess, and introduced her to me. She responded, "Oh yes, Peter and I know each other already", or words to that effect, because I had of course played with the "Jazz Gentlemen", (and also the "Downtown Jazzmen" on one occasion), at some of Lady Baillie's house parties in Leeds Castle, where the Princess was a frequent visitor. I hate to say it, but the headmaster's face at that second was the highlight of my school career.

with H.R.H. Princess Marina at Sutton Valence School. Photo: Kent Messenger

Talking of things American, as Lady Baillie originally was, our next-door neighbour in Maidstone had an American car, the only one I had ever seen until performing at the US air bases in Britain. He was a smallish man, who was a solicitor, and had a beautiful big Saint Bernard dog who went to work with him every day and sat next to him in the front seat. Of course, the steering wheel was on the other side of the car to that which was normal to us, and I would always take great delight in watching other people's reactions whenever he drove by; sometimes it was the highlight of the day.

As in many private schools, there was a large cadet force, to which 99% of the school and some of the staff belonged. There was a fairly large armoury of some 300 or more late World War II Lee Enfield Mark II rifles, all fully operational. I got along well with the ex-army officer Jack Sergison who was in charge, in addition to being our PE instructor, and was offered the position of armourer, (security and maintenance), also checking on the field gun that we had on semi-permanent loan from the regular army. He was a onetime tenor sax player, and we spent hours together discussing music, especially that of Duke Ellington, which was his personal favourite, and subsequently became one of mine.

At one time, one of the French masters married a house matron, and the following morning, a pair of pyjama bottoms and a night dress, (yes, theirs), were seen tied in a lover's knot, billowing from the school flagpole. On another occasion, some boys who were leaving that term managed to get the Art teacher's car on top of one of the school towers during the night, with the aid of the regular army, who looked upon it as a challenge. It was soon taken down with no harm done, but it had many people puzzled, and made the national press.

The cadet force had a good band as well, but, as I remember it, they played "Men of Harlech" beautifully, and that was the entire repertoire for many years, until Paul got involved as M.D. There have been a few times when they have come to mind, especially once when sharing accommodation with the "Happy Dolls" from Japan or Korea, while performing in Halifax, Nova Scotia, so many years later. This group would swap instruments to play one song perfectly, then change back quickly, and they are mentioned in more detail later in this book.

But the ultimate purpose of the cadet force was probably that Britain had been recently through two devastating World Wars, and it was vital that the youth of the country should be semi-prepared, should such a thing ever happen again. Also, if one left school and wanted a military career, the qualifications were already in place to enter officers' training school. The same would apply if there were to be conscription, plus several students went on to take the Eastern Command leadership course, which was run by the regular Army, and considerably more advanced.

My one regret from school days was that I was unable to get music lessons from the teacher that I wanted. There were two music teachers at the school. The senior one was not really one to whom I could relate, while the junior played clarinet in the school jazz band, for which I played banjo, and, together with the French master, wrote really good songs, rather like the old act of Flanders & Swann, with him on the piano, brightening up many a dull assembly. My aunt, who taught music up in Derby, wanted to sponsor my lessons, and he really wanted to teach me, since we were both definitely on the same page.

All seemed perfect, and we discussed things at length, BUT (the capitals are intentional), the senior music master had a vacancy, and try as we might, it was impossible to get permission for me to have instruction from the teacher that I really wanted. So that idea was dropped, and my ears became my teacher (and did I listen - so hard to every note, every nuance that I could, in so many styles). I did have two lessons in Bermuda, many years later, where the teacher, Leon Jones, and I, swapped many ideas, had a good visit with each other, and I took grades one and two exams on the second lesson. Thus ended my formal musical education.

There was a dance for leavers and other upper sixth form members at the end of one summer term, which was as close as we got to a "Grad". Doris Pullen's band, a 4 or 5 piece, was always in attendance, and a bus load of girls came, with chaperone of course, from another school. The seniors at S.V. decidedly did not want a chaperone monitoring their every breath, and the popular schoolmaster at our end, who had either volunteered or been coerced into a similar position, was "bribed" with a bottle of Johnnie Walker to escort the girls' chaperone, very slowly, on a tour of the entire school, arriving back at the hall shortly before the last piece of music. This was not during my final year; I had stayed on late at school that day, a Saturday, in order to hear the band, as, unusually, neither the "Jazz Gentlemen" nor the "Travellers" were playing on that particular night. I volunteered to sit in with the band for a while, a little nervously, as I had never done such a thing before. The music was typical of a small dance band of the time, very structured, adequate but a little wooden, and I did my best to help things move, also contributing a couple of vocals, "Peggy Sue", and "All I have to do is Dream", since I don't remember that they played any of "our" music. A couple of the musicians suggested that I should become a permanent feature, but I could quite see how David Gentle had wanted to get out of a similar band, which was why we joined together; to play music with some room for individual self expression, including compositions of our own, during the early days of the "Travellers", which I am so glad that we did.

Aside note: At a later point of the evening, our helpful staff member appeared at the edge of the dance floor, tired and possibly a little the worse for wear, to renegotiate his "honorarium", which was of course promptly done, with laughs all around, and everything ended as it should.

When one reached the upper sixth form at school, one became eligible for a shared study with two others. Philip Charlton, (of tea-chest bass fame), Roger Bowdler and I got together, and furnished our communal cubbyhole with necessities such as a small cooking ring, a saucepan, utensils for tea and coffee, as well as a table and some comfortable, if somewhat dilapidated, chairs. This meant we could take our daily 11:00 AM government issue third of a pint of milk each and turn it into a hot, acceptable drink, especially in winter, when the milk had been reposing in an unheated changing room for some time, one could quickly turn it into coffee or hot chocolate. This was our haven for at least a year, where we had some great times together and did quite a bit of work, when I wasn't off in a music rehearsal room trying to nail the latest rendition from Buddy Holly. Philip had by now deservedly become head boy of the school, which of course meant he was very busy as well, but it still was a special time to share before individually heading off into the somewhat scary world outside.

Some of us in the "Jazz Gentlemen" used to smoke those Black Russian cigarettes with the gold tips, occasionally in a cigarette holder. It was an "image" thing, and visual rather than actual inhaling, but I must admit that they did taste good at the time. That is, except for Paul, who had a curly Meerschaum pipe from which he would take the odd drag, then place the pipe in his pocket. Every so often smoke would start to come out of his pocket, and there would be a big performance of extinguishing the smouldering jacket, to great amusement, and it became part of the show.

One great thing about working in the City of London was that it was sometimes possible to have a slightly longer lunch break, and take the subway, (or tube), to the West End, in order to check out the music shops. I had fallen in love with a valve amplifier at Selmer's of Charing Cross Road -2 channels, 4 inputs, long Hammond spring reverb, and a very satisfactory tremolo, which in the early 60s was essential, especially for "Surf" music. Plus 30 watts and 2 - 12" Goodman speakers, it was to die for.

Out of curiosity, I sat down one evening to work out what had been spent in the previous year on Black Russian cigarettes. Imagine my amazement to find that the amount was exactly the same, to the penny, as the cost of this "superamp". That, of course, did it, and I cashed in my British Rail season ticket the following day, (buying monthly was the same price anyway), and proudly took home the "superamp", which was used for many years, and travelled all over Europe. Because I now had the amp, I was not going to allow myself to smoke for a year, and with the exception of a few Henri Winterman's cigarillos in Germany, never smoked again.

Returning to the 2 1/2 years commute, the early part of which had the days spent doing a form of mental suicide behind an adding machine, (think of the "unhappy" part of the song "I wanna be a Producer" from the brilliant Mel Brooks musical "The Producers"), when suddenly there was a burst of glorious light at the end of the tunnel. One person in a different area asked if I would like to assist him in proofing complex legal documents, which then had to be printed. It was imperative that these were perfect; they had to be physically typeset, as there was no computerized printing, and were therefore expensive to produce. The top copy was on a parchment, plus there would be six copies on a high-quality white paper called Croxley. This was enjoyable, yet with very high concentration and much talking, so one was allowed to go out for a coffee briefly when needed.

I discovered rapidly that my new co-worker, Ken Swain, had been pianist in the Royal Marines dance band for several years and had especially researched and studied the playing of an early musician named Pinetop Smith, whose sound of course he could produce on request. I recall him telling of the "bandleader" they had, who was hardly musical and far more interested in his appearance. He would say things like "On the command four, you will swing!" so the band would intentionally come in, perfectly together, on three, or seven, just to maintain their sanity. Unfortunately, Ken lived in a totally different direction to me, but one night he came out to join in a "Jazz Gentlemen" performance, to the delight of all who played.

Ken and I worked together for a couple of years, also went for lunch at the excellent staff canteen, which probably had something to do with why people stayed loyal to the company for so long.

"COME AGAIN" AND "FREE AS AIR"

There was a Dramatic and Operatic society of good quality among the staff, some of whom had worked the boards professionally earlier in life and were more than ready to share their skills with the less fortunate. I had a friend in another section of the office called Brian Curling, who was a fine modern jazz guitarist. During my first year the society put on a review called," Come Again!". Brian and I managed to find some mutual ground between our very different musical styles - with versions of "Lady is a Tramp" and "Summertime" -and volunteered our services. The performances were held in a beautiful old-fashioned theatre in the City called King George's Hall, ran for a few days, and were great fun. The next year proved to be even better, with the production of Julian Slade and Dorothy Reynolds' musical "Free as Air", which had run in the West End a few years previously. A good quality show accompanist was brought in for final rehearsals as well as for the actual performance, while Brian and I came in on guitars, plus there was a drummer and accordionist. There was obviously a hole with the lack of bass, so I borrowed Paul's bass guitar, got hold of the West End cast recording, and played along with this at home, since there was only going to be one afternoon of run-throughs on the day of the first performance.

The first night was an amazing experience. Only the pianist had a full score, the rest of us were just doing what we felt the music needed at the time. Imagine our amazement at the show's end when a gentleman came out of the audience to see our little group, full of warmth and friendship, saying how much he had enjoyed our arrangements of his music. We could not tell him, there are some bubbles in life that never need bursting.

As if this wasn't sufficient, my supervisor in the insurance company was a fine church organist by the name of George Woolams. I went one day to St. Paul's Cathedral, where he was playing a lunchtime concert for city workers and was struck by the depth and sensitivity he would put into such well known pieces.

For those of you who do not know, a Cockney is a Londoner who has been born within the sound of "Bow Bells", i.e., Bow Church on Cheapside, in the City of London. The bells hadn't rung since World War II, because of the incessant bombing of the City, but when repairs were finally completed, and the bells rehung, it was George Woolams who was called upon to play for the re-dedication service, a tribute that was so well deserved. He probably understood more than most why I had no choice but to take my music to the next level, no matter how difficult this might be.

There was one winter where the clouds hung low over London, seemingly not moving, below which was thick, orange-coloured swirling smog, so thick that you could almost grab lumps of what would normally be fresh air. Hundreds of thousands of commuters, including me, came into Town daily by rail, the stench was appalling, and many would be instantly ill upon leaving the train.

The Prime Minister was Edward Heath, known as Ted, and not to be confused with the leader of Britain's premier Big Band at the time. The P.M. too, was a brilliant organist, who received a scholarship to Balliol College, Oxford, with his musical skills, and is remembered more for his sailboat prowess than much else that is positive. Constantly battling with the Unions, to his downfall, and eventually reducing Britain to a 3-day work week, he did one incredibly courageous thing for a politician, that should guarantee a place in history. He announced that, by the following October, all houses that used coal, which was everybody, would only be permitted to burn smokeless briquettes, and industry must radically clean up. There would be limited emissions allowed from power stations, all of which would have a filtering "cap" on each smokestack, thus considerably lessening pollution, and any industrial plant that did not abide by the new rules would not be fined, they would be permanently closed. Many thought he would not stick with this, until one plant was shut - I saw the notice on the locked gates - putting many out of work, and others jumped to obey. There were also restrictions on what could be pumped into the Thames River, to the extent that, five years later, there were fish swimming in the Pool of London, for the first time since the Industrial Revolution, though I wonder if that is still the case today.

One time we had a party at "Kitscot". My parents went away together for a long weekend, the only time in my life they had a break together, and it was fine to have a few folks round. So, on a beautiful summer evening, the "Jazz Gentlemen" were set up on the back lawn, and we invited all our friends. We, of course, invited the neighbours, who were used to hearing the band anyway, as there were practice sessions in my bedroom when I couldn't get either of the two Church halls. There were around 50 guests, which seems to be what we always have at a gathering, and there was some good music, as, for example, we had three trumpet players, very different to each other, but all excellent, who had never met before. Brian Epstein drove down from London in his Rolls, (which looked good outside the house), as he knew a couple of the guests, with apologies for gatecrashing, but he brought extra food and drink, and would have been very welcome anyway. He loved New Orleans Jazz, having had the NEMS record shop in Liverpool before managing The Beatles, and later, other acts, so it was great to meet him, the only time I ever did.

During my school days, the cheapest newspaper you could get with any news was "The Times", as it was sold for almost nothing to students. When I started commuting to London, I could still get it for this inexpensive price, because I was going to a special school in Surbiton to obtain insurance qualifications, studying all aspects, including Tort and Contract law, which was to prove so useful in years to come. One day, whilst on the train to London in the early morning, I saw to my amazement an ad. for a not too large replica Mississippi sternwheeler, currently moored in the area of Oxford. My brain immediately kicked into high gear, and I envisioned such a boat cruising the inland waterways of Great Britain, offering a Dixieland Dinner Dance at each port of call, for one or more nights. By the end of the week, I had been in touch for the first of several meetings/phone calls with the Inland Waterways Commission, who were enthusiastic about the idea, and offered help in any way possible, since it would draw huge attention to the canals and waterways, some of which were in disrepair, and needed publicity to encourage restoration. There would have been help with posters and other marketing, and possibly even financial assistance for the start-up.

The "Travellers" (i.e., the rhythm section of the "Jazz Gentlemen"), were all keen. I had a chef who looked at the boat, and said it would be easy to operate, the drummer was also a mechanic, but the problem was that the front three instrumentalists were not going to be available, for various reasons. I looked around at the various musicians I knew, but the concept was not going to work, and I was not experienced enough to put together a new front line, and deal with possible conflicts of personality or other issues that could arise from people unused to working together. So regretfully the idea died, and I got together the "Travellers" to be the basis of a new 6-piece professional band, possibly with a girl singer, to be called 'Band Seven'.

ACT TWO

"Band Seven"

The "Manish Boys"

The "PeeJay Sound System"

The "After Three", (France)

"Peter, Jan, & Jon"

"Band Seven" in rehearsal. Woolf Byrne, David Webber, Sheila Baker, Graham Penney, Me, Bob Solly, Paul Rodriguez.

"The Manish Boys", Bob Solly, Graham Penney, Me, Woolf Byrne, in front: John Watson, Paul Rodriguez. Below: Another rehearsal picture.

"BAND SEVEN" / "MANISH BOYS"

The first thing was that there had to be a hook for promotion. In the way that the "Travellers" had been marketed as "Britain's Brightest Beat", (hey, I was only 16 at the time), I came up with the line "Tune into Band Seven", and had leaflets printed with "Now in rehearsal; blowing your way soon!" and of course a phone number. The manager of the record department in Broadmead's, Maidstone, Angela Harrison, was a very supportive friend, and she made sure that one of these leaflets went out with every record sold for about 8 months. Angela would often appear at "Jazz Gentlemen" gigs, and she would bring into the store any record she thought we ought to hear in the little booth, regardless of whether we bought it or not.

This new band was to be loosely based on "Sounds Incorporated", who were part of the Epstein stable, and really blew your socks off, with high powered versions of things like the "William Tell Overture", or "Hall of the Mountain King", which both Paul and I wanted to have a crack at, as soon as we could.

We also used to often see the "John Barry Seven," with whose guitar player, Vic Flick, I used to sometimes hang out when we shared gigs with them at the Royal Star Hotel. John Barry, of course, got the job of composing and conducting music for the James Bond films, in addition to many others, and there can be few people in the western world who have never heard Vic playing the James Bond theme - I wouldn't be surprised if he plays it in his sleep even now! It is very noticeable in recent Bond films, since Vic's retirement, how his trademark guitar sound is absent. They have got it close, but it will never be Vic.

Vic went on to be a top session player for his career, including much of the guitar work on Sgt. Pepper, considered by many to be the number one popular music album of all time.

We found a tenor sax player locally, and Woolf Byrne, a friend who had been coming out with the band for some time, and helping out with his car, wanted very much to be part of the action. The two of us went into the Star one night to hear the Humphrey Lyttleton band, currently playing Mainstream jazz; as opposed to the New Orleans style of an earlier line-up, when Wally Fawkes (cartoonist "Trog", who drew "Flook" for the Daily Mail) used to do spectacular clarinet duets with Humph., probably never bettered. The line-up that we saw had Tony Coe on tenor sax/clarinet, and Joe Temperley on baritone, Humph. of course, mostly on trumpet. But it was Scottish-born Joe Temperley who truly blew us away, with his technique, creativity and control of the huge instrument. "Sounds Incorporated" of course had a baritone player, which was needed for "Band Seven", and Woolf had already purchased one, which he was learning, now further inspired by Joe's music, and even a blow on his horn.

Aside note: I talked with Joe a couple of times at the Star, and life took me in different directions, but many years later I saw a concert of "Jazz at Lincoln Center" fronted of course by Wynton Marsalis, arguably the world's finest trumpet player, and the only musician to ever be awarded both classical and jazz "Grammys" on the same night. I immediately recognized Joe's playing, which had always been tucked away in the recesses of my mind, and we had a chat later, as we have on occasion since. He had a stellar career, and I was delighted to see him in the world's premier jazz orchestra, which was so richly deserved.

Rehearsals started in earnest; a new drummer, Graham Penney, (brilliant), came in to replace our previous one, who had a day job with British Rail, and slowly things began to take shape. The tenor player was sadly not going to work, so we found another bassist, John Watson, who was also an excellent Blues and R&B singer, and a very accomplished classical pianist, while the indefatigable Paul obtained a tenor sax, and got it to performance level in no time flat. Jackets were made, photos taken, and the energy was building that this band was really going to turn fully professional, at which time our rhythm player Peter Marriott stepped down regretfully, but had family commitments, and this would have been impossible for him. His place was taken by Bob Solly on rhythm, then subsequently organ, and we were ready to go.

For a while, the Royal Star Ballroom was not run by the hotel, but by a production company operating in several towns called McKiernan Enterprises. In the case of the Star, this company was represented by an organist named Alan Haven, plus drummer, who would alternate with the evening's band. When I say organ, I do not mean of the "I do like to be beside the seaside" variety. Alan and his drummer were both excellent jazz musicians who produced a huge show, and the dancers would all cram up front to watch them, which was well deserved. He would usually open with "The Happy Organ" – the Dave "Baby" Cortez hit, which had been covered in Britain by Cherry Wainer, and then would go from there with a magnificent set, including many light changes, which were a new thing. As some performers do, he behaved like a star, and was therefore instantly treated as one, which is effective, should that be the route you wish to take. But a brilliant musician, and a fine man. He married Miss World, Lesley Langley, in the 60s and worked with John Barry on many of the Bond films.

We had a huge crowd at the Royal Star ballroom on our very first appearance, thanks to a big article by David Wigg of the Kent Messenger, and also the 8 month "blitz" of flyers put in every record sold at Broadmead's record store. Bob Solly had only had his little Solette organ for a couple of weeks, but we opened with "Green Onions", played of course on organ, with a wall of sound from the two saxophones and the rest of us. The response was phenomenal, and from then on, we could do no wrong. This followed us all over Kent, especially at the Astor Theatre in Deal, on the south coast, where we opened to a sellout show. Ground floor theatre seats had been removed to facilitate dancing, while the circle was packed, and the screams were to the level of a Beatles concert. One song, originally of Shane Fenton's, (later renamed Alvin Stardust), whom we knew, included a little sigh that I had to do. There was one girl in the front who had been staring at me since the start, and totally passed out when the sigh took place. In a way, this was gratifying, but also spelt out in block capitals, the incredible and very scary power that a band could have over some members of an audience.

We were so lucky to have an amazing fan club from the very beginning, organized by Pam Longhurst and Cynthia Porter, (now Robertson), who wrote for the local pop magazine "Beat 64". They would be at virtually every venue in the area, and Cynthia remains a special friend to this day.

I must mention John Watson, our brilliant bass player/vocalist. Sometimes at the Royal Star, there would be a baby grand piano on the stage. One night, between sets, John went up to the piano and started to play Beethoven's "Moonlight Sonata", impeccably. The ballroom went totally quiet and were mesmerized by his playing, added to which, his long, almost white hair gave the feeling that Beethoven himself had come back to play for us that evening. I had previously heard Benno Moiseiwitsch play the same piece when he visited my school, but world-class as he was, it didn't have the magic of that night at the "Star".

"Band Seven" did one or two "warm-up" gigs, one back at Tonbridge Road Methodist church hall, where the "Cherrypips", had appeared several years previously. We were blowing up a storm, and I saw my mother standing quietly at the back, watching, and giving so much support in her face. She had been in difficult health for many years, and went out very little, certainly not to a crowded, loud hall, so this was something treasured and never to be forgotten. Another event took place at what seemed a very short time afterwards, at my twenty-first birthday party, but it might have been months later. My mother had mercifully passed on, but two of her sisters that I had not seen for years came as her "representatives" for the evening, along with my friends, both musical and from school days. "Band Seven" did a set, and the "Jazz Gentlemen" also, but somewhat depleted on that evening. Nevertheless, it was a great night, and a good "launch" for the new band, even if we were still a "work in progress".

The first fully professional gig for "Band Seven", (i.e., no more day jobs), was on December 31st, 1963, at the Hermitage Ballroom, in Hitchin, Hertfordshire, which was also a huge and valuable lesson. We had all given up our "gainful employment" at the end of that year, intentionally, for accounting purposes, except for Paul, who went part-time for the Chatham News, covering weddings, funerals, and occasionally writing the horoscopes! They did not have a replacement for him, so he had agreed to stay on for a while and help out where possible.

Back to the Hermitage, it was a great night, about 350 people, good food and drink, and we were very well looked after; I still think back to it as a very special event. The BUT to the proceedings was that we were bought and sold at least five times before the job reached us, plus, we were also charged commission on the final one, which was illegal; it being one or the other. We still received a fee with which we could live, but it was under half of what had actually been paid, and we resolved to do more research in the future on this type of job. In North America, agents split commission if they must pass an event to another agent, which is fair. If there is a "buy and sell" event, which is rare, there is never a commission involved as well. It was a good lesson to learn, which I am sure has stayed with every one of us.

We got down to some very serious rehearsals, at least five days a week, "nine to five" with a lunch break, when we could afford food, if not, it was just a cup of tea. The band improved by leaps and bounds and we started to get some good work, but the London clubs such as the Marquee and Flamingo - which were world famous - were very hard to crack. If one approached any of the half dozen or so top clubs, they wanted to see you work in one of the others, or there was no interest. Eventually we talked one of them into letting us do a free set, (one only), which broke down the barriers a bit, as we managed to get two or three of the others to come and see us.

We did get some good things. The Astoria ballroom in Charing Cross Road had dancing and meals from midday onwards, run by a Latin bandleader called Chico Arnez, who had a top-class band with a very fine horn section. He asked if we would do alternate sets with him, plus got us some other venues, but not enough, and things were pretty tight for several months.

On a couple of occasions "Band Seven" even played ice rinks. One was "Silver Blades", in Streatham, where the skaters all went around the edge to an organist, except the few who knew what they were doing, and occupied the middle. Then we came on, and the skaters crowded up to the stage for the whole set. Amazingly, it was fun, and very different.

Of course, this was the time of the Mods and the Rockers, exemplified by the outfits that various stage bands wore, and carried on in the clothing of teens and early twenties throughout the country. In the case of bands all was friendly, but in the rest of the world the Rockers, who wore black leather, sometimes carried chains and knuckle dusters, and usually travelled by Harley-Davidson or equivalent, looked down on the Mods, who wore bright colours of the Carnaby Street style, were into fairly light pop, and usually travelled by scooter. Prime musical examples of the latter would be the "Small Faces" or the "Who" in their early days.

There would be huge battles between the Mods and Rockers in various parts of the country, Brighton on the south coast often being a prime spot. One Saturday, the underground telegraph had let us know that there was to be one of these battles in the ballroom of the Royal Star Hotel, where we were due to play that night. The Mods came into town the previous evening and camped, quite legally, in a park area, so the police could do nothing. On the Saturday morning, the normally busy downtown streets were virtually deserted, with everyone staying home. The Rockers came in sometime around mid-afternoon, with the huge roar of their high-powered bikes. The plan was, with both groups, that someone would buy a ticket, and open the door to the underground parking lot, when the rest would come in.

The hotel made sure that the parking lot was empty, and, as soon as everyone was in there, closed the doors behind them, also to the ballroom. We had meanwhile arranged that the fire department would be waiting, inconspicuously, with hoses at the ready, as we did not want all of our instruments and equipment smashed. The hoses were duly turned on, and in retrospect we felt a little sorry for the Mods, who got by far the worst end of things. But the outcome was that the fight never took place, and the only damage was a little wounded pride. For our part, we had another good evening at the "Star"; the one or two who had actually paid admission left to join their compatriots, and none of them were ever seen again.

We were playing a big social club somewhere, with a cabaret-style audience, and the Concert Secretary came out to introduce us, plus do his spiel about upcoming events. He said (or words to this effect), "Ladies and Gentlemen, I am very sorry to have to tell you that our vice-chairman Bill Snodgrass, (or whoever it was), passed away last Thursday. So, we'll have two minutes silence, followed by this evening's turn", (turn being a colloquialism for an act). Follow that!!!

We did some decent recordings, both for Bob Potter at Camberley, and for Joe Meek, who used his entire house as the studio. He also had amplifiers set up with all the controls soldered, so every band would crank their instruments full on, and he could get the sound that he wanted. The music industry was shocked at his passing some time later, and every one of us wished we could have done more for him, to this day, if we had known more.

One day "Band Seven" was performing in a hall out in the country from our home area, which was run on a non-profit basis for local youth. It was a packed evening, and we were just finishing our first set, when the organizer came up and asked to use the mic. He told us of the assassination of John F. Kennedy, at which time the room went deathly quiet. Everybody was given a refund and went home, also we were paid in full, which we felt showed great class, as he was a volunteer, and the hall probably had to be paid as well.

There was a big difference in bands from the Liverpool/Manchester area, and those from London. Liverpool was more pop oriented: "Beatles", "Hollies", "Swinging Blue Jeans", and "Beatles" spin-offs, initially playing Lennon/McCartney songs, such as "Gerry and the Pacemakers," and "Billy J Kramer and the Dakotas". London was more blues and R&B; instigated mostly by Alexis Korner, who had once led a blues quartet within the Chris Barber band. Charlie Watts, Robert Plant, Graham Bond, Jack Bruce, Ginger Baker, Cyril Davies, and many others all started working with Alexis Korner. The London scene included Georgie Fame, Cliff Bennett, "The Yardbirds", "Rolling Stones", Zoot Money, Chris Farlowe etc., so there was a totally different "feel". Obviously, there are many exceptions - John Mayall was from Newcastle, the "Kinks" were a London band, and Manfred Mann was playing jazz piano in South Africa before putting his UK group together.

It was fairly inevitable that "Band Seven" would be highly influenced by the London sound; especially with 2 saxes and Bob Solly on organ, so the band fitted right in. John Watson was an excellent blues/R&B singer, and there was a feeling among some of the members that this was the direction in which the band should go, aiming at the London Club scene, (at the time, the "Stones" played the 6 Bells in Chelsea on Tuesday nights, and "Pink Floyd" had started doing lunchtime sets in the Rainbow, I think on a Thursday). In "Band Seven", we had now long ago ditched the jackets, unlike the Liverpool bands, and changed our name to the "Manish Boys", after a Muddy Waters song of the same title.

There was a vast labyrinth of caves at Chislehurst, south of London, into which one could walk and possibly never be seen again. Live music was featured weekly, and the "Jazz Gentlemen" performed there more than once. I remember the music echoing around the caves, in addition to the often damp walls, sometimes with water trickling down. When the "Manish Boys" were asked to play, we were ultra-careful of our electrical equipment and made sure that nobody ever touched anything; I think we even had thick socks over the vocal mics!

These weren't actually caves, but ancient chalk and flint mines from the Saxon era, an amazing 22 underground miles of them, and many tunnels were cordoned off for safety.

During World War one, the 'caves' had been a huge ammunition storage facility, while between the wars the damp surroundings were perfect for the commercial growing of mushrooms. Now, there was music, with 'Humph', Acker Bilk, Kenny Ball, and a couple of times, us! Lonnie Donegan played there after leaving the Barber band, and a little later, the "Rolling Stones", "Pink Floyd", Hendrix and more, including the "Manish Boys", until the band's dissolution a while later. Radio Caroline sometimes held popular Saturday nights, and the 'caves' continued to be a magical haven for music and youth into the new millennium.

Graham Penny, our brilliant drummer, was going to have to leave the band - I believe his wife was expecting and he couldn't afford to stay on, plus there were some difficulties with material, so both he and I decided to pull out, me because I didn't really "feel" the music sufficiently at the time, much as I had immersed myself in Muddy Waters recordings borrowed from Bob Solly. So, I pulled out, and Johnny Flux from another Maidstone group "The Cortinas", came in. He was an excellent player, but I do not really think that style of music was his forté either, which was proved some time later when Jimmy Page was brought in to play lead on their first single.

I needed to rethink direction somewhat; I was not in love at all with what I had experienced of the British Pop scene, and needed a complete change, which, unbeknownst to me, was just around the corner.

Meanwhile, it was necessary to get money to keep body and soul together. There was a huge Smedley's cannery locally, who always advertised their vegetables – peas, broad beans etc. as "picked and canned in a day"! Amazingly, this was true, and I applied to work during the broad bean season.

Imagine a huge, round cheese grater, about 8' in diameter, on a slight incline, with the sharp bits going inwards, probably between 15' and 20' in length. Sacks of broad beans are being constantly emptied into the upper end of the cheese grater, which is rotating slowly, with warm water coming through the holes above. The beans drop through the holes below onto a conveyor, while the outside is removed by the sharp bits, and carried out at the bottom by the water for composting.

Somebody in oilskins is constantly walking inside this with a broom, making sure the outsides are going as they should, and the beans through the holes. This was my job. The shifts were 14 hours, through the night, and included one half hour break, and two fifteen-minute breaks, plus there was some time in each shift to remove discoloured beans from the conveyor, before canning.

I only worked at Smedley's for a very few days. I had an apartment a couple of doors from the house in which I had grown up, which was empty and up for sale. My dad had remarried a while after my mother's passing, and moved to Yorkshire in the northeast, which was not going to work for me, as I needed to be close to, or subsequently in, London.

Still, it was strange to be by the house that had been home since the age of five, have a key, and go through all those empty rooms, especially the room that had been "Kitscot Private Theatre" for so long.

Back to Smedley's. I don't think I have ever been as tired in my life, before or since. I used to arrive home at around 10:30 a.m., but one day, I came in at the front door, and did not even make it to the bed. I woke up something like 30 hours later, to find several phone messages awaiting me. Naturally, somebody else had been put in my position, but I had made enough money for several month's rent and was so glad to never go back.

The "Manish Boys" continued for about a year in total, which included a package tour with Gene Pitney, Marianne Faithfull, and "Gerry and the Pacemakers"; the "Manish Boys" opening the show. Artist manager Leslie Conn had a young vocalist/tenor sax player called Davy Jones under contract with Decca (which usually meant 3 singles, then re-evaluate the situation), and suggested he go in with them, which was duly done. Paul and Davy used to visit my apartment in Maidstone on occasion, and he was a nice guy, just recently left Bromley Art College, and eager to make musical performances into a more theatrical experience, with no artistic boundaries.

One day the three of us, together with Bob and Woolf, I think, were sitting in the Giaconda coffee bar, the musician's gathering place, when Paul said, "We've got to get a new name for Dave". Davy Jones of "The Monkees" had just opened in the West End as the Artful Dodger in "Oliver" for Lionel Bart; there was a "Davy Jones and the Cabin boys" up North, and a Blues singer in the U.S. with the same name. There was general discussion, then someone said ,"Well "The Rolling Stones" aren't doing too bad - Jagger, that's like a little knife with a crooked blade", someone else said "Bowie", that's a knife too, you can be Bowie! David was at that time fixated on characters from American history, so to be named after one of them would of course be appealing. The name stuck, and no, you will not find this in any books on David, my guess being that his publicist did not want any references or comparisons to Mick Jagger. But the band stayed together for about ten months, producing a single and did some good work; however, it was economically impossible for them to survive, and they sadly had to call it a day.

Paul went into Philips records as a song plugger, Johnny Flux went to Radio London as a Deejay, calling himself John Edward, while Woolf Byrne went on to the BBC overseas service and other stations. Dave stayed in London, living mostly in an old Bedford ambulance which was parked in Soho Square at night, when the parking meters had stopped running. I had better explain about the ambulances.

During the first half of the 60s in Britain, the health services were selling off older ambulances. The Bedfords went for £65, and (if you were rich), sometimes a Daimler would come on sale for £85 or £90. They were always in perfect working order, and immaculate inside and out. Frequently the bell, (no sirens yet), was still connected, which was of course very useful in heavy traffic if en route to a gig. One band took this to the ultimate, and even carried their own parking meter in the back, which could be placed at the side of the road when needed. This worked for years with no questions asked, until yellow lines started appearing all over the country, and the parking meter had to go. In Maidstone area the "Zephyrs" had an ambulance (which they painted yellow), also the "Whirlwinds", one of whose members was a friend called Mick Stevens. His father had an awesome homemade pie and chips shop, and was so supportive of struggling musicians, never to be forgotten. Both bands put their names where the word "ambulance" would normally be, lit up above the windshield. Pop groups and jazz bands all over the country had these, and there must have been what felt like hundreds of ambulances taking musicians to each day's venue. I like to think that these ambulances were still being used as part of the health service, in that they were bringing music and entertainment to brighten people's lives.

"THE PEEJAY SOUND SYSTEM"

Meanwhile, I was in Maidstone for a little while longer, having put together the nucleus of a possible new group, with the working title of the "PeeJay Sound System". George Waggett lived up the road and came in on tenor sax, (his father was principal flautist with the Royal Philharmonic Orchestra), also we had Mike Dixon, Chris Hocking and Renny Rye as vocalist. Renny would be the main attraction in the band for girls in the audience, rather as Woolf Byrne was in "Band Seven/ Manish Boys".

I had a call for a "Jive Jamboree" at Charing, in Kent, which was the only show we ever did, and pulled in a session bassist, as we had not found one of our own. But it was a great day, with loads of publicity, and several thousand totally energized young folk having an amazing time in the sun.

We all had different projects coming up. I had been contacted by Midlands agent Billy Forrest to put together a band for a tour of the U.S. bases in France, which I eagerly accepted, allowing for the necessary time to organize things.

Renny subsequently went to "Blue Peter" on BBC TV and had a huge career directing and producing series such as "Poirot", "Midsomer Murders" and so many more, which I believe he still does.

"THE AFTER THREE"

So it was time to put this next outfit together, bearing in mind that I had never lived in London, and knew very few people there, even though the "Jazz Gentlemen", (and later, the "Manish Boys"), had done several gigs ,and we had found the musicians' coffee bar/restaurant "La Giaconda", in Denmark Street, which was the current hub, much as the 2I's had been a few years earlier, although in this case there was no stage. I still had a lot to learn but knew enough to put an ad. in the "Melody Maker", which at that time was the working musician's paper for all except classical musicians, unlike the "Record Mirror" (from which the national charts were drawn), or the "New Musical Express", which were both aimed at the general public and fan market. There were several responses to this, and to a similar ad. placed in "The Stage". Meetings were arranged. First, I met with a fine bass player named John Edwards, who had a very good ear, and we were instantly able to sing songs together with very little effort. Not only that, but wonder of wonders, John had an almost new Ford Transit van - loads of room for everyone, plus clothes and the usual mountain of gear. I also met with a female drummer called Jan Dean, who had been for some time with a now defunct group called "Vicky Rowe and the Ladybirds"; Britain's first all girl pop group, (not counting the Ivy Benson orchestra!), and had toured extensively throughout the U.K. The three of us fitted well together from the word "go"; however, having worked on the U.S. Navy base at West Malling in Kent, and other bases with the "Jazz Gentlemen", I knew that for the U.S. service clubs, the band would be far more viable if we also had a vocalist who could cover the black R&B or blues numbers – "Midnight Hour", etc. Fortunately, there were two excellent solo singers in the Maidstone area, who worked with various outfits, Dave Kirby and Tony Bathurst. I discussed the upcoming tour with both singers (the tour to be 2 or 3 months, a month at each venue), and Dave was really interested, so the band was complete.

We settled on the name "The After Three", because there were four of us, and we were also unlikely to see a bed until after 3 A.M. most mornings.

Time was tight, we had a couple of "get-togethers", but realized quickly that we could "wing" the first few nights, and still put on a good show.

All was going great, then, about a week and a half before we were to drive to take the ferry across the channel, (no Chunnel yet), John's van was stolen. Fortunately, it was completely empty except for a mic. in the glove compartment. But we were distraught. Then, two or three days later, he was contacted by police. The van had been found, abandoned. There had been a huge jewel robbery at Hatton Garden in London, and John's van had been the escape vehicle. Of course, the mic. was gone, but on the plus side, the van had been totally tuned and gone over, obviously by an expert mechanic, and was more than ready for the road.

Off to the ferry. The first venue was to be at the U.S. Army base at Koligny Caserne, Orleans, France, for the month of December 1964, exactly 10 months after the "Manish Boys" had turned fully professional. It was decidedly winter, and we were impressed by the dead straight snow-covered highways, with Lombardy poplars on each side, planted by Napoleon to move his troops in all weathers, so many years before.

We had heavy blowing snow that night, to the extent that there was a large overhang of snow from the tops of the high hedge at one side of the road, underneath which we were travelling. We drove slowly, not daring to cough or speak, and awaiting the inevitable. Suddenly there was a big "crrump" and we were no longer going along, just completely buried. With a little difficulty, we got out of the van, armed with a paperback book each, and proceeded to dig our way out of the snow heap we had just created, clearing the exhaust pipe first, and feeling very guilty about any damage to the books. Eventually we shifted enough snow to move, and continued slowly up the wrong side of the road, which was totally clear, there being zero traffic because of the storm. Then, in the darkness, we came upon this huge facility, with a big lit up star rushing around the perimeter fence at great speed. This was the base, and we soon got used to looking for a star such as this, together with rotating searchlight, that would let us know that a U.S. forces camp was imminent.

We reached Orleans and attempted to find a reasonable hotel in our price range for a month. If we had stayed at the Hilton there would have been no problem, but this was out of the question, and the cheaper hotels would not take us because we came from Britain, and the British had once done unthinkable things to Joan of Arc, who was, quite rightly, a heroine in the area. So, we found a parking space, covered ourselves with anything we could find, and settled down for the night, being prepared to run the engine from time to time. The following morning before sunup found us in the first available café/bar, having a huge coffee each, with a cognac in it. This seemed to work, and we were ready to meet the day, and head to the base to set up for the month.

We had been told by the agent that there could be some black people in the audience, not that we cared, apart from having appropriate music, and looked forward to meeting everyone. What we were not told, was that this was a totally black base of several thousand, apart from a handful of other draftees, and the one ex-serviceman who ran the enlisted men's club, plus one or two officers and the MPs. There were still some U.S. bases that were almost totally segregated, and this was sadly one of them. Having said all this, we were made so very welcome, and popular, both with Dave's excellent vocals, and long instrumental sessions of things like "Night Train", "Green Onions", "Moanin'", and many more.

But there was still no place to sleep, and every night, (or very early morning), we would return to our first parking spot, (having borrowed some blankets and cushions), to settle down in the van seats, and get some shuteye, until we could get that first cognac-infused cup of coffee.

The commanding officer and his wife heard of our predicament, and she came so very kindly to find us, with an invitation for the four of us to stay at their house, until such time as a hotel could be found, which we gratefully accepted, probably staying for about a week. Apart from really getting to know them both well, and experiencing their generous hospitality, the colonel's wife spent much time playing tracks from LPs by U.S. artists that we did not necessarily know, which was so hugely helpful at the time. I remember she also played some material by a budding new comedian named Bob Newhart, whose work I have loved ever since.

Our contact in Paris during the tour ran a popular jazz club, also had a couple of apartments two doors away to accommodate visiting musicians. At one time, Miles Davis was working the club, and one night did not show up, when he was going through a bad period. By the following night, there was a luminous, or fluorescent line, painted from the apartment door to the door of the club, and there was never again a "no show" by any visiting artist.

A hotel was eventually found "Hotel Sauvage", that was not really top end - closer to bottom, but the rooms were adequate, reasonably clean, and most importantly, warm. One room had an issue with bedbugs, but a change of mattress rectified that problem. There were extra-curricular activities in the downstairs bar and adjacent rooms, involving U.S. personnel, that did not affect the upstairs. There was another rather dodgy U.K. band staying there as well, that we didn't get to know, (they used to threaten people with cutthroat razors and were eventually thrown off the circuit), apart from their female singer that had been put with them by the agent, (yes, there had to be a girl in the band on the NATO circuit). Her name was Barbara Champion, and, in addition to a busy musical career, she went on to become a leading writer for "The Stage" newspaper, especially covering seasonal pantomimes all over Britain, and we have kept in close touch over the years.

It was quite funny. We would watch from the upstairs window of the hotel on the nights that the U.S. military police would come roaring up to catch any miscreant servicemen in the bar, and cart them off. Meanwhile the gendarmes would wait at the end of the road, lights off, until the M.P.s had left, (with their charges, if any), then turn on the lights, sirens, and anything else they could find, to make as big an arrival as possible, having first made sure that there would be nobody there with whom to get involved. Thus, there were never any conflicts between the two law enforcement agencies – such a sensible precaution.

Chelsea football club was one of the top clubs in Britain, as they usually are, and had a very active supporters' club, whose dedicated volunteer secretary would call the then captain Terry Venables after each game, or he would call to give the final score and a brief chat. This was our drummer, Jan, and fortunately Chelsea nearly always won. The four of us thought a lot of each other, but if Chelsea lost, let's just say that having Jan behind the drum kit made life slightly more challenging for the other three of us that night, with maybe one or two broken drumsticks littering the stage, to say nothing of some sticky Sloe Gin fizz around the floor area of the drum stool.

"PETER, JAN, AND JON"

The tour was successful. Dave returned to the U.K. after the Orleans job, while the three of us continued, (under the new name of "Peter, Jan, and John"), for a couple of months, ending up in the town of Verdun, that had been so heavily bombed, especially in World War One. I remember one day it was raining, and there was a large group of people with umbrellas, standing outside a T.V. retailer, watching the funeral of Sir Winston Churchill on a large screen in the window. Many of them were crying, and one could only speculate as to what horrors they might be recalling, in addition to the passing of such a great leader, without whom the world might have been a very different place. The town had been so devastated in both wars, but was now rebounding with its remarkable resilience, even so, in 1965, many folks still washed their clothes in the river with a washboard; there was a long way to go.

I only once made any money off international foreign exchange. I saw then Prime Minister Harold Wilson on a French T.V. station where he said, unequivocally no less, that Britain was not going to devalue the pound. I looked at his eyes as he said it, took all the U.K. money we had between us, and changed it into French francs. A couple of days later the pound was devalued and I changed it back, giving the three of us roughly 2 week's extra salary each, which was very helpful at the time.

    The tour was drawing to an end, and I had a tipoff that the agent in Paris, who paid us throughout the tour, was liable to come up with the line that we would be paid when back in the U.K. for the final payment, then pocket the last two week's salary. So, we didn't give him the chance; John and I turned up at his house, and I said we were in Paris on business, so to save him the trouble of having to send the money to Britain.... he knew he had been "had" but also respected the way in which we had handled things, and to my knowledge, was straight in his dealings from then on. I have frequently found that if you can offer someone an escape route from a compromising situation, they will not only take it, but will behave more positively in the future.

    Before moving permanently back to London, we visited my sister and brother-in-law, who had a dairy farm in Devon, for a few days. It had been pre- arranged that we would set up in the garage and rehearse some extra material for a bit, which we did, very productively, in such an idyllic surrounding. None of us had been in a garage band before, so this was something for the resumé. I do not know if milk production went up or down during our visit, but the cows did not appear to be in the least bothered, and more than a little interested in what was happening.

Incidentally, while in Paris we saw General de Gaulle, in his immaculate uniform as always, in the back of a car. He saw somebody or something obviously important to him, stood up in the car and saluted. A giant of a man, in more ways than one.

Then it was time for London. Jan was already sharing a bed-sit with a friend, Julie Phillips, who was daytime nanny to Anthea Askey's daughter, (and therefore Arthur's granddaughter), so John and I decided to get the same, as close as we could, which we did, 2 doors away in West Kensington. Note: Arthur Askey was arguably the leading actor/comedian of the time in Britain, one-time president of the two leading charity organisations in showbiz, the "Water Rats" and the "Variety Club"; therefore, a huge force in the entertainment industry. The largest agency/production organization was of three brothers, Lew and Leslie Grade, plus Bernard Delfont. Lew owned ITV, Leslie had the largest entertainment agency, and brother Bernard owned the London Palladium; Britain's no, 1 variety Theatre. If you annoyed the Grade organization you ceased to be in show business, unless you were a pop singer with international hit records, regardless of what had taken place between you, and this happened on occasion, their power was so colossal.

Our trio had just done over 3 months of work together, plus the garage rehearsals, 6 nights per week, 4 or 5 hours a night, so we were by now pretty tight musically. John and I both took lead vocals, with the other backing up as needed, or close harmonies in Everly Brothers' style, plus Jan would occasionally do a vocal on her own, when we could find a suitable song. We wrote some original songs, plus did treatments of old folk and skiffle numbers, but in our own way, which was high energy and fairly jazzy. We met up with an agent called Peter Harrison, who was really pleasant and straight as a die. He had a circuit in pubs all over London, but not the noisy places that were a bit of a zoo. These were venues where customers took their drinks, quietly sat down, and actually listened to the music. Any musician will be aware that in situations like this, the quality of our show would go up fast.

One night we were performing at a venue in southeast London, where there was a couple really into what we were doing, with whom we sat during our break. He was an accountant, and she had a home-based business of some kind. They asked us back to their place when we had finished, which normally we never did, but these two were really pleasant. He also said, "You can bring your guitars if you like" to which my immediate response was "I'll bring my guitar and you can do my taxes". His wife said, "Good for you", and we went to their home anyway and had a good visit. The only reason this is even being mentioned, is that in conversation, it became clear that this lady could see pretty much everything there was to know about me, including things I had forgotten, which initially was a bit unnerving. She basically said, "Don't worry about it, it's a gift that I have", which reminded me, not for the first time, of how very little we know, of what our brains, and those of many other species, can accomplish.

There was one venue where we had appeared three times without payment and went in one morning to collect. We had a pianist friend who was a qualified solicitor, but music was his life. He worked for Cunard, plus for Peter Harrison between cruises. I had been given a few of his cards to use for problem payers and was advised that the cards would be all I would ever need. The three of us went in and were warmly greeted, as always, and told that our cheque had just been mailed!!! We left the premises, but I held back and proffered the card with a big smile, saying, "Just in case the cheque doesn't arrive, you might be needing this", then walked out to join the other two in the van. Before we could leave the parking lot he ran out and paid us in cash, plus more, with profuse apologies for the delay. It was a venue we liked, and there was never a problem again.

We were performing for 3 or 4 nights per week, which was fine, then we met up with a studio engineer named Vic Keary, who owned Chalk Farm Studios, just by the roundhouse, where Andrew Lloyd Webber first produced his early musicals. A roundhouse is a large building, where steam locomotives would be stored or serviced, in a radial pattern, still on tracks of course. This one had been converted to a "theatre in the round" and held many productions, big and small, some of which would see the bright lights of the West End in years to come.

We hit it off with Vic straightaway. He did all kinds of recording: opera, jazz, folk, pop, and blues. He had a good ear, and was very adept at splicing tape, a thing of the past, where sections of recording tape would be cut at an angle and joined together perfectly, so the joint was inaudible, and the timing remained perfect. In those days there was only 1/4" tape, and any overdubs had to be exact, or the whole thing would have to be redone from scratch. When the project was completed, an acetate disc would be cut and sent off to the record company – E.M.I., Decca, or whoever. We recorded with HMV ourselves, doing our first single, "Mountain Boy" in Vic's studio one evening, backing track and vocals first, then it was my turn to overdub a solo. There was an old twelve-string guitar in the corner with only three or four strings on it, which I felt might sound good, so I tuned the remaining strings to the pitch of the recording and produced an appropriate piece. Then I flipped the guitar over and thumped gently on the back in time with the bass drum, letting the strings vibrate for a bigger sound. The record was released, the Melody Maker and New Musical Express gave us good reviews, and David Jacobs especially liked it, playing the song whenever possible. I don't remember if we made "Juke Box Jury", but one thing that happened was that it was released on the same day as a new Beatles single, and all the EMI presses were, not surprisingly, going flat out on producing that as fast as they could. We sold a few thousand quickly that were already available, which was followed by the appearance of letters in the musical press from people saying they were trying to buy "Mountain Boy", but nobody had it in stock, or could get it. Things happen, and we all move on.

Vic did a lot of work with Radio Caroline, which had started transmissions from a ship outside British territorial waters, in February 1964. At that time, all broadcasting in the U.K. was controlled by the Post Office, and nobody else was allowed to broadcast, as was T.V., for which you had to buy a licence, and there would be 'detector' vans driving all over Britain to find anyone who was daring to watch T.V. without a licence, (which paid for the B.B.C., who had no advertising).

Commercial T.V. had not long been going, and there was as yet no commercial radio. The only way that young folk could hear "their" music was on Radio Luxembourg, or later Radio Caroline as well. There were one or two radio offerings on the BBC - Saturday Club on a Saturday morning with Brian Matthew, or the Top 20 with Alan Freeman on Friday evening. BBC T.V. had Six-Five special, with Pete Murray and Jo Douglas, also Juke Box Jury, with David Jacobs, (nice guy). Later ITV upped the ante on a Friday, (after school), with Ready, Steady, Go, which made a household name of Cathy McGowan. The programme was probably the first to have any serious energy from a British Music T.V. show and sowed the seed for other shows to come.

We were doing assorted "jingles" for Radio Caroline through Vic's auspices, often with me writing pieces for each of the Deejays; Tony Blackburn, Garry Kemp, Keith Skues, and Simon Dee. Sometimes there would be a call from one of them saying what someone else had done, and I would dutifully write a jingle on it, that we would record and get to the ship. Then there would be another call, "That's nothing, let me tell you this", and off to the studio again. Plus, we did a personal jingle as an I.D. for each of them, and several for the station.

On one day, there was supposed to be a "boarding party" from the G.P.O., who were coming out to take over the ship. Large supplies of ice cream were taken on board, for use as weapons when the "invasion" took place. Southern England virtually ground to a halt, as everyone listened to the blow by blow, (not really), account, broadcast "live" from the crow's nest. (Radio Caroline by now had another ship as well, off Liverpool). After a few tubs of ice cream had been hurled, the G.P.O. invaders were helped on board for drinks and supper. When commercial radio was eventually permitted in the U.K., Radio Caroline's ship was sold, moved over to the coast of Holland, and I believe became a part of the Radio Veronica setup in Europe for a while.

Prince Buster was a big artist in Jamaica and the Caribbean, and we made backing tracks for him at Vic's studio. Basically, anything we could find in the charts that could be given a Caribbean or "Blue Beat" backing, we made a track in what seemed a reasonable key, and it was sent off for him to put a vocal on the ones he liked and release them. Some were O.K. I think the one we liked best was the Sam Cooke song "Cupid", which leant so well to that "feel". In any event we had a great time putting all these songs down, some of which did not work at all, no matter how hard we tried.

Talking of Blue Beat, on one occasion we were booked to play a basement West Indian Club in Soho. We were to play all our usual material, but infused with the Blue Beat wherever possible, i.e., songs like "The Ballad of Jesse James" became Caribbean in sound, which we could easily do after our many sessions for Prince Buster. The dance floor was packed solid, with everyone having a good time. At the end of one piece, we stopped playing, and one of the dancers fell to the floor, having been stabbed at some point of the song. There was a narrow flight of stairs up to the main entrance, also an emergency exit behind Jan's drum kit, but the drums would have needed moving to access this. Suffice to say that, by the time the police arrived, the body was no longer to be seen. London in the 60s was not all flower power, sweetness, and light. As a musician one didn't feel threatened, any more than Duke

Ellington would have done with some of his "Cotton Club" clientele in the 20s; nevertheless, it was prudent to keep one's eyes open, and one's mouth preferably closed.

One time, I think at Vic's, we'd put down a fairly simple instrumental piece as a background to the dialogue on a cream commercial. I was asked if I wanted to go in, when they filmed a hand pouring cream from a jug over some strawberries. They filmed it several times but were not happy with how the cream looked, so some smart Alec; you can probably guess who, said "There's a paint shop up the road, why don't you get a can of Dulux and use that?" I was semi-joking, but this was duly done, and the commercial went out on national television of a can of white paint being poured onto a beautiful bowl of strawberries. Little do people know.......

Many stories from that studio. On one occasion Ken Sims (ex Acker Bilk trumpet player, whom I knew), Ian Wheeler (clarinet), and Mac Duncan (trombone), from the Ken Colyer band, had formed a new outfit, called "The Sims-Wheeler Vintage Jazz band", with Long John Baldry on guitar/banjo and vocals - in my opinion the U.K.'s finest band - and made a terrific L.P. off the floor, with Vic. It was so good, but was never released, owing to contractual difficulties with different record labels. Such a great shame, and the classic master was eventually destroyed.

Another time Vic had recorded and produced a hit called "Young, gifted and black!". One time a few of us were in the studio and some music was playing. Someone asked what it was, and Vic said it was the backing track to "Young, gifted and black!". General feeling was that it sounded good, and the label thought so too, to the extent that it was released, and became a hit, though I am not sure under what title.

My favourite story of all is of an opera singer who came in to record. Very much the diva/prima donna, she was quite good, but so very full of herself, and Vic stayed up all night splicing tape to get the good bits, at which he was so skilled. When she came back to hear the run-through, she was justifiably amazed at the finished product, and was expounding on her skills. Vic, who had been working all night on the recording, and had not yet been to bed, eventually caved in and said "Yes, don't you wish you could sing like that?"

Acker Bilk's office ('Acker', being English West Country slang for "mate" or "friend"), was in Wardour Street, London. Run by his brother David, plus Mick Mulligan's old trombonist Frank Parr, (who could amazingly whip through the Times crossword at great speed even when totally smashed, and then sink gently to the floor), also a very adept lady called Wendy - I regret not having her last name - who was the "front" of the office, did all the accounts, and essentially held the whole enterprise together, which would have failed miserably without her. The office was called the Bilk Marketing Board, (if you are not from the U.K. ask any Brit to explain this). I am not certain how we connected, but they, and especially Frank, wanted to handle our affairs and manage us, which we accepted.

The leading Traditional Jazz Club in Britain was the 100 club, below ground level in Oxford Street, London. All the greats played there, not only British, but luminaries like Louis Armstrong, Henry "Red" Allen, and George Lewis, also Sydney Bechet, who was on a semi-residency at the Paris "Blue Note" at the time. It was a hugely popular venue, with a good Chinese food kitchen as part of the club. We started playing there twice a week; usually the "star" band would do two sets, and we would do two; sometimes there was a more "free for all" set at the end, which everyone enjoyed; even the audience.

Manager at the time was Roger Horton, who subsequently took over proprietorship, and is one of the most amenable people I have ever known. In addition to "Trad" jazz, blues artists such as Muddy Waters, Howlin' Wolf, and B.B. King would appear, plus in later years the 17-piece Big Band of Montreal-born Maynard Ferguson, whose technique with trumpet and other brass instruments was incredible. Some say he could play 3 octaves higher than anyone else; certainly, he could hit a double high "C" and more with ease. Others say he could play beyond the range of human hearing, with which it would of course be very difficult to argue! Very loud and 'showy' when working, some of the critics didn't like him, but he was a consummate musician who knew exactly what he was doing, and I feel privileged to have heard and talked with him in a club atmosphere, where there would always be instantly recognisable horn players standing close to the stage, in total awe of his presence.

We were connected to another booker, who started to get us cabaret-style venues throughout England and Scotland, (where we built quite a following). I recall the first time we played in Dundee, we were put in a long hall, with the stage laterally across the middle, so that no matter what you did, half the audience was behind you. We did our first number; turned the p.a. speakers and drum kit around, and played it again, to the delight of the audience. From then on, we could do no wrong, and the next time we appeared in Dundee, the stage was back to the wall, where it should have been in the first place.

Dundee was always hard logistically, because we would be there on a Saturday night, and frequently in the 100 club in Oxford Street, (pre motorway), on the Sunday. John did the driving and loved it. At some point near the Scottish border, he would say "I must stop!", pull the van over, Jan and I would get out, and he would sleep very deeply for 10 or 15 minutes, then say, "I'm O.K. now!" and continue as though he'd had a full night's sleep, which he could always do.

It was impossible to get food on a Saturday night after midnight in Scotland. The Lord's Day Observance Society was very strong, and the service of food was totally illegal. So, the first venue was over the border in England, in a somewhat challenging transport café at Scotch Corner, which was always very busy on a Sunday morning.

We went in, ordered three teas off the lady behind the counter, (who was possibly an ex- Russian weightlifter), and John also asked for one of the big sausage rolls that were in the cabinet behind. This was duly given to him on a plate, and we went to our table, where John attempted taking a large bite from the sausage roll. This proved to be impossible, (who knows how old it was), and John took it back to the counter with the words, "I can't bite this". The Russian weightlifter went to the kitchen, came back armed with a large meat cleaver, put the sausage roll on the (very questionable) counter, and with three large thwacks cut it into four equal pieces. John looked at her size, at the meat cleaver, and said "Thank you very much", putting the sausage roll back on the plate, and returning meekly to his seat. I think we took it with us and left it somewhere at the side of the road - resolving never to stop at Scotch Corner again. We shared the story with Frank Parr at the 100 club that night.

Talking about Frank, (who had his own armchair at the 100 club with his name on it, to which he could be carried comatose whenever he was there), and also the Bilk band setup, I must mention a totally brilliant publicist named Peter Leslie. Bernard "Acker" Bilk had a good band, there is no doubt, but there were several good bands at the time struggling to be noticed. Peter came up with the idea of the name Mr. Acker Bilk, the bowler hat, and the waistcoats, also did amazing sleeve notes and articles in a Victorian style, which were instantly successful.

In much of his writing, he would say, "If there had been no Mr. Bilk, it would have been necessary to invent one!", which of course was exactly what he had done, and the band became one of the top three in Britain, along with Chris Barber & Kenny Ball. All three bands produced rather "poppy" jazz for the commercial market, but were capable of playing really good music, should one be fortunate enough to catch them in a club situation.

We stayed with the Bilk office, as "Peter, Jan, and Jon", for quite a while, and were building some degree of a following, especially in the 100 club, but then two major things happened. John had a girlfriend, who had two bunches of hair at the back of her head; therefore nicknamed "Bunches", that he announced he was intending to marry, and that he would be leaving the act. Prior to this there had been a break in at the solicitor's flat where John and I had a bed-sit, and my prized Burns TR2 guitar was stolen, nothing else; somebody knew what they wanted. This was a very sad time for the three of us, although we of course understood that John needed to get off the road, and into his new life.

One thing before leaving "Peter, Jan, and Jon". We were invited to be a part of a big fundraiser for the Stars Organization for Spastics, at Battersea Park. We dutifully showed up in the provided limo, and went into a huge marquee, which was full of stage luminaries that we immediately recognized, but no musicians like ourselves. We were standing in the entrance looking for a friendly face. At the extreme back of the tent was a little group of Sidney James, Laurence (Larry) Olivier, Liz Fraser, and Bernard Bresslaw. Sid saw us a long way away, and immediately left his group, worked his way through the crowd, and came straight up to us, saying "Hello, I'm Sid, come with me and I'll introduce you to some people!" We were so grateful for his thoughtfulness at the time, and I for one will never forget it.

The way that money for the charity was raised, was that there were several tables in a long line. People lined up, paid an admission fee, or more if they wished, and went through the line clutching autograph books, speaking to everyone, including some huge names, and collecting signatures. The three of us were together, with Jan on the left, next to Michael Caine, who had just done the "Ipcress File", and was obviously destined for great things. He had lost his name tag, so Jan put an extra bit on hers, so that it now said "Jan" then underneath: "loves Michael Caine", in big letters, and an arrow to the left, which rectified the situation. This fundraiser was incredibly successful, yet I have never seen the concept repeated, I wonder why?

Mentioning the 100 club again, we used to play once a week on a programme for Radio Luxembourg, hosted by Muriel Young, with big names coming in to "mime" their latest record for the club audience, which was also going out on the air. We would get to do 2 or 3 songs interspersed through the programme, which was the only "live" music in the show. Ken Evans, then head of CBS records in the U.K., used to always be there, and introduced me to Diana Ross, then of "The Supremes", who had their second single out. She was saying how incredibly lucky the three of us were to play "live", as they were expected to mime to their record, which they hated. But they had been truly creative and worked out three extra vocal harmonies to go with the record, which of course would only be heard by those present at the club. We also worked alongside "The Marvelettes", Gladys Knight, and many more, but never saw anyone as creative as them again.

So, the three of us moved on, with many good times to recall, especially getting used to doing studio work with Vic, for ourselves, for Radio Caroline, for Prince Buster, and others. I didn't see John and "Bunches" again for very many years, when playing at the Banff Park Lodge in Canada, but kept in touch with Jan, who was now working for Westminster Marketing, run by the original "Ladybirds" manager, and will appear again later in the story.

I sometimes used to interview stars for Radio Caroline in a "live" situation at the 100 club, except that it was too noisy in the club itself, but we could stand in the entryway on Oxford Street and the sound was great, with some music from below, and a little traffic for ambience.

"Peter, Jan & Jon". Photo: K.H. Kiehlmann, Madrid

"Peter & Elisabeth"

ACT THREE

The Giaconda Years

"Westminster City Sound", (France)

"Peter & Elisabeth", (Germany and U.K.)

"Swinging London"

"THE GIACONDA YEARS"

During the various times that I lived in London, there were two main gathering places for musicians. One was in Archer Street, on a Monday, where mostly pit, orchestral and dance band musicians would hang out, discuss ideas for jobs, and generally compare notes. I was fortunate to get a good contact there once, for the Norwegian Seaman's Club, where there was a pickup band on one day of every week, and I went in on several occasions when times were a bit tight, sometimes to front the evening, (which could be challenging, depending on who was on the stage that night), and sometimes to provide backup.

The other gathering venue, mostly for pop and a few session musicians, was "La Giaconda" restaurant in Denmark Street, Britain's version of Tin Pan Alley in New York. Most of the music publishers were in Denmark Street, and there were several top-quality studios, often in the basements of these publishers. Instrument shops abounded on Charing Cross Road and Shaftesbury Avenue, plus the largest sheet music store in the country. For a budding musician, this restaurant was heaven. Apart from U.S. visitors, (I saw Dylan, Baez, Sonny & Cher, plus several others there), it was the gathering place in the daytime, mostly for the many upcoming, and already established, pop groups.

It was owned by a slightly older Jewish lady named Julie, and her husband. Julie absolutely loved having this little restaurant, packed with musicians and their associates, and was everybody's grandmother, often their best friend too. I recall several of the Liverpool bands asking about bread pudding, which was a more Northern thing, and Julie asking everyone about recipes. Billy J. Kramer proffered his mum's recipe as being the very best, and it went onto the menu at great speed, to everyone's delight.

Julie had another restaurant near Mansion House tube station, in the City of London, which made a fortune selling buns, sandwiches, also take-out teas and coffee for office workers in a hurry, in addition to a sit-down menu. I often think this other venue subsidized "La Giaconda" somewhat, her prices were so reasonable.

I absolutely must mention Albert, the elderly waiter, who frequently wore tails, (but not white tie). Albert was a beautiful human being, who sometimes could get a little confused. It was possible to order egg and chips, (the most basic item on the menu), and Albert would return with a large piece of gooseberry pie, with custard or cream on top. Nobody would ever question what he brought; we all knew that he was an older gentleman doing his absolute best, and none of us wanted to hurt him in any way.

I used to see David (now Bowie) there quite a bit, both in his ambulance days and later, also I became friendly with Marc Bolan, ("T Rex"), who, if you ever needed to cast an elf in a part, would have been the absolute ultimate, and we used to talk for aeons. It was so tragic when he was killed in a car accident sometime later. Marc's girlfriend, with whom he was living at the time, was driving, but they were not legally married under U.K. law, and despite Marc by now being a big name, she was to get nothing, as he died intestate, and Britain so far does not recognize common law marriages, unlike Canada and many other countries. David had also been a friend to both of them, and when he later found out that she was having a difficult time, he set up a financial arrangement that would make sure she was well looked after for life. I only found this out recently and wish I could have thanked Dave for this before he sadly passed as well.

There are so many people to write of during this time frame, all important, and they all made a difference to those years around London.

Herbert Wilcox, film producer/husband of Dame Anna Neagle, was one. We met in "La Giaconda" over a cup of tea, then a few days later

I popped up to his nearby office to meet his beautiful St. Bernard dog, who of course, instantly became a best buddy, and I would happily take him for walks around Soho Square, which was grassed, if Herbert had a busy schedule. I looked forward to my visits to both, and Herbert very kindly tried to assist me in my career, but our hats were so very different.

Just off Charing Cross Road was a small variety/vaudeville style agency, run by Joe Cohen and his partner Philip Hankinson. Joe was very much an old school variety performer, who had actually been in the "Keystone Cops", before being joined with Oliver Hardy for a while as a double act. But Joe was also a big man, and the future pairing of Oliver with Stan Laurel was hardly surprising, since it opened the door to so much physical comedy, with the contrast between the two of them. Joe was such an interesting man, who got me a fair bit of work, mostly as a solo musical act, also I loved looking through his photographs of a bygone era, of which he was such an integral part.

Another small agency, I think in the same block as music publishers Francis, Day & Hunter, was that of Max Mundy, who was a good and supportive friend for several years. Max helped Jon McGrath with L'Hirondelle, a good quality supper club close by with cabaret, and had a finger in several pies in the industry. We'd be trying to fix the world, then he'd say, "Let's have a cuppa tea" and we would head into the Giaconda, where Julie would instantly lay two teas in front of us, knowing we were busy with something.....

I recall meeting Jack Hawkins, a hugely popular British actor, probably around 1967, at a gathering in London. Jack was wearing a jacket with open shirt and a cravat, and when he started talking, I immediately realized that he was talking through a hole where his larynx had once been, as a result of throat cancer. I was so incredibly saddened by this; such a fine man and resolved that tobacco would never play a major role in my life. Jack continued his movie career with his voice dubbed, and a mechanical device for private conversation, until his passing in 1973.

So many faces…. There was Maureen O'Grady, of the flaming red hair, who was editor of "Rave" magazine, a high-quality pop and lifestyle publication, rather of the style of "Salut les Copains" in France, which one could get in London, but you had to know where to go. Maureen had spectacular parties at her apartment, quite dressy and black tie for the men if possible. The parties were under the auspices of "Rave" magazine, and sometimes I'd be asked to read poetry that I'd written, the only times I ever did this, apart from at gathering of Frankfurter Allgemeine staff and others in Germany during 1968, whilst on tour.

The leading girl vocal trio, who backed up so many hit records, was that of Leslie Duncan, Kiki Dee, and Madeline Bell. Leslie, I knew fairly well, Kiki a bit, (who had a No. 1 hit with Elton John), but I didn't know Madeline. All three were part of the nucleus of "regulars" at the Giaconda, who were almost a family, of which I was fortunate to be a part. Dennis "T-Cup" Taylor, (yes, he drank a lot of tea), had a trio with the Merseybeats ex-drummer, and a bassist. When the "Manish Boys" folded, and David wanted to do some live performances of his own material, he joined up with Dennis. I was looking at a "100 club" schedule that had been kept from an ancient copy of the "Melody Maker", and saw that "Peter, Jan and Jon" had been in on the Tuesday and Thursday of one week, while David had been in, (with Dennis' group "The Lower Third"), on the Wednesday. Wish I had known that all those years ago. I never heard Dennis play and would have loved to have seen the trio and Dave together.

They did a single, then eventually Dave moved on without a band for a while, while the Lower Third did a house job in the Middle East. Mandy Rice-Davies (Christine Keeler's friend - remember the Profumo affair that brought down the government?), was a Giaconda regular, and had recently married into a Middle Eastern family - receiving a nightclub as a wedding gift. She immediately thought of her somewhat impoverished friends at the Giaconda, and the "Lower Third" went out for a residency- top notch treatment, great salary, all expenses paid, but the small catch was that you couldn't bring any money back home. Nevertheless, I believe they had a good time, and certainly came back in a far better state of health than when they had left.

The Giaconda had a payphone in the doorway, which took incoming calls. There were no cell phones yet, and so the restaurant was an office to many folks, of which I was one. I still did the odd session for Vic, always having my guitar close by in a music shop, and was often called upon to play a session at one of the local studios, sometimes a demo, sometimes a master, one didn't always know. I remember when Tom Jones did the demo for "It's not unusual" (no, I was not the guitarist, I think it was Jim Sullivan) for Gordon Mills' office, it was pitched to Presley, and I believe P.J. Proby, but nobody picked it up, so they put the brass on and put it out, anyway that's how the story goes.

Another story that did the rounds was ostensibly about Tony Bennett, but, as with many stories, it is quite possible that he knows nothing about it. It seems Tony was working one of the big Northern clubs, such as the "Talk of the North", or the "Fiesta", in Stockton. Many of the clubs, both big and small, had a pie shop close by, who would deliver copious amounts of meat pies to the club at a designated time, which, after a couple of beers, were very popular with the clientele, and no doubt kept the pie shop in business.

One night, Tony was working with a full band, to an appreciative audience, who were enjoying his brilliant music. Suddenly, most of the audience got up and made for the door as fast as they could, to Tony's chagrin. The Concert Secretary came up to the stage, where the show had stopped, and everyone was wondering what on earth had happened, to which he replied, "Don't you worry, Mr. Bennett, the pies have come".

The "Walker Brothers" from the U.S. (Scott Engel, John Maus and Gary Leeds), were regulars, and probably the only act in the U.K. to absolutely guarantee a crowd of screaming girls. We often had to pile out and help them get from their publisher's office across to the restaurant. In this part of London at the time, the Beatles could almost pass unnoticed in comparison. Plus of course many more. Jimi Hendrix would be in most days with Chas Chandler, the "Animals" ex-bassist, who had left the band to bring Jimi to Britain. We used to joke that Jimi was one of the few regulars who always bought tea, even though he could afford coffee! (Footnote: this was the mid-60s, and U.K. restaurants had yet to learn how to make a decent cup of coffee. We're now in the 2020's and some places in the country still serve instant!!) Many more; the "Small Faces" were big; Wayne Fontana, Donovan, the "Pretty Things", the "Kinks"; Clem Cattini from the "Tornadoes" had started doing some sessions, also Brian Locking, bassist from the "Shadows", who replaced Jet Harris, when Jet and Tony Meehan left the band, was a friend during his "Shadows" period of a year, then left to work with Jehovah's Witnesses, being replaced by John Rostill. To me, the "Shadows" were at their best when Brian Locking and Brian Bennett were playing with Hank and Bruce. Jet and Tony were marketed separately, with a friend for life, David Burns, on guitar, except at this point of the story, we have not met yet.

The "Shadows" had a very active fan club, run by Lynn Anderson, who now shared the bed-sit in West Kensington with Jan and Julie. She also drew several thousand rabbits for the movie "Watership Down". Another Giaconda friend, Barbara Cavanaugh, was in this loop, and there was a short period when Lynn, Barbara, and I shared the bed-sit. Barb had a bed, and whoever contributed the most to the rent got the other, although I was usually quite happy with two armchairs facing each other. I remember well the three of us having the most unbelievable stomach "flu" at one time. There was no food in the kitchen except a bag of rice - not that we could have touched even that for several days. Barbara had a job to go to, I had a session, Lynn had commitments, we were broke at the time, because we couldn't do our work, not that money would have helped anyway. Eventually we put some hot water on the rice, which was instant, and somehow the three of us survived.

We had a friend on the floor below, Lyn Grant, who went on to write for the Evening Standard for some years. She wrote a song called "Time on My Hands", and I put together a session at Vic's, where she sang it, with full backing, but no intention on her part of doing any more, except that she now had a couple of acetates of her own professionally produced song. I recall that she shared her flat with a girl called Margaret Oban, who was with the G.P.O., and if you got Margaret on the line as operator when trying to make a long-distance call from the communal pay phone in the hallway, there was never any charge. I kept in touch with Lyn for many years, but as sometimes happens when one travels, the link was sadly severed along the way.

In Canada, except on freeways or very busy main roads, traffic will often stop for a pedestrian, which doesn't happen in many countries. I was once in a taxi coming up Charing Cross Road, in London, when Field Marshal Viscount Montgomery, now a frail elderly man, came out of Foyles' bookshop to cross the road. All the traffic literally screeched to a halt; a couple of people got rapidly out of their vehicles to salute him, which was quickly and smartly returned. I have never forgotten that; he was wearing his ubiquitous black beret, which he still wore when I saw him in Bournemouth, sitting quietly on the seafront in a wheelchair, some years later.

Sandie Shaw was sometimes in the Giaconda, and she would be visiting Phil Coulter, ("Puppet on a String" etc.), in Southern Music next door. One time she had been booked to do cabaret at the Savoy, which was a big deal, and she was inexperienced, and more than a little nervous. A bunch of us found out about this, so we went in on her first night to be supportive, not that we knew her, broke as usual, and ordered a portion of mashed potato each, the cheapest thing on the menu. Being the Savoy, the waiter had class, and did not blink an eyelid. The mashed potato was duly brought out, presented with other vegetables around it, a ring of parsley and a nice sauce, so that it became an enjoyable meal. The maître 'd' looked after us impeccably with complimentary tea or coffee flowing, and thanked us for coming, even though the gratuity was somewhat small. They understood exactly why we were there and treated us all so very well. There are many people in life one would like to go back in time and thank again, these gentlemen were certainly two of them.

One character of the era, who absolutely needs mentioning, is David "Screaming Lord" Sutch, an eccentric rocker, who was an integral part of the British pop scene. The "Screaming", and much of the approach to his act, was plagiarized from "Screamin' Jay Hawkins" in the U.S., even to the extent of being brought on in a smoking coffin, but on occasion he took the horror aspect to a whole new level; for example, in his song "Jack the Ripper", he would pretend to cut out heart and liver from one of the band members, which would then be flung into the audience, having been obtained from a butcher's shop prior to the show. The "Screaming" part of his name was also attributed to the fact that he used to run up and down subway escalators doing just that, while the "Lord" was legally added by Deed Poll. Fiercely British, he stood for Parliament 39 times, earning himself a place in the Guinness Book of records, with his "Monster Raving Loony Party". He knew he would never be chosen yet wanted to prick the pomposity of the ruling classes; pushing for votes at 18, local and commercial radio, all day pubs, passports for pets, and knighthoods for the Beatles, much of which came to pass. At one point he tried to change his name to Margaret Thatcher, but this was rejected, on the grounds that there might be confusion if he were elected.

His band "The Savages" variously contained some huge stars to be: Jeff Beck, (Yardbirds), Ritchie Blackmore, (Deep Purple), Matthew Fisher, (Procol Harum), Mitch Mitchell and Noel Redding, (The Jimi Hendrix Experience), and others all worked with him; drummer Carlo Little even turned down the Rolling Stones to stay where he was.

Both his grandfather and his father, (a policeman who was killed in the Blitz when David was 10 months old), were regulars at Speaker's Corner in Hyde Park, so it is not surprising that he tried to make a difference, in his own way. When Radio Caroline was up and running, he too started a station with his manager, on the "Shivering Sands Fort", off the coast of Essex, as part of his push for commercial radio.

He made many records with Joe Meek, and a couple of his albums made the U.S. charts, where he had somewhat of a "cult" following - including the single "Big Black Coffin", considered to be one of the best U.K. rock singles ever. But it is his eccentricities that are most remembered.

As an avid tea-drinker, (at least 20 cups per day), he was of course in the Giaconda frequently, so we were kept abreast of his activities. My two favourites were, that once, he set up a little workmen's tent in the middle of Oxford Street, together with the obligatory brazier for warmth/cooking chestnuts/ preparing tea. He had a couple of signs around the tent, while police kindly directed traffic appropriately, and he sat inside and played cards; I think he may have dug a very small hole as well. He and his friends spent 3 or 4 days there, then packed everything up, presumably filled the hole, and left. His point was, that nobody questions anything if you are open enough, and he also said that the moles "needed to come up for a breathe anyway".

Another time he had an apartment in Chelsea, which he decided to turn upside down. Yes, completely. The carpet and chairs, side tables, lamps etc., were all fixed to the ceiling, while the main light stuck up vertically from the floor. Even the curtains were reversed, with curtain rods at the bottom of the window, and the actual curtains going upwards, (helped by very thin string). When the newspaper came around, he and three others were upside down in the chairs, (strapped in), playing with magnetic cards. That picture never made the press, because the reporter screamed and ran away.

A larger-than-life character, if a bit scary on occasion, but the 60s would not have been the 60s without him.

A couple of other occasional Giaconda visitors were actor Marty Feldman, instantly recognizable by his prominent mis-aligned eyes. Born in London in 1934, he seemed a nice chap, and I wish I had known him more. He did a fair amount of work, and his appearance did not seem to be a handicap, even though some of his parts might be described as "character". He passed in 1982 in a Mexico City hotel, still in his 40s, and definitely left a "hole" in the London scene, that belonged to him alone.

The other was Spike Milligan, beloved writer of the "Goon Show" from 1951 - 1960, as well as many books. When I first saw him, he was riding an ancient ladies' bicycle with very large wheels along Denmark Street. His apartment had not long previously had a break-in, and, while nothing of importance had been touched, he now understandably carried all of his writings with him, in two large saddlebags which hung on each side of the back wheel, with yet another bag on the rear luggage rack. When he came into the Giaconda, it was quite an entrance, as the overloaded bags would all be stacked by the payphone, with Spike getting the closest booth whenever possible, which was pretty much always, as it would be instantly vacated so that he could keep an eye on such prized possessions.

The "Goons" evolved over a period of years. Spike and comedian/singer Harry Secombe became friends while in the Royal artillery during WWII, with many stories surviving of their times together. Spike met up with Peter Sellers at a Harry Secombe show after the war, and the three subsequently became arguably the most important force that British comedy had ever seen. The three of them used to get together, putting on a "live" comedy show at Grafton's pub in London, one night a week, in the late 40s. All three of them now wrote for the B.B.C., and it was not long before the "Goon Show" was launched as an experiment on the radio, with Spike as writer, but ad-libs were liable to appear at any time. This "experiment" was hugely successful, with comedian Michael Bentine also a cast member for the first three years. It was broadcast in Australia, South Africa, New Zealand, India and Canada, but was often sadly edited somewhat overseas. By the mid-50s, it was on the air in the U.S.A. (N.B.C.) with a "cult" following that lasted many years.

The Beatles "patter" in their movies and interviews owes a huge amount to the "Goons", as does "Firesign" theatre in the U.S., and "Monty Python's Flying Circus", which might well have not existed at all, had the "Goons" not first paved the way.

I only saw Spike perform "live" once, opposite brilliant stage actress Joan Greenwood, who would try in vain to play her part "straight" without "corpsing", which means eventually spluttering and giving up in gales of laughter, usually along with the audience. The play was called "Son of Oblomov" very freely adapted from Ricardo Aragno's play; itself based on the Russian novel of Ivan Goncharov, and somewhat different every performance.

The play opened with Spike asleep in a huge four poster-bed, totally covered apart from two different socks, and emitting "ZZZZZZZ" sounds, which he did for a while, by which time the entire audience was in paroxysms of laughter. When he eventually got out of bed, he asked where people were from, and I was sharing a box with three Aussies, who yelled out "Sydney" at the top of their voices. Spike left the stage, and almost immediately appeared in the box, where he started talking to the delighted Australians. Then he leaned over the edge of the box, and yelled out, "I've been here 5 minutes (more like 2) and nothing's happened on the stage yet, I'm going to ask for my money back"; and of course, more of the same onstage later. Another time, Joan Greenwood had left the stage in a huff, and Spike said, "Shall I follow her folks?" at which point a voice in the audience, possibly a plant, shouted "no".

Immediately all the scenery came down, and the entire cast and tech. crew was on stage, discussing the early night, and whether to go to a pub.

Spike Milligan, K.B.E., thank you for making us laugh.

One time I had not been in the Giaconda for several days. I was not on tour; I was trying to find a new bed-sit and was hanging on tight to the little bit of cash I did have, in case a suitable place came up. About six musicians were sleeping in Hyde Park; the weather was lovely; and a Lyons delivery van, headed for the Serpentine restaurant, used to stop early each morning with a box containing individual meat and fruit pies to help us through the day, which was gratefully received. Eventually I found a bed-sit and headed off to the Giaconda to catch up on events and have an egg and chips, which was duly ordered. A few minutes later, Julie came out from the back with a platter of steak, egg, mushrooms, tomatoes, vegetables and chips, plus coffee, and said, "Don't you ever not come in here again just because you have no money!". There were one or two of us that she really supported, and her friendship at that time meant so much.

I remember one evening, probably at around the same time frame, when I had nowhere to sleep, and spent the night walking the streets of London, guitar case in one hand, and a small suitcase in the other, trying to refocus and sort my next move. I ended up sitting on the Thames embankment at dawn, as the sun rose from behind Tower Bridge to welcome an incredibly clear and vibrant morning. Later I returned to Denmark street with my batteries fully charged, not remotely tired, and so grateful not to have missed such a truly unforgettable sight, such as most people have never seen.

There was always world-class music to be found. R & B at the Marquee, with the Animals or similar. Maybe the Flamingo with Georgie Fame. Mostly jazz at the 100 Club, plus of course Ronnie Scott's. I especially remember Stephane Grappelli playing with Diz Disley (born Winnipeg, brought up mostly in Wales) at Les Cousins, a basement club that was the centre of the Universe for British contemporary folk and blues. Bert Jansch, John Renbourn, Ralph McTell, Long John Baldry, Cat Stevens, Julie Felix, all were there; with overseas visitors Bob Dylan, Paul Simon, Joni Mitchell, Arlo Guthrie and more dropping by. Another memory is of sitting immediately behind the sax section of the powerful Buddy Rich Orchestra at Ronnie Scott's, which positively exploded into each set at the packed supper club.

I always used to take my passport with me up to the West End. Not only did I not want to leave it in the bed-sit, even though the door was locked; (having learned that with "Peter, Jan and Jon"); there was always the chance that it might be suddenly needed, plus I kept a couple of basic toiletries in my guitar case. One day it actually paid off. There was a group going over to the Star Club in Hamburg just for a short gig of a couple of weeks or so, to back Jerry Lee Lewis for one set, plus do other sets each day, and their planned lead player was sick. They already had the obligatory mohair band suits in the van, so I quickly bought some underwear and a couple of shirts from the tailor on the corner, grabbed my guitar from the music shop where it was stored, and we were off.

Everybody at that time played the rock 'n' roll standards in pretty much the same way and in the same keys, so swapping a musician was not a serious difficulty. This was a plus when we got there, as we discovered that the club ran almost round the clock, with a brief stop for cleanup. The schedule with other groups was something like one hour on, three hours off, so everyone was permanently tired. Plus, you lived on the premises, sleeping above or close by the stage. Very soon the band members started replacing their counterparts in different groups, depending on how awake one was, and somehow, we all got through it.

Somebody, I'm not sure that I remember who, told me of an agency that sent 'resting' actors or musicians out on cleaning jobs to private homes. It was regular house cleaning, with nothing strenuous, and one could pick mornings, afternoons, or both as required, to fit in with personal commitments, for good money, which was very helpful at the time.

After about an hour and a half's work there would usually be the appearance of tea or coffee, with cake and biscuits, and a sit-down with the lady of the house, frequently spending the remainder of the time chatting about show-biz or music, in which there was always a great interest. It saddened me incredibly that some of the people one met, who were clearly comfortably off, but almost certainly living alone, were possibly finding it necessary to pay for conversation with another human being . . .

There is so little that we know about life. At the age of four, my mother started to take me to a playschool/kindergarten on the back of her bike, but I obviously didn't fancy the idea, and on two consecutive days started for home at the earliest opportunity. This clearly was not going to work, however, a few days later, when in bed one night, I found myself above the school, looking down on a small barn or shed, where the school dog had just had puppies. The next morning, I was up and dressed, very excited, and told my mother about the new puppies. She was so pleased that I wanted to go to school, which was just a little one in a private house called Shumach Cottage, and off we went on her bicycle, to be met by the lady who ran the school, with "I'm so glad Peter's come today, the dog has just had puppies!" This was the first of many such experiences, one or two of which need sharing.

The next one was a few years later. I suddenly awoke in the middle of the night and went into my mother to tell her that her father had just died, many miles away. I remember that she looked at me with awareness that I had an ability which I had obviously got from her, and a couple of hours later, the telegram came. There were many other instances during my school days of seeing minor things, but I shall fast forward to the Giaconda years, where I had a pianist friend called Stan Harding, who played in the Cumberland Hotel by Marble Arch. We used to meet regularly for coffee; Stan had a home phone; I lived on the top floor of a large block which had only a phone on the ground floor, and the chances of someone coming all that way to tell a resident there was a phone call were slim indeed. Yet we devised a system. At the far end of the Giaconda, on the wall, was a large clock, then the counter, and a bench seat in front of the counter with its back to the clock. I would visualize the clock, set to the time of the desired meeting, with the empty seat in front, or Stan would, and concentrate on it, then show up at the appointed time. Which worked well for about a year and a half; if there was a time that the other could not make it, that person would phone at the time of the meeting to the restaurant, but this rarely happened.

By this time, I was seeing many things that I really did not want to see, nearly every day; things like road accidents, and once a train crash, most of which were subsequently verifiable. This was, to put it mildly, very disturbing. My awareness had been increasing for several years, and culminated in the day that I was chatting with Stan over a cup of coffee and suddenly said "Vicky's going to die", to which he said, "Wow, that was a strong one, who is she?", to which I replied, "It isn't a she, it's a he; he's the cartoonist in the Evening Standard", (a London newspaper), and I knew nothing whatever about him, or what he looked like. As soon as the next evening's paper came out, I grabbed a copy, and sure enough, Vicky had gone. This was simply too much for me to carry, and I asked that the burden could be removed, unless there was a special reason that it was needed. Immediately there was a huge weight lifted off me; I felt full of light, and happier than I had been for a long time. I stopped seeing bad things, although could occasionally still find myself "above" somewhere when in my "sleep", always at the same angle, and often subsequently verifiable. As many people know, this is called Astral Projection, and does not appear to have a harmful side in any way.

One thing that we used to do, which was fun, was attempt to mentally send each other pictures. Some were better than others; the very best was of a seascape and a bay, with a few houses and a couple of sailboats. We got this one almost right, except I believe that one of us put an aircraft where the original drawing had a seagull, also the angle of view was slightly different.

There was a world champion light heavyweight boxer at the time, who was a big star, often on chat shows or panel games, and a hero in Britain. He had a small basement club near the Giaconda, so was an occasional visitor around lunchtime. He used to say that he was not going to pay "protection" to the Kray brothers, the equivalent of Mafia in London at the time. Equally well, they might have left him alone, as one of them was starstruck, and wanted nothing more than to pose for pictures with celebrities. One day, the boxer was found dead in his car. The official report was suicide, but it could have been a gangland killing, also there was much talk that more than one weapon had been involved.

In later years it was found that he had been a serial killer of at least eight women, so there could have been many who wanted him out of the way, and the only reason he is being mentioned at all, is again a reminder that London in the 60s, and the people one met, were not all necessarily as they seemed.

On a lighter note, there was one female performer who went out as a singer in the greater London area. Half English, half Spanish, she was completely tone deaf, and made one see Mrs. Miller or Florence Foster Jenkins in a whole new light. She had a nice warm personality but would be fortunate indeed to pitch a sound even remotely in the correct octave, having absolutely no concept of music in any form. She vocalized loudly and distinctly on every note possible, plus frequently many that were not. The worse she got; the more they loved her; and her encores, while totally indescribable, will never – ever – be forgotten, by those who have witnessed one. But she was nice, and took her applause so graciously, that one had no choice but to be supportive.

She wanted to record, and approached a couple of studios, but once they realized that she had no awareness at all of what she was doing, they kindly made excuses not to do the session, as she could well have been devastated upon hearing the result.

"WESTMINSTER CITY SOUND"

During all this period, in addition to doing a few sessions and one or two solo cabarets, I had met a girl named Linda via a notice in "The Stage", (hers I think), who was aching to be part of a band. We met up, got along, there was a vocal gel, and although there was going to be some serious work involved, we decided to give it a go. She lived in Streatham, in Southwest London, with her mum, so some rehearsals were at her place, some in Denmark St./Charing X Rd area, wherever I could borrow a space, which amazingly, turned out to be much easier than I had thought. We worked very hard; I did the arranging; she practiced and learned everything she possibly could, and after a little while we had a very tight sound, so could start attempting a few gigs in the London area.

I was incredibly fortunate at this time to have as a friend a song plugger named Eddie Rogers, probably one of the most beloved people "backstage" in the history of British show business. An example of this can be found in his autobiographical book "Tin Pan Alley", when he wanted to put in a 2-page picture of Britain's top band leaders, all with their instruments. Several of them had to come great distances, but when they found it was for Eddie, no less than 27 came to the session, with profuse apologies from the few who simply could not make it. It took 350 phone calls to set the optimum time, but this historic photograph could not have been achieved by anyone else in the industry.

I'm not sure how we met, but I remember the first day I went into his office there was a photo of him on the wall with two others, on the day they were "liberated" from a German camp at the end of WWII. The three of them were so thin and emaciated, they were almost skeletons, and it is amazing how they had survived.

After some rehearsal, I took Linda down to meet Eddie. He was really delighted to see us and wanted to see how the act was progressing. He made a quick phone call to the Arts Theatre, and a couple of days later we were in there during the afternoon in costume, doing a set just for him. During the time that I was rehearsing with Linda, I was contacted once again to take a band for the U.S. forces in Europe. I managed to come up with an amazingly talented young organist, Dick Winters, who was very much in the Jimmy Smith style, also Steve Sutherland on bass, and John Williams on drums. Dick had a small Farfisa organ, but he made it sound huge, everybody else was good, and the band was tight in no time flat.

We called ourselves "Westminster City Sound"; Linda decided on "Toni Adams" as a stage name, and our first venue was to be at a large army base at Toul, near Nancy, in France, where we would be accommodated on base in bachelor officers' quarters, as there were no hotels nearby. So, we were fortunate to have the option of meals in the club or use our own kitchens as we wished. The day we were to leave London I had my case, with passport and everything, but fortunately not wallet, stolen, on the tube, (or subway). In those days, potential thieves would carry an empty case with the back removed, and legs that would come out and clip under your case, when this was lowered over it. So, the passport had to be replaced, plus something to wear, in time for the ferry, which amazingly was done after about 4 1/2 hours in the passport office, which I doubt could be done now.

After Toul, we went for a month residency at Chateauroux, where we lived in the town centre at "Hotel Bar des P.T.T.", owned by a M. and Mme. Perrin, who quickly became friends with all of us, including Alex, who was a budding solicitor in his father's London firm, and had taken 3 months off to come and "roadie" for us, the only time I have ever had such a luxury! M. Perrin was the chef, while his wife ran the hotel, and on our days off we gave them carte blanche to do a spectacular dinner for all six of us, which they did, with great delight, and so inexpensively! We had an amazing month at their little hotel and the base. Mme. Perrin kept in touch for several years, which kept my French reasonably up to "snuff".

While on Chateauroux, I must mention the totally brilliant idea of a little bar/club down the road from the hotel, that had a jukebox that ran non-stop, especially late at night. The owner had also put in a blank record for people who did not like the jukebox, for which, of course, you had to pay, and it was used frequently. Amazing!

For the tour to happen, I had to get special permits for Dick and Linda to work outside of the U.K., as they were both under 18. I got the requisite documents duly signed by parents, and we had a meeting in chambers with the judge, who said that we had to come back and see her at the end of the first month, which we did, flying from Le Touquet both ways on Dick's 18th birthday- which meant that he no longer needed a permit, as he had now reached the required age, and we got back in time for the evening show, if somewhat exhausted!

"PETER & ELISABETH"

The third, and last venue, was at Laon. Linda (Toni) had some health issues and went home; we needed a girl singer, so Dick's sister came, and everything worked out. We had already decided between us that Dick, Steve and John would stay together and see what they could find as an instrumental group, while Linda and myself would attempt the cabaret circuit, plus do tours as part of a floorshow on the European forces' camps, with which I was now very familiar.

Once back in London, Linda and I reconnected, and we started to do some serious work on putting the act together, plus I started knocking on a few doors of people I knew.

We went through our paces, with a few of my different arrangements, discussed costuming to fit our approach, also our new name, which we had decided was "Peter and Elisabeth"; (note the "s", we thought it sounded classy and slightly European). Eddie was very supportive and spent some time teaching us how to take a bow together that was fitting to our new image. By the time he had finished with us we could have read half a page from the phone book and still got tremendous applause.

I have always believed that top quality photographs are one's lifeblood in any theatrical pursuit. They get you in the door for meetings, they attract the newspapers and T.V., also, they bring in the public if in a showcase outside the venue. This maybe does not apply quite as it used to, now that much marketing is done via social media, but then it was essential. Eddie thought so too; he made a quick call and borrowed the Empire Theatre, Leicester Square, also laid on the photographer of his choice, for a session. Eddie knew exactly what he wanted, and worked with the photographer to achieve this, including one shot from the circle to show the two of us alone on the huge stage, which was incredibly effective.

We started to get some work; there was not a great deal around London, most of it was in the North of England, where the big social clubs were. We found a fairly upmarket Cricket Club in Kenton, who fell in love with us, and we went in once a month, which was helpful in the early days of the new act. (Still with my Selmer amp, one mic. on a stand, and a Burns Vibraslim guitar, which I had bought off Jim Burns personally, and whom I used to spend quite a bit of time visiting in his shop, a stone's throw from La Giaconda).

As one knows, elections in some countries are sometimes "rigged", and this can apply no less to a few aspects of show business, be it a T.V. talent show, a game show, or the charts, called the "Hit Parade", back in this era. The national charts were published in a now defunct paper called "The Record Mirror" and were compiled from record sales in larger record stores, mostly in London, with shops being changed every week. Of course, the labels would somehow get hold of the list of shops, and several teenagers would be paid to go and buy certain records, which would go back to the distributor (unplayed), and quickly be reissued to the shops from which they had just been purchased, when a different group would go in to buy them again, thus giving the impression of much bigger sales. Once the record started "moving" it would probably keep going on its own impetus if it was any good, but there was the odd case of a record being bought right up to number 1 in order to "push" a specific act.

The two leading show business papers were and still are "The Stage" and "The Melody Maker", although the latter no longer aims at professional musicians quite as much as it did in the earlier days. There was a writer for "The Stage" called Tommy Kane, who occasionally wrote small supportive reviews on "Peter and Elisabeth" much to our delight. He also wrote on another act, "David and Nina Burns", and after a few of these reviews, it became clear that he was a bit confused, and thought David and I were the same person. There was a good showcase on Sundays at Willesden Working Men's Club in north London, where several legitimate bookers would be in attendance, and one Sunday, both acts were on the roster, to the amazement of Tommy, who covered the showcase for "The Stage". David had for a long time been lead player for the "Echoes", who, in addition to their own show and records, backed up virtually all the visiting U.S. stars, as The Musicians' Union wouldn't in those days allow foreign backup groups into the country. They also backed many U.K. acts on tour, especially Dusty Springfield, after the "Springfields" had to break up, with David being involved in the production of several of her huge hits. He then went on to play guitar for Jet Harris and Tony Meehan, after they split from the "Shadows", Britain's number one instrumental group. David and I never quite got that people thought we were the same person. To us, we look and sound very different, but this confusion has arisen so many times throughout our lives that there must be something in it.

I should explain about "The Springfields"...

"The Springfields" were a very popular folk trio, with several mega hits, starting with "Island of Dreams". There was brother and sister Tom and Dusty, plus Mike Hurst, whom I knew somewhat. (One of Tom's songs, "Mountain Boy", already mentioned, was a single for "Peter Jan and Jon"). They unfortunately had signed with an agent who gave them a small flat fee, and pocketed the rest, so after a while, the only way that they could get out of the contract was to disband, which they eventually did. Dusty went on her own, while Tom went on to form and manage "The New Seekers", after the Australian group of the same name had broken up. Some years later "The Springfields" were asked to reunite for a special T.V. show, to commemorate the anniversary of "Thank Your Lucky Stars", at which point the agent said that if this were to happen, they would owe him all the money they had earned that was over their original flat fee, which created a big conundrum. However, it was got around by a) not using their name, and b) making sure that at no time were the three of them seen on T.V. simultaneously. Be careful what you sign, is the lesson from this story.

A couple of friends had started doing what were called adventure tours, aimed at a more youthful market than regular bus tours, which included camping, hiking, all sorts of things. They used Land Rovers for transportation, so it was all very small groups, and business was growing fast. One of their drivers, who was presumably Australian, had dropped off a group in London, and, as he was driving a brand-new Land Rover, decided to hightail it back to Australia as fast as possible. We received a call that they were going to follow him to bring back their vehicle, and since we had a bit of time available, would we like to come with them, as there would be plenty of space. They asked Elisabeth's mum too, who was still in her 30s and jumped at the idea, once she talked her employers into giving her the time off.

We headed off to France the next day, driving through and seeing various countries in pursuit of the stolen vehicle, but still with some time for stops. At each border crossing we could easily find out at exactly what time the other vehicle had gone through, plus there were designated pick-up spots where we needed to stop for mail, leave instructions for other drivers etc., as this was well before the arrival of cell phones or the internet. We slept en route mostly, but I recall one evening at a hotel in Salzburg, with the five of us walking around a high parapet and looking down on the old city in the setting sun.

Through Yugoslavia, where we stopped for lunch one sunny day, and fried our eggs on the hood of the Land Rover, then to Sofia in Bulgaria, when we had a sumptuous meal in the old Royal Palace, which was now I believe a part of the train station.

We eventually arrived at the BP Mocamp, just outside Istanbul, and stopped for the night, visiting a small restaurant close by, that amazingly, had signed photographs of Laurence Olivier, Stanley Holloway, Tessie O'Shea, Malcolm Sargent, and also several Hollywood stars on the wall. The proprietor could speak no English, and of course we couldn't read the menu, so he very resourcefully gave each of us a large piece of fresh bread, and escorted us into his kitchen, where several large pots were bubbling. Lids were removed, and we were invited to "dunk" our bread into each pot in turn, which we duly did, and each of us had a delicious meal, which practice was to be repeated several times over the next few days. The following day we headed into Istanbul, saw the beautiful Blue Mosque, and visited the huge market, which was where one changed money with street traders, never the bank, as the foreign exchange was needed in order for locals to work in other countries. At the same time, we were very careful of personal items, as we had been warned both by our friends, and the staff at BP Mocamp. By now we were very close to the stolen vehicle, whose driver had no idea that he was being followed. The plan was that we would await a different Land Rover on its return journey, while they would go ahead to the next border and await the arrival of their vehicle, where there would also be the advantage of police and border guards, if needed.

So, we settled down to wait for the returning Land Rover, which was due in the next couple of days, and had items to pick up. We made a little tent against the fence to save our remaining money. It was still hot in the day but cold at night, being early October, but somehow, we managed to keep warm, using all the clothes we possessed.

In every trip, there is frequently a point where Murphy's Law appears, and this was to be no exception. After three days there was no vehicle, we were almost out of money - no international credit cards in those days - and had enough tiny glasses of ceremonial sweet Chai tea to last a lifetime, also the lethally strong Turkish coffee, that one could almost chew.

So, I called the British Consulate, and arranged that the three of us would go in and discuss repatriation, which they said could be very simply done. There was a large indoor shopping centre near the Consulate, which had a food area with many samples, a few of which I collected, in order to give us a meal before our meeting. The consulate was extremely helpful, realized there had been some mistake, and booked us on the Orient Express route to London, but not of course on the famous train. They also gave us sufficient money, the proviso being that our passports would be "temporarily impounded" on arrival in the U.K., until such time as we had refunded their costs, which we of course gratefully did as soon as we possibly could, which took a little while, but amazingly there was no interest charged.

"Peter and Elisabeth" were by now starting to get some good work in the Northeast England Social Clubs, some of which we did by train, but Elisabeth had a friend, Richard Reader Harris, M.P., who was more than happy to drive us when commitments allowed. Turning up at a social club or other venue in his Rolls Royce, with House of Commons Insignia (a portcullis) on the front, certainly did us no harm, and Richard even went out and bought a chauffeur's hat to complete the illusion. He always used to say that we were all three in the same business, and there was more than a little truth in that.

To add to this, we looked at all the "pop" and "teenybop" acts around, which definitely wasn't us, so we decided from square one that Elisabeth would always wear a full-length dress or skirt on stage, and once we could afford it made sure these were as good as possible. It made a huge difference to how we were received, by both management and audiences alike. We started getting some really good supper clubs, (The Barn in Braintree, Essex, with mine host Bob Patience, was our favourite), and were now more than ready to do floor show cabaret on the European forces circuit.

We based in Frankfurt at the Nord Hotel on Eckenheimer Landrasse, which was full of performers from different parts of the world. Usually, 2 or 3 acts would make up a show, some were bigger than others, sometimes one act would carry the whole show, depending on the act. Most nights there would only be one club, but it was possible on occasion to get all three i.e., Officers', NCOs and enlisted men. Fortunately, this didn't happen too often, as it could be difficult having the varied audiences back-to-back, and pretty exhausting.

The Gisela Günther Agency booked the floor shows, and always provided a top-class pianist. The house band drummer would often slide in, and maybe the bassist. We didn't need to have a pianist, but one especially, Pierre Hengelmolen, from Belgium, used to quietly slip in some extra tasteful backing, and we wished we could always have him with us.

We worked with so many good acts: "The Tau Moe Family" from Hawaii; a comedy strong man and his wife "Duo De Mille", (he had consistently come second in the Mr. Universe contest and loved carrying amps. and speakers); also "Gladys & Norman Brock", (she would bring her husband on under one arm dressed as the base commander or a senior N.C.O., and proceed to knock him all over the stage, to great delight from lower ranks in the audience). There were many U.S. comedians, some of whom later moved on to host T.V. game shows stateside. Dinah Washington and her husband, (also a comedian), had an apartment in Oder Weg, as did some other semi-permanent acts based in Frankfurt, and we used to visit there sometimes.

Tour buses stopped outside this block, to show their passengers where "all the rich American performers" lived. Little did they know that many of the U.S. acts were working for almost nothing; instead, they were given a tax credit by the U.S. government at year end.

The main club in Frankfurt at the time, where we frequently played, was the "Plantation Club", a large venue which was the premiere appearance for all the name acts coming in from the U.S. Which of course included comedians, and sadly, some of those that had been on the circuit for a considerable time, would go into the Plantation Club in search of extra material, to the extent that one comic, freshly arrived from the U.S., was on in the big N.C.O. club in Wiesbaden with us, and only received polite applause. He was subsequently told by the club manager that his act was really good, but they had had an act just like his the previous week, because his had been stolen, virtually intact. The next time he appeared in the Plantation Club he sent waiters out, with pads and pencils, to any comedians in the house, with the club manager's aid of course, and was very careful not to use his best stuff, but I doubt that anyone wrote down a single word.

Many more acts on the circuit while we were there: Duane Eddy, Dottie West, ventriloquist Jimmy Nelson, (with Farfel the dog of course), Magician Paul Denver, plus many good bands from Germany, the U.K. and the U.S. We covered a great deal of Germany in a very short time, but probably didn't see very much, as we were either sleeping in the minibus, on an air base, or preparing for the next event. Also, some of our shows were "fly-in": Thule, Greenland, in the north, and "Wheelus" AFB, by Tripoli, in Libya.

At the end of the tour, it was back to London. We had already booked a summer season via Capable Management, (who handled the "Walker Bros."), plus there was a chance at variety, which we followed up immediately. For the latter we were definitely in the right place at the right time. We were booked for two West End theatres; The Arts Theatre, which Eddie Rogers had first borrowed to see us, and the Lyceum, a little while later, because the Arts shows were so popular that they had to move to a larger venue. We also did some variety up North, including the venerable City Varieties in Leeds, where the rake of the stage was so steep that we had to unscrew the castors from my Selmer amp., or it would have crashed into the footlights during our performance.

Then it was time for our first (and only) Summer Season, which was to be in a smallish theatre, (possibly 250 seats), on the coast in Filey, Yorkshire. Six nights per week, two weeks rehearsal, and we needed every minute of it, as apart from the opening number Monday - Friday, every show was completely different. Sunday was Old Time Music Hall, (Vaudeville), while our day off was on a Saturday, as in Britain people tend to come and go on this day. A small cast of eight, (including piano/vocalist and drums); we did everything. Sketches, musical comedy songs, a soubrette, comedian, soprano and tenor, dance routines, (which were practiced on the beach at night when the tide was out), all kinds of stuff. We had in the cast Kim Jackley, (Nat's niece), who came straight to us from being head girl of the famed Tiller girls at the London Palladium, in addition to helping Bruce Forsyth with the "Beat the Clock" segment of the Sunday night live T.V. show, along with Angela Bracewell, (who was not a Tiller). She put us all through our paces, and very cleverly gave those of us who were no good, (of which I was clearly one), very simple moves to dress the stage, three a bit more complex, and then she could do what she liked in front with her amazing talent.

Our soprano, Patricia Allwood, had trained under Maria Callas at a school connected with La Scala. While nobody would question Callas' talent and skill, she was well known to be something of a prima donna, which students found out to their chagrin. There was a production of Tosca, with Maria in the lead. At the end of the opera, Maria had to throw herself off the balcony on to a big pile of pillows and rugs to break her fall. On the final night of the production, all the pillows and rugs had been removed, and a trampoline put in, to glorious effect. She of course went absolutely ballistic afterwards, but the students all thought it was so well worth it.

The producer of the show was Bill Scott-Coomber, who had once been a cast member at the Abbey Theatre in Dublin, before moving to London as banjo player for the Savoy Orpheans dance band, who had the distinction of being the first musical group to play live on B.B.C. Radio. Then he created a four-piece vocal group, who worked at the London Palladium, mainly as backup, and occasionally as a fill-in act when needed. Bill was also a songwriter, who wrote under the name of Billy O'Brien, and had already had a hit with "Painting the Clouds with Sunshine", (which my sister used to play on piano all the time when I was small). One day, he wanted to take a girl somewhere really special, so he approached the music publishers with whom he worked and asked if he could have £100 advance on his next song, which was a large sum of money in those days. The publisher said "Yes, Bill, you write good songs; let's hear it", to which Bill replied "Oh, I haven't written it yet!". The publisher said, "Well I can't really give you the advance without hearing the song, but I'll get the money, and if you come in tomorrow morning with a good song, that money is yours".

The next day, Bill came in, played his new song and got the money (he never did tell me the outcome of his date). But the big news was that three months or so later Bing Crosby got hold of the song, and it became huge, making a sizeable difference to Bill's life at that time. It was called "Wi' me shillelagh under me arm"; and I have done this in nearly every seniors' show that we do nowadays, as a tribute to Bill, who was a good friend. He included the song as part of an Irish Scena in the Filey season, which we all enjoyed.

Once Bill and I started talking music, I was given quite a bit of leeway in putting parts of the show together, which was good for both of us, as Bill was also simultaneously producing a season in Minehead, Somerset, which was a long way away. There was going to be a "Carnaby Street" sequence, for which I offered to write a song, plus a "Rain" sequence, where I would again produce an original piece. Plus, I was given a couple of second half openings to do with what I wanted, so Elisabeth and I co-opted Patricia and Kim into a four-piece vocal group, doing a high energy version of "Hello, Young Lovers", (in 4 not 3), for one show, and "Chattanooga Choo Choo", for the other.

On Sunday nights we had an "Old Time Music Hall", which was always popular, and Bill had written a song to open the show. One week, having done the song many times and learned it backwards, forwards, and inside out, I knew for the first, and hopefully only, time what it is to "dry"! It was my cue for some solo lines, but not only did I not know the lines, or the song, but I did not know what I was doing there, who all these people on the stage were, or what was happening in any part of the proceedings. Kim was opposite to me on the stage, and seemed vaguely familiar, so I looked at her, and she, being the seasoned "pro" that she was, picked up my cue and all continued as planned. She said that the actual gap had been maybe a second, but to me, it felt like a week.

Sometimes folks on holiday for a while would try to catch all the different shows. On one occasion a group of regulars approached us before curtain time and asked if we could include "Where have all the flowers gone?", the classic Malvina Reynolds song, in our act. We got permission, and had a run-through in the dressing room, during which time I had the idea of speaking part of it, to make it more of a theatre piece, rather than solely music. This worked beyond our wildest dreams, and, in show business parlance, stopped the show. Bill was delighted, and from then on, we could do whatever we liked for each performance, as long as all six shows were different, and he had the titles for any appropriate royalties to be paid. It was quite a long season, and the company jelled well. The show was called "The 8 o'clock show" and you would be amazed at the number of people who contacted the box office to check on show times! Towards the end of the season there was one special night where dignitaries from all over were invited. Seating was removed, and the theatre set up cabaret-style for dinner and speeches, to be followed by a piece from the show, which in this case was the "Carnaby Street" routine I had written. The company received a standing ovation, as they did again on the final night, followed by the presentation of small gifts, and the inevitable tears and hugs all around, with promises to keep in touch forever.

This, sadly, included "Peter and Elisabeth", for various reasons, but we did keep in close touch until her passing in 2018, with me occasionally being part of a small group of performers who shared her central London apartment, where all had a good time together, and there were some very special gatherings with "friends in the business". On more than one occasion, we looked at re-forming the act that we both knew had been successful, but this never happened.

Bill wanted to buy the "Carnaby Street" number from me and put it on a BBC programme that he produced, called, I believe, "Variety Bandbox", under his name as composer. I know this has happened before to other songwriters, but I didn't accept. Somehow, I felt that this cheapened my efforts, and those of the company, in creating a routine that had been the hit of the season, even if I never played it again. Bill understood my feelings, and we remained friends.

"SWINGING LONDON"

*B*ack to London, where my initial intent was to put together another European forces' floorshow, at which by now I was experienced, and started looking around for dancers, singers, organist, drummer etc. John Williams, who had been drummer on the "Westminster City Sound" tour, wanted to come, and Kim Jackley, who had been in the Filey show also, to produce the dancers, before she was shortly to go into a West End show, starring Betty Grable. We had a couple of week's rehearsal and got things tight, but sadly Gisela Günther, with whom I had always worked direct, now had everyone going through Jack Fallon, a Canadian musician/variety agent living in London. Jack was a nice guy, and a superb musician, having spent much of his career playing bass for Lena Horne and a few others, but really didn't have the "feel" for the forces' circuit, and our show, plus some other good ones, didn't go, while others that were unsuitable were picked up. The show would have been called "Swinging London", and Tony Hatch (who wrote most of Pet Clark's hits) had kindly given me permission to use his song of the same name, never published, that he had written for a T.V. show broadcast "live" from the London Palladium, but ours sadly never took place. Kim's agent, Al Heath, (also her parents' Vaudeville agent), came to see the show, loved it, and couldn't understand why it hadn't been picked up. These things happen.

I should mention a bit about Earl's Court, West Kensington, and other areas of London that were "bed-sit" land. The quality of these varied hugely, the only common factor being that they were almost impossible to get. London in the 60s was booming; there was employment available in virtually any chosen field, and one could get a new job in hours, either by personal application, or by dropping into one of the many employment agencies that seemed to be everywhere, and checking to see what they had on offer. The very tiny hiccup in this amazing period, was that one still needed somewhere to sleep; therefore, much of London became a plethora of bed-sitting rooms, which were advertised either in the evening papers or on large communal notice boards, usually by entrances to the subway (tube) stations, where there would always be a group of young folks standing, awaiting a new card to be affixed to the board. Some cards had a phone number, some were by personal application only, in which case it was often necessary to travel a considerable distance, as fast as possible, to try and reach that given address before the room was gone. There were no cell phones, so there was usually a line-up at any operational telephone box, and once fortunate enough to get in the box, the room was frequently no longer available. If an appointment was arranged, it was prudent to run to the meeting, in case somebody else on the street was also headed for the same place.

One time in London I had a large, relatively comfortable room, in Earls Court, which had both a Baby Belling cooker AND a sink, so I was extremely lucky. Not only that, but I had French doors that led into a somewhat dishevelled private back garden, which were still nice to open on a sunny day. The small drawback was that once the lights were off at night, the other residents, of the small furry kind, that also lived in the building, would appear from under the baseboards and scamper all over the bed, which made sleep somewhat challenging. However, this particular bed-sit thankfully didn't have a coin slot for electricity, and by leaving just one small lamp on at night the problem was easily sorted, and I stayed here happily for quite a while.

Of course, all of this was happening during the "flower power" era, which was not nearly as visible in London as it was in L.A. A few performers in the Giaconda were obviously flower children – Donovan, also Sonny and Cher when they were in town, and a few others. But much more important was the thoughts and attitudes behind the movement, which were shared by so many.

Firstly, if you were one of the "chosen" which was not difficult, as you could decide on this for yourself, you had to have identification, for instant recognition by like-minded people. This was achieved by at all times carrying a copy of "The Lord of the Rings" under your arm, which enabled in-depth conversations with perfect strangers on a daily basis. There was a magazine out in London called "Gandalf's Garden", with much good stuff in it, and also stickers of Gandalf that could be placed in a window. If at any time you saw a Gandalf sticker, it meant that you were invited to that house, apartment, bed-sit, or whatever; for a meal, conversation about life, and frequently a place to sleep, should you need it. Not only this, but somebody opened a restaurant on Cambridge Circus, right by the Palace Theatre. It was a restaurant of inexpensive to produce pasta items, plus a couple of soups, bread, buns etc. There were no prices on the menu, instead, there was what appeared to be a large goldfish bowl near the entrance. If you had lots of money, please put in lots; if you had none; that was fine as well. Richard Burton and Elizabeth Taylor were playing in "Foxes" at the Palace, and were in this little restaurant frequently, loving both the simple food, and the concept behind it. (They were also doing the play receiving only Equity minimum wage, putting the rest of their income into actors' charities).

Richard and Elizabeth had borrowed the "Christina" from Aristotle Onassis and were living on it in the pool of London, just by Tower Bridge. Elizabeth had her two beloved little poodles with her, who were very happy on this large boat, (which had an outdoor garden), and were not subjected to British quarantine laws, provided that they didn't come ashore.

It was an amazing time to be in London, where there was so much sharing and giving among perfect strangers. The restaurant lasted possibly about three years, then the wrong people found it, and money started to go out of the bowl rather than in, and they sadly had to close, as probably did an era at the same time.

Because the Giaconda was surrounded by music publishers, one would also see the leading songwriters of the period, not that they were necessarily recognizable by sight. Of all the many composers, nobody had their finger on the current pulse of pop music like Tony Macaulay, who wrote tuneful, enjoyable, catchy melodies and lyrics, both on his own and with others, that would positively rocket into the charts on release. On occasion during the 60s, some songs would be first recorded by session singers, and then a group put on the road, who would probably be involved in subsequent recordings. Unlike some of the material that was out, Tony's songs never became annoying after repeated plays; they just made you feel better about yourself and your day.

Just a few:
- Build me up Buttercup (Foundations)
- Love grows (where my Rosemary goes) (Jefferson, Edison Lighthouse)
- (Last night) I didn't get to sleep at all (5th Dimension)
- You won't find another fool like me (New Seekers)
- Here comes that rainy day feeling again (Fortunes)
- Home lovin' man (Andy Williams)
- Sorry, Suzanne (Hollies)
- That same old feeling (Pickettywitch)
- Love me, love the life I lead (Elvis Presley)

Heaven knows, I'm missing him now (Sandie Shaw) which was her 23rd single in the U.K., and although not a hit, made her the most recorded female singer of the era.

Lights of Cincinnati (Scott Walker)

Baby, now that I've found you (Fortunes)

Let the heartaches begin (Long John Baldry) and

I'll be home on Christmas Day (Elvis Presley), which kicks off the Macy's Thanksgiving Parade even now.

Tony was "Songwriter of the year" in both 1970 and 1977, also won the Ivor Novello award no less than nine times. His songs when recorded also frequently had very catchy string passages, done by a brilliant arranger of the time, Les Reed, whose trademark sound was also heard on recordings of Tom Jones, Engelbert Humperdinck, The Walker Brothers, and many more.

Just up Charing X Road, by Tottenham Court Road tube station, there was a large block of phone boxes. One day, Jonathan Routh, who hosted the U.K. version of the popular American T.V. show "Candid Camera", simply put a sign on each phone box saying, "Please use other door", set up the cameras out of sight and waited. He got some hilarious footage, and several of the Giaconda regulars were watching from a distance.

It reminded me of a few years previously, when Richard Dimbleby, undoubtedly Britain's most trusted broadcaster, who had a T.V. show called "Panorama", did a show one April Fools' Day on the spaghetti farms in Italy. Italian restaurants were few and far between, most people had never seen pasta, so he did a program showing all these people going round bushes and cutting off pasta, which was hanging everywhere, with scissors. Probably 85 or 90% of the country was taken in with this. If they had seen pasta at all it was in two-inch lengths with "Heinz" on the can, surrounded by tomato sauce. A magnificent programme, which Richard did with a totally straight face, and never to be forgotten.

During this period, either when working with Elisabeth, or subsequently when doing solo cabaret, I joined what was called the Variety Artists' Federation, later to merge with Equity, an absolute necessity for theatre, the better club performances, radio and T.V. One of the truly amazing fringe benefits of an Equity card, was that you could present yourself to the front of house manager of virtually any London Theatre (of which there were over 100), approximately half an hour before curtain, and be shown to the best available seat in the house at no charge, on production of your card, (preferably having called first). Thus, I was so fortunate to see "live" some of the finest actors of the time, including Alec Guinness, Robertson Hare, Cicely Courtneidge, Judi Dench, Albert Finney, Anthony Newley, Vanessa Redgrave, Edward Woodward, Leo McKern, Glenda Jackson, Lauren Bacall, Ingrid Bergman, Joan Rice, Claire Bloom, Peter Ustinov, Max Wall, Beryl Reid, John Mills, Joss Ackland, Dorothy Tutin, Tommy Steele, Annie Ross, Joan Greenwood, Richard Briers, Geraldine McEwan, Robert Morley, Heather Sears, Sally Ann Howes, Anna Calder-Marshall, Joe Melia, Irene Handl, Avril Angers, Jean Kent, David Jason, Shani Wallis, Diane Todd, the list goes on and on, and practically all these consummate actors and singers were seen in "house" seats, reserved for special guests, merely by production of an Equity card.

Only at two theatres, that were virtually sell-outs, was I sent to the "Gods" (extreme upper circle). One was in Richmond, where I first saw Glenda Jackson, and the other at the Theatre Royal Drury Lane, reputed to be the World's oldest continuously running theatre, constructed originally in 1663, where I saw Diane Todd in "The Great Waltz". To give an idea of how high one was in the Theatre Royal "Gods", the head of the person in front of you is roughly level with your knees, and there were very few rows at this height. When seated it wasn't too bad, but more than one person crawled on their hands and knees to get to and from their seat.

Ingrid Bergman was doing the George Bernard Shaw play "Captain Brassbound's Conversion", with which I was unfamiliar. I was waiting for a friend after the performance in the lobby, when things had quieted down a bit, as was Lauren Bacall, who was doing the musical "Applause" down the road. She graciously came over, and we had a good chat about this play and other Shaw works, as well as different things to see in London, as she had virtually gone straight into rehearsal on leaving the plane. A special visit - maybe ten or fifteen minutes, but it has always stayed with me.

In addition to Equity, I also joined the Concert Artistes' Association, who had their own club premises in Bedford Street, just off the Strand. This was the gathering place for variety artists and cabaret performers in general, many of whom had been "in the business" going back to Vaudeville/Music Hall days. Thinking of a few: Leslie Sarony, (whose son Neville was at school with me but several years ahead), Jack Warner, (who got J. Arthur Rank to stand surety for the club's mortgage), Gladys Morgan, Cardew Robinson, Max Bygraves, Jon Pertwee, John Le Mesurier, Alma Cogan, Arthur Askey, Judi Dench, Cyril Fletcher, Pamela Cundell, and so many more.

There was a well-stocked little bar, cheaper than the pubs, tea and coffee, and a variety of sandwiches, pork pies, and other delectables, plus every week the members would put on a variety show for each other, which was always packed. I had the privilege of doing two or three of these, (one had to be recommended, do a performance, and be up to a certain standard to get voted into the association), and there was nothing like working in this room, where every single person was a performer, was on your side, and gave you everything that they possessed to help you do your ultimate best, or even more.

The society was started in 1897 by an entertainer called George Robbins, who realized the need for a benevolent fund to assist performers in difficulty, (i.e., stranded, the week was cancelled, can't pay the landlady etc.), in addition to having a gathering place at a reasonable price for all. It started with 55 members, all male, then in 1900 expanded to include female performers as well, and still runs as a vibrant society for all members of the profession.

After the forces' floorshow "Swinging London" was sadly not picked up, I was a little unsure of my direction, the only time this had happened since the day I first heard Lonnie Donegan. Elisabeth, who had dropped the "s" and substituted a "z", also a new last name Sands, her real name being Sanders, had got a house gig at L'Hirondelle supper club, as she wanted to stay in town. Kim was preparing for the Betty Grable musical under the new name of Georgia Gee, Gee being her parents last name when they had toured in Vaudeville for many years, where Kim was born backstage "in a theatrical trunk", so one could truly say she was born into the business.

"The Zephyrs" Peter (I think) who replaced Denny Lofthouse,
Bryan and Pam Bridge, Me, Neil Carter.

"Lee Binder Trio", Gill Lavis, Lee, Me. Photo: Dezo Hoffman, London

ACT FOUR

"The Zephyrs", and Germany

"London Country"

Sue Thompson tour

London's Viceroy Hotel

Lee Binder Trio (Jazz organ trio, Isle of Wight)

Serpentine Rest., Hyde Park

Peter Jansen Four (back to the Island)

"THE ZEPHYRS" AND GERMANY

I saw an ad. in the "Melody Maker" for a guitarist/vocalist to join a forces' showband currently touring in Germany. The band was run by a tenor sax/clarinet/keyboard player named Bryan Bridge, who had worked for Cunard for many years, and his wife Pam had been a founding member of the popular group "The Kaye Sisters". This sounded like a job from heaven - maybe it was - where I would be playing all kinds of music, and, for the first time since starting the "Cherrypips", not in charge, and having to sort venues, legalities, letters, phone calls and work permits, to say nothing of personal issues that might arise. I couldn't wait, although there were some misgivings about going to another country to become part of a band where I knew nobody. But it was going to be a stretch, hard work initially, but a really good stretch, both mentally and musically, which I so needed at that time.

Thus, December 27th, 1967, saw me leaving London by rail en route to Frankfurt once again, clutching my trusty Selmer amp., a suitcase, and a Gibson Jumbo J160e guitar that I had recently acquired. It was several years old and well "played in", so I was really looking forward to making music, along with the tenor sax, on standards such as "Misty", "Harlem Nocturne", "Don't get around much anymore", "Whisper Not", and others that would be new to me, in addition to the usual pop, country and R&B. The journey was uneventful, and I had until the end of December to listen to the existing line-up - with guitarist - at night, plus rehearse with the band in the day. In a small combo of tenor, guitar, bass and drums, plus of course Pam's vocals, a change of any instrumentalist can be challenging for all, but rehearsals went smoothly. My predecessor was a better sight reader than me, but I was good with chord charts, and definitely knew a whole raft of songs, having done the various solo dining room residencies in London and on the south coast.

All was going to be well; we bade farewell to the guitarist who was headed home, and drove off to our first month's residency, which I believe was the N.C.O. club in Sembach, Bryan and Pam had a trailer in which to live, while the other three of us would stay in a country hotel near the base. There was virtually a circuit of preferred hotels for touring musicians to stop for a month, and one was constantly conferring with other bands for good places to stay. In this case we stopped at Haus Haaman, where Neil and Denny (bass and drums) were already known and welcomed with open arms. I was given an upstairs room in an adjacent building, very comfortable, with a large stove that heated all the rooms. This was maintained by a young lady named Gerda, who lived on the same level, and worked for the hotel. She always made sure that the stove was full, and the room toasty warm, when we came back from a long night's work, followed by the trek through snowy lanes to the welcoming lights of our log-built hotel.

Overall, it was a good tour, with each residency lasting a month, and I stayed in the band (called the "Zephyrs", but no relation to the Maidstone one), for a little over a year, and covered most of Germany, except the extreme North. The biggest bases were usually in the middle of nowhere, as in the U.K., and our hotel was always a little restaurant/bar on its own in the country, with maybe half a dozen Fremdenzimmer (travellers' rooms) upstairs, plus accommodation for the family adjacent. But without exception, we could not have been treated better, therefore Neil, Denny, and I took great pains to blend in wherever we stayed, being helpful if we possibly could.

Of course, 1968 was sadly during the time of the Vietnam War, of which one definitely felt aware at some bases. Mainz was a huge base where many of the draftees from the U.S. went en route to the war zone, and we played for so many young men, some of whom seemed no more than children, awaiting their turn to be sent off, and wondering what on earth they were doing there. Some returnees came back this way too, but it was not normal for this to happen. One of the clubs we worked was a basement club, with a bar carved out of solid rock, that had a grenade under it one night. There was much broken glass around, but the bar very fortunately cushioned most of the shock; it was after the evening had finished, and nobody was seriously hurt, which was miraculous. The explosion was probably instigated by some poor unfortunate with P.T.S.D., we will never know.

Many of the returnees went to the hospital base at Landstuhl, or to Lakenheath in England, until considered "fit" to return to the U.S. We played in Landstuhl, in the huge deserted N.C.O. club, where there would only be a bartender in the distance, unless it was on officers' wives' bingo night once a week, when the place was packed. We very quickly learned to play as if there were a huge party happening, as our music was being transferred, at low volume, to some of the wards, where these poor shattered remnants of humanity lay listening, so our contribution was important, even though we could not see the listeners. Bryan and I stood next to each other, and had a chess set on a little table between us when playing, which became a permanent part of the evening when we moved on to other venues, and there was always great interest in the progress of the game.

There were so many other places. At one base there was an elderly black janitor, who had stayed on as a civilian after his time in the service and was much respected by all. He asked one night if he could come onstage near the end of the evening to sing about his day, so we laid down a blues sequence as requested, and he did exactly this. There is no other word to describe this except "magic". He composed as he went along, blending perfectly with us, and in exact rhyme. Needless to say, we asked him up every night for the rest of the month. I don't know if he did this with the other bands; I hope so, for he had a huge gift to share.

This was the year of the assassinations of both Bobby Kennedy and Martin Luther King, in a short space of time. When Bobby was killed, there was no bugler on the base, so Bryan volunteered to play the "Last Post" on sax, which was mic'd and broadcast over the speakers, as the C.O. felt it disrespectful to use a recording, with which we so agreed. The death of Martin Luther King shocked everyone even more, if that were possible. A man who simply wanted peace and equality, therefore had to be destroyed, as has happened so many times before.

Of course, this was the time when the "Beatles" were huge, and people in Germany would see us, hear the accent, and say "Are you a 'Beatle'?" much in the same way that somebody might say "Can I borrow your Hoover?", for the word "Beatle" had become the generic term for anybody from Britain who played popular music. Not only that, but because of the image projected by the Liverpool group, one was expected to behave in a somewhat eccentric manner, which we naturally milked to the full. We had a month in a town called Hof, at the borders of Czechoslovakia, East, and West Germany. We were living on the U.S. base by the West German border in deep winter, and could see the East German base with ease, as all the trees had been removed to create a clear strip between the two camps. Every morning, troops from both sides would go out and remove snow off tanks and other vehicles, then go back indoors. Shortly later, a vehicle would leave the East German side and meet with a U.S. truck somewhere in the middle, for the trading of bourbon, vodka, cigarettes, cigars, caviar, and all manner of things. We were very impressed with what we saw, as the Cold War had been going on for a while, and this seemed to offer hope for the future. On mentioning this, we were told "You ain't seen nothing yet", as we were to find out the following weekend.

When we pressed the electronic button to open the tabs for our first number, there were seated several Russian officers, some with their wives, along with those from the U.S. base, all in dress uniforms, and they obviously knew each other well, as we were to see every weekend.

The base was a long way from any area that might be deemed sensitive, and both sides were, very impressively, trying to keep it that way.

To give an example of the eccentricity that one was expected to show in order to maintain popularity, one night - or I should say more like at 3:00 a.m., after the night's music was over, it was pitch dark when Neil, Denny and I turned up at the border, where the East German border guard requested our passports and asked where we were headed, as this was a direct corridor to West Berlin, but through East Germany. We said that we wanted to look at the East. He looked at our passports, said "Ah, musica", which of course explained everything. Our passports were stamped for entering East Germany; the barrier was lifted, and we were waved in - it was by now snowing steadily - with a car in front of us, and motorcycle behind. When we had gone maybe 200 yards, the car pulled across the road, and we were signalled to turn around, which we of course did. When we arrived back at the checkpoint, the East German border guard was laughing his head off with, "So you see East Germany; what you think?" and waved us through. I was now the possessor of a passport that showed me entering East Germany, but no exit stamp, and had all kinds of fun a year later explaining to British Customs that an East German border guard could have a sense of humour.

There seemed at that time in Germany to be a marked difference between the attitudes of town and state police, unless our experiences were coincidental. Some of the town police appeared to be looking for problems, with a totally different approach from the state police, who were courteous and helpful, while still professional at all times.

An example of each happened during the same period, when we had rented a farmhouse close by the base of Siegelbach for a couple of months. We were in the main town of Kaiserslautern on our night off, and a policeman came over at a traffic light, yelling at us. We established eventually that the problem was that a rear light bulb had gone, and offered to pull over and rectify the situation immediately, since we carried spares. This was not acceptable to him, and we were told to bring the vehicle a day later, when he started his shift at 6 a.m. or thereabouts, to show the light had been fixed; a really awkward time for us. Our command of the language was not the best, so we did what was asked of us, mumbling a bit to put it mildly, and wondering if it was the U.K. licence plate that had caused his attitude.

Two or three weeks later it was New Year's Eve. We had just finished our run at Siegelbach, which was a communications base, tracking the Apollo 8 mission at one time we were there, and obviously a cut above other places. There was one N.C.O. club for all ranks to share, which I have never seen at any other military post, but here it worked, and the club atmosphere was terrific. We had had a busy evening, being New Year's Eve. Firstly, there was a big dinner, with a traditional lederhosen-clad German band in front of us on the floor for a couple of sets. Then we were on, to have later a visit from the amazing jazz singer Dakota Staton, who was coming with her own group, a band from Frankfurt, with whom she was touring. We got a message that her band was stuck in the snow somewhere, and could we help out by backing her up, to which we swallowed hard, and said we would of course do our very best. Neil was totally awesome on bass, and could read or follow anything, even if he hadn't heard it before, and Bryan was equally adept at doing this type of thing.

Maybe half an hour later, at the end of a set, a smallish black lady with a headscarf came to the stage and said "Hi I'm Dakota; sorry, but all the band parts are with the band in the snowdrift. How about 'A foggy day in London Town', Eb. 1..2..3..4". I think I lost about twenty pounds during that song, which was a difficult transposition from the norm, but we got there, and went into things like "Lady is a Tramp" and some blues and other simpler standards. The set ended up being great, but quite the hardest thing I had ever done, to this day.

At the end of the evening, we packed and headed off on the autobahn to the farmhouse, where there was a gathering of some friends from the base, also the village. Part way down the road we saw the German band, who had played for dinner, at the side of the road, and two state police cars (Bundespolizei) with their lights flashing. We were of course concerned that there had been an accident, but no, the band had some cases of inexpensive Deutsche Sekt "champagne" in their van, and the police were stopping everyone to have a drink and say, "Happy New Year!".

So very different to the Stadtpolizei, but I somehow doubt that would happen nowadays.

A little background on Bryan and Neil. Bryan had worked on Cunard ships for some time, and often talked of the fact that they didn't like to pay overtime, preferring instead to have extra musicians on board. This meant that quite frequently he would have to tap another sax player on the shoulder, mid-song, who would get up from his seat, still playing, while Bryan sat down, and they would cue each other for the takeover.

Neil came to us from a short spell with Billy Smart's Circus, then was with the house band at the famed Latin Quarter club in London, where Princess Margaret, whom the "Jazz Gentlemen" had several years before entertained at Leeds Castle, would sometimes be a visitor, with her friends. He talked of the night where she was sharing a table that included Ronnie Kray, boss of the notorious Mafia-style London protection rackets, and praying that she wouldn't get involved with him, which fortunately never happened.

Of course, on a tour which for me was thirteen months, we met many floorshows, both from the U.K. and "name" acts from the U.S., some of which we backed up. Many brought just a pianist, and we would slide in as appropriate to fill things out. Occasionally there would be a large band - Rosemary Clooney for example brought in a studio level ten piece - Billy Daniels had a large band, and country stars such as

Johnny Cash, Hank Thompson, plus the up-and-coming Charlie Pride, all brought their own backup.

Timi Yuro just brought in a pianist, as did two huge stars from the 40s and 50s, Helen O'Connell, and Dick Haymes. Helen was the star female singer in the Tommy Dorsey band at the same time that Sinatra did the male vocals, and had many huge hits, including "Tangerine", "All of me", "I'm getting sentimental over you", and more. Dick Haymes was no less big in this period, with "You'll never know", "The more I see you", "Put your arms around me honey", "Come rain or come shine", and a recording of songs from the original movie of Rodgers & Hammerstein's "State Fair" in which Dick co-starred. He had also worked with Harry James, Benny Goodman, and later, Tommy Dorsey. Plus, there were guitarist Billy Lorento, (Billy Lawrence), Allan Sherman (Hello Muddah), and others, including a two-week stint with Leslie Townes Hope, from the east end of London, better known to the world as Bob. Amazingly, none of the U.S. forces seemed to know he was originally a Brit., and we certainly weren't about to burst his bubble. At the time, there were two scriptwriters travelling with him, who would hit the ground running at each base in search of current material and camp gossip that could be used in Bob's set. This was hugely popular with the servicemen; the two writers would sometimes have a little board on which they could write ideas during the show, unknown to the audience. Sometimes we travelled together, sometimes not. At first Bob would be telling jokes during the night when others were trying to sleep, but Gladys Brock, who was fairly large, and you may remember had an act of knocking her husband all over the stage, soon rectified that, after which peace and camaraderie reigned throughout the bus, although we always deferred to Bob in public, and had a good time together.

Who else? There were the "Shirelles", which we had to do "cold" without a rehearsal, just a quick chat, and Red Sovine, "Phantom 309", plus other "talking" pieces. A couple of sibling acts on the circuit, with their own groups, were Ike Cole, (brother of Nat), and Erma Franklin (sister of Aretha); both very talented. Plus, we shared an evening with the original "Platters", the "McGuire sisters", Ricky Nelson, Johnny Ray, and Ferlin Husky, who all brought their own bands, Ricky Nelson bringing Scotty Moore with him, who was a treat to see and hear. The most fun I ever had was at an earlier time, in France, with Sonny Boy Williamson II. He came on stage with an old doctors' bag full of harmonicas; the band started with a blues in the key and tempo requested, and he would blow each harp in turn until he found one with which he was happy. At the end of his set, we spent our break picking up harmonicas from all over the stage, but what a set it was!! The mostly back audience was enraptured, but the four honkies on the stage had a good time too.

When at Saarbrücken we used to head into Kaiserslautern for fish, chips, and coleslaw at the Nordsee, a really good quality chain all over Germany, that wasn't greasy like so many places. We would also visit Schaller's music shop, run at that time by Helmut Schaller himself, together with his daughter, (who was an excellent flautist). He had begun his company in 1945 at Feucht, near Nuremberg, as a radio repair shop, then went into amplifiers and speakers, starting on guitar pickups in 1953 for Framus, followed shortly after by Höfner and Hoyer. By the 60s, he was producing pickups for Fender, Gibson, Martin and Ovation, and was a giant in the industry. At the time we were in Kaiserslautern, the company was moving into a new production site at Postbauer-Heng, where they still are. Helmut and his daughter were such very nice, unassuming people, and they always had a coffee pot on, often with cake too (!) for visiting musicians, together with a truly warm welcome.

At one venue whilst on tour, we were staying in the usual small country hotel. At the time, we used to wear suits most days, with a tie, which impressed the owners, as most bands didn't dress this way in the daytime, and we had a standing joke that we would never be seen without a collar and tie. It was New Year's Eve, or more accurately, about 3:30 a.m. on New Year's Day. We had just finished a long night, plus packed all the equipment and our personal stuff for the road, and the party in the lounge bar, immediately below where we were trying to get some sleep, was still in full swing. I couldn't resist it. I had one shirt that had a separate collar, so I put on the collar, having slept au nature to this point, added a bow tie, and went down to the bar to ask them, very politely, if they would mind keeping the noise down a bit.

Probably no comedian on earth has ever received a more gratifying response than I was given at that second. When the applause and laughter had died down, there was a promise to be quieter, plus I was given a bottle of top-quality champagne from all present, which was carried carefully to the next town.

Of course, we met many other bands, some of which were truly excellent, and I have photos, but sadly not many names. One Turkish band we really liked, plus an amazingly good, blues-based outfit called "Power", from Glasgow, Scotland. Lead guitarist Les Harvey (brother of Alex), would have definitely become one of the "greats" along with Clapton and Page, while their singer, Maggie Bell, went on to receive several well-deserved accolades, "Top girl singer of the year", etc. in the British music press. They worked the European circuit for quite a while, then went back to England and renamed themselves "Stone the Crows", under the production of Peter Grant, who also managed "Led Zeppelin".

Maggie was often compared to Janis Joplin, but I felt that to be unfair, because she had a much bigger sound, and was always totally in control of her performance. The brilliant guitarist Les was tragically electrocuted during a concert in Swansea sometime later, which was such a huge loss to music, to Maggie and the band, and to all of us who had known him, however briefly.

In those days, before the Common Market, or E.U., was born, one could work in Germany for three calendar months, then had to leave the country for 24 hours in order to do it again. So, at the end of each month, if you happened to be in the main square of Luxembourg, where in summer there were numerous outdoor bar/restaurants, you would see bands, not only from the U.K., but other parts of Europe as well, all enjoying the ambience, and a few hours much needed break together.

One time we were coming out of Germany to fulfill our 24 hrs. away, when we were stopped at Customs for a quick check of what we were carrying, which in our case, was probably everything that we possessed. They didn't care if you were carrying alcohol of a reasonable amount, or even pot - not that we ever did the latter; the big thing at the time they wanted, which sounds really weird, was coffee, because there were huge differences in prices, producers, and taxes at the time. It was very early morning, because we had played the night before, and there was the sound of a guitar and mandolin, plus some nice smells, coming from the customs shed.

We were asked if we were in a hurry, which we weren't, as long as we did the 24-hour thing, so were invited into the customs office, where there was a huge pot of goulash soup simmering, which I can still smell as I write. They phoned the Luxembourg customs office, who all came over and stamped our passports with the time. Probably we had about an hour or maybe two together, playing folk songs and blues songs, in both English and German, plus enjoying delicious soup in the early morning, where the sun was just starting to rise. The barriers on both the Luxembourg and German side of Customs had been lifted, and there was the zoom, zoom of traffic going both ways, but nobody seemed to care; they were all in the room with us.

We saw so many things on that tour. At one base there were miles of fir trees all around. One morning we were in the club early, and a large block of these trees had gone flat, and slid underground, to reveal a silo, and the heads of many large missiles pointing upwards, aimed at who knows where? An hour later all was normal again.....

At one point of the tour, we were having some engine problems with our old Bedford van. A few of the airmen where we happened to be working said, "Oh we've got an engine like that in the motor pool", and they installed it for us one evening - and most of the night, using the headlights of two military trucks to finish the job; this in the driveway of our home for the month, so we could head off the following day to our next venue. We were treated with such kindness everywhere we went. In this case, which would have probably cost thousands of dollars on the commercial market, they would only accept a bottle of bourbon, which was available very cheaply in the p.x.

We had a "knob twiddler" at one venue, which has to be every musician's greatest fear on a residency, where you come in for an evening's performance, only to find that all the sound needs re-balancing, which is a huge job. When this had happened more than once, by which time we had the settings written down, it was decided to wire all the amplifier handles together and run a current through them as an overnight security. The following evening the very gentle, elderly janitor approached us to warn us to be careful of our equipment, or we might get a shock, as he had found out when cleaning the stage for us. We felt so very bad, and never did this again, however I have learned to write down settings for all residency engagements, which has been done to this day.

On another occasion, we were performing at a base near the East German border, as in Hof, where we used to get visitors from the other side. One day, two visiting officers were walking across the parade ground, when there was a surprise visit from a U.S. General, who was coming to see the commanding officer. The General, not surprisingly, queried what he had just seen, and the Colonel called the officer of the guard to come and explain this, which of course gave the unfortunate officer time to think. He arrived at the Colonel's office with the not very plausible explanation that there were new uniforms on the Soviet side, of which they had a couple, and two men were walking about to familiarize U.S. airmen with the "new look". Amazingly the General said, "Very good, carry on", or words to that effect, and, once he had concluded his business, left the base. There was a sigh of relief all round, as had the General visited the officers' club, he would have seen several more of these uniforms, that were definitely not being worn by U.S. personnel.

We were based by Trier, in the Moselle Valley, for a month, where there are so many amazing historical sites, some dating back to Roman times. While exploring the town, we came upon a small music shop, where I was looking at a reasonably priced 12 string guitar in the window – and really wanted to play "Walk right in" on it. We went in, and to our amazement, found that 95% of the instruments were crafted by the owner of the shop, who was a luthier par excellence. He gave me a Spanish style guitar to play, which was incredibly easy, and much better than anything I had ever played before. Then he handed me another. All I can say, is that I picked it up, and if anything, it played me. There was absolutely zero effort involved; whatever ideas I had could be executed instantly. Sadly, this instrument was justifiably way out of my price range, and a Spanish, so unsuitable for band work, but I did leave his shop clutching the 12 string, and played "Walk right in" that night, and every subsequent night, together with a few other things.

While in Trier, we visited Bernkastel for the wine fest on our day off. The town fountain had been thoroughly cleansed, and was running with new Riesling day and night, which was free to all. Around the fountain were stands with various Wurstchen, (we loved the currywurst), and a traditional style German band was on the stage. It always used to amaze us that German people could party all night and then go to work, but it seems to be what they have always done, and there is no doubt that Germany is consistently the most productive country in Europe, so they must be doing something right.

By this time, I had been in Bryan's band for a full year and was feeling a strong pull from the London "scene", although I can't for the life of me remember the plan I had at the time. I gave my notice, allowing for the fact that I would stay on until a suitable replacement had been found. All was very amicable between us, as it would always be, and I headed back to Britain on the ferry a few weeks later, with, amazingly, a private function booked for my first night back, which was a Sunday. I had called my insurance company regarding extending the musical instrument insurance, and they advised me that I would have to go into an affiliate office in London after the weekend.

I was playing the private function; all was good, and I had done a couple of sets, when I was invited into the next room to get some food, which, of course, I accepted. Imagine my horror when twenty minutes later I returned to the sight of a totally empty stage. Three men in matching overalls had quickly come in, packed everything, and left. Not one person had questioned them, because they were efficient, and totally open about what they were doing, so it appeared that they were meant to be there. All the music that I had written over the years was in a wires bag, as were the acetates for a special version of "Wabash Cannonball" (Peter Jan, and Jon) and "I like the Wintertime" a bossa nova I had written, with John McLaughlin on guitar, Pete McGurk and Chris Karan from the Dudley Moore trio on bass and drums, Duncan Lamont on alto flute, and a brilliant pianist whose name sadly escapes me. This was recorded by "Peter & Elisabeth", with me doing rhythm, and both recordings were irreplaceable. There was no coverage on any of it; I did some research and found there was a group of people going around London clearing stages like this - two nights previously they would have got Georgie Fame's Hammond C3 from the Flamingo, but for the fact that Chris Farlowe used it for his set, rather than bringing in an identical instrument. A small reprieve from all of this, but important to me, was that a few days later, I got a message to go to a specific phone box at a designated time, which I did, and there was all my music, though sadly, no acetates.

I was staying at Elizabeth's for a few days while sorting things out. She was by now singing with the Joe Loss Orchestra , and sharing her apartment with best friend, Billie Davis, (who did the U.K. covers of "Tell him", and "Angel of the morning" and had huge hits with both), plus Billie's boyfriend Alan David, and as always, several theatre folks dropping by; including actress Wendy Craig with writer husband Jack Bentley, Tony Newley and Joan Collins, Tony Barrow and Bess Coleman, (publicists for the "Beatles" and also for Prime Minister Harold Wilson - yes, they thought up the idea of his ubiquitous Gannex coat), and others. Bess kindly gave me comp. tickets for many Albert Hall events, where I first saw Gordon Lightfoot, also the Edwin Hawkins singers, together with the "Desper Steel Orchestra" of Trinidad, both amazing concerts.

Gordon's music was impossibly beautiful, with a concept of melody like no other before him. He had an instantly recognizable sound, both vocally and musically, with his guitar and that of Red Shea, and then the late Terry Clements, fused together as one. Of course there have been brilliant songwriters - from Berlin, Porter, and the Gershwins before, to contemporary singer-songwriters such as Lennon & McCartney, Dylan, Paul Simon, Kristofferson, Carol King, Leonard Cohen, and others, but that night I moved inside Gordon's mind, and experienced for the first time the crashing waves of the Great Lakes, I saw the ribbon of steel winding its way through the snow covered forests, and gazed with awe at the majestic peaks caressing the sky, all through his eyes.

The Edwin Hawkins singers concert was equally amazing - the first time I had seen a black southern gospel choir, a large one, and did they ever make the heavens move, with their incredible sound and energy, while the Desper Steel Orchestra, having over 35 musicians, and up to four or five steel drums each, positively rocked the building, going from Mozart and Bach to Neil Diamond and the William Tell Overture, making me a lover of steel drums for evermore.

One day, I walked back into the flat, to find everyone very excited, as I had received a call from Buckingham Palace. To this day, I have no idea of how that call came through. I had probably been back from Germany for 1 1/2 - 2 weeks, but I dutifully called the person back, who, first of all, was very sorry at the theft of my instruments and equipment, and wondered if I could come in to see him. I presented myself at the designated entrance to the Palace, where I was expected, and escorted via some of the state areas to a downstairs office, where a senior member of the household was awaiting me, together with a sumptuous traditional afternoon tea. He, very pleasantly, explained that they had already been in touch with Bryan in Europe, who had given a glowing reference, also obtained another reference, but I am not sure from who. They wanted to offer me a job in the Royal Household, where I would ultimately train to possibly be assistant to the Master of the Household, except that my function would be to travel ahead of whichever senior member of the Family was to be touring, and check menus, accommodation, bottled water, and any personal things that might be required. From what I recall of the meeting, there would of course be social skills involved, unlike "The Page of the Backstairs" in the Downton Abbey movie, whom one feels was not qualified in this respect for his position.

I would have an apartment in the Palace, but cell phones had not yet come about, and I would have been on call 24 hours per day, seven days a week, except when on holiday. So, if I decided to go to a movie, I would have to check in to say where I was, and in what seat. The same in a restaurant, a club, anywhere at all, I had to be available. Training was initially to be 6 months or so, then I would start travelling with an existing staff member to watch how things were done.

I did think about it for a few days, but eventually turned the offer down, saying that music was my calling, and it would be unfair to them if I went through all this training and then let them down in the future. The person with whom I was dealing was very understanding, but also said that my responsible feelings on this were exactly why they had contacted me in the first place.

So many years later, I have no inkling of how they knew of me, where I was temporarily living in London, and the phone number. The fact that I had been in Europe for over a year with Bryan and how to contact him - our contact at German American agency in Wiesbaden was certainly not involved - the theft of my equipment and instruments; so many questions will always be unanswered. I did learn that if you are not hiding per se, and the powers that be want to find you, they can do so very quickly, which I was to see again in the not too distant future.

I got myself a "temp." position with a Lloyds' broker in London, Lowndes Lambert, where I would be working full time, but if a session or something came up, I could take the time off to do it, for which privilege I took a slightly lower fee. This company was light years better for me than the one I had been with when I left school; I was dealing directly with the clients, many of whom I met personally, and it was a perfect fit.

I soon got myself a Gibson B45 twelve string, well played in, and prepared for my next move, which was to be a duo, possibly in the style of "Peter and Elisabeth". An ad. was put in "The Stage"; I rented one of the Max Rivers rehearsal rooms in Charing X Rd and set up 5 appointments one February afternoon.

I can't remember three of the people who came at all; also, one of the others had been doing the cruise circuit for years and wanted to change to another act with the same work ready to go. But the fifth girl, who came all the way from the south west on her boyfriend's scooter, was more than of interest. She was only just planning to start "in the business" and had no experience, but I knew for certain that we had to keep in close touch. Unknown to me, this was to be my musical and life mate Mary Kingsley, and we decided to join together permanently, in more ways than one, some 4 1/2 years later in Bermuda. But I am jumping the gun, and there are one or two things to happen before that.

"LONDON COUNTRY"

I decided to put together a harmony country/folk outfit, a six piece. Jan wanted to come in again on drums, plus I had found two girls, Angela and Marlene, who wanted to come in on vocals, and the three of us blended well from the word go, so would be really good after some work together. I also found an excellent 5 string banjo player, plus a bassist, and we had a photo session to get the word out whilst in rehearsal. Sadly, this band never appeared. Jan had a business offer that she could hardly refuse, and the bass player had another commitment. Fine, so I found another bass and drums, but they had come down from Yorkshire, and couldn't afford to stay for the time it would take to launch a new group. It was to be called "London Country", after the green buses, and we did one "off the floor" recording session with Vic Keary - from Radio Caroline days - that sounded half decent, considering the small amount of rehearsal we had done to date. We actually did one gig, somewhere in North London. I had my twelve string Gibson, which sounded great, also an older Burns Tri-sonic, that kept on changing volume levels that night, drove me insane, and I got rid of it the following week. I have kept in touch with Angela over the years, who has a beautiful family in Ireland, while she keeps in close contact with Marlene, who operates a successful performing arts agency in the U.K.

I remember July 20th of that year, 1969, as so many of us do, because it was the day of the first moon landing. I went to a "moon party" at Elizabeth's, with maybe up to a dozen of us crowded round the T.V. to share "live" this momentous event. It was also my 27th birthday, and it was nice to think that much of the world was celebrating at the same time.

SUE THOMPSON TOUR

I got another call from the European circuit. This was to go to Mannheim, in Germany, to base there for a forces' tour with Country singer Sue Thompson, who often worked and recorded with Don Gibson. Sue had all the "boys name" hits, (covered in the U.K. by band singer Susan Maughan), such as "Bobby's Girl", "James (hold the ladder steady)", "Norman", and more, plus filled the set with Country standards. Originally, I was going to play lead, but we swapped it about a bit, with me often playing rhythm on the Gibson twelve string, which drove the band much better, while their rhythm player was a more proficient country lead than I was. Sue had also had the country hit of "You belong to me", sung on the commercial market by Patti Page. We had great fun doing this together in harmony, with me doing some jazzy stuff, completely different from the rest of the show.

At Christmas itself I was off for a few days. Three of the group were servicemen, (two had worked some with Glen Campbell), and had families locally, plus we also had a German guitarist, Helmut, who played on several of the gigs. I was alone in Mannheim, but really enjoyed exploring the Christmas markets, and experiencing the magical atmosphere of Heidelberg, which was not too far away.

VICEROY HOTEL, LONDON

*B*ack to London, and a little while later, I got a house gig at the Viceroy hotel, in Lancaster Park. A restaurant/lounge, and I was quite happy there several nights a week, in addition to Lowndes Lambert's head office in Monkwell square. Mary had moved into the area of Earl's Court the previous November, where I also lived, and we saw each other on occasion, with the odd supper at "The Pot", which served rice, chips, and peas with every main dish. It was inexpensive, and had a terrific atmosphere, as it was the meeting place for Australians who had worked their various ways around the world.

Mary was to get her first ever summer season at "Sunshine Holidays", Hayling Island, on the south coast, starting in April, to which she was looking forward, and was sharing a flat in Primrose Gardens with some other girls prior to this.

LEE BINDER TRIO

I completed my summer at the Viceroy, and, at the end of the season, Mary and her boyfriend, Andy, came in for supper one night. We had a good visit, by the end of which we had decided to share an apartment together, as the three of us could afford a much better apartment than two, and we had got along well from the beginning. So, we moved into the Queen's Park area of London, and at some point, I introduced Mary to Lowndes Lambert, where she was also able to get a job as a full-time temp. We stayed there until the following spring, and Mary's return to Sunshine. Meanwhile I had been entertaining in the very upmarket Shore House, Shoeburyness, on the Essex coast, for I think three nights per week, then joined up with top class jazz organist Lee Binder, and a positively brilliant show drummer, Gil Lavis, quite the best show drummer with whom I have ever worked. They had a weekend house gig somewhere, and I easily slid into the band, also backing up a cabaret singer called Mike, who was very competent and knew how to work the entire floor.

We got a summer season in "Le Beau Monde" nightclub at "Cliff Tops" hotel on the Isle of Wight, so the three of us headed off there, each arranging our own accommodation. The season was very successful, and we made some good music. Lee had a Lowrey organ, with a Leslie of course, but had the Hammond percussion and reverb put in, so we had the best of both worlds, and the three of us had a big sound. Mike came down two nights a week from London to do his spot, and I did solo cabaret two nights a week, with Lee and Gil backing up. It worked really well, as Mike went out as hard as he could to the audience, whereas I would sit on a bar stool in the middle of the floor with a spotlight and bring them to me. There was a huge contrast between us, and it was such a joy to work with Gil, who would be with you with a little accentuation every time you put one in yourself.

I lucked out on accommodation, which doesn't always happen. The family that was suggested to me had a nice home a couple of minutes' walk from the sea, and usually took in members of the Shanklin theatre cast, of which there was one already booked, but still a room available for me.

The theatre company was run by a very powerful and pleasant actor, Geoffrey Reed, while his wife Joan Frances (Reed), who had been a regular in the early days of Coronation Street, kept a pub in Shanklin, which was popular with theatre folk and musicians alike.

There was a second-hand book shop in the town, and one day I was fortunate to come across a copy of J.B. Priestley's "Good Companions", about a touring theatre troupe, which somehow, I had never read. Nearly every afternoon after that I would head out across the hills in the direction of Bonchurch, a tiny village with the very old church of St. Boniface hiding close by. Built in 1071, this was a delight as well. I never saw anyone there, but I would explore around, then get a coffee and cake from the little restaurant, and sit alone quietly high up overlooking the sea, living for a while in the world of J.B. Priestley, before heading back to prepare for the evening's entertainment.

I got to know the Shanklin Theatre company well and managed to see every production. Judith Fielding, the juvenile lead, was staying at the same place as I was, so it was a short time before I got to know the others.

In Shanklin, there was a clairvoyant lady whom several locals told me that I absolutely must see. I was a little skeptical because she was operating under the name of Madame Astra, which sounded too close to Noel Coward's Madame Arcati. However, I need not have worried. This lady immediately put me at ease and said that she had tried working under her real name, but it was impossible to make ends meet until she had selected something more theatrical.

Unlike many who are in this field, some for a living, some not - and some characters talking of "tall dark strangers", Madame Astra was the real thing, and instantly started telling me of very specific and accurate events, every single one of which subsequently took place.

Initially she told me of a long-haired Irish girl who had been thinking of me and would be in touch very shortly. Angela, from "London Country", was Irish, and there was a letter, the first I had ever had from her, awaiting me on the doormat an hour later.

I was told of many hundreds of legal documents, which turned out to be performing contracts, mostly from North America, that would be a huge part of my life. I was warned to get the strongest and best vehicle I could, as there was at some time to be an accident with the vehicle rolling in the snow, but that nobody would be hurt. This too, was to take place, in Newfoundland, some years later.

She told me everything, of songwriting, of recordings, and even of reviewing festivals for a magazine, which I did on more than one occasion, with the huge International Festival of Country Music at Wembley, in London, especially recalling an evening spent with Mooney Lynn, Loretta's late husband, that we both really enjoyed. Loretta moved out of the family home that she had shared with Mooney after his passing, subsequently making it, as was, into a museum. I visited one time, remembering the evening shared with her husband years before, and felt like an intruder into the private life that they were no longer able to have together.

Madame Astra talked of other things. She said, "Islands are good for you", which the Isle of Wight certainly was, also Bermuda, Prince Edward Island, visits to Santorini and Mykonos, and larger ones such as Vancouver Island and Newfoundland.

She advised me of back issues that I was to have spasmodically in later life and most important of all, told me with whom I should share my life. How incredibly right she was!

Ann and Mike, with whom I stayed, had two lovely daughters, for whom I felt a little sorry, having 2 strangers in their home for nearly 1/3 of each year, but they bore it with remarkable resilience, and spent most of their time together away from the house, as one often does in those formative years.

The family was completed by a large black Labrador cross named Whiskey, who was a delight. Whiskey was known pretty much all over Shanklin, and used to go for long walks on his own, over much of the island, sometimes not coming home for a night or even two. But nobody in those days was worried; all the Shanklin taxi drivers knew Whiskey, and if he was seen several miles away, which sometimes happened, a friendly taxi would always give him a lift home.

Whiskey would get up in the mornings and head off to the town centre, where there were maybe four butcher's shops who all knew him, and would save him a treat, to which of course Whiskey was very partial. The second year that I went to "Cliff Tops", one of the shops had changed ownership, and didn't know of Whiskey's semi-Mafia setup, so no treat, which Whiskey couldn't understand. Quickly, he grabbed a leg of lamb, and headed home as fast as he knew how. When Mike heard about this, he went straight down to pay for it, and they both had a good laugh. Mike was co-manager of the Halland Hotel not too far away, which probably had the finest dining room on the island, and I have little doubt that the couple who owned the shop were treated to an evening in a way that only Mike could. In any event, all returned to normal, and Whiskey continued with his regular circuit until he could do it no more.

And so, the first season in Shanklin drew to a close, which had been very successful. I had made good friends with Ann and Mike, also with Geoffrey Reed, leading lady Geraldine Hart, and male lead Barry Ashton of the theatre company. I had got interested in the old Manor houses on the Wight, of which there were many, and visited several of them, often accompanied by Geraldine, although this was to happen more on the following season. Barry Ashton - such a nice talented man - was the first person I knew who would subsequently pass away from AIDS, some twenty years later. But that was a long way off, and fortunately none of us was aware of it, so we all said goodbye to each other and the island, knowing that every company or group of musicians on a season is always very different, and no matter how often one returns, it will never be the same again.

It was time to head to Ryde, and back across the Solent. Maybe a four-mile crossing, but in lifestyle and culture a great deal wider than that. In the early 70s, the Isle of Wight still had a relatively peaceful feel; there was far less traffic than the mainland, and people still had time for each other. Many Islanders didn't bother with a car, not necessarily for economic reasons, more because there was a friendly and efficient bus service, and why hurry anyway? Sandown was a busy seaside town in the season, but all the others less so, and there were plenty of beaches where one could find a quiet spot, if desired. All those years ago, the hustle and bustle of modern life had yet to work its inexorable way across that little strip of water, as we all knew it someday would.

Upon returning to London, I was introduced to a very pleasant female singer from north London, who unbeknownst to me, had actually been awaiting my return from the Isle of Wight. We got together for a run-through two or three times, and I was offered some top-quality cruise work - including several trips of the QE2 - but it sadly wasn't going to work. She was Jewish, and her father had a busy tailoring business in Tottenham. Her parents were so kind and welcoming, however, we both knew that this was not to be a musical fit, no matter how many offers we received.

At this time, I was living in what had once been famed actors Dame Sybil Thorndike and Sir Lewis Casson's beautiful country home in Roehampton Vale. The house was exactly as they had left it, and had become available to "persons of a theatrical background", who would have respect for both the house and beautiful gardens. Elizabeth and her fiancée Bernard were offered the property and took it for a while, with myself having a bedroom, and a long-standing friend of Elizabeth's, Caroline Haynes, having another. We four moved into the house and were awed at the many classic theatre photos all around, to say nothing of the priceless antique furniture, but even more, we felt the incredible warmth and love that had been left as a legacy by one of the London theatre's most cherished couples. We had been told we could put things how we wished, as long as all was cared for, so we moved the furniture into the sunny back garden, one room at a time, cleaned the house from top to bottom to perfection, and returned everything to exactly where it was found, as it would have been criminal to even think of doing otherwise.

Caroline was definitely a character. I recall her collecting glasses once at a gathering in Gloucester Place, when a glass fell from her fully loaded tray. She said, "Oh, I am a silly cow", and bent down to move the broken bits, totally oblivious of the full tray balanced on her other hand... Another time, there was a fancy dress "do", which Caroline attended with a deck of cards glued all over her body. As the evening went on, it got warm and fuggy, so the cards started to fall, one at a time, to the floor... The last occasion to be mentioned, was when Elizabeth and I were asked to meet Caroline at a specific coffee bar in London, where a table had been reserved, with designated seats. She came in, wearing a fancy new coat, walked over to the table, and flung the coat open, revealing nothing or everything, depending on your perspective, and said, "I've wanted to do that for my whole life", bearing in mind that the two of us were the only ones to actually witness her performance.

It was a short but very memorable stay at the house in Roehampton Vale. The weather was perfect, and the four of us, plus occasional visitors, always dressed for dinner on the spacious lawns, with candlesticks and linen napkins being de rigeur, as we felt that might be what they would have done...

I have just realized that I am the only one of the four left to chronicle this, so it is a little bittersweet to write, and I do it with the greatest respect to my friends, and, of course, to Dame Sybil and Sir Lewis.

Shortly afterwards, one of my two aunts, Irene, who lived in Derby, which in those days was considered a long way from London, developed phlebitis, which now is relatively easily treated with a course of pills - I have had it - but not so then. Her leg was hugely swollen and had to be kept up, while her sister Kathleen was still busy teaching music all day and into the evening. So, I packed up what I was doing, (which included a couple of rehearsals with another singer, Lynn Russell, who was far more promising), and headed off to Derby to attempt taking over house and meals, at which I had little, if any, experience. All went well; I learned quickly to produce small plates of food, especially for Kathleen, but to have a second and possibly third helping awaiting in the kitchen. They had two boxrooms, untouched since they had purchased the house, where all their parents' things had been stored away. I went through the 3-storey house top to bottom, which was a huge job, but proved helpful when I had to do it all again, shortly after.

SERPENTINE RESTAURANT, HYDE PARK

Upon returning to London, I was fortunate to secure a residency at the Serpentine restaurant in Hyde Park, a stone's throw from where I had slept on the grass for a few nights not so long ago. It was a beautiful job, lots of glass, lots of light, and loads of happy people enjoying the park. I had already been offered the summer season on the Isle of Wight, where I had worked the previous year with Lee and Gil. She and the lady who owned the hotel had not seen eye to eye, so Lee was more than happy for me to take over the venue. I put together a four piece, with tenor sax/guitarist, bass, and a female drummer. I had hoped to get Jan again, but we were unable to make contact with each other. The bass player did a stand-up comedy routine, in addition, for two nights per week, plus I did a solo cabaret for two nights. All was well, and in budget.

PETER JANSEN FOUR

I stayed with Ann and Mike again, plus kids, and Whiskey of course, and the season was lovely. Elizabeth Lynne from the theatre company stayed there also, and we got to know each other well. Geraldine Hart was back as leading lady, and we spent much time exploring manor houses, often taking along Samson, her elderly long-haired dachshund. Joan Frances (Reed) who had the pub "The Green Dragon", the previous year, had renamed it "The Plough and Barleycorn". I was told that "The Green Dragon" had become a bit of a nickname for Joan rather than the pub, so it is hardly surprising that the name was changed.

The nearby pier show had, among others, the "Temperance Seven", and Billy J. Kramer and the "Dakotas". The "Temps" as they were called, sometimes came into the pub with instruments at lunch time, so I occasionally sat in. Sadly, their leader, on trumpet, had severe alcohol problems. Some nights he wouldn't show up at all, some nights he'd spend 85% of the set talking, while the band waited behind, somewhat exasperated, and some nights they were their normal brilliant selves. Somehow Will Hastie, their excellent clarinettist, managed to hold things together, for which he deserves a huge medal. One Saturday we decided to have a Christmas celebration. Joan did a huge Christmas dinner, the pub was decorated, and a whole slew of musicians had a ball playing all the Christmas favourites. Trombonist/pianist Bert Murray became a friend of both Geraldine and me, and we met up with him both on the island, and back in London sometime later.

My aunt Irene, who had phlebitis the previous year, had passed on that April. Her sister Kathleen, ever the dedicated teacher of music, had somehow managed to continue her busy life, but I persuaded her to come down to the island for a couple of weeks, where I found a small family-run hotel right next to "Cliff Tops", where I knew she would be well looked after. I showed her all my favourite haunts, including the tiny Church of Saint Boniface, in Bonchurch, where she played briefly the minuscule organ. I hope to this day I was able to lift her, even slightly, from her terrible loss. She decided to retire that October and go to live with my sister's family in the West Country. Kathleen passed away at her table, as she was writing a farewell to each of her students, which was probably as it should be, although I wish I could have been with her at that time. This would have happened, had my sister not somehow put her hand through a window shortly before, meaning that I was helping to do meals down there, with a view to returning as soon as possible.

Eras reach an end, and this was the end of that generation for me; I still had a younger aunt on my mother's side, but not in regular contact, although this would be renewed a little in years to come.

Over the years I had done one or two brief things to keep body and soul together, if a gap needed filling, as many of us have. The first I can recall was when living in the Earl's Court area, where I had to visit pubs and hotels over quite a wide area of London, to approach customers and buy them a specific drink, which was a product of Courage & Barclay. It was kind of a strong ale, rather like a barley wine, and the conclusion was that it was quite good, but a little sweet. Shortly after that, the brewery marketed an even sweeter version of the same drink, which, needless to say, didn't last very long. I recall that there was an older chap demo-ing the same product in a different area of London. He actually made a living going to various pubs and lounges where he would subsequently eat the glass, which brought large crowds, but they still didn't buy the drink, and I doubt he's still with us.

On another occasion I went into Fortnum and Mason's, in their grocery department, generally stocking shelves, and helping with the display for the busy Christmas season. Servers all wore morning suit or black tie, which I did sometimes, also sometimes a sandy-coloured long coat, the length of a dressing gown, when re-stocking. I got along well with the grocery manager, and we would take meals together. One day, he was discussing the fact that some good quality grapes, which had been reduced because they needed the space, would not sell, to which I replied, "Of course not, this is Fortnum's, they are used to paying high prices". He looked at me, the price was raised, and the grapes were all gone by day's end. On another occasion it was Christmas Eve morning, and there were still too many of the world famous (really, not like the signs one sees all over North America and Britain for world famous apple pie), but Fortnum's Christmas puddings, in their distinctive two and three pound red boxes. He approached me for ideas, because they did not want to reduce the price of puddings after Christmas. There was a major traffic light outside on Piccadilly, so I suggested that he give me a couple of helpers, we'd dress appropriately, and when the traffic stopped, we'd knock on people's car windows, say "Happy Christmas, compliments of Fortnum and Mason", and hand them a pudding. We also included a few taxi drivers, to their delight. Did this ever work, and made the national T.V. news that evening, probably along with the current location of Santa Claus. By the way, I had phoned the newsrooms, but Fortnum's didn't need to know about that.

 The following year until springtime was spent sharing a house in Wimbledon Park, which reminded me of Brook Cottage, where I had spent the first five years of my life; except that here it was the subway, (tube), that went past the bottom of the garden, while in the village of Little Kimble it had been British Rail, with especially the T.P.O. (travelling post office), thundering through at great speed every night, and snatching its bag of mail from the hanging "perch".

 There was a phone to which I had access when in the house at Wimbledon Park, but sometimes I would go to a nearby phone box for privacy. On one occasion I went in to find a ladies' wallet, or "clutch" as they used to be called, sitting in the box on the shelf. It had a large amount of money in it, and I confess to looking at it for a few minutes before taking it to the nearest police station. While on the subject of money, I should mention that some years before there was one particular day where things were pretty low. I had a very small amount of cash to my name, which I took and placed in a charity collection box. At that moment I felt strangely elated, as I felt I had now reached bottom, and there was only one possible direction left, which was up. On the same day I got booked for a good recording session, and things were never that bad again.

ACT FIVE

The Bermuda Years
Mary Arrives

"Peter & Mary" our very first picture. Photo: Gertraud Fendler, Bermuda Sun

THE BERMUDA YEARS

While living in Wimbledon Park, I was contacted by an office for whom I had worked regularly regarding a residency in St. George, Bermuda. They basically wanted exactly what I could offer, with the added proviso that if I was able to entertain an international clientele with songs in several languages, this would be a huge plus in the speedy processing of the necessary work permit. I have always loved the sounds of different languages and could provide two or three songs each in Spanish, French, German, Hebrew and Italian, which no Islander could do, so the permit was granted pretty much instantly, with approval from Hubert Smith, renowned singer and composer, then president of the Bermuda Musicians' Union.

There were several ships, such as that of Cable & Wireless, that came into the town of St. George with an international crew, especially Spanish and Greek, but speaking other languages as well, so that even one song would make them feel welcome and involved.

Off to Bermuda. Mary kindly came to collect me and all my stuff, instruments etc., from Wimbledon Park, and run me to my sister's farm, where I could sort out what was needed for the trip and store the rest. I had a 4 x 12 Impact speaker cabinet plus amplifier, also a Burns p.a. amp., my Gibson 12, and a Commodore semi-acoustic, which was identical to an Epiphone from the same factory, but a different name, so about 30% of the price. Plus of course mic., stands, etc., which were duly sent to Heathrow air cargo ahead of time. Came the day when I was to leave, and all went well with the flight. I will forever remember the aircraft door opening, and warmth and humidity flooding in, together with the smells of Hibiscus, Oleander, and the sound of a steel band welcoming people to the island, a sound I was to hear so many times in the future.

However, there was a hitch, as one learns quickly if doing flights fairly regularly. In this case none of my equipment or instruments had arrived, although my clothes had. The maître-d' of the venue where I was to work, Patrick, was not in the least concerned, said that it would show up shortly, and ran me in on his scooter, clutching a case, to St. George's, where I would be living for the foreseeable future. There was a staff apartment above Outerbridge's Supermarket, directly opposite the "Barbarela" Restaurant, which was joined with the "Pub on the Square", also named "Somers' Tavern", where I would be performing.

Bermuda was discovered in 1503 by Juan De Bermudez, a Spanish mariner, but the first people to permanently settle the island had been on board "Sea Venture"; flagship of a flotilla of eight ships bound for Virginia in 1609, with a total of 600 settlers. The 60-year-old admiral, Sir George Somers, had in his earlier years sailed with Drake and Raleigh, and at that time of the voyage was Member of Parliament for Lyme Regis, in Dorset, England. There was a colossal storm, and the "Sea Venture" was wrecked on a reef, about a mile from the Bermuda coast, till then called "The Isle of Devils", which was uninhabited except for some pigs, that had been left on the island many years before, and hugely increased in numbers.

Two small ships, "The Deliverance" and "The Patience", were ultimately built to complete the journey to Jamestown, which they did, leaving two settlers in Bermuda. Sir George returned to the Island he had come to love, ostensibly to bring some of the pigs to Jamestown, but died in Bermuda on arrival. Hence the name "Somers' Tavern", which was on the square, close to the beautiful gardens where Sir George's heart was supposedly interred.

I had a large room in the staff apartment, which had been re-decorated for my arrival, and was very comfortable. There was the occasional cockroach come under the bedroom door, but I soon learned that a little salt across the bottom of the door rectified this problem, and settled into island life, while awaiting the arrival of my "stuff".

It was eventually found, sitting in JFK airport, New York, after about 10 days, and sent to Bermuda. There was some damage to the Commodore, which I had to tune with pliers for my first season, as no parts were available, but all else was good, and I set up, a little nervously, for my first night of music.

After the first two or three songs, I thought "Now what do I do?", as one sometimes does in a new venue. The place was just about empty, and I was perched on a stool on the little stage with the bartender and maybe half a dozen customers. Then the door opened, in came a solid wall of cruise ship passengers, who had finished dinner on the ship docked the other side of the square and had come for an evening out. I was home and dry, and never concerned again if an evening should start slowly, or indeed, remain that way.

The staff were terrific. The Bermudian owner, a Mr. Gilmour, one only saw maybe once every couple of months, but the manager Leon "Jimmy" Williams was very popular in St. George's, and it was easy to become a part of the team. The restaurant maître-d', Patrick, was also an Islander, as were the three bartenders, a lady who was assistant to the chef, the girl who served food in the pub during the day, and a general helper that one didn't often see. The chef, Joseph, was Austrian, while the two restaurant servers, Patrick and Mohammed, were French and Moroccan respectively, and the last three shared the apartment with me. Quite a mixture, and we all got along really well.

Bermuda was, and remains, idyllic, possibly even more so during that very first visit, when things were not as busy as they are in the third millennium. The speed limit was 20 m.p.h., cars limited to one smallish vehicle per household, except for necessary work vehicles, and I well recall the fuss when the Island's first traffic light was installed, at what seemed a few feet from my window. Wherever one looked, it was picture perfect, with a blaze of tropical blooms and pastel-coloured houses during the day, and the never to be forgotten sound created by millions of tiny tree frogs through the night.

It was impossible to rent a car; there were taxis, and an efficient bus service, but the majority of Islanders and tourists scudded around on mopeds or scooters, frequently on the wrong side of the road, especially when at a roundabout. I didn't get a moped to start with; some venues, such as the Bermudiana hotel, wrote in their contracts that their performers were not to use one. Mine wasn't quite that strict, but it was made clear that it would be preferable if I didn't, as they naturally didn't want their entertainer to be missing for a night or more during the high season, because of Bermuda "Road Rash".

To my surprise, there were already other musicians that I knew on the island. David & Nina Burns, who I had met some seven years previously at Willesden Working Men's club showcase in North London, were at the Holiday Inn a short walk away, while Joanne Iddins, whom I had met when with "Band Seven", was at the Hog Penny in Hamilton, the capital. Joanne had been a dancer back in her U.K. years, and came up with a dance called the "Zizzle" that she tried like crazy to promote, but sadly it never quite "clicked".

Joanne's "stage" was unbelievable. There was what was little more than a shelf above the bar, with a small railing in the front, onto which Joanne would crawl from a little door at the side, almost flat on her stomach, for each set. Once seated behind her little keyboard she was O.K., but if she had ever stood up in a hurry, there would have been serious and permanent damage, as her head was only about three inches from the ceiling. Her years as a dancer had obviously been of use, as she could perform the contortions necessary to get on the shelf with ease, and had it down to a fine art.

Some of the cruise ships I got to see every week when they docked in St. George, only a few feet away from the "Pub on the Square", where

I was performing, so naturally I got to know a few of the officers, who became regulars. The Cunard Ambassador was one of these ships, and on one cruise they had a new doctor, whom the other officers definitely felt needed initiating into shipboard life. On the Island there was one man who used to dress, very spectacularly, in ladies' clothes, and come out to mingle with the tourists, who didn't know, especially when the ships were in. Bermudians all called him "Miss World", (or sometimes "The Duchess"), which title was truly justified - little knowing that they would have a real "Miss World" in St. George, Gina Swainson, a year or two later.

The officers, including the ship's doctor, came in one night, for which "Miss World" had already been primed. They were duly introduced, and the doctor was instantly smitten, as everyone knew he would be. Many of the Island regulars were in that night, but I cut way back on the show, because we were all watching the show that was taking place immediately in front of the stage. Of course, the cruise ship passengers had no clue of what was happening, but when Miss World and the ship's doctor left together, I just very quietly said, "Somebody's going to get a surprise", and the place broke up. The officers were, of course, delighted, and we didn't see the doctor for a couple of weeks, but eventually he came back in, knowing that he had been "had", and could laugh about it with the others. He, quite rightly, never had to pay for a drink again, as the staff always made sure it was "on the house".

It would be impossible to write of Bermuda during this time without mentioning Johnnie Barnes. Johnnie used to drive one of the ubiquitous pink buses that are seen all over the Island, always with a friendly greeting to every passenger, as all the drivers will. When Johnnie retired, he couldn't bear the thought of not seeing his so very many friends every day, so he positioned himself on the Crow Lane roundabout, at the east end of Hamilton's Front Street, to wave at those going to and from work, as well as during much of the day. He did this virtually every day, rain or shine, for the rest of his life, and if Johnnie was not seen on the roundabout, there would be concern that he might be sick. On occasion, in my first year in Bermuda, the chef, Joseph, and I would take the bus into Hamilton, where there was an amazing delicatessen in the Washington Mall, with a sumptuous array of cheeses and some excellent coffees, where we would stock up on treats, for both ourselves and the restaurant. After our coffee one day, Joseph went to the counter, in order to take away coffee and a sandwich, which he said was for Johnnie. When we boarded the bus back to St. George, Joseph asked if he could get off at Paget roundabout, as he wanted to give something to Johnnie, and asked what time the next bus would be. He was told by the driver that they would be pleased to wait while Joseph delivered the coffee and sandwich and had a little chat. That small instance tells one more about Bermuda and its people than many a large book.

When Johnnie passed on, a bronze statue of him was put on the roundabout in memoriam. Many Islanders still wave as they pass it, which I hope they always will.

Occasionally, there would be a submarine come to dock in St. George, possibly from the U.S., but more likely Canadian, out of Halifax, Nova Scotia. Submarine crews are always looking for a little fun, which is hardly surprising, considering their cramped conditions for long periods of time. One regular was the "Okanagan", whose crew were notable in that, once they had been in the pub for a while, had a drink or two, and it was time to head back to the sub., they would drop to their knees and go out of the building in line, singing "Heigh-ho heigh-ho, it's off to work we go"...... I don't know if they stood up once outside, as I was working, but I like to think they navigated the entire town square in true dwarf style before reaching the submarine moored on the opposite side.

One time, two crew members from the same sub, came in fairly early in the evening, before things got busy, and headed to the washroom at the back. After a few minutes, one of them came out clutching a pile of clothes, so that it became obvious what was going to happen next. Then the main door to the square opened, and in came the usual solid wall of cruise ship passengers, having finished dinner, to completely pack the place. The other crew member came out of the washroom in order to do his "streak", saw that the room was full, and had to say "excuse me…….excuse me" in order to get through the room, which took a long time, as the other customers were in no hurry to create space. Of course, when he got out of the door, his friend had gone back to the submarine carrying all the clothes, so he had to cross the main square stark naked, much to the amusement of two Bermuda police officers who were passing at the time. They, of course, had to say something to this poor unfortunate, but it was all in good humour, which was shared by the police officers, once they were out of uniform and could come in to tell us all how the story ended. In this case, I believe a towel or a tablecloth was borrowed, either from us or the White Horse Tavern, in which to wrap the sailor, while he was escorted back to the submarine, which had a military "guard" from the Bermuda regiment on it for the rest of their stay; I'm not sure why….

There was a duo in the early sixties, called "The Allisons", (John Alford and Bob Day), who had won the Eurovision Song Contest, and subsequently had a no. 1 hit, with their composition "Are You Sure?" They did extremely tight harmonies in the style of the Everly Brothers, and occasionally short tours, but not often. One of them was now a flight attendant for British Airways and used to come into the "Pub on the Square" when in Bermuda. I never asked anyone onto the stage, but in this case, it was a mutual idea, and I could see the blend would be easy, so we did several Everlys' songs for about twenty minutes and had a really good time. He was especially pleased that I could nail "Are You

Sure?", which we sang together, without the audience ever knowing the identity of my guest.

When working in Bermuda as a musician or performer, it was part of government regulations that the situation be "all found" for the length of the contract, i.e., accommodation, meals, etc. I was lucky for the two years I spent there, in that there was an excellent chef for each season, who would be happy to do anything requested, especially if it were not on the menu, as this would be something different for him to prepare.

I was so fortunate to have a "following" in the "Pub on the Square", of up to 13 "regulars", who came in several times per week, and we had some great evenings together. There were two key couples, Doug and Carolyn (subsequently married, and special friends over the years), plus Tom and Sharon, (also subsequently married). Sometimes Carolyn's mum Madlin came, also her brother Jonny, and several others, a group that any performer would love to have out front. Many songs, if not all, were "sing along" from the 50s to 70s, or "join in" songs, i.e., "Knock three times" involved huge noise with ashtrays -and many others like it. By now I also had "Never on a Sunday" down, for the Greek crew who came in every week. Only one song in Greek, but they all joined in, and the Greek chef brought me a much appreciated jar of pickled eggs that he had prepared in the ship's galley.

Mornings could be a little challenging at first. The staff apartment was on a crossroads, where there would be a small amount of traffic. The traffic wasn't a problem, even though it was close to 3:00 a.m. when I went to bed. No, the problem was that there used to be a local, who obviously had some problems, and stood in the centre of the intersection waving his arms and shouting at the vehicles first thing every morning. There were very few of these, especially in those days, but it was impossible to sleep, so I invested in an air conditioner, which not only covered the noise, it also meant that some of the humidity was removed from the room. Even so, I still had to change all instrument strings every week.

The town of St. George was a paradise, as is the whole of Bermuda, and I soon got to know several people who worked in the little shops. Robertson's drug store had a 50s style soda fountain at one end of the shop - the only one I had ever seen - and it was nice to go into their air-conditioned space for a soda or float on a hot afternoon. Plus, they had newspapers from both London and New York every day, if one needed the occasional catch-up on world affairs.

There were a couple of late night, (or early morning), watering holes in St. George. One was a small locals' restaurant called Clyde's, which did the most amazing hot fish sandwiches for a dollar, and the other was a short walk away, known as the Gunpowder Cavern, and carved out of the solid limestone rock.

Originally, the gunpowder magazine for the Island had been in the State House, which was built in 1620, and had immense limestone walls. Members of the Assembly who convened there were somewhat uncomfortable about sharing their meetings with a potential bomb, so the Governor had the supply moved to the grounds of his own residence on Retreat Hill. During the war between Britain and America in 1775, the American Continental Congress had stopped the export of food to British colonies, of which Bermuda was one, so a group of prominent Bermudians, led by Sir Henry Tucker, and unbeknownst to the Governor, went to plead their cause with the Congress, offering to bring salt to America, which was an important article of war. Congress turned down the Bermudians but said they would be interested in gunpowder. So, on 14th August, there was a clandestine landing at Tobacco Bay, helped by the Tucker family and others, and a large supply of gunpowder was sold to a grateful General George Washington, who made sure that Bermuda's food supply continued.

The Gunpowder Cavern in St. George was constructed sometime later as the magazine for the Island, but was by now a large, mostly empty cavern, with several rooms built out of bare rock, lots of old flags hanging over a bar, and a simple restaurant. It was very basic, yet the atmosphere was terrific, and it was a good place to unwind after a long evening's work. Several of our staff used to go up there, as did musicians and staff from other restaurants and hotels in the area, with one or two tourists thrown in for good measure. Lyle, who ran the place, was a musician himself, always very welcoming, and sometimes I would pop in for a brief visit over a cup of coffee in the afternoon, usually en route to or from a cooling swim in Tobacco Bay.

Our Austrian chef, Joseph, used to go up there, having prepared meals for both the "Barbarela" and the "Pub on the Square" all evening, with just one helper, and in need of a break. I remember Joseph reading the books of Maria Von Trapp, and being especially taken with them, even more so because of their shared nationality. Maria by now had a beautiful lodge in Stowe, Vermont, and Joseph felt driven to write to her, about her writings and her life, also sharing parts of his own life. She was very touched by his letter, and wrote him a long one back, asking him to come and visit her, see the lodge, and join the "family" of staff who helped her to run it. Joseph was overwhelmed by her offer, and we all said that he should at least go and meet with her, and see the place, but sadly, it was too big an event for him; even though Vermont is so close to Bermuda, it never happened.

Bermuda is a magical Island, with pastel painted cottages nestling amongst the trees, many of which are ablaze with colour, or hibiscus filled hedgerows. Even the cracks in an old limestone wall at the roadside will probably be home to a purple Bermudiana, and there is always the sound of birds, especially the yellow and black Kiskadees, whose sound is so welcoming, no matter where you go.

But even more spectacular than all of this is the sight that can be seen by donning a snorkel mask and looking just a very few inches below the surface of the ocean, where a myriad of multi-coloured fish flash in and out of the coral reefs. My favorite spot has always been Tobacco Bay, in St. George's, which is shallow near the beach, but has a huge drop off after the rocks, enabling one to see Queen Angel Fish, Parrot Fish, Sergeant Majors, Squirrel Fish, Yellowtail, Trumpet Fish, and so many others. On one occasion I was looking near some rocks, and the head of a huge green Moray eel came out of a cleft, and almost to my mask, or so it felt. I had possibly got a little too close to his home, and resolved to be very respectful, should I ever meet one again.

In those days, the big Bermuda hotels, of which there were several, all put on a truly sumptuous complimentary afternoon tea for tourists visiting the Islands, both for their current guests, and as an introduction to others for the future. I tried a couple of them, but my afternoons were much too busy exploring, watching cruise ships navigate the "cut" into St. George's, or swimming in Tobacco Bay. Plus, the Globe Hotel, opposite the staff apartment, was being turned into the Confederate Museum, later to be renamed the Bermuda National Trust Museum, and I was sometimes assisting with the setup.

If in Hamilton, there would occasionally be a visit to the "Hog Penny", where Joanne performed nightly, or to the "Horse and Buggy", which had Phil & Jackie Devon as the resident act. Raymond White, proprietor of the "Horse and Buggy", whom I got to know quite well, approached me regarding a replacement or replacements for Phil & Jackie, who were shortly to leave Bermuda. He was initially looking at two solo performers, so as to have continuous music throughout the evening, which no other venue had done, and I of course suggested Mary as one, and showed him a picture of her posing with guitar and hot pants! This immediately completed the deal, if she was interested, but he said he would like to meet her on his upcoming visit to England.

I contacted her - I believe she had to think for nearly a second over such a momentous offer - and wheels were put in place to start the whole thing going. I also suggested Barbara Champion, whom I had met in France so many years before, and now wrote for "The Stage", in addition to her live performing, as a possible act to alternate with Mary. I had never seen her work, but knew she was constantly busy, and Raymond was specifically looking for two solo female performers at that time. Mary was booked as planned, except the other act booked, which was a brother and sister duo, was going via an agent, through whom I had originally gone into Europe, and he somehow deviously got to do the contract for Mary as well, and expected a commission for the job he hadn't got. However, he was a long way from Bermuda, and there was no point in falling out, so Mary, very sensibly, took her agreed fee, with his percentage added on top, so there was no loss to her, and all, ultimately, was well. Paperwork started, and she was due to come to the Islands the following November, when Phil & Jackie would be leaving, a time that would change both of our lives forever.

But I still had many performances to go before this happened. The main cruise ship season was winding down, and there were only a few left, plus of course the Cable and Wireless ship that maintained the undersea telephone cables that were still in use. Pretty well all my nights were busy, and I had got used to most of the locals, who were regular visitors. There were in those days both a Canadian and U.S. base on the island, in addition to the British navy sometimes using the old facilities in Dockyard, at the far end. The Canadian base was close by, and I recall meeting one very pleasant service woman named Ellen, of whom we will hear more later. Plus, there was a member of the J. Arthur Guinness family, a co-owner of the brewery, who now lived on the Island. I always knew if he was in, as a glass of Guinness would appear by my side, which I didn't really want, as it was too heavy, but wanted to be polite, and always surreptitiously found a home for it. The other, surprising, resident always talked about his work with the C.I.A. after a couple of drinks. I couldn't believe such a loose tongue, but most of the locals knew him, and said that he was definitely legit, and still a part of the agency. He was an older man, and I wonder if he had been deliberately put where he could do no harm for his final working years, as I have seen with a couple of hotel managers over time.

I had of course got totally used to the humidity by now - which was very hard on amplifiers and sound systems in general, leaving a thick white buildup on controls and other connections, thus needing constant maintenance - plus most people kept a light on in their clothes closets, not the cool L.E.D. bulbs that are in use today, but the old incandescent bulbs that gave out 90% of their energy in heat, and were sufficient to avoid any dampness.

That fall I experienced my first hurricane. In Bermuda, houses are built of solid limestone blocks. The State House in St. George's, built in 1620, still stands as proudly today as when it was first built, but there is a definite procedure which all Islanders know to follow. Firstly, small craft - and huge cruise ships - are taken from their moorings, and away from the shore, to lessen any chance of damage. Every home has a battery powered radio, as the power will almost certainly go off, and there is an emergency radio station telling residents what to do. All shutters, which in Bermuda are real, not ornamental, and louvered, are tightly latched on the side of the building that is to be hit by the storm first, with the windows behind wide open. On the lee side, both shutters and windows remain open. The first shutters on the storm side will filter the wind somewhat as it roars through the house, while having them both open on the lee side prevents any buildup of pressure inside. When the eye of the hurricane is reached, there is around twenty minutes of total calm and silence, not one leaf moves, or one bird makes a sound. During this period, it is time to go out and reverse the shutter positions, as when the wind returns, it will be going full bore in the opposite direction. Of course, all breakables and anything loose need putting away safely, and sometimes furniture may need moving into a solid block by a wall. There are usually trees down, and many thousands of flowers decimated, with possible damage to the occasional chimney, but once the storm is through, everybody on the Island turns out for the big cleanup. The sun is back out, new buds bloom, and within a few days there is often no evidence that the storm has ever been.

Having said all this, there can sometimes be damage to hotels that have not been built in the same way, and certainly don't have shutters. Mermaid Beach, which was a smaller hotel, had an extension of several rooms put on it by the non-Bermudian owner, who was warned by the locals of what might happen. And happen it did, the day of my first storm, when the extension simply wasn't there anymore. Also, one year a huge hurricane did colossal damage to the 300 room Sonesta Beach Hotel, in Southampton, to the extent that the hotel was subsequently removed, and the site returned to grassland.

But I will never forget leaving the apartment during the eerie silence as the eye passed over, and helping Jimmy Williams with the shutters, at the same time watching the clouds, to be well out of the way myself before the colossal roar of wind that was about to take place, all over again, in the opposite direction.

With the possible exception of the Mermaid Beach extension, the Islands were returned to their pristine beauty by the time that Mary was due to arrive from the U.K. for her residency at the "Horse & Buggy" in Hamilton that November, to which I had been looking forward for so very long. By now I had got to know David & Nina Burns, musicians from the St. George Holiday Inn, pretty well, and we often visited each other's venues, or ran into each other in the square during the day.

Every corner in Bermuda has perfection just around the other side, and I couldn't wait to share the innumerable treasures of these Islands with Mary, to say nothing of introducing her to David & Nina, as well as to Joanne Iddins, (of the "shelf"), and to some of the other people with whom I had been working since May.

Before she was due to arrive, we had Remembrance Day on the Island, and I was to see something I had seen in no other part of the world. At 11 a.m., when there is traditionally a 2-minute silence in Cenotaph or Church services, all traffic in Bermuda was stopped by police, excepting emergency vehicles, for 2 minutes. Engines off, there actually was silence, and it really made me think. Such a simple gesture, yet so powerful; I wish everyone did that.

MARY ARRIVES

I was up bright and early the day of Mary's arrival, bearing in mind that I probably hadn't been in bed much before 3:00 a.m. We had had a busy night at the "Pub on the Square". Several of my regulars had been in, Doug & Carolyn, Tom & Sharon, and others, who had all become such good friends, and knew of Mary's imminent arrival, with a promise to go and be supportive at the "Horse & Buggy", once she had settled in. Plan for the day was that I would go to the airport and meet Raymond in good time for the flight to arrive from Heathrow, where we would welcome her, also Chrissie & Nigel, the new duo, then take them to the Swizzle Inn, just over the causeway, for a relaxing visit, where everyone could get to know each other.

At which point I should probably explain the constituents of a "Swizzle", that harmless little drink that is often given to new arrivals in Bermuda. Firstly, comes a can of orange juice, another can, of equal or slightly lesser size, of pineapple juice. This is followed by copious amounts of a gold rum plus an equivalent amount of dark rum for good measure. Then, variously, some add a little grenadine, for colour, or angostura bitters - or not. Occasionally, if preparing a large punch bowl, some put in ginger ale as well; the recipe varies somewhat from place to place. This seemingly innocuous and very pleasant tasting drink is quite relaxing; however, many folks find that on standing up, the legs from knees downwards may be completely dysfunctional, a symptom that can spread upwards as far as the hips. It is usually served in jugs, of various sizes.

Added to that, the fact that Mary, Chrissie and Nigel had been up since 4:00 a.m. U.K. time, navigated Heathrow airport and all its joys, followed by the long flight to Bermuda, made it clear that they were very tired after their visit to the Swizzle Inn, and ready for a good sleep. However, this was not to happen. They were deposited at a guest house for a couple of hours, then Raymond collected them, to go to where Phil & Jackie Devon were still playing, at the "Horse & Buggy" for supper, to meet many, many people, and to introduce their music, with zero setup time. What an incredibly hard first evening, so very different to mine with Jimmy Williams in St. George.

Phil and Jackie left Bermuda, and Mary, plus Chrissie and Nigel, moved into their beautiful location at "Springfield", where there were huge gardens replete with grapefruit, lemons, bananas, and the sound of many birds. Brightly coloured lizards lay in the sun by day, and of course, there was always the magical sound of tree frogs at night.

Springfield was, however, a little way from the "Horse & Buggy", so it was necessary for Mary to get a moped as soon as possible, unlike me, who had only to cross the street. Nigel moved into an alternative accommodation, as there were only two small bedrooms in the apartment, and the three of them started their run.

Lewis Carroll's Cheshire Cat was a positive amateur compared to the grin that Mary wore that first time she came into St. Georges' on her

Honda moped; a grin that was to stay with her at all times throughout her year on the Island, and instantly reappear on subsequent visits, of which there have been many.

The next three weeks were life-altering for both of us. Not only were there the joys of seeing each other again, and sharing some of the delights of this beautiful Island, we also spent a good many afternoons in Springfield going through music to fit the "Horse & Buggy" clientele, which, in addition to mostly American and Canadian tourists, also included servicemen from the U.S., Canadian, British and French navies, all eager for a night out, a good pint or two, and some fun.

My season was drawing to a close, as St George's was much quieter than Hamilton in the winter season, so under Bermuda law I had to leave the Island if not working, to reappear in the early spring, as I could not class as a tourist.

We became very close in those three weeks. Mary came to my end of the Island on her day off, and also came to see me work, after which I introduced her to the "Gunpowder Cavern". On my first day off after her arrival, I went to see her, (plus Chrissie and Nigel), at the "Horse & Buggy"; plus one evening we went on her moped to check out "The Robin Hood", which was the late night venue where many ex-pat British hung out, close to Hamilton, being very careful to avoid the huge toads that could sometimes be seen on the roads at night, especially after rainfall.

Mary was duly introduced to David & Nina Burns at the "Holiday Inn", Joanne Iddins at the "Hog Penny", and several of my "regulars" at the "Pub on the Square", also Jimmy Williams welcomed her with open arms, and any time we had a meal together, it was always "on the house". Such a nice man, and we kept in touch sporadically for the rest of his life, which was sadly curtailed far too soon.

The weeks went by fast, but we managed to cram in a huge amount, including sharing for the first time together the unbelievable joys of snorkelling in Tobacco Bay, or sitting out on the deck at the "White Horse Tavern", so it was with a somewhat heavy heart that I boarded a plane for the U.K., clutching 2 guitars, as I intended to make an album for the Bermuda tourist market before my return.

Come the New Year, I based partially with Geraldine Hart, from the Shanklin Theatre Company, who lived in the heart of the West End, and everything one could possibly need was within easy walking distance. She was trying like crazy to crack the London theatre market, having done loads of good work throughout the U.K., with luminaries such as Charles Dance, Mark Eden, (both several times), and many others. In those days there were no such things as answering machines, cell phones, personal computers etc., so if you were awaiting that all important life-altering phone call, you had to do just that, wait...... Consequently, there were many experienced and talented actors around London who lived by their phones and hardly dared go out in the day, unless for an audition. Geraldine was one of these, groceries were close by, and Samson, her beloved long-haired Dachshund, could be walked locally, other than that, it was stay home.

Although there are over 100 theatres in London, it is probably even harder to get into a West End theatre production than to appear in the Marquee, Flamingo, or any other top club with a rhythm and blues outfit, as I so well recall from "Manish Boys" days.

Geraldine wanted to take a couple of courses - Shakespearean stage fighting was one of them - and I needed quiet time to prepare charts for the upcoming recording, so was happy to look after both Samson and the phone while she was doing the courses, and all was to go smoothly.

I was also out researching studios, as Vic was not available, and came upon Studio Republic, in Pinner, Middlesex, owned and run by a fine engineer named John Bales, where I was to go again when doing the first album with Mary a little while later. The plan was to do an album where the two sides were somewhat different in style to each other, and my first call was to a steel player, Peter Willsher, that I had known for some time, both because he used to work with Jim Burns, (Burns guitars), and also because he had the European hit with "Sleepwalk"; the U.S. hits being "Santo and Johnny" plus "Ferrante & Teicher". Peter was fast becoming the number one session steel player in the U.K., so I felt incredibly lucky to get him for my sessions. I was recommended to Ian Pearce on guitar, who was also doing some pretty major recording, plus working with a good quality band on a house gig. This particular album, aimed at tourists, was to be mostly "covers", so Ian's bass and drums came in as well, as they were used to playing together, which I always feel is a huge plus. Also, there was vocal backing on some cuts from Samantha Timbs, and her friend Ian Johnson. The two of them had done quite a bit of studio work together and certainly added to the album. All went well, and I returned to Bermuda having completed the master, and awaiting arrival of the finished product.

Geraldine did subsequently crack the West End market and had her name in lights on many a London theatre marquee, as well as being a frequent guest on the popular Michael Parkinson T.V. chat show, for the rest of her career.

It was such a joy to get back to the Island that is so easy to love, and of course to Mary that had been hugely missed whilst I was in London and other parts of the U.K. I had visited the Giaconda a couple of times, but the regulars had changed, and even Julie was not there, so it seemed like an era had passed. I had enjoyed doing the album, but Peter Willsher and Samantha Timbs were the only people involved that I knew at all, and I was ready to leave.

Mary had, of course, fallen in love with Bermuda, as I knew she would, and we settled back into Island life. She had received a surprise visit from Andy, the three of us having of course shared the London apartment some years before, and we had good times catching up with each other's activities, as has happened many times since. He had gone into theatre management, which he was to do in various civic positions for many years.

I set up ready to go for my first night back, which Jimmy had made sure would be packed with all my regulars. I now had a "sound to light" unit, to be mounted on the ceiling, which for its time, was very clever. There were three lights, I believe red, blue, and green, which responded to pitch on the guitar. Low notes were red, middle green, and high notes blue, or you could alter things as desired. I only used it once or twice a night, when I would give the bartender a cue, and lights over the audience would be dimmed while I did a certain piece, complete with colours changing to fit the music. It was very effective, and certainly a case of "less is more", to be used minimally.

David and Nina, up at the Holiday Inn, had become very close friends. At one time they were recording an album in their apartment, with equipment everywhere, much of which had been purpose built by David, who loved electronics. It reminded me so much of when I had worked with Joe Meek, who had gadgets and musicians all over his house; I think even the bathroom was used on occasion.

The four of us would do all kinds of things together, both in the day and after work. On one occasion we went out with marine biologist Bronson Hartley on his boat, just a short distance from Flatt's inlet. He had diving helmets that received air from a machine on deck, and we were walking on the seabed, maybe only in about ten or fifteen feet of water, being shown the various fish and corals. There was one Bermuda Queen Angel Fish that he had amazingly taught to come and get morsels of food from his lips, and she looked for him daily. He also had some rings, rather like a magician's linking rings, and she would flip in and out of them to get goodies at the end.

We of course snorkelled a lot in Tobacco Bay, which in those days was a quiet area, and sometimes visited a family who lived by the beach in Shelly Bay, further towards Hamilton, and were friends of David and Nina.

There were many cruise ships, both in Hamilton and St. George; some of which would spend two or three nights in each place. Two ships had been purpose built to navigate the shallow "cut" into St. George's, these were the "Sea Venture" and "Island Venture" and were the "official" ships with preferred berths, a Bermuda company. Some years later Holland America obtained this status instead, at which point the two ships were sold to P & O, and became the beginning of Princess Cruises, the "Pacific Princess" of "Love Boat" fame, on which we were to work later - and the "Island Princess", her twin sister.

An occasional St. George visitor was the "Alexandr Pushkin", home port Leningrad, running out of New York. One night, the captain and several officers came into where I was working; the purser approached me and said, "Our captain wishes to sing". In other circumstances I would have found a reason to say "no", but this was obviously a very big deal, plus several of his passengers were in, so I of course agreed, and asked what his choice of song would be. The purser came back to me with "Toreador Song, Carmen", which I didn't know at all, and gave minimal, not very good, back up. He had a huge voice, and thanked me very politely, returning to his group. I found out that the ship was to return in a couple of weeks, so, having a record player in my room, I purchased a recording of "Carmen" and did some serious work in producing a half decent accompaniment.

When the ship came back in, I approached the purser and asked if he could request that the captain sing his song again, as everyone had enjoyed it so much the last time, which was of course agreed. The captain's face positively lit up when he saw that I had worked on the piece and invited me back on the ship for a visit. I think we chatted the world around till about 5:00 a.m., sampling Russian delectables. When I left, he said "Anytime you wish to sing on my ship" …. and gave me a couple of phone numbers, and a name to use. Within a couple of years this was to take place more than once, and we got to know some of the officers as friends. There was a big thunderstorm a few weeks after the ship had left, and I returned to my room one day to find an unbelievable smell, plus the record player had completely melted, teaching me to unplug, or to use a power bar that contained a fuse.

Mary and I were getting together a great deal, both in St George's and at Springfield, where we could sit out in the beautiful gardens to look at music, or just relax. We had decided our lives were to be together, both in and out of music, and, since we had different nights off, we would play together at each other's venues most weeks. Nigel was by now doing the first "Horse & Buggy" set on solo piano, with he and Chrissie alternating with Mary the rest of the night. I seem to recall the two of us doing the St. George venue more, but could be wrong in this.

Together with David and Nina, we devised a system of "house points", rather like one sometimes gets at school. To obtain a "house point", all you had to do was something truly eccentric, which would be judged accordingly by those not involved. For example, one day Mary and I were down at Springfield, and she had just taken a shower and washed her hair, which was being dried with a hairdryer. I offered her an iced tea, so she swapped the dryer to the other hand, took the iced tea, and poured it all over her head. This, of course, was a house point by unanimous agreement, and there were many others. Mary, David, and Nina were down at the "Pub on the Square" one night and were heading out to their apartment to prepare snacks for when I had finished work. I duly showed up at the apartment to find the street door open, and the three of them in bed with parasols and Christmas lights all around, doing a routine on "Singin' in the Rain!" This was an excellent house point, but I was now behind, and had to catch up, so when we left their place at around 3:00 a.m., I asked Mary to hold all of my clothes, and went back to knock on the door. David opened it and broke up, calling for Nina to come and see; the response was "I'm doing my teeth", but I, for one, hoped she would come quickly, before anyone else came past.

The major holiday on the Island of Bermuda is a cricket match that takes place between St. George and Somerset - further down the Island - on the Thursday and Friday before the first Monday of August, thus creating a four day holiday, called appropriately, "Cup Match". This is a party in which the cricket, while playing a major part, also has to compete with Crown & Anchor tables, Conch Stew, or Curried Mussel Pie, with music extending well into the night, and many camped out for the weekend. Between twelve and fifteen thousand attend, and the Island virtually stops for this, although of course the big tourist venues continue as usual.

Chrissie and Nigel, who worked with Mary, were leaving the Island, so she agreed to continue on her own, which she was more than capable of doing. A couple of months later, David and Nina were also leaving, to see if they could get into the U.S. resort market. The Bermuda Union had a local trio available, who therefore were given David and Nina's job, but within a few weeks the night club was closed and turned into a coffee bar plus convention room, as the clientele had all gone. Good Bermudian musicians, of which there are many, like the influx of others to learn new things and keep standards up; unfortunately, there were some Island musicians at the time of lesser quality, who still had to be employed, regardless of ability. This trio had become available and was put by the Holiday Inn swimming pool during afternoon tea, when the area was empty, and they could do no harm, but when David and Nina left, they had to be given the nightclub slot, to disastrous effect.

Joanne Iddins was still on the Island, and amongst her many projects for the community, had written a musical about Bermuda, called initially "Dream Bermuda", that was staged in Hamilton a little while after we left. She did so much work on it, and it was very close to being a movie, but like many projects it never quite happened, even though she tried for many years. We met her again sometime after leaving the Island, now married to Steve Diaz, who at that time was in the Guinness Book of Records for going under the lowest ever limbo pole. In later years she lived in Orpington, Kent, in the U.K., close to the Austrian chef, Joseph, who had been working in the "Barbarela" on my first season in Bermuda.

Joanne was offered Bermudian citizenship, which was very rare, and meant she would have been exempt from work permits amongst other things, but I don't think she ever took it. We sadly missed her at the "Pub on the Square" when having lunch many years later, by about 15 minutes, not knowing that she was on the Island.

Bermuda is very different to other places, in that there is no income tax. Instead, revenue is generated via import duties, which means groceries cost quite a bit more, and there are large duties on other things - such as buying a boat, car, or house. Some people find it necessary to maintain two jobs, but the Island lifestyle is idyllic. Mark Twain lived there much of his time; Noël Coward once had a house, and while we were there, Gordon Mills had a property which was shared with the two main artists that he managed, Tom Jones and Engelbert Humperdinck. David Bowie, one time of the "Manish Boys", lived on the Island, with his house at Cambridge Beaches, but this was many years later, and he subsequently moved to Mustique, in the Grenadines, just by Princess Margaret.

One day, there was going to be a T.V. shoot of Engelbert and Anne Murray, partly on the Hamilton waterfront, and partly at Elbow Beach hotel, so Mary and I went down to watch for a bit, especially as the technical side was so interesting. In the case of Engelbert, I think it was the first time we had ever seen a performer come on with the seams of his pants open, which were pulled tight immediately before the shot.

The main large hotels on the Island were undoubtedly the two Princesses, Hamilton and Southampton - now Fairmont - and the musical director of Princess hotels, (no connection with the future cruise line), Joe Wylie, whom we knew well, approached us with an offer to appear as a resident act in the Southampton Princess. There was to be a new wine bar in the basement, soft lights, and entertainment of a style aimed at a listening audience. He showed us the venue and we were delighted. Mary needed to catch up with her family first if we were able to take this on, so decided to leave the Island in late September, with me still having about two months to go at the "Pub on the Square". I was very sad to see her go, but we were excited about the forthcoming Princess residency, which is exactly what we wanted, possibly better....

Douglas & Carolyn, friends and favorite customers, were getting married, which unfortunately Mary was going to miss, but I went to the service and took a couple of photos of them with the traditional Bermuda wedding Horse & Buggy. Imagine my surprise when the entire wedding group turned up later in the evening at the "Pub on the Square", with Carolyn still in her wedding dress. Jimmy, of course, made sure there was champagne for everyone in the house, and I'm not sure that we closed on time that night.

One day Connie Francis, whom I had met while still at school all those years ago, in Caxton Hall, London, on her first tour, came in for lunch. I sadly missed her, but Jimmy took a picture of her on the little stage, with my album sleeves on the wall behind.

My last night at the "Pub on the Square" was amazing. The place was packed solid, there were lots of hugs and kisses, and of course, Jimmy kept the champagne flowing. There was a big cake and a gift from Tommy, the chef, also my regulars, headed by the newly married Doug & Carolyn Shirley, plus the soon to be married Tom & Sharon (Trimingham), presented me with an engraved tankard, with everybody's name on, which is used to this day.

I was sad to be leaving St. George's, but looking forward to the residency with Mary at the Southampton Princess, and Joe Wylie was going ahead with the permit applications, which were still in process when I left the Island. However, the outcome eventually was that a local trio was available - possibly the same one that had caused the demise of the Holiday Inn nightclub - and try as he might, Joe was unable to find anywhere to place them.

So, the whole concept of the venue was permanently shelved, and it was time for us to rethink....

ACT SIX

"Peter & Mary" – at last!

Cruising: "Monte Toledo"

Atlantic Canada Tour

Cruising: "Alexandr Pushkin"

Remzi's, Oxford, England

Molly's

The Royal York

West to the Rockies

Country Music tours, Britain

In the woods near Saint John, New Brunswick. Photo: Garey Pridham

"PETER & MARY" – AT LAST!

Just about the very first thing we had done in Bermuda from the point of view of promotion, once we decided to join together, was to sort out a top-quality photo shoot. We knew a very talented lady who photographed the fashion pages for the Bermuda Sun, Gertraud Fendler, and she did a session for us, including of course, a spread in the Sun, a picture in the Royal Gazette, and articles in both papers. One of her pictures also went into the Stage, in the U.K., with information regarding us individually, the new act, types of venue we planned on working, and, of course, contact information.

"MONTE TOLEDO"

This actually paid off. We had been back in Britain for a very short while, when we got a call from the Al Heath office, regarding what was to be our first ever cruise. At that time Spain was trying hard to get into what was then called the Common Market, (now the European Union), and correctly thought that having a cruise line would earn them a few brownie points. But this was a cruise line with a difference. The lower deck was a car deck, the next deck mostly bananas and tomatoes, plus other produce, and the rest, a cruise ship. Relatively small, even in those days, (the lines running to Bermuda from the U.S. were 20,000 tons or more); these were two ships of 14,000 tons each, the "Monte Toledo" and the "Monte Granada", running from London via various ports in France, Spain, Portugal, Madeira, Canary Islands, and North Africa. We were offered a two-week Christmas and New Year's cruise, which, in addition to ourselves, would include magicians Richard and Lara Jarmaine, plus a house band of organ, bass, and drums, called "We Three", who were resident with the line. So, Dec. 23rd, 1974, saw us at Millwall docks, and boarding the Monte Toledo, ready for a new experience, and of course, our very first together!

The Bay of Biscay is famous, (or infamous if you prefer), for being sometimes one of the more challenging stretches of water on the European coastline, or, occasionally, one of the calmest. We were to see both of its moods on this trip, starting with a force 11 gale, (13 being a full hurricane), which saw the bow of the Monte Toledo completely submerged with every wave, only to rise totally out of the water in between.

Fortunately, this was not on our first night, which had gone smoothly in all senses of the word, as had the second, Christmas Eve, and all of the performers blended well together, so it was going to be a good run. No, this was on the third night, Christmas Day itself, which saw very few passengers in the dining room, maybe 35, with even less when cold lobster was served as a starter. The ship was heaving mightily, but Richard and I managed to work a couple of spots together, with me holding props. or whatever as needed, making sure nothing fell off the stage, then him lying on the floor holding a mic. stand with one hand, and the bottom of my stool with the other, without which I would have crashed into the railings that surrounded the dance floor. Mary and Lara were both totally incapacitated and recumbent in our respective cabins, as were two rabbits, and one performing chicken, who would normally have been helping Richard and Lara with their show.

On Boxing Day, we reached Vigo, on the Atlantic coast of Spain, where we stopped to pick up Spanish passengers for the trip, and had a few hours exploring the old town, once we had all stopped lurching around, and somewhat regained our equilibrium.

We were lucky to have "We Three" as musical backup. Jim Hewson was a fine organist/pianist, who subsequently renamed himself "Jimmy Keys", and did a residency at "Henry VIII" in Bermuda for several years, where he was very popular, both for the amount of community "shooters" that would be consumed by customers every night, and for his risqué comedy material, that resulted in an ongoing battle with the local Musicians' Union. Rick Champion on bass was very competent, and deservedly got a permanent "house" job at Caesar's Palace in Las Vegas, backing all the big shows. I'm not sure what happened to the drummer, Steve Faithful, but he held his own in the trio, and, for our first ever backup band, we felt very fortunate.

Richard and Lara were great folks; they had a good show, and we worked out quite a few bits with the four of us to keep things moving, and everybody involved. I remember we were given bottles of Spanish "Champagne" as give-aways, which the passengers rapidly learned they would rather not have, and there was much good-natured banter between audience and stage as to what could be done with these, as there was at other times; it was that kind of crowd.

We visited various places, the high spot probably being the Portuguese island of Madeira, very beautiful, and famous for large toboggans carrying tourists at breakneck speeds down steep cobbled streets to the waterfront, with drivers kicking at the wall where necessary to keep everyone vaguely upright. Views from the top of the island were spectacular, and one could quite see how Winston Churchill on occasion during WWII would get the R.A.F. to bring him out here for a few hours, so that he could sit and paint, in total solitude, and recharge his batteries. Back on board, with many people of course clutching bottles of Madeira, that used to be so very popular a while back - "Have some Madeira, m' dear," (Michael Flanders & Donald Swann). A bit sweet, but it grows on you. Other stops: La Palma, where we climbed our first volcano, Las Palmas, very busy, almost like a smaller Miami, Tenerife, and more. On the final night of the cruise, the four of us, plus "We Three", did an Old Time Musical Hall, having already left our Spanish passengers at La Coruna, who might not have related to that type of show. But I must talk about the rabbits - yes, and the performing chicken!

When we'd been on the cruise a few days, we were talking with Richard and Lara, and they were worried, as they had been advised by British Customs that they wouldn't be able to bring their two rabbits back into the U.K. at the end of the cruise, because they might have contracted rabies, which we all thought was officialdom at its most ridiculous, since the rabbits would only be loose in the cabin occasionally with them, or briefly on the stage in a magic box, certainly never off the ship. One of the rabbits had been with them for years, and was definitely a pet, but they had reluctantly decided that the only thing to do was find a nice Spanish family with kids while on the boat, and the rabbits would get a new home. The chicken was not a problem, as it couldn't carry rabies anyway.

You are, of course, wondering about the chicken's act, which was very creative. Imagine a tiny piano, or some such, with only a very few notes, all hollowed out, into which individual grains of corn or other seed could roll, one at a time, from out of sight, to be pecked out by the chicken as they appeared, and thus produce a musical note. This is exactly what happened, and the notes could be controlled by the order in which the corn was fed to different keys. The chicken was not in the least bothered by the audience and had learned to do this over a period of time, thus making a beautiful bit of "business", and no, it was not "food deprived" to make it play. It could even pick out the first few notes of "Edelweiss", which of course the audience loved.

The rabbits would not have even been brought to the ship had Richard and Lara known there would be a problem, but they soon found a family who would be more than happy to take them, so all was well - until they realized that their special rabbits were far more likely to end up on the dinner table then be family pets.

The way the cruise lines used to operate with musicians, and performers with props., is that, when leaving the ship, all one's equipment would be spread out, either in the ballroom, or sometimes on the dockside, and a checklist gone through with the Customs officer, to confirm that nothing had been added. This was duly done with all our instruments and amps., as with Richard and Lara's magic props., where more than one box was shown to be completely empty, but in fact had a rabbit in the secret compartment behind. This worked perfectly, and the rabbits went home, for a long and happy life in Britain, never to go near a cruise ship again!

ATLANTIC CANADA TOUR

Back home, after a glass-like crossing of the Bay of Biscay, we quickly set to work visiting, and if necessary auditioning, for all the top agencies who booked long-term engagements in resorts, or on cruises, as well as doing cabaret spots in the south west, where we were based. There were of course many visits to London, and in the middle of January we met up with David & Nina Burns, in the Giaconda, to discuss life in general. They had been exploring resort venues in the eastern U.S., and had been offered work, but found it impossible to get into the Musicians' Union as non-Americans, which was essential for the requisite work permit. So, they headed northwards over the border into Canada, where they found an excellent agency in Halifax, Nova Scotia, who were more than ready to book them all over the Maritimes and Newfoundland, on one or two week engagements. Although it was the same union as in the U.S., there were far less restrictions on joining in Canada, and they were so excited to share this information with us. David was going to follow up with Halifax to see if there was room for us on the circuit as well; meanwhile we continued to follow up other things for the next couple of weeks. The first actual offer we received was for a summer on the island of Jersey, which we probably would have taken, had the offer been a little more realistic. At the end of January, we ran into David and Nina again, to be told that there was great interest from one of the bookers in the Halifax office, and David would call as soon as they were back in Canada, in a few days' time.

Which he did, 4 days later, with the exciting news that we were to start a six-month tour in the Maritimes and Newfoundland on April 28th, with the agency sorting the work permit by phone with us, and David liaising if necessary.

The following day, we had yet another call, with the offer of a one-month residency in Kuwait, starting on the 1st of March, which we also accepted; it seemed to be all happening at once. We started to prepare our things for the flight, and were actually packed ready to go, on March 1st, awaiting our flight details, when we got the call saying that this job was not happening; we never found out why, maybe sometimes it is better not to know.

Two days later David called to say that our work permit had been approved, and we were to start our first week, as planned, in late April.

Yet another call a few days later, from Leslie Douglas, who definitely bears mentioning. Leslie was a fine man and musician who had been in charge of the big band for R.A.F. Bomber Command during WWII, which did many concerts, and broadcasts on the BBC, to help raise morale. He now had an office in London, and offered us the summer season at the Villa Marina, Douglas, on the Isle of Man. This was off the west coast of Britain, and a job we might well have taken, had we not already got the permit sorted out for Canada, which was going to be something completely new.

Once again, the phone rang. This time it was the Al Heath office, asking if we could fly immediately to join the "Monte Granada" on another cruise. We would have loved this, and just had the time available, but there was a bad flu bug going around, which Mary had unfortunately contracted, so we sadly had to pass. In any event, we were so busy, and as soon as Mary recovered, we took all of our sound equipment, lights, transformer, plus instruments, packed with as much padding as we could find, up to Air Cargo, so that it would be in Halifax for us to collect on arrival in Canada.

One thing of which we were unaware before crossing the Atlantic for the first time, is that the seasons on both sides are not quite in sync. with each other. When we left England, it was April 21st, and spring with all its glories had truly arrived, but flying over Newfoundland and Cape Breton, the land was still reawakening from a long winter's sleep, and the mountainous terrain had patches of snow and ice as far as the eye could see. When William Shakespeare wrote "A Midsummer Night's Dream", he was referring to the June solstice, which in North America is considered to be summer's first day, a full six weeks later than in Britain. Nevertheless, we landed in Halifax safely, and joined the lineup for customs.

As we were standing waiting, there was a Customs and Immigration officer walking up the line clutching a "10 by 8" photograph, who came up to us and said, "Peter and Mary, welcome to Canada", gave us his name and shook hands. What a pleasant way to arrive in another country! We went to his office, did some necessary paperwork relating to the permit, then left, saying we had to make a call. At which point he put his hand in his pocket and gave us a dime for the phone, as we only had paper money, having just arrived off the plane. A nice man, whom we would see again several times, and one who made a difference by the way in which he did his job.

The call was duly made, to Ellen Ewonchuk, from the Canadian Navy, that I had met at the "Pub on the Square" in Bermuda, and her husband Dan, also Navy. Ellen had got to know David and Nina when they were playing the Holiday Inn, and she had visited the resort with her Navy compatriots on more than one occasion. We had been told that she generously expected us to stay for a couple of days, while we sorted ourselves out. Dan answered and said to get a cab down to their place, and that they were looking forward to seeing us. We had a warm welcome, and they went off to work the next morning, so kindly giving us a key to their house, and an invitation to help ourselves to anything we needed.

This was our first taste of the unbelievable hospitality to be found in Atlantic Canada, as we found out some years later that Dan and Ellen had not been particularly expecting us at that time, but had opened their home, and their hearts, to us instantly, without a second thought.

We visited the agency, where all was well, and collected the details of our first engagement, which was to be a good quality dining room, "The Cameo", just a few doors away, with accommodation booked close at hand.

A second evening was spent with Dan and Ellen, when we went with them to another venue in Armdale, where we would soon be playing, having first had a tour of Halifax and the waterfront. There was an Acadian duo onstage, Cornelia and Billy, who were doing mostly covers, but also several of Cornelia's own songs, and I remember well being struck by the quality of her writing.

The next day we flew to Sydney, with our equipment. David and Nina met us at the airport, and we had an evening together at the local Holiday Inn, where they worked regularly, and we were also shortly to appear. Then to their recently purchased home in Hay Cove, where we set up to make sure everything worked after the flight. All was good, except the drum unit, (which was a mandatory part of the engagements), but David with his audio electronic skills was soon able to fix this, as well as installing a vernier dial for totally accurate beat adjustments, essential to our show.

On the Sunday, after a good visit and catch up, it was time to fly back to Halifax, except that I never put the drum unit in checked baggage again!

At which point I must elaborate on where we were staying. It was a large house, quite extravagant in a chintzy sort of way, where the lady who owned it, a Mrs. Nixon, let out a few rooms, some permanently, some for shorter lets of only one week. A strange lady, who used to undress you with her eyes every time you walked through the door, and each one of us thought we were individually fancied by her; that is, until we compared notes, and decided she probably did it to everybody. One of the harbour pilots stayed with her full time, plus during our visit there was an all-girl band called "The Happy Dolls", from Japan or Korea, good musicians all, who were playing in a club called "The Misty Moon". They were one of those bands who each played a regular instrument, but would swap instruments just for one song, (the only one they could play), then go back to normal, a practice often seen with bands from the Far East and sometimes Hawaii.

Their culinary skills were amazing. It seemed that the whole band could descend upon the kitchen, with pots and pans flying all over the place, whip up a meal, clean up and be out, while the two of us had just buttered our first slice of bread. There is possibly slight exaggeration in this, but I am just trying to illustrate what it felt like. We went to see them work after we had finished one evening; they were very good, but it was decidedly the type of venue where it was best to look directly at the stage and make eye contact with nobody at all.

Our week was good; Dan and Ellen came in on the first night, and again later in the week, when they brought in a group of friends to see us. We also had our first lesson in the many differences between phraseology from one side of the Atlantic to the other. We went into the agency, and they asked us how things were going, to which I replied, "It went a bomb". On the following day, they again asked, and I said, "It's going a bomb!" Let me explain. This expression, in the U.K., implies an explosion upwards, which is a good thing, whereas the North American expression, "It bombed", implies the exact opposite. A subtle distinction which took a couple of days to sort out, and only when the Cameo called to ask if we could stay an extra week was the difference discovered, and we all had a good laugh.

We met another couple at the restaurant the first week: Harvey and Mary Johnson. Harvey was also Navy, and remained with them until well after normal retirement, as he was able to write easily understandable instruction books on rather important things, (like lifeboats), which are vital if one is in a hurry, but rarely done. He was also a good musician on accordion and banjo, and we hit it off with them immediately, as we had with Dan and Ellen.

We looked around for a vehicle, with Harvey's assistance, and nearly bought a VW Minibus, but on our second week, found a Mazda station wagon in excellent condition, and Mary took it for a test drive with Harvey and me in the back, and Bill Frew from the garage in the front.

Of course, she was now sitting, for the very first time in her life, on the opposite side of the car to that which was normal for her, so, when going to change gear, she understandably opened the window instead. Bill Frew nearly got out at this point, but gritted his teeth and held on, which was probably good for him, as the rest of the drive went perfectly, and we purchased the car in good time to get used to it before our first road trip to Yarmouth.

I should mention that whilst doing our first job in Halifax, in May 1975, we sent a postcard to our friend Barbara Champion, musician and writer for "The Stage", in London, England, then promptly forgot all about it. It was eventually delivered, with a rubber-stamped apology from the Post Office for the delay, in October 2013, some 38 1/2 years later. Fortunately, the address was still the same!

    Sunday saw us loaded up and on the idyllic drive along the south shore of Nova Scotia to Yarmouth, including a stop off at the picture-perfect village of Lunenburg, that we had been told we absolutely must see. At one point, we were surprised, because we saw a sign for Yarmouth saying a certain distance, then 20 minutes later, another sign that said it was further. When arriving at the Grand Hotel, we mentioned this, and were told, "Yes, I know, it's been that way for years", almost as though it had been deliberately left like that as a conversation piece!

    We quickly learned on this tour that in each town folks would come out, often on a Monday, to check out the acts at each venue, and plan their weekends accordingly. If there was a slow night it was Tuesday, but by the time Friday and Saturday rolled around most places were packed solid, with a clientele that was a perfect fit with our programme. The Grand was a beautiful hotel for its time, however the bedroom walls were paper thin, to the extent that if someone even spoke in the next room, you would just about go through the roof, as you expected them to be standing right by the bed. On subsequent visits, of which there were many, we would always try to get a quiet room, with hopefully no chance of neighbours, especially if a young couple!

    After Yarmouth, we continued around the coast to Digby, and took the ferry across to Saint John, New Brunswick. As the ferry approached the terminal there was firstly an awful smell, then a big orange cloud over the city, somewhat reminiscent of London smog, which we were told was Atlantic Canada's biggest pulp and paper mill, on the Saint John River. Right next to it was the Red Rose Tea plant, a subsidiary of Brooke Bond, and possibly Canada's best-selling tea. Their T.V. commercials showed people in London in a Rolls Royce drinking this tea with "Only in Canada, eh? Pity". Of course, we soon came out with comedy material relating to its distinctive flavour, with the pulp mill next door!

The tour got better and better, and we were grateful to find that on a return visit somewhere, there would often be a full house all week. We adjusted our material to fit each room; if in a lounge it would be varied, if more of a "pub" venue, such as Dick Turpin's in the Chateau Halifax, it would be totally high energy Irish, Scottish, or Maritime music.

Dick Turpin's bears a mention. In the leading hotel in town, owned by Canadian Pacific, it was THE hub of Irish-style party music, packed every night with navy and nurses, and the tables constantly kept full of draught beer. In front of the stage was a large round three-legged table, of which the top was very loose, and could be turned at will. This table, when full, as it always was, could probably seat 16 party-goers at one time, all singing, and occasionally jumping on the table, should there be a space amongst the beer glasses. We very soon learned that if you played just to this table, they would carry the room for you. Of course, if anyone ran out of beer, all they had to do was swivel the table top a little, as there was always plenty more, close at hand.

I well recall our first appearance at the Holiday Inn, close to David and Nina. There was a fairly large dining room, but the lounge/pub was somewhat smaller. After the Monday night, it was obvious that we were going to be very busy, so the licenses were swapped over, as was the furniture, and we moved to the larger room. The clientele in Sydney were funny, as they all went to the nearby town of Glace Bay to party, because they didn't want to be seen partying on their own doorstep, while the folks from Glace Bay came to Sydney. One morning, we were called to the front desk quite early, bearing in mind the time one got to bed, as there were two immigration officers to see us. Somebody had obviously tipped them off that we were probably working illegally, and they had come to check things out. Of course, all our paperwork was perfectly in order, and I think they felt a little embarrassed that they had got us out of bed. It reminded me of a situation in Germany, with Bryan and Pam, where our drummer Denny was suddenly invaded by armed police at about 4:00 a.m., because they had been told he was with an underage German girl, who turned out to be his elder sister from England, visiting for a couple of days.

On this tour we had stage outfits and lighting, as did our friends David and Nina. We soon knew of many acts on the circuit, but the only other act that tried to make a theatrical presentation of the evening was Mike and Pam Blakeney, from Halifax, who went under the name of "Blakeney Still". It made such a difference to how one was treated, and we wondered why others didn't do it more often.

Aside note: In previous years, everyone used to wear stage clothes, until one night, the "Lovin Spoonful" were doing a concert, and their clothes didn't arrive with them at the airport, so they had to appear as they were. They still had a tremendous response, and on that day much of show business changed forever, not necessarily for the better. I suppose on the lounge circuit it really depended on whether one thought of one's act as "wallpaper", or more of a show, where the idea was that the clientele would be actually looking in the direction of the stage.

To give an idea of how things were in the Maritimes back in that era, in the smaller communities most people never locked their homes, and if we were with friends, we would always lock the car very surreptitiously, so as not to offend anyone. How times have changed!

We had our first visit to Newfoundland on this tour as well, taking the long ferry ride to Port-aux- Basques, and heading up the west coast, which is the only major highway. Apart from other places, we played in the picturesque port town of Corner Brook for a couple of weeks, where an occasional visitor was the cruise ship "Alexandr Pushkin", whose captain I had previously met in Bermuda, and it reminded us of his offer, which we decided to follow up. We also stopped at Gander, which was such a key airport in WWII, and again became world famous on 9/11, when New York bound aircraft were re-routed to Gander, and Newfoundlanders opened their homes to stranded travellers. Many of them became friends for life, which of course is so well remembered in the musical: "Come from Away".

It was time to connect with March Shipping, in Montreal, who were the Canadian agents for the Alexandr Pushkin, which was operated by Baltic Shipping out of the then Leningrad. We had decided, after much thought and discussion, to apply for Canadian Landed Immigrant Status, the first stage of becoming a Canadian citizen, which would in no way affect our U.K. status. The live entertainment scene in Britain was a mess, and very few performers were working full-time. The industrial North, and therefore the thousands of social clubs that went with them, had virtually collapsed, as had many of the repertory theatres that dotted the country, due to the policies of Maggie Thatcher, and the writing was on the wall. Literally anyone we knew of in the performing arts in Britain said how lucky we were to be working at all, so this seemed a no-brainer, plus the people we had met in Atlantic Canada were some of the warmest that either of us had known in our entire lives.

We called March Shipping and told them of the offer I had received from the captain, to which the response was that this was impossible, and that there was solely Russian food, Russian entertainment, and Russian music. I quoted the name I had been told to give, at which point there were profuse apologies, and that they would call back immediately. Which they did, within a day, and asked which crossing we would like, from Montreal to Tilbury, (London). Apart from wanting to work on the ship anyway, it was a method of getting our equipment back to the U.K. in safety, as the drum unit had been damaged on the flight out, and only David's expertise had saved us from a big problem.

All was in process, and we continued the tour, including another run in the port of Sydney, Nova Scotia. The sight of a dance floor in the Maritimes could be amazing. The local girls would all come out, dressed to the nines, while many of the men looked like they had just come from work; some even in their fishing boat wellies! The dance didn't really change with the tempo, it was a pumping of his partner's arm by the man, which would be adapted to fit, i.e., if a slow dance, the arm could be pumped in double time, if a fast dance, the speed could be halved. If a waltz time, then a general shuffle around the floor would suffice, but these were kept to an absolute minimum.

One night, we were playing away, and a large man in a smart grey coat and an astrakhan hat, Russian style, came in and stood at the back for a while. He turned out to be the captain of a Russian cargo ship, docked in Sydney, who had been sent in to check us out. The slightly unnerving bit of this was that nobody had contacted the agency to see where we were, and nobody had contacted our friends in Halifax either, but the KGB, or whoever they chose to use, knew exactly where to find us. Not that this created any problem, but it reminded me of the time I had been called by Buckingham Palace, in a somewhat different situation.

We continued with our tour, and were working at the Lord Beaverbrook hotel, a favorite venue right opposite the Provincial Legislature in New Brunswick, where we had got to know several of the customers. One day, Mary and I went into the local music store, and saw both six and twelve string Ovation acoustic/electric guitars on the wall, which we had been interested in trying for some time. We asked to have a look and received the very non-Maritime response of "Put your money on the counter and you can try them!" We immediately left the store, (the owner apologized profusely when we got to know him later) and decided to go another route to see instruments of this type.

In New York City there are two world famous musical instrument shops, Manny's and Sam Ash, both close to each other, where even musicians from London would come shopping, both for the prices, and the fact that they both often had custom-made instruments that were unavailable anywhere else.

So, David & Nina, plus ourselves, decided to take a week off, and spend three nights each in both New York and Boston, see a few shows, and get the things that both acts needed. We flew to New York, where there was a hotel, called "The Piccadilly", right close to Broadway, that had amazingly special rates for actors auditioning or musicians, and the booking had been made for three nights – at $23 U.S. a night per couple! The four of us did our shopping, which included buying two higher quality Ovation guitars than those we had seen in Fredericton, plus went to the musical "Shenandoah", and also to Radio City, marvelling at the amazing quality of the 76-piece theatre orchestra, as well as other things. Then it was time for the 4 1/2-hour Amtrak ride to Boston, in which the train's air conditioning had quit, so we loosened the strings on our new instruments for safety, also on an old Gibson guitar that I had picked up in a second-hand shop, which became my instrument for life.

Boston was just as enjoyable. We had all the equipment that was needed, so just played tourist, seeing a couple of theatre shows and generally exploring Boston and Cambridge, including the buildings of Harvard, and of course, "Old Ironsides", in Boston harbor.

It was an uneventful flight back, arriving in time to see the Engelbert Humperdinck/Anne Murray special on T.V. that we had seen in production on the Bermuda waterfront not long ago, but they didn't include the bit where his pants were sewn up!

By the way, the punch line was that we had all obtained the equipment and instruments that were needed in New York, plus paid for our 6 days holiday, and legally imported everything into Canada, yet still saved money on buying lesser instruments in Fredericton. Probably about 20 cents!

"ALEXANDR PUSHKIN"

We finished the tour, and headed off to Montreal to join the Alexandr Pushkin, for our first of several trans-Atlantic crossings. In those days, driving through Montreal on the freeway was difficult, as there were no warning notices of upcoming exits, only at the exit itself, which was impossible if you were in one of the faster lanes and traffic was heavy. Anyway, we got off, and a kindly CN rail driver guided us right to the ship. Yet another person one would like to thank again, and to him it probably meant nothing.

Everything was loaded onto the ship, with all our instruments and equipment packed into an easily accessible part of the baggage hold. We arranged with the purser that we would do one concert for the passengers and asked if we might do one for the crew, which was warmly received, and our treatment onboard was second to none. Sadly for me, the captain that I knew from Bermuda was now on a different ship, and we never got to know this one, but nevertheless made friends with several of the officers, two of whom we would see nightly in the "White Knights" lounge, when the other passengers had gone to bed, and the four of us could have a quiet chat. Being a Russian ship, the beverage of choice was of course Vodka. Interestingly, the bottles that were sold to the passengers had screw tops, while those sold to the officers and crew had tear-off tops, it being inconceivable that one could possibly open a bottle without it being finished. So, we would get four tumblers, four slices of lemon, and a refrigerated bottle of Mosovskaya, (which has a flavour), - and fix the world, until the next day.

There were some fine musicians on the ship, including several brass players, whose function would be to stand at the rail, and play the ship out of port with appropriate sounds. From the dockside, the musicians would appear to be in resplendent uniforms, with gold braid everywhere, including hats, but of course one could only see them to waist level. Below that, unseen by those on the quay, it was blue jeans and desert boots, the current uniform of choice for a classy Russian sailor! All the singers, dancers, or musicians on the ship also had other functions onboard; this is not to belittle their expertise and professionalism in any way, but it was an opportunity for them to travel with their art, and still reach people. Most, if not all of the dancers, came from the Ukraine, while our cabin stewardess, Ludmila Ganiushkina, was a professionally trained singer, who was deservedly the star among the Russian artistes on every trip we took. She favoured a huge amount of echo in her presentations, unusually to us, but somewhat reminiscent of the Marino Marini quartet some years before. A beautiful person, and we were so lucky to see her on a daily basis, in the quiet of our cabin.

REMZI'S

We arrived safely in London, (Tilbury), and started to look for a residency, rather than doing one night stand cabarets dotted all over the place. A couple of auditions were set up during the first week, including one at "Remzi's", a Greek/Turkish nightclub in Oxford. It was quite a place; the nightclub was downstairs, with a Turkish Bouzouki player and organist alternating with another act, who did most of the evening, and provided general entertainment. Interspersed with a belly dancer, the place was very successful, with good food and a great atmosphere. On the ground floor there was a bistro, above which was a disco, then staff accommodation, (us), and more staff on the top floor. We hit it off with the owner immediately, and signed a three-month renewable contract, to start shortly.

Plus, we got the paperwork moving on our "Landed Immigrant" status for Canada, which we put through the Birmingham office, as this took about six months max., as opposed to two years in London, where there was a long waiting list.

Remzi's skill as a host/maître'd was a sight to behold. It was usually necessary to reserve, as the place was very popular, and customers would always be warmly greeted before being escorted to their table, which was always "the best in the house". For example: "best table, because it is best view of band", "best table for a quiet tête à tête", "best view of belly dancer", "closest to bar", (you couldn't serve yourself anyway), "best table because..." Very occasionally a table would be removed from obscurity and brought to the edge of the dance floor, with much show attached, especially for someone new. If you were new, there would always be a bottle of wine, "Compliments of the house", on your table, or very rapidly delivered, (for which you would pay, by the time the evening was through, several times over!). But everybody loved the place, the wine list was extensive, and the service good.

Before we moved in to Remzi's however, we had a few other venues, a couple of which need mentioning. The first of these was the never-to-be-forgotten Keynsham British legion, in the Bristol area. This was having extensive renovations when we arrived to do our cabaret one cold day, to the degree that an outside wall had been almost completely removed, and there was plastic sheeting billowing in its place. The hall was full, and we asked where we might change, only to be shown to a grimy boiler room, with a large pile of office papers, edges curling, sitting on top of the boiler, and ready to burst into flames at any second. We managed with great difficulty to change into our immaculate outfits without them touching the floor, which was made even harder by the fact that in the main club room there was a large fish tank, behind which was - the boiler room, and anyone looking closely at the beautiful fish swimming around, might well have seen two semi-naked performers trying desperately to get dressed for a show in some semblance of privacy.

However, we made it, and came out for our spot, to be asked for a bit of background, as always, at which point we mentioned our work in Bermuda, the tour in Canada, and that we had just come from a trans-Atlantic cruise. The Concert Secretary, as they are called in Britain, went to the microphone and said, "Ladies and gentlemen, you're not going to believe this", (thus negating anything he was about to say, no matter what it was), "this duo has done everything, they've been all over the world, they've been on all the cruise ships, (2), and now here they are in our club". There was a bit more of this, but I was looking at the billowing plastic sheeting and wondering if the guitars would stay enough in tune for our first set. All I remember, is that we had to work our brains out for that show, or we would never have reached the audience as we always did. By the time we reached our second set they were well in sync with us, but we were still so pleased to be packed and out of there, with a vow never to return.

Also relating to water, another event we did a few days later was at the prestigious Cadbury Country Club. We arrived and were somewhat surprised to be asked to set up poolside in the huge indoor swimming area, where all the bar stools were below water level, and each person was given a little lifebelt to put around their drink, so that it would not immediately become a part of the pool water. The chlorine level in the area was inordinately high, with little or no extraction, and we wondered how we would manage to get through the evening with so many vocals. After the first set we were approached by the management with the offer of a permanent residency. If there had been another space in the club, we might have looked at it sometime, as it was a beautiful venue, but this area was impossible, and definitely not to be.

Back to Remzi's, where we stayed for a total of six months. The agent, Jack Fallon, (the bass player), had wanted to move us to one of the Lyons' Corner Houses in central London, with a huge dance floor, but we preferred where we were, and Remzi wanted us to stay. We'd had a really good and productive time so far and increased our repertoire quite a bit. Remzi no longer had the bouzouki/organ duo, but had bought an old bouzouki himself, and put a speaker behind the sound hole, with the cable going off to a player of some kind which had bouzouki music on it. He would do a sort of dance on the floor, but, like my "circus" with Martin Sharp at age about 6 or 7, it was probably much better in his head than in real life; I hope so. He also did another dance with many plates stacked alternately on his head and a glass of wine on top, which he would suddenly catch, and then start breaking the plates, (unglazed rejects), over the heads of those customers unfortunate enough to be next to the dance floor. On one occasion we had friends visiting from Hereford, some distance away, and I will always remember the expression of one of them, as Remzi repeatedly tried to break an extra-strong plate over his head.

The dancing could get quite wild, especially with things like "Zorba" or "Hava Nagila", and one night, one of our column speakers went crashing to the floor with a broken horn and a somewhat inebriated reveller lying on top, to the sound of Mary, who was at that side of the stage, yelling "Get off my speaker", which I am sure was never heard. Remzi, very efficiently, had a carpenter come in on the next day, to put a balustrade along the front of the stage, with strong poles going to the ceiling, thus making sure that such a thing could never happen again, plus of course, our horn was fixed.

The belly dancers who came in every Friday and Saturday were pretty, and popular with the male customers, but possibly less so with the women, for obvious reasons. One weekend, he tried out a slightly older lady, who did a perfectly good dance, and it was about as threatening to the female audience as Shirley Temple. I was to introduce her as being "direct from the Kervansary Night Club in Istanbul". I looked at her, and put the lights fairly low for her routine. A larger lady, as is sometimes the case with belly dancers, she was competent enough, even to the extent of swirling two tassels in opposite directions, one on the end of each breast, with all the delight of a six-year-old. One solo customer, sitting alone having supper, (very unusual), held up a glass of wine for her, to which she said, "Sorry ducks, but when I've finished me dance, I'll come and sit wiv you, awright?", a sound straight from the east end of London. So much for Istanbul, but the audience, especially women, all loved her, and she stayed for many weeks. Her name was Kazara, plus her husband, Reg, was always there looking out for her, and she added hugely to the success of the place.

By mid-April, we had finished our very successful run at Remzi's; our landed Immigrant papers had been accepted the previous January, and we were ready for a break, before again meeting our Russian friends on the "Alexandr Pushkin", en route to Montreal.

We were so glad to see the spring again, as it had been a long, wet, and cold winter. Our old Vauxhall that we had bought to get us through the season had served us well, but the heater was toast, and we had spent our day off each week driving to visit Mary's folks in the West Country, stopping overnight and returning the next day. This involved driving through the town of Swindon, which was where the air mass from over the North Sea seemed to collide with the air mass from the Atlantic, with maybe a gentle nudge from the air mass over northern France as well. It appeared to us to be the fog capital of Europe that winter, and there were many very cold and huddled up journeys to and from Oxford, with the fog swirling thickly around us in Swindon, or just laying over the town like a freezing grey velvet blanket, as we drove ever so slowly through.

But now it was spring. Snowdrops and crocuses had been out along the banks of the River Isis, close to Remzi's, and daffodils were exploding in profusion. Apart from one concert, we had a little time to prepare for the next chapter in our lives, as well as catching up with friends and relatives, plus playing tourist, all of which we did wholeheartedly. Then we rented a van, and Mary's indefatigable brother, John, drove us and our gear up to London, (Tilbury), to board the ship.

It was a good sendoff from John, also Mary's mum, plus my sister's family, and our so very helpful cockney friend Ronnie, who had rescued us from more than one stranded situation. After the grand tour of the ship, there were somewhat bittersweet goodbyes between us, but we all knew we would see each other again soon.

Our cabin was at the very front of the ship, by which I mean there was a sharp narrow point opposite the bed, and we were fairly near the waterline. We left the Thames estuary, the same river that flows through Oxford as the Isis, and headed south into the English Channel, before turning westwards towards the Atlantic. There were heavy seas, which we probably felt more than some, and the first full day of the voyage was spent totally out of action. The second day we managed to get a cabin amidships, which was a huge improvement, and we were able to do a cabaret show in the music salon for an hour that evening, by which time we had left the Channel into calmer waters. We again offered a crew show, which was hugely popular, and having got to know some of them on the previous crossing, we knew to give them a much "rockier" programme than we gave the passengers.

There was the usual excitement on the first sighting of Newfoundland; the Atlantic crossing had again been good, and we had done a couple of dance evenings that were much appreciated, to the extent that we had an open offer from the Purser, on behalf of the shipping line, to travel with them at any time we wished. A couple of postcards of the ship had been mailed to friends, including Dan and Ellen, who were of course in the Navy, based in Halifax. Theirs arrived sometime later, marked up that it had been examined by security, or some such, I believe with a few words blacked out, even though it was all very innocuous. Talking of security, two of the officers on the ship, that we had got to know, told us of a security agent who would be pretending to work on the docks, when the Alexandr Pushkin was pulling into the Montreal quay. Sure enough, there he was, exactly as described - and I wished the world could be a more friendly and open place.

We took the overnight train to Halifax, having a beautiful view of Quebec City, which we vowed to return and explore very soon. Our station wagon, which by now had a roof rack and a small Coleman trailer to carry extra speakers, had been left with David and Nina in their barn at Hay Cove, Cape Breton, so we headed in that direction to pick it up. Having collected all our equipment and instruments, we then headed back into Sydney for a three-week run at the Holiday Inn. It was very different at first to be playing in these familiar places, but no longer on a work permit, which had to be tied to a specific booking office, but of course we continued to work with the same agency whenever in the area. Many of the venues we had previously done for a week were now for two or three week engagements, and we were starting to build a strong following on return visits.

There were some great acts on the Maritime circuit, which was good for all of us, as it kept standards high, with everyone constantly honing their craft in friendly competition. One of them was "Finnigan", Jimmy Flynn from Newfoundland, and Peter Stoney from Ireland. Jimmy did a high-powered barrage of edgy comedy, literally thousands of jokes, with Peter more as a "straight man", and a fine musician. The comedy was interspersed with all the Maritime folk standards and sea shanties you could imagine, delivered with high energy. If you missed one of

Jimmy's jokes it didn't matter, as you were still laughing at the previous one, and we were to run into both Jimmy and Peter many times over the years.

Then it was off to Fredericton again; provincial capital of New Brunswick, and a beautiful city of wide streets, stately elms, and magnificent old houses on the banks of the Saint John River, which flowed gently through. We played the Lord Beaverbrook hotel, named after Max Aitken, who amongst other things, was owner/editor of the London "Daily Express" during my childhood years, as well as instigating the "Children's Newspaper" in Britain, very popular at the time, and a brilliant idea, now sadly defunct. There was another hotel, of the same chain, close by, where we also had good crowds, and a little younger than the clientele at the Beaverbrook, which was opposite the legislature and possibly more conservative, though not necessarily politically! In years to come Richard Hatfield, long time premier of New Brunswick, would always come and sit with Mary's mother if she were touring with us from England, and listening to our music at a table on her own. Such a very kind and caring man.

We were to buy a house just outside Fredericton a few years later, but there was yet to be another five years of living "on the road" first, performing all over this vast country, with occasional breaks in between, on both sides of the Atlantic.

During this period, we had our first experience of a "double booking", where we had a two-week run booked at a certain venue, while the second week was also covered by a different agent. We immediately contacted the Musicians' Union, and both acts were paid in full, as was fair, as both had legal contracts on the same week. It has been very fortunate for us that we have only needed the legal services of the

Union twice in our entire career to date, but in both cases, they were there for us instantly, as they always are....

Several new things were on the agenda that summer; firstly, we went over for bookings on Prince Edward Island, delighting in the pastoral scenery, red roads, and also the warmth of our welcome, including a "dinner theatre" venue in Summerside, where the cast also served supper, and there was a guest act, (us), as part of the nightly show. Very different. We also worked in Cavendish, location of the famed "Green Gables" stories of Lucy Maud Montgomery, and once her childhood home.

Our top priority on returning to Halifax was to prepare a good quality introductory promo. recording that could be given to potential bookers, so we went into a studio and recorded segments of about a dozen or so different styles of music, including some in other languages. We had met a good quality radio broadcaster, with an impressive voice, whom we hired to link the whole thing together, and the project was successful. There was one point in the script, totally my fault, where I had written "Mary has developed a lot since her early folk days", at which point we all broke up, but it was left in, and the recording was helpful in our early touring days, partially because nobody else had ever done anything like it.

The tour continued until the fall, with trips to the extreme north of New Brunswick and into Québec, constantly adjusting our programme to fit different venues, which was a huge learning curve, also adding a low octave bass pedal to my guitar to fill things out, which was used for many years and a huge plus, once I had got used to it. Then there was a family trip to the U.K., during which time we dropped into Remzi's in Oxford to check out our friends, but were soon back in New

Brunswick for our first three-week appearance at the "Coachmen" in Bathurst, for Billy Noble and Floyd Gallant, over the Christmas and New Year's season. This quickly became one of our favorite venues in Atlantic Canada, and we spent both Christmas Day and the following Thanksgiving with Billy, his mother, and a few others.

It is amazing the difference that a few miles can make to a language! There we were, enjoying a sumptuous Christmas dinner, when Mrs. Noble said, "Have some more Cranberry sauce; there's all kinds of Cranberry sauce". I dutifully looked at the table and took some more sauce, even though I could only see one type. Only a few minutes later, when she told us there was "all kinds of mashed potato", did the penny drop, and we were able to have a good laugh about it.

Of course, there are many of these; a couple of classics being that in Britain "I'll knock you up in the morning", means "I'll be around early to wake you," for some reason or other, - totally unlike North America, where the connotation would be very different. Or "Randy", which would be a common abbreviation for "Randolph" west of the Atlantic, but unusable in Britain.

Shortly after, we were driving to the North shore of New Brunswick yet again, and near Moncton, when the snow got really intense, and the Trans-Canada highway was closed both in front and behind us. There was a motel where we could hole up for the duration of the storm, with a garage/restaurant within walking distance, even in this weather, so we thankfully pulled in. The following morning, we looked out of the window onto a deep blanket of white, with only a very slight kink in the snow where our station wagon and trailer lay covered. The road was closed that day too, and when we dug out the following day, there was no way we were going anywhere. Somebody from the garage showed up with a can of what was called "Quick Start", of which we'd never heard, and proceeded to empty the bulk of the can into the appropriate place. The car fired up like a Saturn rocket, and got us to where we were headed, then died, never to go again, rather like "My Grandfather's Clock", as the strain on the engine had been too much.

We were set up ready to go in the afternoon at the venue in Atholville, by Campbellton, thinking that after such a huge storm there would be very few people coming out for dinner and our show that night, but we had forgotten where we were, and there were many snowmobiles parked outside when we returned to perform, as the roads had not yet been cleared.

One of the customers worked in a local car dealership, a nice French-Canadian man named Guy Picard. I'm not sure if we met in the dealership, or where we were working, but the outcome was, that he said, "what you really need is this", showing us a beautiful shiny blue Suburban, which to the uninitiated is rather like going into a garage to look at a small Ford and being presented with the keys to a Rolls Royce. He showed us how we could make this work, and we duly contacted our bank in Halifax, but they didn't want to know, as we were newly arrived landed immigrants, living at that time strictly on the road. Guy called his bank manager at the Bank of Nova Scotia, who came out for supper with his wife that night, enjoyed our evening, and said "You'll keep working; come in tomorrow and tell me what you need". Years later, we ran into him, and he said that he'd really gone out on a limb for us, which we of course knew, but had never missed a payment.

The venue not being a hotel gig, there were pluses and minuses to this. The plus was that we had a fully equipped house trailer, close to our work, which was a treat after many weeks of hotel rooms, no matter how good. The minus was that it was in the dead of winter, and we no longer had a vehicle, having not yet purchased the Suburban. I seem to remember that we walked over once, in the way below freezing temperatures and biting wind, but that could have been somewhere else.

Hiding underneath the trailer in the bitter cold was a large orange tomcat, who was decidedly the worse for wear, and very hungry. The ends of his ears were frostbitten, and there were pitiful attempts at a meow, yet one couldn't get near him. We started to put food down; first under the trailer, then on the step, and he gradually came to trust us over a few days, eventually being coaxed into the trailer. He was a bit concerned for the first couple of minutes, but soon settled into having a real drink, instead of snow, with some much-needed warmth, and sleep.

In no time at all he was happy in the house trailer, going out when necessary, and lying between us with a loud purring, or draping himself across Mary as she slept. His fur was soon to regain its lustre, thanks to Mary's constant brushing, which I was to see more than once, if waking in the early hours.

We left Atholville after 2 weeks, not only in a brand-new three-quarter ton Suburban, but also one that contained a cat, who by now was christened Sam, or Sammy. It was a euphoric feeling, heading south into the sun, not thinking of his future or ours, living for the moment. We left the colossal snow banks that were higher than our vehicle, and headed towards Saint John, on the Bay of Fundy, location of our next venue. This again was not a hotel gig, so we had booked into Keddy's Motor Inn, one of our favourite places to play, and where we knew so many of the staff. Sam was great, he always stayed close when we took him for walks, and the week was uneventful.

That is, until Saturday, when we took him down through the open-sided garage for his walk, prior to our matinèe, which for us was to be the end of our working week. Sammy took off like a rocket, and try as we might, he was not to be found. We had to do our show, followed by the packup, and coming back to the hotel sometime later.

There was Sam, meowing, waiting where we had seen him earlier. He was in a really bad state, possibly from a fight, and we needed to take him to a vet. quickly. Which we did. The vet wanted to put him down, saying that he was just an alley cat, but we had been living with him for three weeks, and could see so much more. We put the required fee down in advance, and Sam was soon returned to us, minus a couple of teeth, that needed coming out anyway. We had already found a home for him with a young couple, so left him there on the following day, and headed north to Fredericton, 100 km. distant, to another Keddy's venue, where we were to stay for two weeks, of course leaving our phone number with Sam's new "parents".

Three days later there was a call, saying that Sammy wouldn't eat. So, we bundled ourselves in the car and headed back to Saint John. As soon as Sammy saw us, there was a big "meow" in welcome, and he headed straight for his food bowl.

There was but one option, and we headed back to Fredericton, and the Eden Roc hotel, once again with a cat on board. The rooms were perfect, as they all had outside access onto a huge lawn, where we walked with Sam for a week or more in the day, or put him out at night after work, when he would always come back if called.

Until one day, when he didn't! We searched and searched, also putting it on the radio; (radio stations have been SO kind to us, "living on the road" as we did, and trying to help animals in distress). There was a call from a lady close by, who said, "I think your cat has been watching my house for the last couple of days, as my cat is on heat." Problem solved. We went to the area, and searched for Sammy, every day, in the woods, and around the nearby cemetery, but he was not to be found. Several times a day we looked, eventually leaving Fredericton somewhat distraught, but at the same time, I wondered if Sam possibly needed to go back to his old life.

Every time we came back to the area, we would always go to see if we could spot Sammy, and make sure that he was all right, scouring the woods and streets around for a considerable time, but he was not to be seen.

Two years later, Mary was up near the cemetery, and a totally magnificent Sammy came out of the woods, in perfect condition; orange fur glistening with health. Mary called "Sam," and he ran towards her, bursting with joy, and she lifted him into her arms. Who knows how long they were together; Mary wanted to show him to me, but Sam now had a new life, which clearly suited him, and headed back into the woods. We were so grateful to have seen him again, and to know that his life was now good. He touched us very deeply over time, and anyone who has been kind enough to buy an L.P., cassette, or CD over the years will know that when we started our own label, it was, and is, called "Sam Cat Records", with a caricature of a somewhat straggly cat on the sleeve.

When we worked in Sydney, at the Holiday Inn, it was sub-contracted through a Toronto agent, who had the Holiday Inn account for Eastern Canada, so we contacted him regarding a summer tour in Ontario, which we had yet to see.

His venues varied hugely, from sumptuous to considerably less so, as we were to find out, and it was amazing that the same act could be sent to such different locations. At one of these, in Chatham, our bedroom was directly above the somewhat smoky tavern, and it was in an old building, so that the smoke permeated directly through the roof during the evening, only to be awaiting us when we went upstairs to bed. Not only that, but it was 117 °F, no A/C, and the humidity was just about off the scale, so we couldn't wait to leave. The only plus was going to the park in the hot afternoon and laying in the shade of a big tree with a cold drink, watching the large black squirrels that we had never seen before.

MOLLY'S

*H*aving by now built up a large repertoire of Irish music with our work in the Maritimes, we were privileged to be invited into Molly McGuire's, Ottawa's number one Irish pub, close to the Parliament buildings, and known throughout Canada, for St. Patrick's Day itself. We'd just been doing a run in Spencerville, with matinée and evening show on the Saturday; then the big pack up, followed by a snowy drive to the Nation's capital, arriving at around 4:00 a.m. We had said farewell to the staff after a good stay, one of whom was a writer, married to one of the McGarrigle sisters. Kate and Anna were by far our favourite "roots" musicians on planet Earth. Their compositions have been covered by luminaries such as Emmylou Harris and Linda Ronstadt, but the simplicity and feeling of the earthy originals will never be replicated.

To play Molly's on St. Patrick's Day, even on a Sunday, meant setting up at some time during the night, as the entrance line would start forming at around 7:30 a.m., after which it was impossible to "load in", through the huge crowd. Extra speakers were put to carry music to the street, with complimentary tea, coffee, and later, sandwiches for those in the queue, who would be dancing in the partially closed off street in order to keep warm. We were supposed to be staying on the premises, but someone had forgotten to leave the appropriate key, so we checked into a nearby hotel for way too few hours of exhausted sleep, before returning, somewhat groggily, to start our music in a packed house at 11 a.m.

The place was beautifully decorated, but we wondered a bit at the huge, old, rather ratty tables, that didn't seem to blend with the room. Then we started playing, and the tables were all immediately filled by dancers, which of course meant that there was now more floor space for people to crowd in through the door. It was an amazing experience;

we played initially for seven hours, with odd breaks and very little voice left. Then something happened, for the first and only time in our lives. The owner came over, handed me a signed blank cheque, and said, "Here, fill it in how you like, but keep playing!" We took a break, then played another hour of mostly instrumental music, after which everything switched to recordings, as we could do no more. And no, we didn't abuse the blank cheque, but charged him pretty much pro rata for the extra time.

Another time we went to a hotel called the "Knob Hill", in Scarborough, by Toronto. Quite a large hotel, it had definitely seen better days, and the bedrooms were clean, but badly maintained. The night clerk who checked us in said, "This isn't the Ritz, you know", and gave us three keys to select a room. So, we picked the best of the three, moved a T.V. from one room, plus a standard lamp and an armchair from another, to make up an acceptable room for ourselves, before returning two sets of keys to the front desk.

THE "ROYAL YORK"

The main hotel in Toronto was of course the Canadian Pacific "Royal York", which, at the time of its opening, was the largest hotel in what is now called the Commonwealth, so, out of courtesy, we called the agent to see if he could get us in there. To give him credit, he didn't actually splutter, but it was all too clear that he thought we lived on a different planet. So, I contacted the hotel, spoke to Zena Cheevers who booked the entertainment, in addition to some other venues, and arranged to see her.

Our next engagement was at a high level Travelodge, in Willowdale, just off the 401, and on our second evening there, Zena came in to see us, with a senior manager from the hotel. We had already had a good meeting, and now arranged that we would go into one of the Royal York entertainment rooms at a mutually convenient time, which we did, on many occasions over the years.

The Royal York was the first of Canada's grand old railway hotels in which we worked, though by no means the last. Opened in 1929, it had an impressive 26 floors and 1,100 guest bedrooms, with an extra wing of 400 more rooms added in the 1950s. The main dining room, the Imperial room, boasted cabaret of the ilk of Frank Sinatra, Ella Fitzgerald, Lena Horne, and Tony Bennett, all backed by the resident Moxie Whitney band, plus there were several lounges, with and without music, and Dick Turpin's, a high energy entertainment room, pub style, but with a focused show, which was our spot in the late 70s. To give you an idea of the ambience, this is the only room we have ever worked where the maître-d' was in white tie, despite the fact that it was a "pub" show. One night, we went into our final song a couple of minutes before closing, which was probably midnight, but could have been later. We finished the song, which was a medley, at about 2 minutes past, and the next day there was a note on our music stand, which also went to the food and beverage office and to the maître-d', with a very polite reminder to finish exactly on time. But they treated us well and staying in the hotel meant we could walk to many downtown locations. However, our first stay there was during a very cold January, so we didn't go too far. Often there would be

a T.V. chat show going on in the vast lobby, with band and sometimes guest singers, so there was usually something to watch. When Arthur Hailey wrote his famous book "Hotel", he moved into the Royal York for the duration, and having stayed there several times we can quite see why he made this perfect choice!

Prior to this, we had been over to the U.K., arriving in time for Mary's dad's 80th, and we managed to have 80 candles, all burning at once, no, not on a cake, but all over the living room, which was no mean feat! We also did our first L.P. together on one trip, "Peter & Mary and Friends", recorded at John Bales' studio in Pinner, where I had recorded my previous solo album for Bermuda, using many of the same musicians, except that this time I did the lead playing, as the finished product needed to have a similar "feel" to our stage performance. I recall John coming to Heathrow to give us the finished master tape, on which he had done great work, and then me getting it to the aircraft without it being scanned by ANYTHING, lest it be rendered useless.

WEST TO THE ROCKIES

*I*t was time for our first trip West, to Alberta. One of Canada's leading musicians, Tommy Banks, who had a national T.V. show at the time, was based in Edmonton, where his wife Ida had a busy agency. We contacted the agency, and one of the bookers there said they would arrange three venues, contracts to be sorted out on arrival. This was followed up by phone, and we set off on the road, having just completed a repeat engagement over Thanksgiving in Bathurst. We had a brief stop to see our friends "Amber", another duo, who were working in Atholville by Campbellton, where we had bought the Suburban, and then headed to Ottawa and points west. En route, we stopped to call the agency again, at which point the booker in question wouldn't come to the phone. We tried several times, to no avail, so it became clear that the ball had been well and truly dropped, and no bookings had been arranged.

However, all was not lost. We had previously met a musician from Newfoundland, Harry Hibbs, who sang slightly old-fashioned comedy songs, mostly of his own composition, and backed up by his own accordion playing, with much banter in between. He was a big name in his home province, and toured extensively coast to coast. He had mentioned to us that he always worked via "Studio City", Edmonton's other leading agency, so we gave them a call. The phone was picked up by a lady named Carol Duke, who was appalled at what had happened, and said she would work on it right away.

Which she did, and called us back where we had stopped overnight, in very short order, to tell us that we were booked into the "Can-Can lounge" at the Hotel MacDonald the following week. The MacDonald was by far the leading hotel in the area, and would be a great start to the tour, which Carol would of course, book for us. Built by the Grand Trunk Pacific railway, the hotel had been open since 1915, and was now the property of Canadian National, with extensive renovations, and beautiful views overlooking the North Saskatchewan River. The term "Can-Can lounge" evokes images of frilly skirts and knickers, as in the Paris "Moulin Rouge", but not so. This was a room of cocktails and relatively quiet conversation, a good place for a mixture of light music, even if inappropriately named. The amazing thing was, that on our first night, Carol came in, and stayed a full two sets, in order to really get a handle on our music, so that she could put us into suitable venues. Unlike the Ontario agent, who would have sent "Peter & Mary", "Andrés Segovia and Yehudi Menhuin", or "The Smothers Brothers" consecutively to the same location, on the grounds that we were all duos. Carol was to handle our Alberta performances for the next six years or more, and always came to see us, however briefly, when we appeared in Edmonton after being away for a while, something that no other agent has ever done in our entire career, and we have kept in touch ever since.

After the MacDonald, we headed into the Canadian Rockies for the very first time and were spellbound by the amazing views in every possible direction, as every newcomer is. We had a three-week run at the Athabasca hotel, one of Jasper townsite's first hotels, and THE place for residents to hang out, especially in the off season. A different lounge, it was on 2 levels, with the performers upstairs, and a mirror at 45 degrees above their heads, so that they could be seen from down below, albeit at a strange angle. We were there for Halloween, which in Jasper was huge at the time, and truly spectacular costumes appeared all evening. One reveller dressed as Frankenstein's monster, and created a costume, using stilts, that allowed him to sit upstairs with his "feet" on the floor below. Very carefully measured and constructed, he of course had to be the winner that year.

In some lounges across the country, hockey ruled, and if there was a big game on T.V., music would not start until the game was over. Not so in Jasper. The only thing that could cause a delay was transmission of the "Carol Burnette Show ", for which everything stopped. Rightly, in our book, as we loved it just as much as everybody else. Especially we loved the "stunts" that she and designer/carpenter/general ideas man Bob Mackie would put together, without the rest of the cast being aware, that were only unveiled on live camera. The supreme classic of these was of course the "Gone with the Wind" parody, when Carol (as "Starlett") comes down the stairs wearing a huge velvet curtain, including a big brass curtain rod across her shoulders, and says in response to the applause and laughter, "Thank you, I saw it in the window, and I just couldn't resist it". This amazing prop. is now in the Smithsonian, where it rightfully belongs. Many years later, after Bob's passing, we were to meet his wife and daughter on a tour in Italy, and were so fortunate to hear several stories of those times.

It was an amazing first visit to Jasper. There were very few visitors; the summer was over, and the community was taking a much-needed collective breath together, before the winter skiers, a smaller group, started to arrive. Instead of tourists, there was wildlife wandering peacefully around the town, especially Elk and Mule Deer, and we quickly fell in love with the place, as yet another "second home", as is Bermuda, where we would recharge our batteries, even if still working.

By now, we of course had our first L.P. record pressed and available, with a front sleeve that to us was very special. We had got to know a couple, Ernest and Nancy Mickelburgh, in Hampton, New Brunswick, who had a lake on their property where lived a couple of beavers. Every evening, they would put a couple of young tree branches down by the water's edge, and retreat indoors to watch; sometimes they would see, sometimes not, but the branches were gone by the next day. After a long time of doing this, they would sit out, but away from the water, and the branches would go. Eventually, Nancy would actually hold one end of a branch, while a beaver came to take away part of it. By the time we met them, they had been doing this for many years and the beavers, especially an older female which they called "Charlie", would come over to eat a carrot from your hand, provided that you were still and quiet. So, the sleeve of the L.P. had just that, with Mary holding Charlie's carrot, and me behind. In some of the photo shoot we had guitars, and were concerned that they might become breakfast, but not in the picture we finally used.

There was a ranger in the Algonquin park, in Ontario, who had heard about Nancy's efforts, and there was a beaver that needed relocating from his area, so he drove all the way to see them with this male beaver, which they immediately named "Peter". The truly amazing thing was that Peter, who had no human contact in his life prior to this, quickly assimilated into the little community, and would take a carrot off Nancy in less than a month.

We had our first experience of a very strange phenomenon shortly after our first visit to Jasper. Some hotels at the time ran for entertainment what came to be called "split rooms", meaning that the dining room and lounge were next to each other, with either a wall or lower partition between, and the stage facing half into each room. If there was a 2-piece musical act, this meant initially that each one of you would sometimes be looking at a totally different audience. Not only that, but often the music needed for the lounge would be inappropriate for dining and vice versa. Very occasionally, the dining room would be busy earlier in the evening and the lounge later, in which case one could make it work, after a fashion, but this was rare. In our case, we learned to face the lounge pretty much all the time, with sometimes a low volume speaker in the dining room, but usually not. The only way it could possibly work would be in a high-end venue where the music in both rooms was quiet and constantly of a dining level, but the high end venues fortunately, didn't do "split rooms" anyway. A truly terrible idea, and I hope there are none of them left.

We encountered our first one at the Continental, a large new hotel in Medicine Hat, Alberta. The hotel itself was good, and we had the pleasure of meeting up with two couples with whom we had shared meals on our last "Alexandr Pushkin" crossing of the Atlantic. These four retirees were true old-style western gentlefolk, I know of no other way to describe them, and were pillars of the Medicine Hat community. There was Doctor Matt Davis and his wife Diana, who lived in a large Victorian style corner house, with a huge weeping birch out back. Matt was highly respected, and it seemed that the whole of Medicine Hat knew of Dr. Davis and his family. The other couple were Gordon and Joanne Simmons, who had built a large hardware business in the area. Gordon was President of the legion and was named "Citizen of the Year" on more than one occasion, for his many endeavors to help others in the community. Of the four, Joanne was fun, and also a little feisty, but I somehow felt that polite, gentle Diana was in fact the strongest of the group, in her quiet way.

They belonged to a fast-vanishing era of which we were fortunate to catch a glimpse, together with a few other older folks in Medicine Hat, and one or two around Lethbridge, not to be seen anywhere else, people you might meet and instantly be aware that you were in the presence of respect and integrity, immaculate both in appearance and especially character.

Matt and Diana's son, Donald, was also a medical specialist, and came to our aid so very quickly once when we needed assistance, which can be problematic when constantly touring.

One morning, before leaving "The Hat", we woke up to find the entire sky a beautiful salmon pink colour, which we had never seen before, but never forgot, as that sight meant both very dry and very cold, (-45°c). Fortunately, a Chinook wind blew in, and the temperature rose over 30°c in the space of an hour, to our amazement.

We were headed northwards that Christmas, not a huge distance, around 460 km. to the town of Grande Prairie, which was new to us. The engagement was from Boxing Day until New Year's Day, but we were loath to travel on Christmas Day itself, mostly because everything would be closed, and it might be hard to get gas. Added to that, we had just completed a short run at Westridge Park Lodge, out in the country west of Edmonton, where we knew the staff, and they wanted us to stay on as long as possible. Somewhat regretfully, we decided that Christmas Eve was the only day to travel and set off. Surprisingly, the roads were very quiet; it seemed that everyone had got to wherever they were going already, or they weren't going in the first place, to the extent that, by early evening, the sight of a vehicle was rare.

Our first album together, picture with the beavers in Hampton, New Brunswick

"Power of the Rockies" – the majestic Moraine Lake

Somewhere between Fox Creek and Valleyview, in the middle of nowhere, it was dark, and we were flagged down by somebody clutching a gas can, who begged us to go back the way we had come to get some fuel, as he had run out. It was suggested that he might want to get someone going in that direction, to which we got the response of, "It's Christmas!", and we, a little reluctantly, took him back to an operating gas station, adding considerably to our journey.

It is said that every good deed is rewarded, and in our case, this was certainly true. We reached the Grande Prairie Motor Inn, our home for a week, with an actual stream running right through it, and went up to our room, to be greeted by the sight of a fully lit up and decorated Christmas tree, which had been transferred from a banquet room by some kind members of staff, who knew we would be alone in the hotel on Christmas Day.

And alone we were. The next day we drove around the town to find a Christmas Dinner, or a meal of any form, but this was years ago, and pretty much everything was closed. However, all was not lost. We found an open convenience store, and, since we always carried an electric skillet, bought some wieners and a can of beans, also a loaf of bread, and settled down in our room to a sumptuous Christmas meal, with carols from the choir at King's College, Cambridge, on the T.V., and a bottle of Moskovskaya, (shades of the "Alexandr Pushkin"), to wash it all down, our only regret being that we had arrived too late for a Christmas service the night before.

We stayed around Alberta for another 3 months, including a return visit to Jasper, which we had learned to love, and our first to Banff, at the old Cascade Inn on Banff Avenue. This was a good hotel, catering mostly to locals at this time of year, as the ski business was yet nothing like the insanity of the summer tourist boom, which we were not to see for a while. One summer, years later, we were playing in the Cascade when a group of tourists, who sounded Parisian rather than French

Canadian, came in and sat near to us. After a couple of songs, we included something in French, which we have always done ever since Bermuda days. A table close to them very pointedly stood up, leaving their drinks and personal possessions, and went out into the hallway until we sang in English again. I wondered then, as I wonder almost every day, if the human race will ever get it together, and live peaceably, with the respect for each other that all deserve.

Time to head east, and another stop for 2 weeks at Toronto's Royal York, to packed houses as always, followed by a few weeks in the Maritimes, before once more boarding the "Alexandr Pushkin" for the trans-Atlantic run, and a big tour of Country Music festivals and clubs in the U.K., playing, of course, appropriate material.

The crossing was good, and we helped with the "Miss Pushkin" pageant, fancy dress competitions, and the passengers' talent show, which can be a little scary. Bear in mind that every contestant has paid for their ticket to be on the ship, no matter how bad they are, and you really cannot do the old Vaudeville/ Music Hall shepherd's crook routine, no matter how tempting this may be. One passenger was attempting a Bob Dylan song - I believe it was "Knocking on Heaven's Door", really slow, draggy, and just plain bad. We could see that the officers and passengers were getting somewhat fidgety, so Mary, who was on one side of the stage, came rapidly out at the end of one verse, when there was a huge gap of just guitar strumming, which maybe sounded good to him, as he could hear other things in his head, grabbed his mic. off the stand and said, "That was truly amazing", (or words to that effect), while I physically semi-lifted him from the stool on which he had been sitting. We clapped a lot and got the audience to clap, with difficulty, but somehow we removed him from the stage, in somewhat of a daze as to what had just happened.

We of course also did our shows for both passengers and crew, but since I brought up the name of Bob Dylan, (Robert Zimmerman), the brilliant songwriter, I should mention that he picked his last name as a writer/performer as more than a tip of the hat to the amazing work of Dylan Thomas, with which I so agree. If I were to be stranded on a desert island, as in the old radio show, and could only take 12 books, one of these, apart from taking "How to survive if stranded on a desert island", which might become useful, would almost certainly be the writings of Dylan Thomas. It was the prolific composer Tom Russell who told me about Bob Dylan. Tom is also a lover of Dylan Thomas, and has written "The Sparrow of Swansea", as a tribute, in his memory.

We docked in Tilbury, the port for London, and started to go through the process of checking all our equipment that was needed for the tour against insurance policy and other lists. The British customs officer was, very unusually, being inordinately slow and difficult, but we swallowed hard and eventually got our paperwork done. However, when the passengers, most of whom we had got to know in various degrees during the crossing, were in line, it became clear that he was being deliberately awkward, and spinning things out as much as possible. The passengers were all Canadian, some disembarking for U.K. holidays, some just for the few hours the ship was in port, including a large group of university students from Montreal, who were headed for an Arts and Culture tour in Russia. This last was being done especially for them by Intourist, the Russian tourist office, at a little over $200 per head, as a promotion, and included the ship, the holiday, and the flight back to Montreal. An amazing deal organized so that the students would both tell their friends, and possibly go back on another trip with spouse and children in the years to come, when they hopefully had enough money to afford it. There was one elderly passenger, of Russian origin but living in Montreal, who was visiting family, probably for the first time since emigrating, and always wore a somewhat dishevelled light grey jacket, that crinkled every time he moved, as he had the savings of many years sewn into the lining, to help family and friends back home. I haven't really thought of him until now, and hope so much that he made it safely to his destination.

Meanwhile, the line of passengers was longer, and moving slower. Some were getting understandably edgy, while one older lady was really getting a hard time from the customs officer, and on the verge of tears.

Something had to be done; these people were all visiting Britain for the first time, the place where I was born, and getting a terrible first impression. I went out in front of the desk where the customs officer was sitting and said, (or words to this effect), "Ladies and gentlemen, for those of you on your first visit to Britain, I must apologize for the behavior of the gentleman behind me. Please do not think he is in any way typical of the people you will meet on your holiday". I then left the ship via the crew exit, found a group of officers, selected the one with the most scrambled eggs on his hat, and reported the incident, checking back a few minutes later, to see, with not a little satisfaction, that the passports were now being stamped at high speed. I'll never know what made him like that. Was it because the ship was Soviet? Certainly the passengers weren't. Or was he just plainly and simply in the wrong job?

This tour was going to be interesting. After a week and a half of "r and r", plus prep. for the road, we had received our schedule, which already showed 65 towns in 75 days, some venues with a barring clause. In many parts of the world, when on tour, the contract will stipulate that you must not appear within a certain distance of the engagement for a specified period of time before, and sometimes after, the performance. In Britain this was usually a 100-mile radius, unless the act was huge, in which case the distance would be much greater. We had hired the largest station wagon we could find, which was small by North American standards, and borrowed an equally small trailer, called a caravan in Britain, from a friend of my sister, Anne, in which the two main speakers would have to travel between gigs. We were ready, or so we thought. The agent who had booked the tour, Mike Storey, was by far the leading booker in Britain for the Country Music circuit of festivals, clubs, and community theatres, with the huge festivals, such as the giant Wembley 3 or 4 day event, being handled by Mervyn Conn, this being virtually a "Who's Who" of the Nashville market. Mike Storey, to his credit, had booked an extremely comprehensive tour for us, and offered to fill any holes, but we declined the latter, preferring an occasional day off.

COUNTRY MUSIC TOURS – BRITAIN

The Country Music scene had evolved considerably since writing magazine articles on the Wembley festivals a few years ago. In those days there had been a very small circuit of concert-style events, with the huge Nashville Room pub in the Earl's Court/West Kensington area of London as the hub, where I first saw George Jones, Loretta Lynn, and Hank Snow. The Wembley festival had very few U.K. or Irish bands in the programme; Country Fever, (with lead player Albert Lee, who was to positively explode on to the world scene with his playing, along with Ricky Skaggs, in Emmylou Harris' Hot Band, and got so many awards from Guitar Player magazine as to become ineligible), The Jonny Young Four (very fine, excellent harmonies in "Sons of The Pioneers" style), also Ray Lynam and Philomena Begley's band from Ireland, who covered all the boy/girl duets and were equally good. Other than that, it was all top Nashville artistes, with the odd insert of someone like Leapy Lee, (Little Arrows), which was hardly Country, or Miki & Griff, who toured with Lonnie Donegan all those years before, and had definitely reached "iconic" status in Britain, with numerous regular T.V. spots.

The British Country Music Association had a regular monthly magazine going out to its members nationwide, with the location of events in towns everywhere. It could be a large rented room in a pub, (hopefully on the ground floor), a hall, a stately home, or even a theatre, anywhere there was a space. Plus, there were a few localized magazines (such as Clive Wynes' "Country Matters" in the southwest) with more information on where to find the music. There were only four BBC Radio programmes per week that were Country, the main one being hosted by Wally Whyton, (once of the "Vipers" skiffle group), so exposure on any one of these would be huge, as there was a big, if very select, following.

The tour started. We loaded everything we could into our rented Toyota station wagon, which was somewhat underpowered, as we were to find out(!), plus a couple of things in the trailer, which looked in good condition, if a little elderly. All the lights worked, tires looked fine, and we were off, towing behind us, attached invisibly to the rear bumper, our own personal rain cloud that we had yet to discover.

It was so very different in the British clubs to venues in the United States, being a blend of Nashville and Wild West, unlike anywhere else. Many of the club attendees would arrive in very authentic looking well-used western attire, as opposed to the immaculate, often rhinestone covered outfits of the performers. Reproduction Colt 45s and Buntline specials were common, which fired very loud smoke emitting blanks. Between two sets of an act or band there would frequently be a mock shoot-out, such as one might see at Goldfield or other Arizona ghost towns today. The most popular singer of all time was Jim Reeves, and it was somewhat of a polite salute to occasionally include one of his songs. I had the privilege of meeting his wife, Mary, on more than one occasion, sometime after his passing, as she always liked to attend the Wembley festival, (backstage), to catch up with her many friends. The Nashville act topping the bill each day at Wembley often finished their set with "How great Thou Art", while on the U.K. circuit the preference was Elvis Presley's "An American Trilogy". We quickly discovered that a rendering of "High Noon" would be treated as reverentially as a beloved hymn, while our instrumental version of "Ghost Riders in the Sky" meant guns out, much noise, and a room full of smoke by the end. Amazing! Historically, there were many somewhat inaccurate things that took place, from the trooping of a Confederate Flag, for some unaccountable reason, to the reading of the Gettysburg address by an actor dressed as Abraham Lincoln, who travelled the country doing just that. But the response to all of it was phenomenal, and there is no doubt that everyone had fun.

Probably the first thing we were to learn on the tour was that it was almost impossible to find somewhere to park overnight, on one occasion driving nearly 50 miles to find a spot to pull in. Lay-bys were not really an option, as large trucks would come thundering past about four inches away, causing the trailer to shake violently. Sometimes there would be a rest parking lot on a motorway stop, which would be a godsend, but whenever possible we would stay close to the venue and pull out the next morning. On our very first concert, we had asked for advice, and it was suggested that we park in an empty square downtown, which we gratefully did. We awoke to the sound of two little boys outside the window, saying, "Ee, I think there's somebody in there", and pulling the curtain open a crack to see that we were now in the middle of a large open-air market, surrounded by stalls of vegetables and handicrafts. I should probably mention at this point that we had just done a full evening the night before, so probably didn't get to bed before 1:00 a.m. or later, and it was hardly surprising that we hadn't heard anything of people arriving. We had to get out of there, as we had a long way to go that day, and several stalls had to be moved, but I don't recall a single complaint, as I rapidly wound up the legs with a somewhat red face, and we ever so slowly made our way out. The market hadn't really got going yet, and I think everybody was amused at our predicament, and somewhat sympathetic, even though we had created extra work for them. It was at least a nice sunny morning, which probably helped, plus we had unwittingly given the stall holders something to talk about, as their setup was completed.

The next problem was food. In those days it was just about impossible to get a meal in Britain, unless it was at what was called a "meal time". If on a motorway it was possible to get very basic food, or a truck stop would suffice, but much of the time we survived on a pretty limited diet, unlike Britain nowadays, where there is a huge choice. Two places stand out that saved us. We seemed to drive through Doncaster frequently, when there was a Canadian run restaurant of hamburgers, fries, coleslaw, and other things, all prepared in house and of decent quality, plus good coffee, which became a regular stop-off, particularly in the pouring rain that seemed to plague much of each day. We struck true gold at the old Roman fortress town of Caerleon, near Newport in Wales, where we found sumptuous home-cooked meals, with what seemed to be unlimited fresh vegetables available at pretty much any time of day. For this we would divert quite a bit from our route, wishing they were somewhere we could pass more regularly, with their warm and friendly welcome.

While on the subject of Wales, we must remember the classic Fish & Chip shop in Bridgend, which had a daily special of a roast beef or chicken dinner, in addition to the usual fare. Having opted for the former, we asked for horseradish sauce from the cheerful waitress, whose response was "eeeuuww! You don't like that, do you?" The rice pudding that was the day's dessert caused an even bigger expletive, but we left rejoicing in the fact that we had met a true character, and we would for sure go back there if ever in the area.

We were part of several festivals on the tour, so got to hear and meet most of the leading U.K. acts of the time. Something unusual to us, which was quite normal to them, was that each act or band would do a full stage set up in the reverse order of their appearance, thus, the closing act, (presumably the headliner), would set up, including p.a., at the rear of the stage, and so on, with the opening act at the front. Each act would do a full sound check as they set up, and remove their own gear, with the help of a stage crew, after the set, leaving the next group ready to go. It was quite efficient and meant that everyone got the sound to which they were used, rather than having a sound engineer, who possibly did not know them, in charge of the mix, which they would only get on monitor, so be unaware of what the audience was actually hearing.

There was one performance at a hall in Staffordshire, where we turned up at the appointed time, and proceeded to wait, and wait, for somebody to show up and unlock the place for us to move in. Then the bride's mother appeared (!) and was so very pleased to see us. Paperwork was checked, and yes, we were in the place designated, and it seemed we were playing at a wedding, which was unusual, but not impossible, which we knew so well having both toured in the U.K. years earlier. In retrospect, it reminds me of a time with "Peter and Elisabeth", where we are both standing in the wings, my amp. on stage, and the Concert Secretary walks out and says, "Ladies and Gentlemen, tonight we've got a grand magic act all the way from London... ", me clutching a guitar which he can actually see! Oh well....

Anyway, it seemed that somebody called Kevin had booked the entertainment, (who was not coming), and nobody else showed up, so we figured that we must be the appointed act. I didn't see any shotguns anywhere, but the two families sat on opposite sides of the long hall and glowered at each other, while we attempted to get the evening moving in any way we could, which it did, slowly, once both sides had a drink or two inside them. They even started actually communicating with each other, and, while we didn't expect to play a dance gig on this tour, we knew we could make it work, with a range of music from ABBA to Zorba the Greek. After a long set, the best man approached us with an offer of some food, drink, and a break, all of which we accepted with alacrity, as it had been one of those days with little time for essentials, bearing in mind that this was only the second day of the tour, and this was the self-same day that we had woken up in the middle of an open-air market, just a few hours before.

We had just sat down for our meal when somebody appeared with a T-shirt advertising a promotion company, and the words, "What the……. do you think you are doing here?" It seemed that we were supposed to be playing, as Top of the Bill, at a big Country Music festival which was now being held at the nearby racetrack. Whether the agent had neglected to tell us of the change in venue, or the promotion company had neglected to tell the agent, we will never know. The promoter said that we had to pack up, and come immediately to the racetrack, or we would be sued, not that it was any fault of ours. The wedding people said that if we left, we would be sued, which was ridiculous, since they hadn't booked us in the first place, and the occupants of the hall might well have come to blows, had we not been there to diffuse the electrically charged atmosphere. Eventually we took half of our fee, and headed off to the racetrack, leaving the wedding party grouped around an old upright piano, singing the music hall songs of yesteryear, while we went through the gargantuan task of loading all our equipment, including p.a., up an elevator to the backstage area.

It was a 6-hour concert in total, with 750 in attendance, and there had been several bus loads of people who were now all leaving, as it was time for the buses to go, regardless of showtimes. One of Britain's top bands was on, and they were milking what was left of the audience and still awake, as hard as they could, with no thought of the evening's schedule. When we eventually got on it was 12:40 a.m. and there was only 20 minutes left, plus a mic. stand had broken in the rush from the wedding, and kept slowly slipping down, despite copious amounts of tape to try and hold it. The buses had all left, and we did the best we could with the 60 or 70 people left, receiving, once again, half of our fee.

Which we could have contested, but were far more interested in getting both food and some sleep before the third day of the tour, when things settled down and everything went smoothly for the remainder of the 24-day first block, which ended with a week in South Wales, and gave us a chance to regroup a little, as distances were shorter.

During the tour there were arranged occasional visits to radio stations to promote ourselves and venues we were playing locally, for which we got a standard fee negotiated by the Musicians' Union in the U.K. I was impressed with this, as we have never been paid for an interview in either Canada or the U.S.A. On this trip I recall a radio spot in Swansea, where we met Daniel O'Donnell for the first time. A nice chap, he had started doing "covers" of the big Nashville hits at a studio in Ireland, and was big on the British Country Music scene, with his albums, sometimes having up to 4 in the charts at one time. In some ways more importantly, we met the label owner who was at that time managing Daniel, and I remember thinking that Daniel could have sung half a page from the phone book, and this man would have made it somehow into a hit, a feeling I have never had from anybody else, in my entire musical career. Daniel many years later made a T.V. special for the Public Broadcasting System in the U.S. and I think 90% of women in the States over the age of 65 fell in love that night of the first transmission, which introduced him to a whole new audience, where he continues to be extremely popular.

The trailer (caravan) was approximately 12 years old and had been kept outside during this time. It was small, and we had to carry our two big Cerwin Vega speakers in it, which went in the front of the station wagon when we put the seats down to create a bed each night. There was no plumbing of any form, and we carried a plastic bucket which was our only loo!

On one occasion, we were driving through a fortunately not busy housing area and swung around to the left for the direction in which we were travelling. The trailer, however, had other ideas, and continued straight forward on its own, to be stopped by the wound-up support pin when it reached the kerb, without which it would have hit an elderly gentleman who was on the sidewalk. We ran over to make sure he was all right, but his first concern was for possible damage to the trailer, which of course had all the electrical wiring totally shredded, and said how lucky we were to have a beautiful little home to take with us, making us see the trailer, and this kind man, in a special light. In those days a trailer in the U.K. had no chains, no lock on the hitch, just a little catch, and no safety brakes, which surely has changed by now.

We continued our journey with a sign on the back of the trailer, as there were now no lights, to a dockers' club in the less salubrious part of Hartlepool, surrounded by broken glass, tin cans, and all manner of rubbish. Pretty much immediately, we were surrounded by kids, who wanted to watch our trailer for us. We looked at them and decided quickly that this was probably a good idea, so gave them a small retainer for starters and proceeded to hump our equipment upstairs into the social club. We had a good evening, as the tour was generally, and were packing up at the end of the show to the familiar sight of a club custodian, arms folded, sitting on a seat watching us. To be fair, he did say we could have torn down in the morning, and didn't come up with the so familiar line to performers in Britain of, "Aven't you got 'omes to go to?", but we not only had to get the trailer wiring repaired, we would have also felt very unsafe leaving everything set up with no security. We had to sleep outside the club, as we had no lights, but were out of there at daybreak to park outside a friendly looking garage, who quickly replaced our wiring harness, and got us on our way.

On another occasion, we were heading up the M1 Motorway, when somebody hooted, and yelled at us. We pulled over and saw that something had happened to the trailer. One corner support had completely disintegrated, and the back was open to the world. Fortunately, it was a day off, somewhere near Morecambe, and we managed to get a real camp site that evening, in the obligatory pouring rain, where we started to properly look at the problem to see what we could do, being watched by many people in their nicely heated trailers clutching cups of tea. But all was not lost. A large Russian man came over to us with the words "You need help". He looked at the problem, took some measurements, and went off, returning with a perfectly cut strut of wood, plus a couple of smaller bits that would be needed. He fixed everything so that any damage was virtually invisible, very skilfully, by which time the rain had pretty much stopped, although the ground was still soggy. He was really interested to know that we had played on a Russian ship, especially that we gave shows to the crew, and would take nothing for the work that he had so very kindly done. It seemed that the guttering on the trailer had a tiny pin hole directly over the corner strut, which had rain going into it for years, turning the strut into nothing more than sawdust, that had now been perfectly repaired, including sealant on the offending hole.

The tour continued, as did the rain. No, it didn't rain all day, just enough to be a nuisance loading in, or loading out, or when trying to find something to eat. Early arrivals to a venue might well have found one of us on the floor trying to press stage outfits with a towel underneath, even in the washroom, where there was usually an electrical outlet, or attempting to dry wet hair.

But once everything was set up, the shows were amazing, and on some occasions, we would see audience members again at another venue, which was truly gratifying. One or two at each show would be really into audio, and were very impressed with our big Cerwin Vega speakers that could move a lot of air, with even a quiet bass note able to put out a candle at considerable distance.

Nearer the end of the tour, we were in the vicinity of the picturesque coastal fishing town of Whitby, in North Yorkshire. There was a steep downwards hill, with a sharp bend at the bottom, then a bridge and an equally steep hill upwards on the other side. We had to come to a stop before navigating the bridge, then attempted the 1 in 4 climb, bearing in mind the trailer and all our gear. This was the point at which we found out that our rented brand-new Toyota station wagon, which had served us so well, was grossly underpowered. We got about half way up, then stopped, with the station wagon refusing to go any further. Mary had her foot on the brake, and we amazingly didn't roll backwards, but it felt that we could at any second. I got out and put wedges behind the wheels of the trailer, then ran up the hill in the direction of a farmhouse that was visible not far away, with Mary still holding onto the brake for dear life. Fortunately, the farmer was home, and came out very rapidly with his tractor, to tow both station wagon plus trailer easily up the hill. This incident was the basis of several dreams in years to come, of rolling backwards down a steep hill, which I am glad to report, has never happened.

We carried a battery-powered radio with us, and on one day I was listening to an interview with the "New Seekers", who were talking about the expenses of touring a show, no matter how careful you are, and that often it was only merchandise sales, C.D.s, T shirts etc., that made the difference between breaking even and actually showing a profit. Mick Jagger said this on occasion as well. On one tour I remember "The Rolling Stones" were using 36 semi-trailers, so the expenses would have been phenomenal, regardless of ticket price. When one time "Manish Boy" David Bowie, with whom I had kept in touch, and seen intermittently over the years since the band sadly folded, brought his "Glass Spider" tour into Edmonton, Canada, he only used about 16 semis, which is positively stingy in comparison!

Our tour came to an end, with so many memories and stories to tell. After the first couple of days everything had settled down, as it usually does, and Mike Storey, together with another agent, Frank Feeney, had done an incredible job, with such a huge schedule.

We were to do another tour, based out of Bristol, a while later, but a great deal smaller, just the south west and Wales, through country singer Kelvin Henderson, who booked this circuit, and had a B.B.C. radio programme on which we appeared a couple of times. The places where you get to do a show are unbelievable. On one occasion we were set up at the end of a skittle alley. The pins had been removed, and we were on the bowling lanes, with amplifiers etc. on the bales of straw behind. Another time we were at Weston -Super-Mare, Mary's home town, in the railway station waiting room/cafeteria, which was very quiet. Then a train pulled in, and all the carriages emptied into the cafeteria, which became a huge party, with everybody singing and joining in for a little over half an hour, when the guard blew his whistle, and all the passengers flooded back onto the train.

But that was another time, and right now we were preparing to join the "Alexandr Pushkin" for the trip back to Canada.

The two officers with whom we had become friends were awaiting our arrival when we boarded the ship. It seemed there was a KGB security officer checking everything out, and, while none of us had in any way said or done anything inappropriate, they felt we should not socialize on this trip, which we of course understood.

It was a calm cruise from Tilbury docks into the English Channel, passing Southampton as the QE2 headed out on its New York run. There was to be a hurricane in the Atlantic, so our captain took the ship well north to go around the top of the storm, while the QE2, which had a much tighter schedule, sustained considerable damage to furniture, and to a grand piano. The arrival in Montreal was on a Sunday, which meant that we were unable to collect our vehicle, parked in the Olympic Stadium, until the following day, so the purser kindly allowed us to keep our cabin. That evening, we left the ship for supper, and returned to find the captain, officers, and crew in the main passenger area, with the KGB officer, who had up to now been masquerading as a deckhand, immaculate in suit and tie, giving everyone else a "pep" talk, in which we did not need to be involved, and went quietly back to the cabin.

We didn't travel on the "Alexandr Pushkin" again; life took us in different directions, but we will never forget the warmth of the Russian crew with whom we worked, and the way that, if one was moving something heavy, like a speaker, a sailor would appear as if by magic, and say "No touch! Hands! Music!" and carry the speaker to wherever it was needed, such is their respect for the performing arts.

It was an amazing fall in the Maritimes, as it always is, with the trees positively exploding in red and gold, and it was good to do a run of some favourite venues, catching up with the staff we knew so well, before heading off to Bermuda for a truly magical Christmas break with Doug and Carolyn - a high spot being when we went for a Boxing Day swim, unthinkable to Bermudians, who traditionally never go in the water until the May long weekend, and receiving huge applause from several of our friends who had been hiding behind trees to see if we would actually do it!

ACT SEVEN

Resorts (East & West)
Cruising: "The Love Boat"
A Bermuda Wedding
Canadian Hunger Foundation concerts
Earth Day Festival (Canada's number one!)
The Kenya Project

Jasper Park Lodge

Banff Springs Hotel

RESORTS (EAST & WEST)
BANFF PARK LODGE

We started performing at the big resort venues in the Rockies by the end of '79, with a month's run at the relatively new Banff Park Lodge. A very different place to work, the performance area was half a flight up, with the musicians backing onto the front desk, though with a frosted glass partition. This meant that the music could also be constantly heard in the lobby, of which one had to be aware at all times. It was a Christmas and New Year's run, and we had a large Christmas repertoire, which was of course welcoming for new arrivals checking in to celebrate the season.

If you are a musician, you not only remember someone's face; more importantly, you remember their music and how they played it. There were many residencies over the years at Banff Park Lodge, but one evening we were playing away, and a couple was checking in at the front desk. The husband said to his wife, "If I didn't know better, I would say that was Pete Jansen playing that guitar", because he of course could not see us through the glass partition. They came up into the lounge area, but I had grown a beard since we last saw each other, so he still wasn't sure, but I was. It was John, from London, of "Peter, Jan and Jon", with his wife "Bunches", (though I don't know if the nickname had stuck). We had a great catch up that evening, which continued over breakfast, after which they were on their way. It was amazing to see them both again after many years, and I will always remember John's fine bass work, plus of course we sang together in harmony for much of the act, the only time I ever did this, except with one of the "Allisons", whilst in Bermuda. Mary and I have of course harmonized over the years, but harmonizing with a female vocalist is in complete contrast to a male, as one automatically selects different parts and range to create an appropriate mix.

Talking of bassists, I have been so fortunate to have worked with some incredibly creative ones in earlier combo situations, who have charged my batteries for life. Paul Rodriguez, with the "Jazz Gentlemen" and the "Travellers", John Watson, with the "Manish Boys", John Edwards, with "Peter, Jan and Jon", Steve Sutherland, with "Westminster City Sound", and Neil Carter, with Bryan Bridge's band in Germany. Incidentally, during this time Neil and myself, together with drummer Denny Lofthouse, would most evenings do a trio segment, in totally different tempos and often keys to each other, but still musically related, which flew all over the place with constantly changing improvisations, then suddenly came together with three very tight choruses at the end. The U.S. servicemen absolutely loved it, and it was never remotely the same twice. How I wish one or two of those sessions had been recorded.

Whilst living in London, I used to on occasion pop into Ronnie Scott's world-famous jazz club, where I sometimes saw vocalist Sheila Jordan, who worked, (and still does), solely with a double bassist. She was right, as nothing else is needed. For many years, Mary and I did a jazz version of "Your Cheatin' Heart". With her vocals and me on bass it was a joy to play, with a full sound, yet the music was still able to breathe, which is so important, and often neglected.

JASPER PARK LODGE

Canada has many old-style truly Grand Hotels all over the country, mostly built between 1890 and 1920 by the various railroads: Canadian Pacific, Canadian National, Grand Trunk Pacific, and Canadian Northern, all of whom wanted their passengers to have total luxury at every major destination, no matter where that might be. There were also lodge style resort hotels, with equally luxurious cabins, at Jasper, in the Rockies, and Minaki, near Kenora, in Northern Ontario, to name just two, both of which we were to see many times. The entertainment for Jasper Park Lodge was booked by Studio City, through whom we worked with Carol Duke. Another agent, who worked alongside her, had the resort contract for the lodge, Margie Zahn, and we soon started with the first of many runs at this palatial mountain hideaway, which became almost a second home to us over the years.

For so many reasons. There was a brilliant in-house jazz pianist, originally from Chicago, Nate Strong, who would work the winter season in the huge Beauvert dining room, overlooking the lake, with the addition of bass and drums, then move as a solo to the downstairs steakhouse, when José Poneira, a more general pianist but also very fine, from Winnipeg, came in for the summer run. José used to have his own T.V. show, and now worked the rest of the year at the venerable Hotel Fort Garry, in Winnipeg, where he had a home with his wife, Gladys; in her younger years a Radio City Rockette in New York. There was also an Austrian zither player, Werner Frey, who came in for much of the summer with Maria, his wife, and they lived in a 60s style VW Campervan, parked just outside J block, which was hotel accommodation where the rest of us lived, separately, but as a musical family, with the occasional tour director from a bus company passing through for a night or two.

We were in another dining room, "The Moose's Nook", usually for a month at a time, for up to three times a year. This had a huge salad bar, a huge dessert bar, and entrées were ordered individually, prepared by an excellent Austrian chef. There are so many stories of Jasper Park Lodge. Nate always took his van from J block to the main lodge every day, both for the evening's performance, and for his meals throughout the day, on the grounds that "There might be a bear out there, Doll", as he would say to Mary regularly. Sometimes it was possible to approach the door from the outside, and Nate would be standing inside the screen door in his tuxedo looking for bears before coming out. His tux was as black as he was, and only the whites of his eyes, plus possibly his shirt collar, would tell you that he was on the other side. A beautiful person and top-class musician; we kept in touch for the rest of his life. With José it always made us laugh that he would say "I want to officially welcome you to Jasper Park Lodge", once the Beauvert dining room was full. Even if guests had been greeted by the CEO of what was then still a CN resort, it was always José's greeting that truly mattered. He was a good chess player who could quickly wipe me out; I won on one occasion, but I think he was just being kind.

Thinking of Nate and the bears reminds me of an earlier time when we were in residency at Jasper's Marmot Lodge. After work we sometimes went for a 2:00 a.m. swim in the indoor swimming pool, along with the maintenance man and a couple of other staff members. One night, I had taken the instruments back to our suite, and was heading for a swim, when I saw that I was being followed by a large black bear. I slightly increased my speed; so did the bear. I reached the glass pool door, and was banging on it to be let in, receiving waves from Mary and the others in the water, who were unaware that I was in somewhat of a hurry, but fortunately, the door was eventually opened.

Another time, I was finishing the "load up" before we moved town, with Ben our dog already in the back seat, when a bear appeared a little way from the truck. Ben leaped over my shoulder, and ran out towards the bear, barking his head off. The bear reared up on his hind legs, (which I now know means to get a better view), then ran off up the hill - known as Bear Hill, for obvious reasons - with huge applause from a busload of seniors who were just pulling out, and an even bigger gasp of relief from me, when Ben returned, unscathed and smiling, a tad sheepishly, as only he could.

Mary fortunately saw none of this, which was the only time in his life that Ben felt he needed to be protective, as he would normally never chase anything, even a rabbit he would sit and quietly watch, then gently walk away.

We had a home in New Brunswick from '81 to '86 with some amazing neighbours, Jan and Fred Phillips, and their two daughters, Shelley and Beth. I say amazing, because they made us feel we were all part of the same family, and we would do anything for each other. Bears coming onto the property from the woods were not unusual, and I remember so well Jan coming over one day, somewhat flustered, to announce that there was a bear in her kitchen.

Returning to the lodge, the "Moose's Nook" was a good room for us. Full most of the time, we became very adept at turning the dining room around if one sitting stayed on for a bit too long, a skill we had previously not known even existed. If the maître'd approached us with a request to change the clientele, we would up the tempo for a couple, then play something really slow to make people feel tired, whatever it took to get the room ready for the next sitting, without anyone being aware that there had been manipulation involved. I still find it scary that we were able to do this. If really stuck, a version of "Rolling in my sweet baby's arms", still at dining room volume, but accelerating to breakneck speed, seemed to work, there would be a room full of empty plates, but this was truly a last resort!

There was quite a varied clientele, as in any resort dining room, including a Mr. Jakobs that we knew well, who owned "Bic"; (pens, razors etc.) The waiters never gave him a menu; he asked for what he wanted, and it appeared. He quite often had requests for us, and we could usually accommodate him. On the subject of requests, one night a waiter came up with a request for "I only have eyes for you", which we hadn't done before, but I had a copy in our cabin, which I could get during intermission, and was sure we could fake adequately.

Then the little light went on. At our next break, I got 4 empty tumblers from the bar, and put 2 ice cubes in one of them, which I gave to the lady who had requested the song, with an empty glass to each of the 3 others, and a promise that I could get the sheet music if needed. It took a few seconds, then there was a roar of laughter from the table, and I seem to remember her putting the 4 glasses together and taking a picture. No, we never did play the song; she said this was so much better.

We really needed some Japanese songs, to accommodate the huge influx of tourists during that era. One night we were chatting with a lady who introduced herself as the Japanese editor of "Cosmopolitan" magazine, who also sang with a band in Tokyo. I asked her if she had any songs that could be easily learned by uninitiated Western ears in phonetic style. We always had a recording system hooked into our p.a., so putting it down was not a problem. The following night, at the end of our evening, she came on stage after the customers had left, and sang three songs a cappella, since I could work out some suitable backing later. Then I got her to say the words to each song slowly, so we could get the pronunciation right. Some weeks later, we were working the Rob Roy room at the prestigious Banff Springs Hotel, and on our first night we had a full house, and only one table not Japanese. I pulled out the recording and worked like crazy the next day getting a couple of them down, with the help of a couple of Japanese staff members. We introduced the new material that night, to a huge response, and everyone singing with us. The only difference was that they knew what they were singing about, whilst we, to this day, had no clue.

Jasper Park Lodge had some amazing accommodation, which, while still log cabins and therefore somewhat rustic, were definitely 5-star. A personal chef would come in to prepare meals, or waiters, absolutely anything that could be needed. There were many rooms, especially in "Point" and "Outlook" cabins, which could easily be made secure from the rest of the resort. King George VI and Queen Elizabeth the Queen Mother stayed there, as have Queen Elizabeth, Prince Philip and other royals, who have been either on honeymoon, or just having a quiet getaway.

Also, several celebrities, with security keeping an unobtrusive, yet watchful eye on their little corner of paradise. Room service at the lodge was always done by bicycle, with trays held high, a nice touch, which continues to this day, when weather permits.

Jasper is different to Banff and Lake Louise in that it is not a resort town first, but a large marshalling yard for CN rail, and a major stop for the "Rocky Mountaineer". It therefore has a permanent community that is not tourism related, so the "feel" of the little town is completely different, and far less transient. Two of the locomotive engineers especially became very close friends. One of them, Gordon Willman, was a lover of all things guitar, and played in his earlier days, until a train coupling was reversed on to his hand, which immediately removed any skill he might once have had. He was a friend of Chet Atkins, who always sent him two copies of any recordings, one to play, one to keep sealed for posterity, and called his eldest son after him. Gordon used to appear at many places we played, not just in Jasper, and we always knew if he was in house by the distinctive smell of his pipe, which was definitely a "one off". We are fortunate to still be in touch with his younger son, Russell, and remember Gordon so well.

Our other friend, Harry Home, was not only an engineer but a true locomotive buff, who could, (and did), strip a huge mountain class locomotive and completely rebuild it. Let me explain. Harry used to take long distance trains all over Canada, and was frequently through Winnipeg, where there was one of the very last of these beautiful behemoths sitting in a siding, slowly deteriorating. He haggled with CN rail for years, because he wanted to restore it, with the aid of a couple of friends, and they eventually sold it to him for a dollar, the condition being that he had to take it away. Harry and a friend, Ernie Ottowell, went up to Winnipeg, and worked on the locomotive for a couple of weeks, also arranging to get a diesel and tow it back to Jasper. Which they did, arriving in the night, and managing to come in under steam, having just disconnected the diesel.

They expected a quiet arrival, being nighttime, but the whole town was out to welcome the two men, and the locomotive - number 6060. I got Harry to sit down with me one day, some twelve years later, when it was fully restored by his dedicated team, to tell me the story from when it was first built, in October 1944. This became the basis for the song "Going back to Jasper", which was featured on one of our albums "Sweet Rocky Mountains", and got extensive radio play, especially in the Far East, including Malaysia. I wanted authentic whistle recordings of the 6060 going through the mountains, which Harry arranged, as I knew that if I used a generic train whistle on the song, this would be spotted instantly, and the song's credibility would be destroyed to all who really mattered.

I must include the fact that when Harry and his friends went to restore the 6060, all the mountain class plans had been destroyed by a fire in Montreal. Some parts they were able to get off the 6015 locomotive, which stands majestically in front of Jasper railroad station, but some were made by removing, and measuring, the old part, and replacing it from scratch, no mean feat!

Two good friends at the lodge were Sally and Eva, who were gardeners constantly beautifying the flower beds. Sally eventually bought the Shell garage in Jasper, which she ran for years, and sold many of our recordings, as did a couple of other gift shops in town. Especially popular was the "Sweet Rocky Mountains" album, recorded in Ottawa, which included musicians Ted Gerow (keys), Gilles "Satch" Rehaume (bass), both from the Carroll Baker band; plus Dave Dennison (engineer, button accordion, 5-string banjo and blues harp), and Gary "Spike" Spicer (steel guitar and dobro), both from the "Family Brown" band. Also there was Sam Henry (drums), Ralph Carlson, (guitar and help with production), not forgetting our friend from Halifax, Harvey Johnson, now residing in Ottawa, also on 5-string banjo.

All songs were originals from yours truly, and the sleeve photography was done by a Hollywood cinematographer, Ron Waller, whom we had got to know whilst doing a run at the Marmot Lodge. What fun we had putting it all together, with Mary on rhythm and me on lead, plus plectrum banjo. The album sold, and continues to sell, on Vinyl, Cassette, CD, and Vinyl again, charting in both Austria and Denmark, still with occasional radio play, so many years later.

A town of characters. One, who had a big black beard and looked like he lived under a tree, was called "Little John the Mountain Man" by all and sundry, and worked for Parks Canada. A nice chap, who, when he had some time off, would go gold panning in a favorite spot up North, known only to him, always coming back with an average of $460.00 per day. Bear in mind that this was in the early 80s, so at the time of writing about $1,700 on current gold prices; not a bad reward for a day enjoying yourself in the mountains. Little John has now left us, and took his secret location, and his so different, but likeable personality with him, but to us, he will never be forgotten.

By this time, we had our first dog, a small Labrador cross which we named Ben, who always had a big smile on his face, and was called "The laughing dog" in more than one venue. He was welcome in all of the grand resorts in which we worked, and the musicians, plus Sally and Eva, loved him. One day, he came nose to nose literally with a coyote outside the lodge, and they just stood for a bit, checking each other out, with no confrontation involved, a skill Ben had, having seen him nose to nose with an adult skunk on two different occasions, and once with a large bull elk bent down to touch his face. Only once did he get sprayed by a very young skunk, in Calgary, where we had great fun trying to clean the elevator we had used to get him back to our room, at 3:00 o'clock in the morning, and then filling the bath with the requisite tomato juice to complete the job, with nobody aware of what had happened.

When we first came to Canada and made friends with Cornelia MacLeod and her husband, Billy, who performed music on the Maritime circuit, she had her little poodle dog always close by, and I will never forget her saying that if it had been a hard night, which some venues were in those early days, you could go back to your room, and there was this little dog, (on whom you had probably checked several times throughout the evening), who was so pleased to see you, and instantly removed any stress you might be feeling. How incredibly right she was!

Sometimes, when a hotel manager changes location, he or she will bring an "in-house" musician with them. This happened with Jasper Park Lodge. José was losing his sight, and moved back to Winnipeg to just do weekends at the Fort Garry hotel, while Nate Strong was in bad health. The new manager was from the Maritimes, and brought Alan Fawcett, a fine pianist that we knew from the Keddy's hotel circuit, as house pianist for the Lodge, who stayed there for several years, followed by the accomplished Morley Fleming. We were doing less residencies at Jasper Park Lodge by now, though still a few special events, and were focusing more on the Canadian Pacific resorts of Chateau Lake Louise and Banff Springs, still in the magnificent Rocky Mountains, but further south.

CHATEAU LAKE LOUISE

The first time we saw the amazing vista that is Lake Louise, we were working at the Cascade Inn, one of Banff's oldest hotels, and had become friendly with a Brewster bus driver, Bill Lougheed, whose brother Peter was a very popular Premier of Alberta. Bill was to collect a party of skiers from the Lake Louise ski lifts and offered to run us to the lake and Chateau whilst up there. The spectacular view as we walked to the edge of the 2-1/2-mile-long lake was unbelievable in the bright sunshine, with the almost sheer face of Mt. Victoria, at 11,365 feet, making an awe-inspiring backdrop. A layer of pristine snow covered everything but the steepest slopes, with not a footprint to be seen, other than ours, and a few by the door of the Chateau, which was not in those days open during winter, and only had a small maintenance staff in residence.

The sight was breathtaking, especially so because there was not a soul to be seen anywhere, and total, complete, silence. We gazed at the huge Chateau and decided this was definitely to be the place for us, in the very near future.

It is possible that the first humans in the area were the Kootenay, coming through the Bow Valley up to 10,000 years ago, but the earliest documented evidence is of the Stoney people, a branch of the Sioux nation, who moved westwards through Blackfoot territory on the prairies and reached the Rockies in the early 1800s. They certainly knew of Lake Louise, which they called the "Lake of little fishes", sitting at an altitude of 5,680 feet. Geologist James Hector was the first non-indigenous person in the area, but the first to actually view the lake was Tom Wilson, on August 21st, 1882, who was taken there by Stoney Edwin (Gold seeker) Hunter; (his English name). The railroad came in

November of the following year, where there was a small construction community known as "Holt City", after the owner of the general store.

In the summer of 1884, the Lake was renamed Lake Louise after Queen Victoria's fourth daughter, and the community officially called "Laggan". A couple of basic cabins had been built by the lakeshore, but the first tourist accommodation was in the form of a small chalet, with two guest bedrooms, opened for the 1890 season; the same year as the first railway station opened in Laggan. The chalet burned down in '93 and was replaced, with an extra floor added a couple of years later. Gradual expansion over time by CPR architects Thomas Sorbey, and later, Francis Rattenbury, culminated in a large 3 and partially 4 story T-shaped mock Tudor building, which was constructed of wood to blend in with the surrounding forest, and completed in the year 1911. The CPR's chief architect, Walter Painter, already known for his work on the Banff Springs Hotel and Cave & Basin complex, added a five-storey wing, built of concrete, for the following season, with sliding metal fire screens to protect it from the rest of the building. Twelve years later, a fire in the kitchen of the staff quarters destroyed all but the Painter wing, which was saved by the fire screens. Over the winter of '24 – '25 a large 10-storey block, also by Painter, and blending with his earlier concrete wing, was constructed, and the hotel now became known as Chateau Lake Louise, rather than Chalet. There were 386 bedrooms, and it was this configuration of the hotel that we first saw when visiting with Bill Lougheed, and where we subsequently performed several times, living either in the Chateau, or in the "Hillside" staff block, with Ben the dog of course, a short walk up from the main building.

Our first two or three visits to the Chateau were for runs in the Glacier lounge, entertaining both guests and staff, but a change of Food & Beverage manager brought us into the dining areas. One Christmas we were coming in for a five-week residency. There had been heavy snow over much of Alberta, and the roads were all closed for our intended travel day, so we waited with bated breath, and several calls to the R.C.M.P. (Mounties) for news that there had been sufficient clearance for us to get through. Which there eventually was, early the next morning, so we arrived, somewhat exhausted after the long snowy drive, in time to join in a very welcoming staff Christmas Eve dinner, which was being served by the management. What an amazing touch; so very much appreciated, and never seen anywhere before or since. We started off with a few nights in the Tom Wilson dining room, on the top floor of the Painter wing, then moved to the larger Edelweiss for New Year's Eve, before settling into a January run in the positively huge Victoria dining room, which we loved.

That five-week run at the Chateau was very special for us, as when at Jasper Park Lodge, because there were other musicians, and like-minded friends, to bounce off occasionally in our "down" time, which makes such a huge difference to the lives of constantly touring performing artists. In the case of Lake Louise, this was usually in the form of a nightly "get together", when we had all finished our various evening's work in different parts of the hotel. On this particular visit we were staying in the Chateau itself, with a room overlooking the lake, so Ben was able to be a part of the "family", once he had been out for his nightly walk in our magical surroundings, where the lakeside fir trees were festooned with hundreds of lights, and hockey games would appear spontaneously on the cleared skating rink in front of the ice castle, which was lit by a spotlight high on the hotel roof. Everywhere else there was deep, deep snow.

Each night we would take our instruments back to the room, where there would be great excitement from Ben, who knew that this meant we would be going outside together. By the time we reached the lakeside, Jon Frolick, drummer/leader of "Cornerpocket", in the Victoria Dining Room, would be out on the ice, as would George Tutt, (nicknamed "King Tut"), who had the bookshop in the Chateau, as he does to this day. The two of them would play some high energy hockey, then come back indoors to join the gathering. "Cornerpocket" was a fine band; the lineup we knew best, apart from Jon, was Ian Clayton, (alto and other saxes, plus flute), who will always be remembered for the slowest and most reverential bow in the history of Planet Earth, should there have been applause to a song from the diners; Karen Crowe, (vocalist), and Bob Kitt, (who was keyboardist at this time). For special events Jon would sometimes augment with brass, to make a very full sounding front line. In the "Cascade" lounge, there was also Suzanne Morley, a very popular vocalist/pianist, who would be married to Jon in '94. They have a beautiful home in Canmore, just outside the National Park gates, but decidedly still in the Rockies, where the "Three Sisters" mountains keep a watchful eye over the community, and we are so pleased to have kept in touch over the years. To complete our little gathering, there was "Artist in Residence" Samara Carrier, who had her studio in the hotel, and could be seen at all hours, painting pictures of the lake, some huge, in different lights and moods, or of wolves, which were a favourite. In the daytime there was in addition Irish harpist Jacqueline Dolan, who performed in the main area overlooking the lake, with its spectacular view. So much music, and it was so special to be a part of that era.

It was New Year's Eve, or more correctly, early morning on New Year's Day. We had all finished our respective performances, and were gathered together, still full of energy from the previous night, and discussing everything one could possibly imagine. The conversation somehow got around to comedy, and Jon Frolick was talking about Monty Python's "The Meaning of Life", especially the hilarious Protestant/Catholic segment, at which point somebody asked where the name "John Thomas" originated. Being a Brit., I knew that the "Daily Telegraph" in London had an information line in those days, for anything you could possibly wish to ask, so we all decided to call the London office, and start their New Year with this question. When the staff had finished rolling around the floor laughing, they said they would call back, which they did a few minutes later, with the news that the name referred to a church minister called John Thomas Bond, who possibly had visited the female members of his parish a little more than he should. A great response, but we were all a little suspicious; I think the use of the name "Bond" suggested that all could be fiction, nevertheless, a great way to start the New Year.

The Victoria Dining Room was an amazing place to play. Full of light from the huge windows by day, and the many bulbs in the polished chandeliers by night, it was truly a sight to behold, with its perfectly set tables and glistening silverware. There had always been special attention to this, the main ballroom for special events, going back to the previous building, when a hydro-electric plant had been built back in 1914, some 3000 feet down the mountain, to provide additional power for refrigeration, the elevator, and of course, the ballroom.

Constantly busy, with visitors from all over the world, it gave us a chance to play a huge variety of music, in many languages and styles, which we have always loved. Talking of languages, Mary has always been very adept at picking up other voices and accents, sometimes subconsciously. On one occasion in the "Vic", we had just come off break, where she had been visiting with a couple from Adelaide, Australia, which has a very distinctive accent all its own. Her songs for the next 50 minutes were sung with a strong Australian accent, a sound I will never forget.

That particular winter, ('87–'88), saw the construction of the Glacier wing, which was an unbelievable sight. Every Monday morning, the parking lot outside the main entrance was completely dug up to huge depths, where large piping was being installed for heating and other necessities for the new block. Late Thursday or early Friday it would all be filled in again, so that the main entrance was perfect for the arrival of weekend visitors. Ivor Petrak, manager of the Banff Springs Hotel, and

Lake Louise from the Chateau

Chateau Lake Louise

Western Canada manager of CP hotels was constantly adamant that, no matter what it cost, standards must always be kept up, and that it would pay off, time and again. How right he was!

The Glacier wing was completed, and in 2004, the separate Mount Temple wing was also completed, giving the Chateau a total of 539 bedrooms. Musician Neil Gow, who had played in all the main Rockies resorts with his band "The Five Knights" for many years, now based for the summer, dressed in Tyrolean style, on the banks of Lake Louise with a large Alpine horn, whose sound would echo up the valley.

Jacqueline Dolan had long moved on, her place as harpist being taken by Deborah Nyack, whose virtuoso playing, and spectacular costumes have become so much a part of visits to Banff or Lake Louise. Another special friend with whom we always hope to keep in contact!

THE BANFF SPRINGS

The Banff Springs Hotel opened in 1888, but not as the huge baronial Scottish castle we see today. The original, as with all the resort hotels, was mostly of wood, and architect Bruce Price sadly neglected to put in a North point on the plan. When William Van Horne, general manager of the Canadian Pacific Railway, came to inspect the property, he discovered that the huge building had been constructed back to front, with the kitchens facing a prime view of the Bow Valley and the distant range of the Fairholme Mountains. Never being one to give up, he grabbed a piece of paper and quickly sketched a rotunda to be built in front of the kitchens, thus saving the priceless view.

House orchestra at the Banff Springs when we first visited was that of Louis Trono, who played for many of his 95 years in the Rob Roy room, where we played later on occasion before it ceased to be an entertainment venue. Born in Bankhead to a family of Italian miners, Louis bought a mail order trombone in 1923 and it became his career. We had the privilege of knowing him, and there is a Gazebo in the park, down by the Bow River, honouring his contribution to music and the arts in Banff, with a special concert every year in his name. Pretty much all the musicians we knew from Chateau Lake Louise also played the "Springs", the only exception being the fine pianist Peter Bertelsen, who has remained solely at the Banff Springs Hotel for many years. We always stayed "in house" at the Springs, recalling one time when our bed shared a wall with the bakery, which started being unbelievably noisy well before 5 each morning, (not nice), with what felt like trollies crashing into the wall a few inches from our heads. Then came the smell of fresh bread and croissants under the door, (better), followed by the sound of bakery carts rushing past our door as they were wheeled off to different parts of the building. We moved the bed away from the wall, which helped a little, and tried to change rooms, but it was a full house, so we had to grin and bear it, sometimes catching up on sleep in the day. Life is not always easy!

FAIRMONT HOT SPRINGS

The other major Rockies resort in which we performed regularly over several years was that of Fairmont Hot Springs, in the Columbia Valley, on the western side of the Rockies. The valley was first inhabited by Kootenay and subsequently Sushwap First Nations people, going back over 7,000 years, with indications of indigenous habitation still in the area. This included bathtubs carved in the rock, which had been created by deposits from the hot mineral springs, and signs of early dwellings, together with many artifacts. The first commercial pool was built in 1923, with a restaurant nearby, which some years later was moved on logs to a different site, and became the beginning of accommodation, (apart from tents), for the resort. By the time we were there, the property was in the hands of the Wilder family, Lloyd and Ward, nice people, with their daughter Carol managing. We initially would work the resort lounge for 2 or 3 week runs, with the excellent Norman Swain on piano, resident in the dining room next door. The golf clubhouse at the time was on Mountainside course, where Hans and Lauren Harb would come in for the main season, and they quickly became good friends.

Hans was Austrian by birth, and his approach to the evening, together with a plethora of instruments, from Tuba to Glockenspiel, perfectly fitted the Austro-German approach one sees throughout the valley. He billed himself, appropriately, as "Happy Hans", and the four of us would usually get together for camaraderie and many laughs when the day's music was done. Sometimes we would be in the clubhouse for a part of the season, when Caribbean-style performer Aubrey Skyers would be brought into the lounge, thus making a complete contrast. We had an apartment in the staff block, as did Hans and Lauren, and enjoyed both the golf course, plus the huge pools, when not exploring with Ben. After a year or two, Hans and Lauren moved permanently to the Banff Springs, so we took over much of the clubhouse season, going into the main dining room for one Christmas.

A very strange thing that happened for a short time, was that the maintenance man was one day playing a few chords and generally running around the piano keyboard when the dining room was closed. Norman Swain was away at the time, so the maintenance man was asked if he would like to play the evenings, which he eagerly accepted. The amazing thing was, that when he came out, he did exactly the same as when the room was empty; a few chords and generally running around the keyboard, to the amazement of the diners. At no time was there any suggestion of melody, or recognizable tune of any kind. Musically, there was absolutely nothing wrong with it, and I suppose it maybe even created a mood of some form, should you ever get over being totally puzzled by the whole endeavour!

MINAKI LODGE

There were two major resorts that we used to work when living in Noonan, by Fredericton, in the 1980s. One of these was Minaki lodge in Northern Ontario, close to Kenora, but decidedly in the "wilds". The original lodge had burned to the ground literally the day before the June 1925 grand opening, but was reconstructed and opened 2 years later. Based on the successful Jasper Park Lodge, it was yet another wooden structure, with a huge Rotunda, and luxurious log cabins all around the property. It belonged to CN until 1974, when the Ontario government took over Minaki, which was constantly plagued by difficulties. Nine years later it re-opened, with additional modern accommodation, and was being managed by Radisson Hotels for a couple of years. This was the period where we used to stay there, usually for a month at a time, playing in the main lodge, with its "log cabin" atmosphere, and business, while we were there at least, seemed to be fine.

One time we were in the resort for Mother's Day. It was our day off, and we had an emergency phone call for help from the manager. It seemed that a new member of staff had been put as hostess, also taking reservations, in the main dining room, where there was a huge buffet running for much of the day. Without realizing what she was doing, she had booked the entire room for - say 12 noon - then much of it again for 12:15 p.m., and so on. The place was packed, so we went into the lounge for as long as it took; there was a complimentary bar and hors d'oeuvres, and we managed to help rectify the situation. The hostess was appalled at what she had done, and certain to be dismissed, but the manager, with whom we got along really well, took her on one side, and assumed full responsibility for the whole fiasco, on the grounds that she should not have been put in that position without proper training. Every so often one meets somebody with true class, as this gentleman had, and I hope life has treated him kindly.

We loved Minaki, as did Ben, with miles of wilderness to explore, and a huge lake, with the sound of loons echoing across the water. It was so sad when the main lodge burned down in 2003, as had the wooden Jasper Park Lodge main building 50 years earlier. The difference being that in Jasper a new lodge was constructed by the following season, while Minaki stays empty to this day. It is maybe too far in the wilderness for some tourists, also pulp mills have caused some leaching of mercury into the lake, poisoning the area's fish. But it was a special place to us, remembering mostly a Thanksgiving weekend, where we, plus the dining room pianist and a couple of other musicians brought in by him, played together in the huge Rotunda to a packed assembly, and had such a memorable evening.

THE ALGONQUIN

The other resort, much closer to home, was the Algonquin, in Saint Andrews-by-the-sea, New Brunswick. Currently owned by the province, it was the flagship hotel of the area, and managed for them by Canadian Pacific, (who added "by-the-sea" to all of their publicity). The first hotel, again of wood, had an observation tower that could be seen for 75 miles along the shoreline. Opened in 1889 to much fanfare, the Algonquin was immediately popular with a high end clientele from both sides of the border. In 1914 the seemingly inevitable happened, and the roof caught fire while tar was being applied. The hotel had gas lighting throughout, which may have been a contributing factor, as the building was gone in half an hour. Despite wartime austerity, a new building was opened the following year, which was where we played residency engagements so many times, until our move westward, with the three of us loving swimming together in the salt waters of Katy's cove. The small community of Saint Andrews, especially in summer, has to be one of the most beautiful places on the North American continent, in fact "U.S.A. Today" once named it the "Best place to visit in Canada". The town was founded by United Empire Loyalists fleeing the American Revolution in 1783, with many of their homes being dismantled and brought up by boat or barge to this idyllic spot, Canada's first seaside resort, which was designated a National Historic Site in 1998. We played the library lounge, with softer music, also "Sir William's", downstairs, with a much higher energy show for one summer, when we brought in a musical university student named George as a more than competent drummer.

The veranda part of the main restaurant, with its incredible views, has to be one of our very favourite places. The summery feel, instigated by Kate Reed in 1915, who did so much for CP hotels, had been maintained, with wicker furniture and flowery designs for a perfect ambience. As with all resorts, we either had "carte blanche" in the restaurants, or there was a staff dining room, usually called "the bean",

"the zoo", or some such, with a duty meal of one's choice attached to each session of music. Sometimes we would have Mary's mother, Lillian, travelling with us on an extended visit from the U.K. of six months to a year. Naturally her meals were not provided, and we did sometimes speculate that it would be cheaper for the three of us to go out locally for a meal, or a bag of chips together, but this rarely, if ever, happened. All the places we worked were not of this standard, and we had enough meals "on the road" to relish the quality of a high end resort whenever the situation could possibly arise. Not only that, but it was a huge treat for us to be able to share with Lillian the best that we could. We booked as many places of this level as possible, and gradually managed to weed out the less desirable ones, which could be a bit challenging!

When at our home near Fredericton, not too far from Saint Andrews, we used to appear regularly at the Oromocto Hotel, which was close to C.F.B. Gagetown, whenever we had a free Sunday, for Roy and Manuela deStecher, who owned the place. Mrs. deStecher, from Vienna, was a first-class chef, who used to put little bowls of assorted nibblies on each table, all smothered with her own secret recipe spicing, guaranteed to keep you drinking all afternoon. When Roy passed, she would sometimes go back to Vienna, book into the main hotel with a multi-bedroom suite, call all her friends and say "I'm here"; the point being, that if they really cared, they would make the effort and come for a visit. Many times on our travels, we have thought of Manuela, and that she possibly had the right idea.

We had a friend on the circuit, Albert Gatto, keyboardist/vocalist, who was the only performer we knew at the time who travelled in a small aircraft, which had room for his keyboard, stool, a small p.a. system, and a suitcase. He wanted to visit the beavers who were on our L.P. sleeve, and asked for directions to drive there, which we of course gave him, in our best English vernacular. We told him the route, then, at an intersection where the road split into two, told him to "Fork off to the left". There was another of these, when we said to "Fork off to the right", by which time he was virtually rolling on the floor in uncontrollable mirth. To cut things short, this became part of a private "culture" between the three of us, and any time we were passing through a town and saw his name on a marquee sign, we would pop in quickly and leave a fork from the dining room on his keyboard, as he did with us for several years, so that we could keep tabs on each other with such busy schedules.

Close to the Oromocto Hotel, and right by the gates to C.F.B. Gagetown, was a pub called the "Down Homer". There was a bunch of young men from both sides of the Atlantic on commando training, and eager to prove their manhood, which it seems could only be done by going into the "Down Homer", which was off base, and smashing up as many people and as much furniture as possible. Into which we were booked, knowing nothing about it. There had been large rock bands previously, but the owners had decided to cut down to a duo, hoping that this would make the clientele less aggressive. And, of course, the first duo on this experiment was "Peter & Mary". We soon established that the experiment had failed, with glasses, bottles, and furniture flying everywhere. Mary was out of the room, but I was really concerned for our equipment, and asked the proprietor if he would pay for horns if necessary, should I turn the p.a. up to feedback levels. Which I did, stopping the fight almost immediately, with people blocking their ears and getting out of the building as fast as they could. Shortly after this event, the proprietor, Kevin Murphy, a nice man from Ireland, sold his share of the business, after an elderly lady tapped him on the shoulder one lunchtime, when all was normal, and he had instinctively reacted by throwing her over his back onto the floor in a "Half Nelson". Fortunately, she was unharmed, if a little shaken, but he was appalled, realizing what the business was doing to him, and was out of there in no time flat, making this quite the worst place in which we ever worked!

NEWFOUNDLAND

It was at the end of the first week in March. We'd just finished a run for the Keddy's hotel chain, at their venue in Dartmouth, Nova Scotia, with a Saturday matinée, and an evening show until 1 a.m. After which we packed, and loaded all our instruments and equipment, in addition to moving out of the hotel, which was a big job. We had no choice but to drive through the night to North Sydney, where we would catch the 11:00 a.m. Newfoundland ferry, as the one we had booked for later had been cancelled.

So, at 4 a.m., we set off on the road, four weary travellers; the two of us, who had played for seven hours and packed the equipment, plus Mary's mother and Ben. There was no alternative, but we had plenty of time.

My new short winter jacket had been stolen from a coat rack during Saturday night's supper, so I would have to manage without a coat, but philosophically thought that spring was on the way. It was normally a 6-hour crossing to Port-Aux-Basques, but this crossing took nine hours, much of which time the ferry, which was also an icebreaker, would go forward, back up a little, and then forward again, to get through the ice, but we arrived unscathed.

David & Nina Burns, our friends from Bermuda, had gone their separate ways. We were still in close touch with both of them, and were to see David, who was working in Port-Aux-Basques with his new trio "Copperwood", which included Mitzi MacDonald on keys and vocals, plus Fonna on drums. We were due to follow them into this venue for our second week, and met for supper, when we found there were some issues relating to the engagement, so stayed over with them to try and sort things on the Monday morning. Lillian had the bed, while the rest of us spread out on chairs, an old settee, and the floor, before driving to Corner Brook for that night's performance.

Road conditions in Newfoundland were decidedly different to those in Halifax/Dartmouth two days earlier, where spring flowers were starting to bloom. Here, it was snowing steadily, there were big snowbanks at the roadside, and it was decidedly icy, so we were taking it easy.

Just by Robertson's, there is an area known as "Wreckhouse", where a very powerful wind can suddenly hurl down between the mountains, and may literally blow a locomotive off the tracks, which has happened on occasion. We knew nothing of this, but were to find out very shortly, when we were suddenly whisked off the icy road with great force, rolling 2-1/2 times before coming to rest upside down in the deep snow.

I can still see that roll, in very slow motion, such as one sees in so many movies, but did not realize that this could take place in real life, until this moment. The windows and windshield were all gone, and we were upside down in our seatbelts, excepting Ben, who was wandering around in the snow outside, and wondering what had happened.

There was a total silence; then we started checking that everybody was all right, at which point Mary's mother, realizing she was upside down, started shouting to be released from her seat belt, which was instantly done.

I had always packed equipment so that nothing could move, also with a clothes bag up each side of the truck, and one across the back. This day it paid off, and none of the truck contents, including us, appeared to be damaged in any way. There was no traffic, but eventually a car came, and the driver called on his C.B. radio for a tow truck and ambulance, both of which came shortly. Newfoundlanders are some of the warmest people on Earth, and two very uncharacteristic things happened. The ambulance arrived first, as we wanted Lillian to be checked over, as a result of the "plop" onto the roof! The driver agreed to take her to the nearest hospital in Stephenville, but only with cash up front, which we couldn't believe. We managed to produce the required amount, and Mary, together with her mum, headed off in the ambulance up the snowy highway, leaving me standing alongside the truck with Ben, wearing just a sweater, and awaiting the tow truck.

Which arrived, after what felt like a long time, and the driver said he would soon flip the Suburban and we'd be on our way. I was concerned about more possible damage to instruments etc., at which point the driver said he would wait while I removed everything, he would flip the truck, then I could repack, and no, he didn't assist, just watched me in my snow-covered sweater, while he sat in his nicely heated truck. In retrospect, this could have had something to do with insurance, but I still couldn't believe his attitude, and nor could the police, who came as I was repacking.

The tow truck took Ben and me to Stephenville, with our loaded vehicle behind. Mary's mum was fine, and we found a dog-friendly hotel, immediately contacting the Corner Brook venue where we were supposed to be performing that night. The owner was, of course, not happy to miss a night's entertainment, but said he would collect us on the following day, which he did, in a somewhat smaller vehicle, but we somehow got everything on board. All four of us were fine, if a little shaken, and we managed to get through the week, using taxis to get to and from the provided apartment.

We rented the largest vehicle we could find, which was a station wagon, and headed back to Port-Aux-Basques, speakers on the roof rack, to the apartment where we had stayed overnight a week earlier with "Copperwood". There was one other permanent resident, who had a room near the front door, and was separate to us. This man worked in the fish plant, and hung his coveralls just inside the doorway, creating the most unbelievable smell when one went in from the outside world. Not only that, but the house was on rocks, and with the depth of snow, it was actually necessary to slide Mary's mum, who was not a small person, down the icy rocks to reach the door on our first arrival, which must have been quite a sight for the locals.

But we made it through the week and headed back to Stephenville for a run at the "Lorelei" lounge. Our truck could possibly have been fixed on the mainland, but not in Newfoundland, and was sadly a write-off. We found a similar half-ton Suburban, the previous one having been three-quarter, which was adequate, if a little pricey. Fred, our next-door neighbour in New Brunswick, on whom we could always rely, checked prices at home, and even offered to meet us at the ferry, but when we looked at the hassles involved with another rental, plus unloading everything somehow onto the ferry and off again, we decided it was worth paying that bit extra.

Back on the ferry to North Sydney, where we were lucky enough to run into "Copperwood", also on their home journey, and we all had a good catchup on our experiences, plus a meal together in Sydney, before the 650 km drive to our house near Fredericton.

There was a huge welcome from Jan, Fred, Shelley, and Beth when we got home, as always, but somehow this one stood out as being a little more poignant, and Ben had a really good bark at the trees to tell all and sundry that he was back!!

So many years later, I think of Madame Astra, on the Isle of Wight, and her warning, wondering what she actually saw.

FREDERICTON

We loved our home in the woods near Fredericton, and worked from it as much as possible, especially when Mary's mother was over on an extended stay. Ben loved it too, and would lie at the end of the driveway watching for action many hours of the day. Sometimes he would head to the other end of the subdivision to visit with Max, who lived with a family down by the mailboxes. We would see him heading off, knowing exactly where he was going, and always imagined him carrying a stick, with all his possessions in a red and white spotted handkerchief, tied to the top. There was also a tame red squirrel who lived in the fir trees behind our house. We gave him nuts, and should we come home early in the morning from a show some distance away and be sleeping in, he would swing on the chain connected to the storm door, holding on to the chain with his front paws, and knocking the glass with the other two, as a gentle reminder that it was past breakfast time. On occasion Ben would come out, and the squirrel would run to the trees, pursued by Ben, who would lie under his tree, waiting. Often Ben would doze off on a hot day, and the squirrel would quietly get a small pine cone, move directly above his head, and drop the pine cone, then explode in mirth at Ben's reaction. We could watch the two of them for hours, and sometimes did.

Ben was as gentle as any dog I have ever known. On one occasion he was eating his meal, and a stray cat came in at the back door, usually open, looking hungry. Ben quietly backed away from his food, allowing the cat to eat, then, after a short time, went back and joined in at the same bowl. We used to get deer on the front lawn, and at one time had a woodchuck visit in the back for a few days, but, while a little shy, none of them ever felt threatened.

Canadian Pacific also had several hotels across the country that went under the name "Red Oak Inn". They were nothing like the grand old hotels of yesteryear, but once in the door, facilities were very similar. We regularly did one at Peterborough, Ontario, when headed east or west, usually for a two or three week stopover. One year, we were there on a run when the World Snowmobile Championship awards were being held at the hotel, as they were every year. The hotel was built as a large square, and we were surprised to see all the lamp shades and some carpeting being removed before the event, when the hotel would be closed to other members of the public. When we heard a snowmobile roaring past our bedroom door in the night, we understood the removal of anything of value, and learned that the hotel tolerated it because of the immense T.V. publicity generated. Plus, all damage was paid for by the organisation, so it was obviously worth it. Early one morning there was a knock on the door, which we opened, to see that some convention-eers had mounted a brand new toilet pedestal on a luggage cart, filled it with vodka and orange, plus a couple of bratwurst sausages for good measure, and were going around the hotel at around 5:30 a.m. asking if anyone would like a drink! Those were the days!!

One of the managers of this hotel, who became a friend over the years, was one day discussing resorts with me, not only CP, but others in different parts of the globe. He gave me one of the huge world-wide hotel indexes put out by Murdoch Magazines, in case this would be helpful, which it was. Every so often, we would send a letter and promo. kit to various resorts, mostly Canada, the U.S., and Europe, that seemed interesting for our kind of work, and decided to do this again when home in Fredericton. We sent off maybe a dozen or more and had an immediate reply from Harrison Hot Springs resort, near Chilliwack,

British Columbia, with an offer to be discussed as soon as possible, and included in our next tour west.

One of our regular cross-country stops was at the Water Tower Inn, a good property in Sault Ste. Marie, at the junction of Lakes Huron and Superior, again usually for two or three weeks. The main dining room was built as an old mill, with wheels and belts constantly in motion on the walls, while the lounge had a very different extraction system, all coming through the same vents. There would be heat, right above our heads, onstage, so that it was hard to keep instruments in tune, followed by the extraction of possible smoke, with cooling at the same time. Since it blew hot and cold all day and night, the staff had long ago christened it "The Menopause Machine".

Across the prairies, we would sometimes stop in a small town, just for a week, and for the totally different feel of playing in a small community. Places like Melita, Manitoba, and Shaunavon, Saskatchewan, spring to mind, and I am so glad we did them. We often did a tour leaving Fredericton in May, and returning just before Halloween, usually stopping off at Lakehead University, in Thunder Bay, for a truly wild students "pub" night, one of which I recall had several of the participants "mooning" at one time, when the tables were all in a competition to see which one was best.

HARRISON HOT SPRINGS

Harrison Hot Springs has been known to the Salish First Nations for a long time, but the first hotel and bathhouse was not opened at the then named St. Alice Springs until 1886. A road cut through to the rail station at Agassiz greatly improved access, plus some families would come up the Harrison River by canoe and river steamer. Again, fire destroyed the hotel in 1920, but by 1926 what we now know as Harrison Hot Springs Resort had appeared on the lakeside, in which building we were to appear so many years later. "The Harrison", as it was called when we first performed there, had a different feel to all of the other resorts in which we worked, in that, despite being a large operation, it came over very much as a huge family, with many of the staff proudly wearing pins to show how long they had been there. The three lounge bartenders were all very popular, Mike and Tony from England, and Gerd from Austria, who could usually be prevailed upon to come and sing "Edelweiss" at some point of each evening.

Frequently, we would be called upon to do a cabaret spot, of about 20 minutes, in the main dining room, "The Copper Room", which had a permanent house band for dinner and dancing year round. Not only did this give the dinner guests a floorshow, it also encouraged them to go into the lounge later on, which was an entertainment venue, as opposed to a "background" room. Behind the hotel, there was an amazing walkway through the Pacific Rain Forest that grew naturally. A beautiful sight, but it also reminded you of the very changeable weather in the area. Nevertheless, Mary, Ben and I loved it, and would go through at least once a day.

It was a Tuesday I think, anyway the quietest night of our stay. The guests had either gone to bed or were lounging in the hot pools, and we were playing a few songs quietly in the empty room before closing.

Seven smartly dressed gentlemen came in, sat down close to us, and after a few minutes one of them asked if we knew "St. Louis Blues", which we of course instantly supplied. They asked us to join them and were talking about their day at Expo '86, in Vancouver, at which we were also performing. We asked how they had managed with the lineups, but they said that they had no lineups, then introduced themselves as the commanding officers for Army, Navy, and Air Force, in both Canada and the U.S., together with the U.S. Chief of Staff. In conversation, it was explained that they considered the world situation far too delicate to be trusted only to politicians, and that they got together maybe two or three times a year to discuss things, over a two-day break. I, for one, thought this was some of the best news in a long time, and we both slept well that night.

The following morning, I was up on the top floor of the new block, where a sumptuous buffet breakfast was served, when our friends from the night before came in, two of them in uniform. Probably about a third of the dining room instantly came to attention, and the U.S. officers were picked up by helicopter shortly after.

The "Harrison" when we first visited was in a time warp, which was undoubtedly its greatest attraction, along with the indoor and outdoor hot pools, also the magnificent main pool, with fir trees stretching skyward close at hand. Many of the staff lived in the little village, or in Agassiz, and an evening spent in the "Copper Room" took one totally into a different era, with a dance band playing the songs of yesteryear. Afternoon tea with cakes was served to guests on the main floor from a large Victorian Samovar, which was constantly replenished, and the atmosphere was one of refined gentility, yet with warmth and friendliness at the same time. Subsequently, the hotel changed hands, and Japanese style hot pools were installed on the property, which were lit in various colours from below the water, adding considerably to the night time ambience. We were accommodated in what was then called a "bungalow", which was in fact a luxurious cabin, and the two of us, plus Ben, were invited to stop over whenever in the area, which we gratefully accepted on several occasions. Moving instruments from the bungalow each night, we always used a side entrance by the "Copper Room", where we would frequently encounter two or three raccoons. We quickly learned to give them space, and of course made sure they were never close to Ben.

When we were first performing in Canada, especially in the Maritimes, people would constantly come up to the stage, and say how much Mary sounded like Marg Osborne, whom we didn't know. Marg was one of the vocalists, along with Charlie Chamberlain, on Don Messer's Jubilee, which in the 60s was the number one T.V. show in the country. We listened to one or two recordings, and could see a resemblance, but didn't really think about it until one night playing in a resort, when we were approached by a couple, John and Evalyne Ricketts. Evalyne was bowled over at the sound of Mary's voice, and introduced herself as a long time friend of Marg's, who would help her get ready for a performance, do her hair, and often sing some backup, though not on camera. Amazing the people one is fortunate enough to meet, and we kept in touch from then onwards.

Another time we were doing an 18-week run at the Mayfield Inn, in Edmonton, where Juliet Mills, John's daughter, was doing "Rattle of a Simple Man", in the dinner theatre, which was a part of the complex. She came in after her performance one night, and after that nearly every night, where we would reminisce about "show-biz" friends, and happenings in the U.K. We both remember seeing her father, playing Jess Oakroyd in a musical version of "The Good Companions", at my favourite London theatre, Her Majesty's, having forgotten that he was a "hoofer" in many of Noël Coward's productions years before, and being awestruck by his still amazing talent.

(Talking of dancers, we also met Cyd Charisse, star of so many Hollywood musicals, at the Mayfield some time later, when she was doing the title role in "Charley's Aunt", which, as Theatre aficionados know, is a relatively small role near the end; therefore, a good vehicle for a performer slowing down a little, for whatever reason).

We of course had Ben with us at the Mayfield, and always took him for a long walk, round about 2:00 a.m. every morning, when our instruments had been taken up to the room. There was a huge Caterpillar depot close by, with millions of dollars worth of machinery, and a guard dog who was probably bored out of his mind with nobody around. The two of us, together with Ben, would have to pass by the depot, and this guard dog would always wake up and slip under the wire fence, which appeared to reach the ground, so that he could join us on our walk. He liked Ben, and we'd have a good walk together, then he would slip back under the fence on our return. We called it his "union break".

At one time, we found a puppy that had been left, probably dumped, in the laundromat near the Mayfield. We took him with us, and advised the various agencies, together with one or two local radio stations, on the following day. Within a few days we had been contacted by a man who instantly fell in love with what was going to be a beautiful dog, and promised to give him a good home. He and his wife had a large sailboat and were preparing for a lengthy round the world cruise with their dog, now with "Puppy" as an added companion. A sky kennel was purchased, and he was in Victoria the next day. They wrote to us before they left, to let us know that he was already an indispensable part of the family and would be well looked after in the future. I have often thought about him, and hope his life was good.

"THE GRENADINES"

During the same run, the theatre production changed to another musical, "I love you, you're perfect, now change!" We met up with the show's drummer one night, who turned out to be Malcolm Page, once of the "Tremeloes", who was the high voice in "Silence is Golden". We became friends with him and his wife Pat, spending time with them on their 43' sailboat "Tainan" in the Caribbean, some years later. This was quite a trip. Malcolm and Pat had both been sailing instructors, running out of Duncan, on Vancouver Island, and had decided to join the world's "Yachties", living full-time on their boat in the Caribbean, which they did for several years. We had been invited to join them for a visit on more than one occasion, so at the beginning of '92, following a Christmas and New Year's run in Fairmont, we headed off to spend a week with them, plus a little break on our own, having arranged with a friend, who thought the world of Ben, to move into our home and make sure all was well. A few weeks prior, we had opened the huge hotel guide given to us at the Red Oak Inn, to see how best to connect. We decided to break the journey in Miami for a couple of days anyway, then came across the island of Grenada, about which we knew nothing, and saw an ad. for holiday apartments, right by Grand Anse beach. Immediately, the call was made, and we booked two stays of three nights each, before and after our visit with Malcolm and Pat. On arrival in Miami, we started calling hotels on the direct lines from the airport. We wanted to go into the older Art Deco area, but found places were full, as there was a big festival in process. The decision was made to wing it, and we got a cab over, being incredibly lucky, in that we got a large seafront room overlooking the beach and festival, because this hotel's phones were down, and they had been unable to take reservations. We quickly went out for an explore and supper in the bustling atmosphere all along

Ocean Drive, with street performers adding to the joyous ambience. The main stage was right on the beach, close to our hotel, and on this Saturday night, featured "Jack Siegel's Noteworthy Orchestra", together with 84-year-old Cab Calloway as headliner.

Cab Calloway, of course, was a legend. He took over from Duke Ellington at the Cotton Club in Harlem in 1931 as house band, which included backing floor shows and many solo entertainers, becoming a major figure on the jazz scene. Considered by many to be the most important vocal stylist of the era, he had a huge career, including movies with stars from Al Jolson to Steve McQueen, culminating in "The Blues Brothers", with Dan Aykroyd and John Belushi, which brought him a whole new generation of fans in later life, with his classic rendition of "Minnie the Moocher". When George Gershwin wrote the immortal "Porgy and Bess", the character of "Sportin' Life" was created as a representation of Cab Calloway. And here we were, able to walk along the beach, and see such a legend, with a top-class swinging orchestra behind, at no charge, courtesy of several sponsors. After Cab's set, we were somewhat tired with the time change, and went to bed with our windows wide open, and the sound of this magnificent orchestra in our ears, never, ever, to be forgotten.

We flew the following day to Grenada, "The Spice Island", where we were immediately struck by an exotic smell when the aircraft door was first opened. There was a warm greeting from the hotel proprietor, and we were driven to "South Winds", where our little apartment had everything that could be needed for a beautiful three days of "r and r", five hundred yards from the beach, and a little less from the supermarket. The restaurant was a long row of tables, surrounded by glass on three sides, and guests chatted happily together over the evening meal, which was mostly Caribbean in style. Grenada is south of the Tropic of Cancer and close to Trinidad, so we were totally amazed at the speed with which the sun set each night, having never been so close to the equator before. We visited the capital, St. George's, so different to St. George's in Bermuda, and watched the Islanders happily haggling over the prices of magnificent fruits and vegetables in the huge open-air market, while tourists probably did the same with crafts and souvenirs.

The owner drove us back to the airport after our third night. He was very impressed with us, as all his visitors over the years had come via travel agencies, or on some sort of package; I think we were just about the first people he had ever seen who picked up the phone and had called him direct.

We boarded one of the Liat "Island Hoppers", and took off for Union Island, where we were to be met by Malcom and Pat. This was probably our first flight ever that hadn't instantly gone to around 35,000 feet, although we might possibly have reached 100. I seem to remember that we collected a bit of tree on either this or the return flight. Anyway, we landed in Union Island, and saw a small shack with "Union Island International Airport" roughly painted on it, so headed there and awaited Customs. There was a bit of a wait, then the Customs officer came in, with his resplendent uniform, welcomed us to the Island, and quickly processed our passports. Malcolm was waiting for us when we left the building, so the three of us headed off to the dockside and "Tainan". After leaving the airport, there was a big wave from a school bus; the driver, now in T-shirt and shorts, being the customs officer who had just greeted us in his immaculate uniform, moments before.

It was good to meet up with Pat again, plus "Moggsly", the "Ship's Cat", and we headed northwards up the Grenadines, with our first stop being the beautiful island of Petit St. Vincent, privately owned, with its 22 cottages scattered over hillside, cliff, and beach, all with total privacy. Run up a yellow flag for room service, or a red flag to be left alone; the resort boasted a fine dining room, with dinner on the beach one night per week, and a local band brought in for the occasion. We anchored offshore, and Malcolm took in the little tender, where he cut us a couple of fresh coconuts to drink, straight from the tree.

The following day we sailed across to the Island of Mayreau, about which there is some necessary background before the story can continue.

Some time before we had been playing at the Holiday Inn, Barrie, a little way north of Toronto. One of the guests that we got to know was an architect, who was very into sailing. A friend of his was to deliver a boat to the Caribbean, and asked if he would like to crew, which he quickly accepted. Their journey took them past Mayreau, where there was a building on Saltwhistle Bay that was a chandlery, i.e., selling parts for the many sailboat owners in the area, with a little restaurant. There was also a "For Sale" sign, with a fabulous expanse of beach. Jumping ahead, by the time we met, he had purchased the property, and built eight units, each for two families, plus a new restaurant, and had a small resort going in this idyllic location. Being in the trade wind belt, just one small wind turbine easily provided all the power needed. He had just produced a brochure, (which I have in front of me), and said that we must drop in, and see him and his wife. Unless you are a sailboat enthusiast, Mayreau is in the middle of nowhere, but sometime later, we were performing on the "Love Boat", the "Pacific Princess", (which had originally been the "Sea Venture" in Bermuda), and one of the reasons we were so excited to be on this particular cruise, was that it was to stop for a few hours off Mayreau. There was a small community on one side of the island, other than that, no roads, but we thought we could easily walk across; it being a small island, and literally "drop in" unannounced. Which we did, following a rainwater gully over the top, and down to their property. Our friend was in Canada, but his wife was there, and we had a good visit before heading back to the ship, at the same time marvelling at their incredible expanse of beach, which was later recognized by National Geographic as being one of the world's ten best.

Now here we were again, with Malcolm and Pat, and were going to anchor offshore, along with a few other sailboats, and visit the island properly. The restaurant was al fresco, each table having its own little thatched roof in case of rain, and we spent four glorious days, sleeping on "Tainan", and going back and forth to the island for meals. We were in the extreme front of the boat, with our bed almost to a point, and our feet semi-entwined, (which wasn't all bad!), but the hatch was open, and we could lie on our backs under the sky, gazing at the thousands of stars above, with not a single light to spoil our view. The blue-green sea was like stepping into a warm bath, the most perfect we had ever known, with its spectacular curve of beach all around. Being novice sailors, the first couple of days had been a little challenging with the ocean swell, but this was the ultimate. We then moved to the adjacent snorkelling area of Tobago Cays, gazing with awe at the many brightly coloured fish, some reminiscent of Bermuda, where we anchored for a couple of nights before heading back to Union Island and the flight to Grenada, in a tiny plane which bobbed and bounced en route to the much larger island ahead. There was more extensive exploration on this visit, including stopping at a nutmeg plantation, where we were appalled to find that the locals received a paltry $1 U.S. per day for their hard work.

Back to Miami, which absolutely needs mentioning. It was a BWIA flight, and the meal was an excellent curry, with all the trimmings. Imagine our surprise when the friendly flight attendant came out of the galley with a ladle and a large saucepan, walking down the aisle offering seconds, which we have never seen on an aircraft before or since! It had been an amazing week with Malcolm and Pat, and I recall his special "travel" drum kit, which could be packed almost flat; also the contortions we all got into each day to make sure that the sun was truly over the yardarm!

THE "LOVE BOAT"

Mentioning "Princess", the cruise we did with them was quite challenging. We have done several cruises over the years, all of which have been fine, but this one was a little different. An agent in Vancouver, with whom we sometimes worked, had put us into Nancy Greene's ski lodge in Whistler, B.C. Nancy was, of course, a world class skier, but the amazing thing was the pictures on her wall, taken at the height of her career, when she looked exactly like Mary at the same age, to the extent that they could have both been twins. We got along with her really well, and were pleased to have been at the lodge, where Nancy wanted us to return, as soon as we were able. The agent was also the principal booker for Princess Cruises and asked us if we could do the Caribbean run on the Pacific Princess, to which we agreed, having found friends to take care of Ben.

So, we flew off to Miami, where we were to be met and taken to the ship. We waited, and waited, taxis not being an option when carrying a full sound system. We paged the shipping line, many times, to no avail. Eventually, we decided to check into the airport hotel, and to put all our instruments and equipment into the left luggage. They gasped in horror when they saw we had 17 pieces, and said there was no room, but I, having spent many years loading amps., speakers, and assorted instruments into vehicles, asked if I might repack one area, as I was sure it would all fit easily. Which was duly done, plus the luggage was all now in numerical order, a definite improvement. The following day, after more pagings, we eventually found a van that was going to the ship, and managed to get ourselves and gear to the dock, where we waited in the sticky humidity and 90° temperature for two hours, before being allowed to board, bearing in mind that we had woken up the day before in the deep snow of a Canadian winter. This time, we paged the Cruise Director, who obviously thought he was way above being paged, and on being told of difficulties so far, simply said "par for the course" a few times.

Once on board, we took all our stuff to where we could re-assemble everything, and check it out, as it had been packed for flight, where there is always a risk of damage. We fortunately didn't have to work the afternoon tea set that day, as it was a changeover day in port, but the schedule was horrendous, and it was subsequently found out that we were replacing two other acts. A typical day was: 11 a.m.-1:00 p.m., Island music, (calypso, ska, reggae), outdoors on the sundeck; 3:30-4:15 p.m., Afternoon tea, background instrumental music, ("Shadow of your smile" etc.); 5-5:45 p.m. and 7-7:45 p.m., (a semi "show" set in the "Starlight Lounge", at the top of the ship before each sitting of dinner); 9:30 p.m.-2 a.m., Dance music in the main ballroom, alternating with a 5-piece band. Every second or third night, when one reached the first "break" of the evening, it was necessary to grab two instruments and play in the showroom between sets there. Not only that, but our main equipment was set up in the ballroom permanently, moving a smaller amount, including mics. and stands, to different parts of the ship for each set.

One could eat at any one of the elaborate buffets on board, but, of course, there was never time for that. On occasion we would grab something en route to the next set up; meals were usually in the crew mess, where all the food sat in tall containers of hot water, which was fine if your schedule allowed you to get the food fresh, not so good if it had been sitting, especially soggy cabbage and totally dissolved potatoes. Also, bed before 3 a.m. was impossible, as one had to wait for the next day's schedule to come under the door! So, it was not a bundle of laughs much of the time. We got along well with the passengers, with whom we could sit at the bar if we wished, to the extent that, by the second full day, about 4 or 5 passengers would appear at the end of every set; one would say, "Right, where to?" and they would grab mic. stands and instruments, speakers, whatever, and help us go to the next location, then disappear until it was time for the next move. To say this was appreciated is such an understatement, but our little group of passengers would not take "no" for an answer and assured us that we in no way interfered with their day; in fact, they were more than pleased to feel useful. Plus, there were the essential drills of watertight doors and lifeboats, which necessarily took priority over other activities, when the Purser pleasantly made the point that he had more rings on his sleeve then did a Cruise Director.

But our days in the various Caribbean ports were heaven. We could relax and explore for a few hours, not working until 5 p.m., and we relished our time away from the ship. We ran into the magician, who was in exactly an opposite situation to us. He did 2 x 20 min. sets per week, plus a bit of table magic on a couple of meals, and was bored out of his mind most of the time. We didn't get to know him, and he was rarely seen. Nowadays a ventriloquist or magician, and possibly a comic, is often taken to more than one ship of the same line by helicopter, which seems, on the surface at least, to be a much better idea.

We have worked with other Cruise Directors of course, but this one was totally lacking in social skills when it came to the passengers, and quite possibly in the wrong position. One of our favourite movies ever is the Jack Lemmon/Walter Matthau "Out to Sea", with the C.D. being brilliantly portrayed by Brent Spiner, and it brings back memories of this particular run, which we couldn't wait to finish. One of our helpers on board had a business which owned a large warehouse in Miami. Our friend who was looking after Ben was on the road with his work, Ben alongside him, and it was just before Christmas, so we called Doug and Carolyn in Bermuda, as we were so close to them, and had a truly amazing Christmas together, with our helper from the ship kindly storing sound equipment in his warehouse whilst we were away. We eventually flew out of Miami ten days later, where a case containing much of our music was stolen in the airport and took several months to rewrite.

By the way, it was mandatory to play the "Love Boat" theme at the beginning and end of every set, which I quite liked before this cruise. I imagine all the passengers were totally "punch drunk" on the song by the time they got off. Hopefully things have changed now, in so many ways, which I am sure they have.

While on our Christmas in Bermuda, amidst the joys of exploring the island again, we dropped into Henry VIII, and found that our friend Peter Stoney, once of "Finnigan" years before, had the house job as a solo entertainer year round, taking a break of several weeks in mid-summer to return to Ireland. John Ferris, owner of this top-class restaurant/pub venue, who became a friend, was really pleased to see us, and discussed the possibility of our filling the so important mid-summer slot.

Which we did, for two consecutive years, taking Ben the first time, who used to travel between us on the communal scooter, draped across Mary's lap on the passenger seat, she of course holding on to make sure that he didn't slip, a sight which was soon familiar throughout the island.

Henry VIII had what was like an apse at one end of the building, with a high roof. As part of our evening's performance, and as one of the highlights, the audience would be built up to a level where we would have a competition to see which was the best group of people, i.e., the best table. At the beginning, there would just be glasses held up, then they would stand, maybe get on the table, or hold the table in the air, but the ultimate best, which I believe was a sports team from the U.S.,

By 1993, we had altered our market considerably. There were many engagements at Fort Edmonton Park, where we would dress in appropriate period costumes, depending on which street we were playing, and perform music with banjo and guitar to fit the period, coupled with a huge amount of interaction with park visitors. In the spring, we played what was to be our last lounge gig, excepting mountain resorts, for a happy Newfoundland and Maritime clientele, but it was time to move on, which we realized when packing on the final night.

That December, we were in the latter part of our always busy Christmas season, when we had to say farewell to Ben, who had been such an integral part of our lives, at home and on the road, for thirteen years. The gap was enormous, and it took us over four years to be ready to welcome a new puppy into our lives, which we did, delightedly, with the arrival of Meggie, a black Cardigan Welsh Corgi cross, who needed a home. We immediately christened her Meggie Shortpaws, and she filled our lives again with joy.

CANADIAN HUNGER FOUNDATION CONCERTS

One of the things we had both long wanted to do was to get involved in a meaningful way with trying to help rectify the food, and more especially water, crisis that constantly affects different parts of the Globe, especially Africa. We of course contributed as we were able to emergency situations, but used to discuss how we could be involved in something more long-term, where results would actually be visible.

When we had the house in New Brunswick, we were on one of our summer tours to Alberta, which usually lasted from early May until just before Halloween, and working at Westridge Park Lodge Golf and Country Club, just outside Edmonton. There was a small convention in progress, of the Canadian Hunger Foundation, and their literature was on a table outside the meeting room, some of which we borrowed after work one night, and read excitedly, as the organization seemed a perfect fit. The following day we sat down with principal organizer Bruce Moore, with whom we were to remain in contact for several years, and discussed their current projects, plus ways in which we could be of use.

In our profession, the more practical approach was to put on a fund-raising concert, which we decided would be more effective if it were done the following winter in Fredericton, where we knew so many performers. Which was duly arranged. On our arrival home we met with the local CHF contact, Flora Dell, booked the Playhouse, and started wheels turning. Just about every performer we approached jumped at the chance to be involved, to the extent that the final roster had no less than 16 acts. The show was to be called "Children of the World", and Paul Lauzon, one of our performers, wrote a song of the same name, which was the finale to the evening, sung by the entire company and most of the audience. Foundation Executive Director John Laidlaw came in from Ottawa, and the commanding officer of C.F.B. Gagetown, Brig. Gen. George Kells, was our patron. A considerable amount of money was raised, which, together with matching grants, went to a project in Senegal, where 3,000 small farms, each with a few trees and an irrigation well, were being installed to stop the westward encroachment of the Sahara Desert.

We did many fund-raising concerts over the years, in Alberta and British Columbia as well as that first concert in Fredericton and were always able to report at or before each performance exactly where those funds were going, and give progress reports afterwards, which was a huge plus.

The Foundation was run very efficiently. I say "was" regretfully, as the work it did has recently been taken over by its "parent" government organization. When we were first involved, only 9% of monies raised went into administration, which eventually went down to 6%, truly a remarkable record. One example of their work was that Bruce Moore was told of what used to be a very lush area of Sri Lanka that was now becoming desertified, despite many attempts to grow different things. He went over there, connected with the locals immediately, and asked what used to be there before it became desert. That was a long time ago, and nobody knew, nor did the libraries. There was a spoken order monastery in the vicinity, meaning all was handed down through the centuries by word of mouth, and he decided to give that a go. This was incredibly successful, and local volunteers were able to replant the land as it had been hundreds of years previously, which was a correct balance for the area, and soon took hold.

Other projects with which we were involved included the planting of shade trees in Kenya, so that crops could be grown in that shade, which was a difficult one, as it involved initially using precious water for nourishment of the trees, but worthwhile once they were established. This was partially administered in Africa by our friend Katie Damphouse, with whom we stayed when visiting the foundation headquarters in Ottawa. All of the more than 800 projects involved collaboration with local village groups, who implemented the various initiatives, and more importantly, kept them going with virtually no overhead, once they had been shown how. Hundreds of thousands of lives were altered, in 52 countries, by the work of the CHF, over a little more than 65 years, and we were so privileged to have been a very small part of this.

While we were doing our fundraisers for the Foundation, another initiative was launched, which would hugely affect our lives for the next 16 years.

"EARTH DAY" FESTIVAL

The first Earth Day had been instigated in the United States by a senator, Gaylord Nelson, who was concerned about the lack of environmental awareness in both business and the general public. A special day was set aside when all seats of learning in the country would look at issues threatening the environment, and what could be done to make things better. That day was April 22nd, 1970, and a young man from Wisconsin, Denis Hayes, was brought on board to coordinate this huge event, which was a resounding success. Some years later, Denis looked at making Earth Day into a global event, and on April 22nd, 1990, Earth Day International was born, with festivals to celebrate the planet, in addition to the launching of many environmental initiatives, in 141 countries worldwide. In the English-speaking world, Julie Gold's song "From a Distance", seemed to be an anchor for the whole movement, and Bette Midler had a colossal hit with it.

It was pretty close to the wire when we got involved with the first ever Earth Day Festival in the City of Edmonton, with maybe only a month to go before the actual day. It seemed that one of the principal organizers, by now removed from the board, had been using the upcoming festival as a personal fund-raiser, so the media, with the exception of K-Lite radio, who was a sponsor and helping with the main stage, wouldn't touch the festival with a barge pole, and a huge amount of damage had been done. I sat in on a committee meeting and was instantly struck by the caring and dedication of those there, which reminded me so much of the 60s Flower Power movement - in fact I wrote a song about it "The Soul of the Sixties", which we sang at many festivals and other shows throughout the years. Conversation was mostly about how the media could be brought back on board, to which I said, "I'll fix it", to which organizers Barb Nicoll and Tom Yohemas heaved a sigh of relief, and the meeting moved on to other things.

Posters had already been printed, but they were pleased to have us as a part of the mainstage show, and the next day I hit the ground running, setting up radio, T.V., and press meetings, to undo the damage, focusing solely on the purpose of the festival. K-Lite had already arranged session guitarist Amos Garrett's "Eh Team", and the popular band "Blackboard Jungle", plus there were a couple of good speakers, also Mayor Jan Reimer was attending, to put the City's stamp of approval on the whole event. This was a huge success, with a sunny day and around 12,000 participants, sowing the first seeds for years to come.

We stayed with the festival for sixteen years. I took over the stage the following year, in addition to media, then subsequently "inherited" the entire festival, having to build most of it again from scratch, and creating my own personal contacts. Earth Day Canada operated within the mandate of being non-political and non-confrontational, which sounds easy on paper, but can in fact be very challenging, when dealing with so many organizations that are not necessarily exactly on the same page.

Initially, tents were a little difficult to obtain, it being expensive to rent so many, and we were determined that the festival remained free for all to attend. Fortunately, the Heritage Festival came to our aid, which was a huge help. Later, the Canadian Armed Forces base at Wainwright stepped in with the loan of military tents, even sending a helper on occasion to make sure that we erected them correctly. These, of course, had to be returned dry and properly folded - on one occasion they were spread out in a gymnasium, on another they were "flown" on a stage when a bit wet, but we had so much fun together putting them up that I can still hear the laughter if I stop to think.

We did not permit food concessions to use disposable plates or cutlery. At first, everything was handheld, or one brought one's own plate and mug. The Edmonton Folk Festival offered the loan of their plates, and we set up a washing station on site, rewashing them again after the festival before they were returned.

The military tents were needed overseas, but we got a large discount from Big Top rentals, who did their own setup and teardown, plus the Friends of the Environment Foundation came forward to sponsor these for many years.

So much support, for which we are eternally grateful.

The stage to me was very important, as the quality of the show had a huge bearing on how many people attended the festival. Once there, the idea was that they would peruse the 65 or so environmental booths, and hopefully learn something, possibly to the extent of joining one of the societies represented: Greenpeace, Western Canada Wilderness Committee, The Solar Energy Society, Sierra Club, Amnesty International, and many more. There were organizations for the rehabilitation of injured wildlife, plus "Earth's General Store", owned and operated by Michael Kalmanovitch, possibly the most highly respected member of the local environmental business community, and an example to all.

Very soon we were exhibiting a snazzy "green" racing car, totally solar, made by the University of Alberta, also demonstrating solar cookers that were being sent to Africa. A wooden box, a reflector, zero pollution, and no cost to run. An inexpensive wind turbine was on show, and so many more things. Each booth was run by knowledgeable people from the society involved, and it was a huge opportunity to learn, and feel informed, about so many global issues.

Wherever possible, there would be a mainstage "headliner", (Valdy, Shari Ulrich, Paul Hann, Laura Vinson, Gary Fjellgaard), not forgetting the magnificent coloratura soprano Irén Bartók (related to the famed Hungarian Composer). Irén had started her career with Edmonton's "Leave it to Jane" theatre company, then, whilst furthering her training at the Banff Centre, she was picked by Harold Prince to take over the lead role of Christine in the original London West End production of "Phantom of the Opera". Which she did, initially for 2 1/2 years, before moving on to the equally prestigious role of "Griddlebone the Operatic Cat", in "Cats", of course another Andrew Lloyd Webber musical. The title role of "Madame Butterfly", for English Festival Opera, ensued, along with many other appearances on both sides of the Atlantic. We knew Irén from Arts Conventions and were so privileged to have her appear at Earth Day, with her friend Sylvia Shadick Taylor on piano. In addition, there were other top class local musicians offering sounds from different parts of the world, in many languages and styles: Dale Ladouceur, Chapman Stick/vocals, and sometimes a band, Incanto, Peruvian music/vocal, Scona Brae, traditional folk music, Jerusalem Ridge, bluegrass, Sandy Kwong, guitar/Chinese and English vocals, John Spearn, guitar and self-penned Canadian historical songs, (also on our committee), and so many others, plus of course, ourselves. Every year I would look at the mainstage audience to see if there was a segment of the local population not represented, in which case I would find an act to bring them in for the next year.

The organizing team was second to none, as of course were the volunteers, always the lifeblood of any festival. There would be a huge oval of tents, with the stage as a part of the oval, so that the music could be felt by all. Sometimes we would have a known guest speaker, author and activist Howard Lyman was one, whom we flew in the day after his historic appearance on the Oprah Winfrey show. Also, Tom Taylor, who had taken over from Bruce Moore at the Canadian Hunger Foundation, and did an excellent presentation on the biogas cooking initiatives he had personally overseen in India, which improved the health and well-being of so many women and children. Another visitor from the CHF was Sandra Adamchuk, who supervised their educational programmes, visiting a few schools whilst in town.

I wish it were possible to put down on paper the energy of those years. There would be some preparation in November of the year prior, then from mid-January on, the festival would build and build, up to a sudden silence a couple of days before the event, telling us that everything was ready. On the day itself, the majority of my time was spent with media, also troubleshooting the inevitable display that didn't quite fit our non-confrontational mandate.

Aside note: One year, I was walking through the booths, and saw a large blow-up of the now famous picture of Premier Ralph Klein, giving the one-finger sign, in front of a display. CBC television was just about to come around the corner, and I gave the picture my finest attempt at a rugby tackle since leaving school, diving at the floor, and whisking the offending picture under a table, to the surprise of all around, before it could be seen.

Mary was by now emceeing the main stage, which she could seemingly do effortlessly over the longest period, unlike some radio deejays who would "dry", once they had completed a script. Sometimes, I would be approached by a committee member with "Did you see ....?", to which I would reply, "No, what was wrong with it?" If their response was, "Nothing", I would usually return with, "That's why I didn't see it", such was my focus for most of the time.

The festival grew and grew, usually blessed, but not always, by good weather. One year we had the stage and all the tents up when there was a huge snow dump. Tent sides were quickly rolled up and snow was kept from the tops through the night, but the event clearly could not happen. All radio and T.V. stations, of which there were many, were immediately contacted, and Global T.V., one of our main sponsors, ran a "crawler" at the bottom of the screen all day, to say that the festival was not taking place. The committee, of course, all went down as usual, and by the time the few who hadn't heard the news showed up, maybe 100 or so, we had the stage front open, heat lamps available if needed, and a drum circle going to keep us all warm. Hot soup and coffee or tea were ready, and everyone was given a tree seedling, plus some reading material to take home, if they wished. There was only a handful of us, but the camaraderie was terrific, and it was a great day, in so many ways.

There was just one solitary complaint, from a man who said we should have put a full-page announcement in the Edmonton Journal. Apart from the fact that this would have been impossible at that notice, I thanked him for his input, and said that should such a thing ever happen again, I would be pleased to try and do this, sending him the invoice, and also suggested that he join the organizing committee, at which point he disappeared, as fast as he could, through the deep snow.

So many names stand out from the organizing team over the years. After my first year as co-ordinator, it was clear that some of the jobs needed "spreading out" for greater efficiency. Anita Naiker, who had come on board the year I took over mainstage, took over the Earth Day tent, a huge job on the festival day itself. Carol Rankin dealt brilliantly with all the booths, passing on to the indispensable Cynthia Berg, who also liaised with volunteers. Shauna Robertson later took over working with the food booths, making sure they all complied with health department and festival guidelines; Janice Boudreau did the kids' area with her friend Lynn Maskell, and subsequently joined the committee some years later. Mary was of course emceeing and supervising main stage. Tracy Grabowksi, who does all of our professional photo shoots, was in charge of a photographic record of the day; so many faces, all

Earth Day Festival – photos Tracy Grabowski

Stage shot on a cold and windy day – Me, Mary, Bob Shortt, one of the sound crew, Dale Ladouceur

of which I can still see, and remember their efforts over so many years with gratitude.

Some came on board for a shorter time: Michael Kalmanovitch, David Parker, from Vegetarians of Alberta, Geoff and Kelly Woodward, who owned several "Body Shops", and some joined later, including Michael Kurylo, who had been in charge of our audio setup for several years, plus John Spearn, a regular on mainstage. Jo and Zig Szady, with their solar powered motorhome, were with us for a while, while our friend Nancy, (who had helped Mary choose her wedding dress back in Bermuda days), introduced her husband Ed Loken to the committee, and he took over site management for several years, which was a great help to me. Plus, Walter Kehl, Edmonton's volunteer "extraordinaire", who is to be seen almost daily at different events throughout the year; Melanie, Amy, Laurelle, none of you will ever be forgotten.

The first major thing to remind the million plus people living in the city area that Earth Day was approaching was the day we put up big banners on several bridges over the main freeways, done by Mary, Anita, and myself, all being very careful and holding on for dear life, as the bridge on which two of us were standing often had heavy traffic, zooming past uncomfortably close. Two of us would put each banner up, while one stood below to watch that it was straight, and would not sag in a few days, meaning we'd have to come back and do it all again. We were the first major festival of the season, and there was much supportive honking from vehicles passing under each bridge; our first indication that the huge work of the last months was all worthwhile.

One of the biggest days was the day that posters were ready at the printers. There would be an emergency meeting, and these would be allocated, 500 for schools, 350 for City sites, plus all shopping centres in Edmonton and satellite communities, museums, media, theatres and more, to be got up as fast as possible. I also created literature each year to be sent to every school, along with the poster, of suggested environmental activities for both students and teachers to study, which ended up with receipt of the Emerald Award "for individual commitment to environmental excellence", for the Province of Alberta, together with numerous citations over the years, (which had nothing to do with my driving!).

The festival continued to grow, with a maximum attendance of 32,000 one year, sometimes with "spin-off" events. For instance, one summer we were given a provincial flag with a huge white border, saying "Alberta is committed to "reuse". We had a ceremony at the legislature at which I arranged for eight schools to be in attendance, and leading figures, plus anyone else who wished, could sign the flag, finishing with Environment Minister Gary Marr. The flag was flown for two weeks, then passed to various schools, which was so effective as an awareness campaign.

I was constantly on the lookout for big name performers to front the mainstage. One year I was trying to get Pete Seeger, arguably the number one folk singer of all time. I had a good relationship with one of the airlines, and transportation would not be a problem. Imagine my surprise and delight when he called me direct, to discuss why it would unfortunately be impossible for him to attend.

Just about the biggest gift an older person can ever give, is their time, which is so precious. We had an in-depth conversation about many things, for around 40 minutes, and it will always stand out among the highlights of my life.

Our personal stage set varied; frequently we played our own environmental children's songs and had many musician friends join the set. Bob Shortt, from Dublin, who has worked with us so many times, on banjo and mandolin, Cynthia Horton or Dale Ladouceur on bass, and either Tony Michaels or Patricia Gavreau deLisle on fiddle. Cynthia and Patricia also joined us for the Emerald Award ceremony, the year following my award, when we were invited to appear at Edmonton's prestigious Winspear Centre, and brought 8 schoolchildren on stage as part of the act.

There are many other speakers and performers I should mention – "Maple Creek", (bluegrass), Maria Dunn, Bob Jahrig, Smokey Fennel's country band "Cheap Suits", John Wort Hannam, Andy Donnelly (from CKUA radio), and Janice's daughter, Michelle Boudreau, but my favourite memories are of Mary, emceeing on a cold day and exhibiting to the audience her bright blue long johns, also our friends Iain and Val Little, dressed as "Captain Zero" and "Mother Nature", the latter being approached by Global T.V., and asked how come she'd allowed such a cold snap. Her instant response was, "That's the trouble with you people. I'm Mother Nature, I do Flora and Fauna; I DON'T do weather!", which the station loved so much that they used it many times.

The close of the festival was always marked by an indigenous drum group on stage, and a huge circle of dancers, sometimes two or even three concentric rings, bringing everyone together, and making a perfect finish to the day.

We lost two giants of the environmental community during my tenure with the festival, one being Leroy Lister, owner of "Veggies", Edmonton's first full-service vegetarian restaurant, who used to cycle an average 80 km. per day and was everybody's friend. He ran the festival food booths for the first five years, then passed away while on a trip to Costa Rica for Earthwatch, to help save the eggs of endangered leatherback sea turtles. He was hugely missed, and his place in the festival team was taken by Shauna Robertson, his friend.

Not with the festival, but undoubtedly our most supportive ally ever, was sometime city councillor Tooker Gomberg, who was described by Earth Day Canada President Jed Goldberg as being "without question the most sophisticated and effective grassroots activist (he had) ever seen". The festival bicycle parking lot was run by Edmonton Bicycle Commuters, started by Tooker. The overnight crew was organized by Eco-city, founded by Tooker, and the fact that Edmonton has the most sophisticated composting facility in North America is also mostly down to Tooker Gomberg. He, together with his wife, Angela Bischoff, was constantly trying to improve the human condition, and more importantly, the condition of Planet Earth, thus leaving a huge legacy for all.

Over 250,000 attended the festival during my tenure, and the biggest thing we have both taken from it is the incredible warmth and support we have received, from attendees, from the rest of the ever-evolving organizing committee, and from the various City departments that became good friends over the years, a warmth we have kept with us ever since.

But it was time to move on, for two reasons. Firstly, I felt that the festival had been taken as far as we could take it and needed new blood and new ideas if it was to progress. Secondly, there was a good winter circuit in the southern U.S. that we badly wanted to work, and had been semi-postponing, because Earth Day took three and a half months of volunteer work to prepare, most of that full-time, meaning little or no income. We had been to Toronto, and got to know Jed Goldberg, President of Earth Day Canada, (who later came to visit us when we did the Legislative flag-raising), also locally there was Karin Piett, executive director of "Kids for Saving Earth" Canada, and Debbie Riopel, who ran the Canadian branch of the "World Kindness Movement", with her friend Cheryl Moskaluk. Amazingly, all three of them lived nearby at the time, which was more than helpful when there were different issues to be discussed, and we are pleased to have remained good friends.

We left the organizing committee, somewhat regretfully, but still continued to play music for the festival, and were always available for consultation. Janice Boudreau took over as co-ordinator, assisted by Michael Kurylo, both experienced with the festival, and already on committee. A trip to Arizona to look at the circuit there had already been successfully undertaken, with no less than 52 meetings over 8 days in Mesa, Yuma, Tucson, Apache Junction, and Casa Grande, after which we had 24 performances contracted for Jan. – March of the following year.

Our hope, more than anything, was that we, through the festival, had actually reached some people, and enabled them to make positive differences in their lives, with some even actually becoming a part of the environmental community. Every one of us can "Tread a little lighter on the Earth", (as in the children's song written by yours truly), regardless of beliefs, religion, politics, or ethnic background, which is all that the festival was about. For several years it was the largest of its type in the country, and we were honoured to have been at the helm.

This is not to say that we were in any way turning our backs on the environmental and awareness communities in which we had become so involved. I had long ago learned, in the words of Rachel Carson, to "Think Globally and act Locally". To this end I had frequently been in touch with environment ministers in various provinces, as well as at a national level. I recall being very concerned when there was talk in Ottawa about environmental jurisdiction being given to each province individually, which to me was truly worrisome, as on a provincial level environmental issues always seemed to be given second place to money and what is questionably called "growth". I wrote to then Federal environment minister Sheila Copps, with my concerns, (c. c. the Prime

Minister, of course), and received a lengthy 'phone call back, where we discussed the ramifications of such a move. I wrote to the BC environment minister, (c. c. all other provincial environment ministers), about the preservation of the rare white "Kermode" bears on Princess Royal Island, to positive effect. I wrote several letters regarding total banning of the horrific "leg-hold traps", I wrote about the appalling treatment of elephants and other species for "entertainment", recalling Neil Carter, bassist in Bryan Bridge's band in Germany, who was for a short time in the orchestra of a large circus in the U.K., and left when he saw what was happening. Thank goodness the world has had street performer Guy Laliberté, who created "Cirque du Soleil", proving to the world that far better performances can be created without animal abuse.

I came in contact with actress Joyce deWitt, ("Three's Company"), who was involved with an organization in L.A., alongside friends Valerie Harper, ("Rhoda", with Mary Tyler Moore), and Dennis Weaver, ("Gun Law/Gunsmoke"), called L.I.F.E., ("Love is feeding everyone"). The Beach Boys had given them an old equipment truck, and they would collect food from supermarkets at the end of each day, for distribution as needed to the homeless and others. An estimated one third of all the fresh food produced is never sold, (how many crooked carrots are there in your local supermarket?) and ends up being destroyed or ploughed back into the ground, (rare), instead of ending up where it is needed most. L.I.F.E. got much bigger, with many vehicles collecting, and many names, (Neil Diamond was one), supporting the cause, to the extent that they were eventually feeding 185,000 people per week! Joyce and I swapped ideas on occasion, and we were so pleased to actually meet when she came into Edmonton to do a play.

I continue to be horrified by the senseless destruction of the Amazon Rain Forest, which I think of, more than anywhere, as being the "lungs" of Planet Earth.

Acting locally, as per Rachel Carson's instructions, we encountered a plan to build a freeway across a large lake, (called "Big Lake"), close to where we live. This lake and adjacent wetlands is well known to be one of the three most important stopping off places in Western Canada for migratory birds, many such "rest stops" having already been destroyed or polluted. We helped in getting signatures against the road, organized by our special friend Elke Blodgett, who would be out in all weathers with the petition, under an umbrella at the recycle centre. This petition, of between 11 and 13,000 signatures, went to City Council. Our contribution was that I wrote a song "Beautiful Big Lake", and it was recorded, bird noises and all, at the studio of our friend Ian Martin, with performers from all over the province coming in on different sessions to "do their bit". (Bob Jahrig, Larry Renn, John Spearn, Maria Dunn, John Wort Hannam, Jill Younghusband, Bill Werthman, Dale Ladouceur, Maurice Gallardo (Flute), plus Ian on drums, bass, and piano, Maria on accordion, John Spearn on guitar, and of course, ourselves).

Then came the huge mix-down, followed by which, copies went to CBC radio, and CKUA radio (the main arts and culture outlets), where they received extensive play. For various reasons, a large kink was eventually put in the road, and it no longer crossed over the lake itself, which was a good compromise, and avoided what was becoming a huge confrontation. Ian especially, plus all the musicians, vocalists and others, donated a large amount of time to our recording project, for which we remain so grateful, and are pleased to say that our small efforts proved worthwhile.

I was approached by more than one Edmonton city councillor during our Earth Day period, to say that my name had been brought up for consideration as "Citizen of the Year", but was not taken any further, as we were not Edmonton residents, but in the adjacent City of St. Albert, therefore not eligible. I felt so honoured by this, not because of the award, but because the importance of the work we were trying to do was being recognized.

But now it was time to connect more with Debbie Riopel, of the "World Kindness Movement", and get involved in a whole new adventure.

THE KENYA PROJECT

Debbie wanted to connect with all the countries of the "Kindness Movement" and strengthen the organization by personal involvement. One November, she was putting on an event for "World Kindness Day", at Edmonton's Muttart Conservatory, where we performed quite regularly, and we volunteered our services for this special day. A guest who would be attending that day and talking of her work, was Wanjiku Kironyo, a Kikuyu lady who did amazing work in the Mathare Valley shanty town area of Nairobi, where over 600,000 people live in corrugated iron shacks, with loads of dust, sand, and of course, no electricity, water, plumbing, sewage disposal, or anything else. Not only had Wanjiku set up a co-operative assistance project for residents of the valley to start a small business, she was also operating three schools, in addition to being a professional family councillor, and we immediately hit it off, both being incredibly interested in her life-altering work for so many. She said that we must come and see what it was that she was trying to achieve, and a flame was ignited in our souls at that moment, which has burned ever since.

Debbie and her life partner, Mark Broscheit, both had homes, and decided to sell up, using the proceeds to personally visit every country in the "Kindness Movement", over the period of a year. Debbie taught school locally, mostly kindergarten, and took a year's sabbatical for the project. Of course, when they both left, we would be in occasional contact to know their whereabouts, and Mary managed to get a flight on Kenya Airways that would deposit us in Nairobi an hour and a half after their arrival from India, where they had just had a traditional wedding ceremony. Wanjiku and her assistant Waigi, who was to act as our "guide" for the visit, were there to meet us, along with Debbie and Mark, and we headed off to the "Hillcrest" hotel, driving through the busy streets of Nairobi, where there were huge new office buildings everywhere, yet with little corrugated iron shacks selling crafts and produce on the sidewalk right in front. When we left the airport, there were many young men waving olive branches and palms, which we initially took to be a welcoming gesture, but when we realized that they were actually trying to hit Wanjiku, who was driving the small pickup in which we travelled, it became clear that this was a country in which one had to be very aware.

The "Hillcrest" was a smaller hotel with a mostly indigenous clientele, very clean, nice staff and oh, so reasonable, at $52 Canadian, bed, breakfast and evening meal, for both of us. It brought back memories of my very early childhood, where my mother's kitchen floor was red, polished with a product called Carnation. The Hillcrest had obviously no shortage of this product, for if one walked to the en suite bathroom in the night, red feet became the norm.

We met up with another friend, Jan Streader, an English actress also resident in Edmonton, whom we had known for several years, plus Jan Carnahan, a schoolteacher from Vancouver Island, and the group was complete. Debbie and Mark needed electrical outlets for charging their equipment, and for extra video lighting, which was not available in the "Hillcrest", so we moved to the "680" downtown, which was where all the volunteers and staff from various organizations, NGO's, Red Cross etc., stayed, yet still reasonable in price. It was a huge plus to meet all these different folks, not that I had disliked the "Hillcrest", apart, possibly, from the fact that it was across the street from a large

mosque, whose first call to prayer was on speakers, loudly, at what felt like 3:00 a.m.

The group stayed together most of the time, except that on the second day, Debbie and Mark moved all of our communal luggage, plus the 2 guitars that had been so very kindly donated to Wanjiku's schools by "Mother's Music" in Edmonton, down to the "680". Meanwhile, we were met by a representative from PLAN who was to take us on a 150 km. drive for a very special meeting.

Stanley Irungu was a young boy who was being sponsored for his schooling by our friend Nancy, and we had promised to look him up, if at all possible, during our trip. We went first in one of those magnificent Toyota 4-wheel drive vehicles, rather like a huge Land Rover, to Embu, where the regional office of PLAN was located, then to Stanley's school, and on to his home to meet the family. I felt so sorry for Stanley, who must have been petrified at strange people from the other side of the

Mathare Valley Slums – Nairobi

world coming to take him off in a truck. However, we reached his home in the country safely, navigating a deep stream and many huge potholes en route. Stanley had lost his father recently, and, in true Kenyan tradition, his unmarried uncle had moved in, and was now responsible for the family's well-being. Such hospitable people, and most of them spoke English in addition to their native Swahili, with Stanley's uncle being educated and very fluent. He proudly showed us a small growth of maize behind their little home, that was both the staple crop for their well-being, and also a source of meagre income. We had a large meal, in which Stanley and I were supposed to share in eating the head of a rooster, as part of the ceremony, but which I somehow managed to avoid, both Mary and I being careful to eat only that which was well cooked, or had a skin, (bananas, for example). Then we bade farewell and headed back to Nairobi, having taken several pictures for Nancy. It was dark when we arrived, and our hospitable driver was booked into a hotel, as it was not considered safe to drive at night.

We visited all of Wanjiku's amazing projects. In the Mathare Valley itself, she and her helpers had set up over 350 families in small business, with an initial "loan", (the quotes are intentional), of $60, plus help in getting things going, then another $60 later on as needed. Examples were, a greengrocer, carpenter, hairdresser, baker etc., but still very simple, in the corrugated iron shack that was also home, with little or no furniture, maybe a couple of old wooden chairs if one was really fortunate. I remember being very impressed by part of an old bicycle, that, when pedalled, made a simple lathe, to produce very good quality table and chair legs, some even with a pattern. The biggest thing one noticed were the children, who had naught but the clothes in which they stood, yet seemed so free and happy. Some had shoes, (a piece of wood with a bit of old car tire underneath) and some did not. Wanjiku was very insistent that any gifts should be something that could be shared, and then put away, such as a football, being rightly concerned that the children should not become competitive as regards possessions, which she had seen so much in other parts of the world.

We visited her Academy on the Maasai land, some distance from Nairobi. At the time, there were 161 students, from kindergarten to grade 8, many being AIDS orphans, or young girls escaping the probability of forced child marriages. The truly amazing thing was that the Maasai elders thought so much of Wanjiku that they encouraged the girls to attend school as well, a very rare thing in tribal culture. We met with the Academy principal, Mr. Wanjohi, and the two Jans donated a bicycle which would be useful with the huge distances that had to be walked for very basic essentials. There was a staff of 12, who were paid when possible, and the dream was that a bore hole could be drilled, thus providing water and lush green crops in the future. Out came the two guitars, and we entertained the children, which, inevitably, was a

Sharing music with Maasai children and AIDS orphans
photo: Mark Broscheit

high spot of our trip. We soon learned that any time we played, or Mary pulled out a ventriloquist puppet, the children always did something in return; it being impossible in their culture to accept without giving back. As regards the puppet, Mary has one she calls "Verna, the Vegetarian Vulture". The children had never seen anything remotely like it, and with Mary's puppetry skills, their eyes were truly like saucers!

There were other schools too. In the Kaserani district of Nairobi, Wanjiku has the Maji Mazuri orphanage, only 7 km. from the City Centre, yet the "roads" are by now deeply rutted, and we were all covered in a film of red dust on arrival. This is an emergency facility for AIDS orphans, handicapped, or street children, who would otherwise be involved in prostitution, and can accommodate 50 at any one time. It includes a dressmaking shop, which enables older children and teenagers to learn a skill and become self-sufficient, creating "uniforms"

I was privileged to take this picture in the Maasai village

for Wanjiku's other schools along the way. Needless to say, we both left the premises having purchased beautifully made traditional Kenyan costumes, which are carefully kept, and worn when possible.

One can hardly go all the way to Kenya without a traditional safari, which was arranged locally through one of Wanjiku's contacts at probably a third or less of the cost of booking the same thing from home. Not only that, but our driver, Bill, who had the six of us privately in his VW minibus, had radio contact with the large commercial tours, which can be bumper to bumper, and made sure that we never, ever, saw one. In fact, we only saw 4 vehicles, (all at a distance), in the whole 5-day tour, except when we stopped at night, in both the Masai Mara, and at Lake Nakuru, where there were many baboons, and also thousands of flamingos, who turned the sky a bright pink as they collectively came in to land on the water. Naturally we saw many animals in both parks, some we stopped and watched quietly for a while, making sure not to invade their "space". Lions, Zebras, Wildebeest, Hippos, Gazelle, Cape Buffalo, Warthogs, Impala, Elephants, (magnificent). and more, possibly remembering most of all, the various giraffe families, who were quietly enjoying a meal, and totally unperturbed by our presence. When back in Nairobi, we saw some of the re-introduced Rothschild's giraffe in a sanctuary, "Giraffe Centre", where one had the amazing experience of meeting these so perfect animals face-to-face!

We got to know 4 girls at the "680", who worked, two at a time, in the coffee shop, and we would always stop for a (sometimes lengthy) visit. Frida, Hana, Esther, and Rose were beautiful people, from different socio-economic backgrounds to each other. Fridah and Hana, especially, were very worried about the AIDS epidemic that was rampant, and were concerned that the disease might be forced upon them, no matter how much they attempted to avoid it. Esther came from a well-off situation, by Kenyan standards, and was therefore far less likely to be exposed. Rose was philosophical, and thought she would be O.K., but Fridah and

Hana wanted to move to a safer part of the world. Fridah was especially interested in Canada, about which she had heard so much, and had worked extensively in both a seniors' home and an orphanage, at the same time, one of which she did without payment, because she cared.

I thought immediately of the many lodges where we continue to entertain the residents, and knew she would be a perfect fit, with her experience, her sunny disposition, and the fact that she could speak English, so we resolved to take this further when home. The spectre of AIDS had not really confronted me full on at this time, although I sadly knew of more than one warm, talented person that had passed away from the disease. One day, we were in a small market somewhere, with many brightly coloured stalls, most with the inevitable rusty corrugated iron covering. One of the stalls sold nothing but simple wooden coffins, many of them very small, which hit me like a ton of bricks, and gave me yet another lesson in the ways of the world.

Hana and Rose came with us to see Wanjiku's projects, with which they were very impressed, and talked of helping, but Hana, at age 25, had lost both parents, and was raising a younger brother and sister on very little money, so, for her at least, this was unlikely. We tried to keep in touch with Hana; the last time we spoke she was in the U.S., with her first baby on the way. There were many attempts to track her whereabouts, which sadly failed.

We spent no less than ten years trying to get Fridah into Canada, jumping through every hoop that was thrown at us. Seniors' lodges wanted her, I recall that the Calgary Zoo wanted her, many other places. The work permit seemed impossible, because of her Kenyan background, whereas if she was from say, the Philippines, there would probably have been no problem. We couldn't even get her in for a holiday, at our expense. She managed to get the requisite $25,000 into her Nairobi bank, deposited by everyone she knew, as a security, but was still told she couldn't come, as she had relatives here, (us!!), and many other excuses. The Kenyan government was known to be corrupt, and we were advised by several sources that this had spread to the embassies and consulates of other countries, which appears possible. In any event, we were reminded that the playing field of life is in no way level.

Some good news is needed, and I am so pleased to say that Fridah is now married and living in Germany with her husband. We remain in regular contact, which, hopefully, we always will.

One Sunday morning we travelled to a school just outside the Mathare Valley slums, where a youth group, co-ordinated through the Maji Mazuri centre, was to put on a performance for us that would illustrate the issues, drugs, AIDS, and crime, that were encountered on a daily basis. We were a little early for them, but there was some beautiful singing, such as you will only hear in Africa, coming from a service in the large, partially open-sided wooden building nearby. This was, of course, a magnet for us both, and within seconds we were quietly standing by a corner of the packed room, listening to the amazing sound. At the end of the song, the minister called to us, and said, "Why are you here?", to which we replied that we were shortly to see a performance by the youth group, and also entertain them with our instruments. The minister asked if we would do something for them, to which we replied that we needed our two guitars. His response was, "We can wait", (we had by now learned that time was not relevant to indigenous Kenyans), and we were shortly back, tuned up and ready to go.

As soon as we started, with an uptempo spiritual number, the place positively exploded with hand-clapping, stamping, swaying, and general chanting along with our song. The floor of the building was dirt and sand, so by the time we reached the second or third verse, with all the stamping, it was just about impossible to see any faces, let alone breathe. But we did about three songs, then left to catch up with the

The beautiful markings of a Maasai giraffe

Proud parents in the Maasai Mara

youth group, full of an incredible energy on which I have drawn so many times.

Before we left Nairobi, we visited famed author Baroness Karen Blixen's home, (pseudonym Isak Dinesen), now with beautiful gardens, and donated to the people of Kenya by the Dutch government. We then headed to Mombasa for a couple of days sightseeing, before heading back to Canada, and had an amazing break at the "Bamburi Beach Hotel", a half hour from the airport, where I especially remember our first night's al fresco supper, under a full moon, and within feet of the Indian Ocean. We explored the strongly Arab influenced Old Mombasa, somewhat run down, but with an ambience like nowhere else. We swam in the almost hot Indian Ocean, just south of the equator, marvelling at the very different fish, and oh so mistakenly removing our T-shirts before laying in the water. Then we visited the famous Akamba co-operative craft village, where well over 100 wood carvers of various skills, carved the animals of Kenya, with master carvers sometimes finishing the carvings if necessary, before they were sent all over the world.

Back to Nairobi for one more night, when we visited the historic Kenya Museum after checking out of the hotel, following which, the guest services manager of the "680", Annette, with whom we had become friendly over our time there, invited us to use her suite to shower and prepare for the journey home. Mary put on her favourite skirt from India, that was very much admired. Needless to say, she immediately took it off, and it remained with Annette in Nairobi!

We had brought to Kenya a case full of things for the children; now we were heading back with the same case full of African crafts, which would be shortly sold, and proceeds sent back to Wanjiku. Not only that, but we had bought a large carved giraffe on Bamburi beach, and also took back many memories, including that of the traditional Maasai Moran, (warrior), dance, which has been an integral part of our children's performances ever since. The crafts sold well, and, every time somebody went to Nairobi, they would return with a case of crafts, which was always opened with great excitement, not only to see the beautiful carvings, but because the case contained the unforgettable smell of Africa!

Us with "MeMe" – photo Tracy Grabowski. Ventriloquist figure by Verna Finley, Florida

Jamming in New Orleans

"Rock and Roll will never die!" – at St. Albert Children's Festival

ACT EIGHT

Schools (fun and learning)

Santa Claus Parades

A "Day out with Thomas"

Festivals, Fairs, Fort Edmonton, and more

Ventriloquism and laughter

Southern Tours: Arizona, California, & Las Vegas

Full Circle

Thousands at the fair.

"Thomas and friends"

SCHOOLS (FUN AND LEARNING)

*O*ur shows for children had started quite a few years before that magical trip to Kenya, somewhat sporadically at first, with the occasional appearance at a shopping centre or some such. In those days, we did already established material such as Tom Paxton's "Going to the Zoo", or Shel Silverstein's "The Unicorn", interspersed with a "jug" band or limbo dance. This expanded considerably when we became involved with the huge Edmonton Fringe Festival; second globally only to Edinburgh, and performed sets in the old Telephone Museum, which was the perfect location for a focused show. There was a gratifying response, which triggered off the idea of starting schools' performances the following year.

We put together a curriculum-based one hour show called "This land is your Land", for grades K to 6, with the Woody Guthrie song of the same name to kick off the performance in high energy, (always a must), and also reprised in the final medley. There was a song from each Province, brief information on what was produced there, and a huge Provincial flag brought out. I'd written a "Song for Saskatchewan", also we made sure to include a song in both French Canadian and Acadian, although, somewhat regretfully, not having one in any of the indigenous languages, of which there are many. We obtained co-sponsorship of the show from the "Musicians' Performance Trust Fund", administered by the American Federation of Musicians, which had been such a huge support when we were living in the Fredericton area of New Brunswick. This enabled us to take our music into schools that might otherwise have been unable to afford a live performance. The show succeeded beyond our wildest dreams, with more than 470 performances in the three Western Provinces over the next few years.

The creative stars must have been aligned for us in that year, 1997, for not only did we create this schools' show, Mary also attended the Citadel Theatre School, performing in an excerpt from "Nicholas Nickleby", on her final night. In addition, there was a trip to Las Vegas for the International Ventriloquists' Convention, which art form would become a huge part of her life, and all of our performances in the future. Funnily enough, in my pre-teen years before I had started in music, I had thought of ventriloquism as a possible future, having seen "live" Bobbie Kimber, (Augustus Peabody),Arthur Worsley, (Charlie Brown) and Saveen, (Daisy May), all of whom I loved, but the first Lonnie Donegan concert fixed that, as it did for probably 95% of other potential musicians who were shortly to appear on the circuit, so great was his influence.

Because of our schools' show, there was a simple adaptation to make a great Canada Day performance, and we did two that year, with our friend Bob Shortt from Ireland on banjo, in both Fort Edmonton Park, (of which we will hear more later), and the neighbouring town of Leduc, with a blind panic in between, as both venues needed a full audio setup.

My stepmother Joan was visiting us at the time from the U.K. with her friend Leni, so talented in artistic needlework. Leni designed and embroidered Jewish Wedding Canopies, which went all over Canada, in addition to her other projects, and lived on Mayne Island in British Columbia. Joan had a professional theatre background. Following her training, she had appeared as a member of the resident company in the New Theatre Oxford, England, for some years, alongside luminaries such as John Neville, who did so much to make the Neptune Theatre, in Halifax, Nova Scotia, into a world-class destination. This was only the second time Joan had seen us perform, so it was an important day for all three of us, and she positively scurried around the Fort Edmonton stage area, taking numerous photographs.

Our Canada Day show grew and grew, being booked into many towns and cities across the Western Provinces, in addition to frequently being seen in Edmonton at or in front of City Hall, the Muttart Conservatory, and other locations.

    On one occasion we were outdoors by the Convention Centre, immediately before the fireworks, which were to be in the river valley below, and the place was packed. There was a large choir in town from Louisville, Kentucky, and I talked to the choir director to see if they would mind doing "O Canada", the National Anthem, at the close of our set, which they were honoured to do. We backed up with some reasonably heavy guitar work, and the fireworks started about halfway through, leaving more than a few people a bit teary on a magnificent summer's evening. Perfect!!

    At that time, Edmonton had a Mississippi-style riverboat on which we also performed, dressed in twenties styled costumes, with firstly a dining set, such as we would have done in the Rockies resorts, followed by a lively guitar and banjo sing-along on the outdoor upper deck. They had an excellent sound system on the boat, and, once we got Mary's keyboard into the act, work in that dining room did a huge amount to polish our music, as one could hear and balance everything so very clearly.

    Aside note: When we first started performing together, we didn't have stage monitors, and had probably never used them, but when we got into bigger, (and rowdier), venues, we got a single monitor amp. that we would mount behind us to put a general "wash" of the mix over the stage, so that we could hear what we were doing. This, of course, had a notch filter, so that we could remove the inevitable feedback, but was definitely a step in the right direction. Then we got more sophisticated, with floor monitors, and ultimately got to the level where, on tour, we would carry two systems, with separate mix and power for monitoring in larger venues, although I always like to have the monitor mix as close as possible to that which is out front, so that we can hear what the audience hears.

The next schools' show that we did arose from our many years with the Earth Day Festival. Called "Planet Kindness", all songs were original, and were based on our experiences both from the festival, and from our tour in Kenya with Debbie from the "World Kindness Movement". By now, our performances had evolved hugely, with the appearance of Mary's ventriloquial figure "MeMe" in her own likeness, created by Verna Finley, who at the time was North America's leading soft puppet maker. This, of course, opened the door for many comedic asides, such as, "If you have a puppet of yourself, you will never need a psychiatrist"! Added to this: we were increasing the magic and participation from the audience at every possible turn, so that they were learning, or reinforcing, their environmental knowledge, but having fun at the same time. The energy created in the room was colossal, as it has been in all of our children's shows, because children cannot wait to give back to you, if you give them your all, which we always will.

The programme also included the introduction of "Verna, the Vegetarian Vulture", which Mary had personally got from Steve Axtell, in Ventura, California, who makes such amazing puppets and props. In our case, Verna would teach the children in depth about water conservation, with a few funnies like, "Take a bath with a friend", always guaranteed to raise a laugh, even though a shower would conserve even more. The show was closed with Mary's song, "Jambo, Jambo, Jambo", (Swahili for "Hello"), and included a version of the dance we had seen in the Maasai village, with three boys dressed in Maasai outfits, competing to see who could jump the highest. Also, a girl, wearing a Maasai wedding necklace, would be standing at the side to pick the winner, little knowing that the two of them would be coupled together, with the inevitable audience response, at the song's end.

SANTA CLAUS PARADES

We created two more schools' programmes, one for Christmas, and one for a general end of term party, which is always popular. All four shows were interactive, and the Christmas show was adapted every year for two or three "Santa's arrival" events at larger shopping centres, where we would always end with kids singing a Christmas song for Santa, followed frequently by a parade around the mall, including Santa, the kids, some parents, and us at the front with guitar and banjo. One year, we'd just done a parade, and went for a break in a little coffee bar which was run by a young Kenyan man. Imagine his and our surprise, when we found that his parents owned and operated the "Bamburi Beach Hotel", where we had stayed when in Mombasa, not so long before.

The ultimate best of these parades was organized for two or three different years in what we have always considered to be Edmonton's number one, though not necessarily largest, shopping centre. At the end of the show, Santa had arrived from the North Pole, and Mary was interviewing him about Mrs. Claus' health, plus his trip down. At the end of this, all the children sang "Jingle Bells", and I had a trumpet (Bob Tildesley or later Joel Gray), clarinet (Doug Innes), and tuba player, hidden separately in the audience, who came up playing on the second verse to join in the festivities. We then left the stage to start the parade, at which time we were joined by local children appearing in the professional production of the "Nutcracker" that was running in town, all in full costume, for the walk around.

We played things like "Winter Wonderland", "Rudolph", "Santa Claus is coming to town", and "White Christmas"; all in true New Orleans style, and had a blast doing it. For the first time in many years, I even removed the mute from my banjo!

Many of the events we have done over the years have been created where we could see a need. There is a large pedway system that connects the main office buildings and two downtown shopping centres in the city, which for over 20 years was host to the "official" Santa Claus parade. Of course, it was all indoors and heated, thus attracting thousands of families with small children, who would be seated or standing on each side of the route, waiting for the parade to start. I could see a huge need for an act to go out, well before the parade started, to get everybody "pumped", which we did, with guitar and banjo, for many years, playing favourites for young and old. We carried a bag of sleigh bells with us, giving them out for a couple of songs as we went along, and when we played an instrumental version of "Sleigh Ride", with the bells jingling, both the sound, and response, was amazing!

There were T.V. cameras throughout the parade route, plus one at the judging area. Sometimes there would be gaps in the parade caused by some minor mishap, (such as a wheel coming off a handcart), when we would endeavour to quickly fill the hole; especially one year in the judging area, where an unmanned static camera was actually transmitting the view of a blank wall to those at home. We arranged two or three bits of "business" to make sure this never, ever, happened again, and always watched the area with great vigilance.

A "DAY OUT WITH THOMAS"

I received my first "Thomas the Tank Engine" book at the age of five, in a Christmas stocking at my aunts' house in Derby, where I instantly fell in love with Wilbert Awdry's pictures, and the fact that, wonder of wonders, all the engines could talk to each other, which to me, seemed perfectly logical at the time. The Rev. Awdry, a railway buff, had written his first book "The Three Railway Engines" as a gift for his son, Christopher, who was ill with the measles. It was subsequently seen by a friend, who immediately asked if he might refer it to a publisher. Both of my grandfathers were Anglican ministers, one of whom slightly knew the Rev. Awdry, and while not essential to this story, it is nice to know of a family link before I became involved.

Fast forward to 2007, Wilbert Awdry had passed on, having written no less than 26 books in the "Railway" series, with son Christopher adding more. T.V. series had ensued, one of which had Ringo Starr as an occasional guest character, and were now on the cartoon version, "Thomas and Friends", aimed at an even younger market. Ringo had purchased the entire concept, along with Pierce Brosnan and others, under the name of "Hit Entertainment".

The business was huge on both sides of the Atlantic, and in 2007, no less than eight full-size replicas of Thomas, one of which was a fully operational locomotive, were to be seen at different locations throughout the U.S. and Canada, to the delight of many thousands of small children.

We got a call from Heritage Park, in Calgary, with whom we had been in touch for some years, to come in, doing six shows a day to packed audiences in a huge tent, right by the railway track on which Thomas would be running, aided by a much larger steam locomotive behind, which was probably invisible to most of the children. Thomas in his bright blue livery, was, and is, magic, with a little white smoke from his funnel, a friendly whistle, a wave from the driver, and, after the first two or three years, a face that worked, with moving eyes and mouth. No wonder the children loved him!

Our dog, Meggie, travelled with us everywhere, and we asked if we might bring in our trailer, both for breaks when time allowed, and also for sleep at night, plus somewhere for Meggie whilst we were performing, which was her "second home", and a very familiar space. This was agreed, and we camped initially in the Tipi area close to the fort, where there was a well-hidden power socket, a site we used for several years.

It would be difficult to describe the ambience of Heritage Park, in which we were to stay each spring for "A Day out with Thomas" for thirteen years. We soon got to know the security guards, two of whom would be the only other human occupants of the park, when evening arrived, and all was closed until the next morning.

The success of any society, and most businesses, is usually determined by the example of the person at the helm, and Heritage Park at this time was no exception. President and C.E.O. for the whole period we worked with Thomas was Alida Visbach, a hugely talented lady whom we had first met when living in Fredericton, N.B., where she was running the nearby "Kings Landing" historical settlement, a somewhat smaller but still very viable facility. She raised incredible amounts of money for additions and improvements to Heritage Park, and was always available very rapidly for any staff member or volunteer who needed a consultation. Not only that, but she would frequently be seen volunteering herself in different positions during the annual visit of Thomas, so it is no wonder that the park ran like a well-oiled machine, with camaraderie throughout.

The tent in which we performed had a large stage with good lighting, always perfectly positioned on our arrival, so that parents and grandparents could get the ultimate shot of any child on the stage, and there were many! Just about everything in our show was interactive, plus, of course, we had an original song about Thomas and the park, which was included in most performances. Several of the children would come back to see us more than once, so we were always on the lookout for familiar faces, which made sure that we changed the programme.

We got to know many of the volunteers and staff like family over the years, and always looked forward to our return, coupled with the welcome that went with it, from our arrival at the security gate to the handing in of our key for showers and other facilities, ten days later.

One time, we were told there might be some members of the Calgary City Police Force coming in for training on the following day. There was a very gentle growl from Meggie, quite early in the morning, and you can imagine our surprise when we looked out of the trailer window to see that we were surrounded by officers in full combat dress, all lying on the ground with semi-automatic weapons, and it looked like a war zone. Fortunately, the weapons were not aimed at our trailer, and it was not a day of Thomas performances, so we made tea and coffee, and remained quiet until all was clear.

During "Thomas" show days, there would be somebody positioned at the side of the stage for the entire event doing announcements, to be broadcast all over the park, of Thomas' next trip, our show schedule, and other attractions, all of which had to be done exactly to time. This was a fine jazz singer from Calgary, Cindy McLeod, who had her own radio show, in addition to running the popular summer and winter Calgary Blues Festivals and she became a good friend. For the first years, her announcements would come out in the tent as well, so I had to be constantly aware that if one was scheduled, our music would be reduced to a very low volume, until completion.

Later, things managed to be wired somewhat differently, and announcements went all over the park, but not in the tent. In addition to our stage, with its theatre-style seating, there were "stations" all around the interior, with face-painting, crafts, pictures with Sir Topham Hatt, a railway set-up for play, and many other things, so there was a constant bubble all day, plus the happy faces of many excited children.

Our camping site was changed after a few years, and we moved in behind the old Canmore Opera House, a working theatre in the park. There was a resident company of players preparing for the upcoming season, with artistic directors husband and wife team Trevor Matheson and Melissa Dorsey, where we would be welcome to "sit in" on rehearsals, watching the current year's productions evolve. The opening weekend was always the Victoria Day holiday, and we were so grateful for the company's warmth and friendship.

Each day would start with hopefully a sunny morning, although during the thirteen years that we stayed in Heritage Park, we managed to have a snow dump on a night before performances in all years but one. We'd be up first thing, and I would take Meggie for a walk through the trees behind the old fort, where one might see deer, rabbits, and possibly the resident coyote. The park would be slowly awakening, with a reproduction 1905 bus, itself almost 60 years old, coming gradually through, and dropping off the first staff members at their respective sites. The park was a haven for wildlife, 127 acres almost in the middle of the city, yet with traffic virtually inaudible, even though it was relatively close. Somebody would always be in early to feed and water the horses, as two of the teams would be busy on "Thomas" days, of which there were initially two, followed by a four-day break, during which time the park would continue preparing for the season's opening, and we would recharge our batteries for the final 18 shows. Mary's birthday usually fell in this period, and we would go with Meggie to Banff, in the Rocky Mountains, if there was an open day, unless performing for the children, which was always her greatest joy.

Thomas would be brought past us from his nighttime shed whilst we were having breakfast, and the "Thomas" music would start up from speakers on top of the old buildings, to check that all was perfect before admission was allowed. I would head over to the Chautauqua tent to set up and warm instruments, prepare the stage, and check that all batteries were ready to go, before our busy day. Cindy would have arrived, the heater would be on, and I would take a huge mental breath before the six performances to come. Mary would come in, walking past the restored Laggan station from Lake Louise, and following the railroad tracks to the village, which was next to the field with our tent. Meggie would have had another walk, and it was time to put out the stage props. as volunteers came in, and everyone said hello. Cindy's first announcement had gone out, dead on cue, and the day had begun.

There would be a sea of faces, from very tiny to grandparents, awaiting our show at different times of the day. For many years we have started with a lively instrumental piece to bring people over to the stage area, which always works so well. This would happen here, or, if we already had a nearly full house, we'd start with our song "Day out with Thomas", before involving kids immediately the song was finished. They were up and down from the stage throughout the performance, as part of a lively "jug" band, assisting with a magic trick, a ventriloquist puppet, or as part of a limbo dance, plus trying out hula hoops on the ground in front. More often than not, there would be a group of 20 or so enthralled children sitting on the stage in front of us, in addition to the audience below.

We loved these performances as much as any we have done in our entire lives. The children loved Mary, as they always do, and anyone could see her delight in working with them. The tent was massive, so we brought in our larger system for crystal clarity and a big sound, plus we had the delight of seeing volunteers, many of whom we got to know so well, who would be dancing, jigging, and generally joining in, all around the tent.

Evenings were special. We'd go back to the trailer, and an excited greeting from Meggie, on whom we had of course checked with a meal and walk at lunchtime. Exhausted from six performances, we'd often sit quietly outside if it was sunny, watching rabbits enjoy the new clover. After supper, it was time for a walk around the now empty park, apart from the two security guards, where especially the horses would always come over to share a friendly greeting with all three of us, and maybe get a handful of spring grass. We'd head down to the Glenmore Reservoir, where Meggie would have a swim, and check out the sternwheeler S.S. Moyie, now raised high out of the water, but back in for the season before we were to leave the park, until next year.

Meggie sadly passed on, at almost 16 years of age, leaving a huge hole in our lives. After a year and a half, we decided it was time to adopt a new family member, which we did with a 3 ½ year old Australian Shepherd from the Humane Society, who took less than a minute to be comfortable in her new home. She also loved her spring visits to

Heritage Park, as had Meggie, and was so excited when the three of us showed up with our trailer at the welcoming security gate. We re-christened her "Jenny", as her original name "Nova" meant absolutely nothing to her. One wonders....

FESTIVALS, FAIRS, FORT EDMONTON, AND MORE...

*A*n absolute high spot of our performances for children each year was when we were involved in Children's Festivals, some of which were huge. These usually took place during a school week, when many brightly coloured yellow busloads of kids would descend upon a town, and several stages would run simultaneously with both curriculum-based and "fun" shows, also occasionally some very different things to amaze all. Seating was, of course, pre-booked, and could be in a theatre, a curling rink, or a huge tent in an adjacent park, often with strolling entertainers adding to the ambience. There would usually be a big outdoor stage as well, and all were great to work, with the added focus provided by a real theatre always being our first choice.

The big plus was that these festivals drew musicians and performers from all parts of the globe, who would come in for a several month run across Canada and the U.S. We would get to see so many different acts, some already known to us, and the camaraderie between all was priceless, as in festivals everywhere.

Our hometown of St. Albert had a world-class Children's Festival. Originally produced in Edmonton, this was transferred to a superior location, with park spaces close to the theatre, and riverside walks where various attractions could be located. We were friends with Arden Theatre Artistic Director Brenda Heatherington, plus Manager Leslie MacNeeley, for many years, in addition to festival co-ordinators Nancy Abrahamson, Paul Moulton, Sandra Moloney, Troy Funk, Vicky Rogers, and so many others, plus, more recently, the Arden's current Artistic Director Caitlin North, who took over when Brenda moved to a theatre in Hamilton, Ontario. We have had the privilege of appearing for the duration of the festival no less than nine times, which is so very special in one's home community, where some audience members, plus many of the volunteers, are like extended family, whom one sees every year, and often in between.

Many other festivals, in the three western provinces especially, including Battleford, (4 times), Prince Albert, (to a mostly indigenous children's audience), Red Deer, Bow Island, Fort MacLeod, and more, including the birth of a new festival north of us in Grand Prairie, where the theatre was a perfect venue, and we were soon friends with festival organizer Aum Nicol and theatre manager Wayne Ayling. As with "Thomas", all ran like a well-oiled machine, so we were especially pleased to be invited back.

Of course, there were thousands of performances over the years, and we also took our children's or family shows to fairs and exhibitions in many parts of Canada and the United States. The night before the opening of one of these, there would often be a parade through the town, when we would be perched on a float or in the back of an open car, with banjo and guitar, or sometimes Mary would have a ventriloquist puppet with her, and when we had Meggie, she would always be an integral part of things, riding along with us, and a huge attraction for all.

A friend for many years that I don't need to embarrass tells of an instance where he was asked to go in a parade dressed as a stick of celery. The friend in question was a well-known musician who had sung lead on a million selling pop song, and agreed to help out provided nobody could see his face. He was to sit on the seat back of an open car, with a bunch of broccoli the other side, and Humpty Dumpty, an egg, between them. The car had to go up a hill, and Humpty did that for which he became famous, i.e., he rolled backwards out of the car, over the trunk (boot), and down the street, unable to stop himself, as his arms were inside the egg. He was, of course, pursued by the broccoli and the celery, and I believe all turned out fine. Our friend's face was not seen by anyone, and he jokingly would talk of this as being the low point of his career.

Aside note: Humpty, (forget Dumpty), was a large, somewhat bulbous cannon in the English Civil War. Humpty was set on the battlements, (sat on a wall), to help repel Cromwell's army. The cannon was only fired once, it partially split, and (had a great fall) backwards with the recoil, never to be used anymore. (All the King's horses and all the King's men couldn't put Humpty together again). So many old rhymes have a story....

Unless commuting to a fair from home, we always moved in the day before with our trailer, to get a good, powered site, hopefully, (but not always), in a quieter location, both for our much-needed break periods, also because the trailer would be Meggie's home during the day. Plus, temperatures could often be up to 100°F, so we constantly needed to cool off and get fresh clothes. If staying overnight on the grounds, we would always make sure to have music in the trailer before any fireworks, but preferred to stay off site. There were so many different hats we wore in working a big fair. We might have two or three family shows, or kids' shows, in the day, usually with our own sound. We might stroll, in various outfits, playing music way back to the 20's with banjo and guitar, or with two electric guitars and Pignose amps. at our waists, playing guitar instrumentals of the 60s.

We might play folks into a big evening concert, or do a crowd "warm up", before wrapping up our day; often we would do the Grandstand show ourselves, sometimes for thousands at a time. We tried to make sure that we always knew what was going on, and appointed ourselves "Ambassadors" for every fair, constantly chatting to participants to make sure they had as good a time as possible. One had to be very resilient to work the fair circuit, but there was great fun to be had, and we got to know the proprietors of many travelling carnivals over the year, whom we would look forward to seeing, also the "Carnies"- roustabouts, side-show and ride operators - who live such different lives, but are always friendly and welcoming to visiting performers.

The vision that stays in my head is of one fair where our trailer was almost directly under a very big wheel, which was constantly revolving, with seats full of people, and hoping all had been constructed properly.

It was nothing to drive 1,000 km. or even miles between fair engagements, although we always tried to get a run of 2 or 3 to make things more viable. One time, it was blazing hot, and we were playing in Coeur d'Alene, Idaho, on an outdoor stage, with the sun directly in our faces, and 3 blocks of metal bleachers out front. These would have caused life-altering damage should anyone have touched or sat on them before the sun went down, when they miraculously became perfectly fine. We had an afternoon set, playing to the empty bleachers, while a few trees off to stage right had as many people who could cram under them as possible in order to try and see our show. The awning to the stage was of a heavy red material, creating even more heat, and it was impossible to keep instruments in any semblance of tune, this being before we had an electronic keyboard, which might well have melted! My twelve string Ovation had sustained a broken headstock courtesy of one particular airline flight, and for extra strength, I had put in a couple of titanium drill bits to connect the neck and headstock, before the whole thing was reglued, which worked fine. However, I was not allowing for this day in Coeur d'Alene, when Grade 3 physics reared its head, and the titanium drill bits got excessively hot, lengthened, and actually pushed the headstock right off the guitar, totally ignoring the over 700 lbs. of string tension in the opposite direction. Not every show was easy!

If the run of a fair included Sunday, there would always be a cowboy service, with country band, readings, and cowboy poetry, (frequently featuring Sid Marty, whom we met so many times). Sometimes there would be a minister, or possibly the headliner from the previous evening would take the service, recalling George Hamilton IV, plus Johnny Cash & June Carter, on different occasions. It seemed that the entire community would come out for such a special gathering, which was often preceded by a free pancake breakfast, and these services were among the most powerful community events we have ever witnessed.

In many towns, both in Canada and the U.S., we would be asked to go into one or two seniors' lodges as a part of the fair's community outreach programme, or we would instigate these events on our own behalf. When performing in these situations, we have always given, and will always give, the absolute best and most professional performance of which we are capable, quite as good as we would offer in a theatre setting, with no corners cut, apart from not bringing lights. So often in senior situations things are not the best, and it can be hard for the residents, so from us, they are always going to receive colourful, sharp-looking outfits, good sound, comedy, involvement, and if there is a resident from another country, we will try to include a song in their native language. I am at a loss to understand how anybody could do less.

The fairs had marketing conventions as well, and the Western Canada Fairs convention always fell on the fall weekend when daylight savings time ended. It was impeccably run by our friend from the Moose Jaw Herald, Joyce Walter, who was loved by all. The hospitality room usually had a true jam session every late night, (i.e., folks playing together, NOT doing party pieces to obtain brownie points from potential bookers), and the atmosphere was probably the best, and the most "down home" of any convention we have ever attended, where all were equal, and pleased to have an annual get-together. Business got done, but it was a true relax for all, and we looked forward to seeing performers and fair committees each year.

A bigger convention that we also attended as "service members" was that of the Rocky Mountain Association of Fairs, which we were recommended to attend by friends at Edmonton's Klondike Days, also Lethbridge, and Medicine Hat, all three being larger venues where we frequently performed. The convention moved to various cities in the northern U.S. and southern Canada, always, if possible, taking over an entire large hotel, with several floors overlooking a central atrium. These rooms would be where service members, i.e., anyone providing a potential service for a fair or exhibition, would be staying, and your room was also your trade booth, to be set up in a way to attract as many potential clients as possible.

Frequently you were expected to provide a complimentary bar(!), plus snacks, and these rooms operated much of the day, (and night), way more than that in the scheduled programme.

We of course got engagements from this convention too, but for me personally the huge attraction was the nighttime jam, run in a big circle, (or two concentric circles on occasion), by singer-songwriter John Dunnigan, whom we got to know well over the years. Fair presenters would attend, but they would sit in total silence, with no applause, respecting that this was private time for the musicians, and they were there as guests. One year, there was a female folk singer who had come for a daytime showcase, with none other than Glenn Frey, lead of "The Eagles", to back her up. At the jam that evening I had Glenn on my immediate left, and Frannie Beecher from Bill Haley's original "Comets" on my immediate right, who had originally been guitarist for the Benny Goodman orchestra.

Then there were three of the "Doo-Wah Riders", a fine Country showband, next to a balloon artist, who had made a traditional "balloon banjo" for the occasion. Many more performers, including John, who was roughly opposite me in the large circle. Most people did standard things such as "Take me back to Tulsa", "Country Roads", or Dylan's "You ain't goin' nowhere" on which we could all build huge walls of harmony and fill the room with sound. Somebody a little more jazzy, suggested "The World is waiting for the Sunrise", the song with which the "Jazz Gentlemen" had reached the finals of "Home Grown" on Southern Television in the U.K. all those years before. I kicked off the sequence in Bb, (we had played enough folk and country keys for a bit), and Frannie Beecher positively flew in, with Glenn Frey close behind. We traded licks, did harmonies, took turns on the chords, or different versions of the chords, then Glenn suggested we tried minoring the whole thing, which was incredible fun, and a true stretch for all. Kenny Lee Benson, keyboardist/accordionist for the "Doo Wah Riders", was providing bass parts, plus our long-time friend Jim Calhoun was in the circle as part of the wall of rhythm behind everything. That one song was truly for me: "The jam of a lifetime", and never to be forgotten.

There have been others - one in a dressing room with the brilliant guitarist Ronnie Prophet on the same song - but to play with Glenn Frey and Frannie Beecher as a trio, no, I will never top that!

I should mention that on another song that same evening, folks were taking solos, and I yelled out "balloon solo", for the "banjo" balloon. Most of us played "stop" chords, and the balloon artist, whom I believe was named Joe, dutifully twanged away, with some of the world's finest backing him up, until we all collapsed laughing. Maybe you had to be there, I wish you had seen it too.

Another convention we attended, which was a real eye-opener, was the Texas fairs convention in Houston. There was a vast indoor space, with booths set up in rows, many with sound systems and live "demos" going on next to each other. If you had an actual showcase, it was probably fine, but all these booths operating at once was mindless. Often booths operate with video or audio on headsets, which is good, but this was like a noisy market. We shared space with our friends the Calhouns, and all agreed that it was a waste of time and money, but still a learning experience.

The big plus to visiting Houston was that we were able to spend time with David Burns, and his so warm new American wife Elizabeth, whom we had first met at Windsor Castle some years before. We explored Galveston, the Space Centre, and spent a little while in San Antonio, sitting out under the stars listening to the Mariachi bands, who would rotate from one restaurant to another along the riverbank, throughout a magical evening.

A short break in New Orleans was an absolute must. It was only a few days from Mardi Gras, and the energy, especially in the French Quarter, was building fast. We had a beautiful hotel with a peaceful central courtyard, and a close walk to everything. I had my banjo for potential "sit-ins" and discovered within a very short time that if one had an instrument case there was no "hustling" from clubs, restaurants, or souvenir stalls to make you spend money. Accordingly, the banjo case travelled with us frequently, but often empty, and we had a far better visit because of this.

We visited Preservation Hall, where the creative director as always was Ben Jaffe, whose parents Allan and Sandra have done such an amazing job in keeping the musical heritage of New Orleans alive and vibrant. The night we went, Preservation Hall Jazz Band was being fronted by Wendell Brunious on trumpet, whose brother John, now sadly passed, we had seen fronting a slightly different line-up in Edmonton, though with Ben on sousaphone or bass and "Lil' Joe" Lastie on drums as usual. It reminded me so much of the differences in the "Jazz Gentlemen", when Brian Jenner, who was much more "out there", was fronting, as opposed to Tony Swift, who liked to stay "inside" the sound of the band. I would love to hear Wendell's interpretation of the Harry James classic "Stardust", though am not sure that Preservation Hall would be a fitting location.

There was a conspicuously British banjo player on the stage that night, both in appearance and the style of playing. He introduced himself as having been with the Mike Cotton band in the U.K., and had moved to New Orleans, as several musicians have, to totally immerse himself in, and live, his music. He played long-neck Plectrum banjo, as do I, which made us both pretty rare birds, a tenor banjo being the norm, and we enjoyed comparing instruments. He spotted that I had a Clifford Essex mute on mine, and I was able to show how I had rectified the inevitable "buzz" problem with two bits of green felt.

The place to "sit-in" in New Orleans was Sweet Kathleen's, at the junction of Decatur and Peters streets. Kathleen played piano for the afternoon and dinner sets, then one of her two sons would front the evening, on clarinet or trumpet. I, of course, had to go down for a few songs, plus Mary had her ventriloquist puppet of herself "MeMe", who came up to do "All of me", and work the crowd.

There was an elderly black gentleman on trombone next to me, who said, "I've been playing this (trombone) all my life, and I ain't never backed up no puppet before!! – but his eyes were twinkling as he said it, and I knew he was enjoying it as much as the rest of us.

I was asked to front with a vocal, and picked, "I'm gonna sit right down and write myself a letter", unusually in the key of F, but Kathleen's son Chuck really rose to the occasion, and did a beautiful trumpet solo, exclaiming afterwards what a great choice of key that was, to really lift the song in a different way, which Mary fortunately recorded, my first ever set in New Orleans.

HEADING WEST....

There had been a great deal of research before we moved westwards, from the tiny hamlet of Noonan, by Fredericton, New Brunswick, to the over 1 million people in the Edmonton area of Alberta. We had fallen in love with the resort towns of Jasper and Banff, in the Canadian Rockies, also Harrison Hot Springs, close to Chilliwack and nearer Vancouver, in B.C. Fairmont in the Columbia Valley we had yet to discover, but we had good quality engagements in both Edmonton and Calgary, so the pull was strong, especially as venues in the Maritimes were dwindling somewhat, and we needed to base near a much larger market. The three main centres were Vancouver, Calgary, and Edmonton, all of which we examined in detail, soon discovering that Edmonton had by far the strongest Arts community at that time of any similar sized city in North America, and seemed a good area in which to base, at least for a while. Theatre-wise, the Citadel was a large modern complex, containing three theatres and a hall, all of which were often in use, with very high-quality productions and well attended, whereas Calgary had more difficulty putting "bottoms on seats", especially if the play was a little more challenging in content. Also, despite the best efforts by Ray Petch, of the Musicians' Union, there were still some venues where musicians were expected to survive solely by selling product, which was not a good sign.

We had some regular locations in Calgary, especially the huge Canadian Pacific, (now Fairmont), Palliser Hotel, and the Marlborough Inn "Widgeon's Pub", which was more of a showroom, with four acts, all British, on rotation: Arden & Masie, from Seattle, Washington, our friends Bernie & Red, from close by Abbottsford, B.C., London Bobby, from Vancouver Island, and ourselves. In both of these venues we generally did around three to four week runs each time, and they were "live-in", for the duration.

In Edmonton there had been "house" gigs as well, but for shorter periods, and we were winding those down anyway, apart from the resorts, where we would continue playing for some years. There was the huge summer "Fringe" festival, (where we did children's performances), and also a fine symphony orchestra resident in the Jubilee auditorium, until a new purpose-built concert hall, named after Francis Winspear, was built, which included a magnificent pipe organ. (Aside note: When the Edmonton Symphony orchestra played their final night at the "Jube" before moving to the new venue, we were honoured to play patrons into this special concert, as well as providing music for the intermission). There was live music in most of the hotel lounges, and much live entertainment put on by the city itself, in various guises, as we were to find out shortly. There were around six other full-time theatre companies in addition to productions at the Citadel. One of these "Rapid Fire", an improv. troupe, was in the Guinness book of world records for the longest continuously running improvised soap opera "Die Nasty", while another company, "Teatro La Quindicina", existed almost exclusively on the works of a prolific local playwright, Stewart Lemoine. There must have been others, but the only other playwright I know who has achieved this, was William Shakespeare, so many years ago.

There was also a Francophone theatre in the mostly French area of the city, where there was an outdoor restaurant with live music for pre-theatre entertainment during the summer, and great atmosphere.

The adjacent town of St. Albert, where we eventually bought a home, had a top-quality Children's Theatre, run by Janice Flower, plus, for those serious about their future, there was in Edmonton the Victoria Composite High School for the Performing Arts, after which one could move on to Grant McEwan college, (now University), which had degree level courses in all aspects of music and theatre.

Edmonton also boasted a full-time jazz venue, the "Yardbird Suite", with world-quality music, and many fine musicians, including the prolific pianist, and later Senator, Tommy Banks, whom we were privileged to know well over the years, trumpeter Bob Tildesley, clarinettist Doug Innes, trombonist Bob Stroup, saxophonists P.J.Perry, Kent Sangster, and Dave Babcock There were also popular folk clubs, as in Calgary and Vancouver.

Vancouver is, of course, a vastly bigger region, heavily into film production and recording, but compared to Edmonton and Calgary at the time, there was far less live music, thus huge competition for any work available. Inevitably, there were more street performing acts, of course weather dependent, and housing costs were through the roof! Edmonton was located in the very centre of the three western provinces, with relatively easy access everywhere, except that one had to watch weather conditions on the mountain passes at some times of the year, and possibly even more so on Highway 2 to Calgary, which we avoided on occasion.

So, we decided to give the area a try, and, somewhat regretfully, put what had been our first home together on the market, in many ways hoping that it wouldn't sell. Some three years before, when doing our first run at Edmonton's Mayfield Inn, we had been in touch with our friend Nina, once of David & Nina Burns back in Bermuda days. She had been working as a solo act over much of Canada, which can be very hard, moving from town to town. Then she had a home on Prince Edward Island, but for various reasons, it was time to move. We had a guitarist/vocalist friend, George Spring, who had long wanted to do a duo situation, and suggested the two should meet. Nina came out to visit us at the Mayfield, we introduced them, and all went well. We took a "pro" photo and came up with the name "Summer Wine", as they wanted a band name which suggested slight maturity!

Incidentally, after that Mayfield Inn run, we went into performances connected with Universiade '83, the World University Games, with performing artists also appearing from many of the participating countries. It was an incredibly bad mosquito season, and we had to do an outdoor set for CBC television one early evening, quite the worst time for being bitten!! Anyway, it went out live, with us both doing this very strange dance, along with our music. It was possibly somewhat Germanic, as it involved much slapping of legs, knees, arms, and even occasionally one's face, whilst still playing and singing at the same time. Fortunately, this was a one-time performance, which has never been repeated.

Aside note: While at Universiade, we met a magician who was also Prime Minister of the Cook Islands, and had a good laugh, agreeing with him that this was probably the only country in the world where one could be Prime Minister, and a professional magician at the same time.

On one occasion, we were doing an extended dining room run for the Edmonton Petroleum Club, (where I had the privilege of sipping champagne from the Stanley Cup after an Oilers win) and had rented a double-wide trailer out in the country by Antler Lake for the spring season, with the amazing sound of all the nesting birds to awaken us each morning, which we soaked up like sponges. Then, a year later, we were heading to look at the possibility of buying a house close to the lake's edge, wondering if this was to be a good move, when a large water delivery truck barrelled up from behind and straight into the rear of our Suburban. To give an idea of the impact, our truck was empty apart from one large speaker cabinet behind the passenger seat, which broke open the rear van-style doors from the inside. Unlike a gasoline-carrying vehicle, this water truck had no baffles, so the contents all moved to the back, then came forward again hard, giving us a whole new appreciation of the term "double whammy". Suffice to say we never did see the house and spent much of the next two years involved with jaw, neck and back therapy, but still managed to do several runs in Fairmont, plus the two summers already mentioned at Henry VIII in Bermuda, which culminated in our marriage ceremony in August 1990.

Once ensconced in the Edmonton area, we became far more aware of community events. Our first visit to the Alberta Showcase had made us realize that we could expand our horizons in different areas, which we started to do as soon as possible, with Arts Council stage concerts immediately added to our touring performances. The first job we did for the city itself was a family event in the centre at Rundle Park, where we made a friend in Parks & Recreation, Heather Johnson, the first of so many over the years to come.

"KLONDIKE DAYS"

Edmonton is called "Canada's Festival City" for a reason, with around 50 festivals, of varying sizes, in the vicinity every year. There was a summer festival called "Klondike Days", harking back to the gold rush era of the 1890's, which started from Edmonton, (the Klondike gold rush was actually 1896-98), and we became very involved for several years. In the huge park area of Northlands, there was a mammoth fun-fair/carnival, with spectacular rides and sideshows. Several stages would operate throughout the day and evening, with big names all included in the ticket price, such as Tommy Hunter, (a regular), "Kiss", "The Beach Boys", "Trooper", "B.T.O.", "The Guess Who", and more, plus always a top-notch hypnotist, one of whom used to regularly send his "subjects" out into the audience searching for their own stolen backsides! There was a "Klondike" stage, the "Silver Slipper", where we did several daily period vaudeville shows, also a "Kids World", where we appeared one year with 30 performances. There was even a stream for gold panning, with real flakes of gold, and an old-timey park, where our friend Tony Michaels, who has often appeared with us, would play traditional fiddle tunes, plus a couple of other musicians for backup, (The "Foggy-Minded Mountain Boys").

There was a huge downtown parade to launch the event, which often took a couple of hours to pass, and floats were frequently brought long distances to participate. In addition to the appearance of local dignitaries, there were two military bases in the area, both of which were well represented, including a top-quality military band, which gave the thousands lining the route the opportunity to acknowledge their service.

The city joined in the fun, separate from Northlands, and many shops, restaurants, or lounges would have their staff dressed in period costumes, as were much of the general public, and there would often be live music to complete the atmosphere. This was put together by the Edmonton Klondike Days Association, and one would agree on a ten-day contract of 40 varied performances for a set fee. Some of the shows would be a proper production, with two or three acts, or we might find just ourselves playing 1890's – 1920's music gently in a bank, with a small sound setup. It could be a service club, a seniors' lodge, or several other places, I recall the lobby of the Westin as well.

Some venues were not very clever. One time we were in front of a white wall at the side of a supermarket on a blazing hot day, with the sun directly on us, and full setup. We both ended up with heatstroke, and were so glad to get out of there. If one met another performer, the initial greeting was always, "How many have you got left?" Four venues a day was hard work, especially if audio equipment was involved, but we all enjoyed it, and were sad when it was over.

Each day had an outdoor pancake breakfast in a different area of town, with stage setup, often a small troupe of dancers, a couple of acts, and of course a visit from that year's "Klondike Kate", who would do a vaudeville spot of about 20 minutes in elaborate 1890s costume, before being whisked off by her friendly escort Rex Moore, to the next venue.

We've worked with several Kates over the years. Sue Whalen (Janzen) was the first, whom we had met when she was in the duo "Randy & Sue", Gillian Campbell, Kennedy Jenson, Maria Manna, and others, including Kate Ryan, no relation to the original "Klondike Kate" of the same name. All put their own "stamp" on the character of Kate, a role which was offered to Mary on occasion, and we have loved interacting on stage with every one of them. The community breakfasts and shows we all did together, usually with an audience of several hundred, and other acts, such as P.J. MacDonald, Bob Shortt, and Dr. Boogie, to name a few, were so much a high spot of each day - if sometimes a little early!

Aside note: The "Klondike Kate" of history, was born in Johnville, N.B., Aug. 20th, 1869. She went to Seattle, Washington, as a nurse, then joined the gold rush, travelling alone and staking three claims. As a special constable, she was the first female member of the Northwest Mounted Police, possibly in Dawson City, also sometime a gold inspector, jail keeper, and restaurateur. An early suffragette, she died at age 63 in Vancouver. During this period, a dance-hall girl working in Dawson City, Kate Rockwell, had picked up on the "Klondike Kate" nickname, and was using it herself, as a performer, which is the Kate remembered at "Klondike Days", not the original.

On the Northlands grounds there was always a particular country that was showcased each year in one of the huge pavilions. One year, it was Britain, and we were asked to head up the mainstage, with three shows daily, having had special costumes made for the occasion, plus the production of a "nostalgia" recording "Over 'Ome", which included the brilliant jazz pianist, Charlie Austin, also of a U.K. background. This was marketed from the stage, and sold out by the end of the festival. Crowds were colossal for every performance, as was the response, and we loved it. There was also an English "Pub", featuring "London Bobby", and Christine Pilgrim, from Barkerville, B.C., who did an act as a Victorian schoolmarm, especially popular in schools, where she would sometimes stay for several days. Christine had an incredible entrance. She would walk through the room to the stage with a tray of glasses, all labelled and with a little cloth on top, calling out "British Air", "only one dollar", in character, of course. Amazingly, people bought them.

Sunday Promenade Day was the best of all. Held at Churchill Square in front of City Hall, many hundreds would stroll through in their finery, all as though they had just walked off the set of "Hello, Dolly". The main street, Jasper Avenue, was closed to traffic, pedestrians were everywhere, and bands of all sorts - Country, Rock, Jazz, and Folk, were on stages at every corner, plus there was a special Klondike stage as well. There would be bathtub races down the street, the strongest man contest, beard contests, and more, also the mayor and members of council would dress up, making this day truly one of the highlights of summer. "Klondike Kate" of course presided over awards and festivities, until all the ceremonies were complete.

The day after "Promenade", while Klondike Days was still running in high gear, the big stage for "A Taste of Edmonton" would be erected in Churchill Square, with lights and a large sound system. Booths would surround the square, and the leading hotels and restaurants offered a small portion of up to two items from their extensive menus at a nominal price. This was initially a five-day festival, and had live music going from mid-day until later at night, with smaller acts during the day. We would usually be featured on this stage as well, our preference being to have the contrast of doing a children's show in mid-afternoon. Many of the other Klondike acts would be in, including our friends "Stratus", (Brock, Merry-Jo, and Murray), a fine act from Calgary, who were popular on the circuit. The evening acts were bigger Country, Rock or Blues bands, who would come on, and, in musician's parlance, "Kick some butt", when the square would erupt with summer fun.

HERITAGE FESTIVAL

Another summer festival where we would occasionally do a mainstage appearance was the huge Heritage Festival. Billed as the "World's largest celebration of multiculturalism", it had close on 100 countries represented each year, with lines of tents stretching into the distance, each containing ethnic crafts and clothing for sale, plus history and tourism information. Food from all over the world was available, reasonably priced, and admission was free, with special buses running from all over the city. A 3-day event, held over the August long weekend, the festival drew over 200,000 participants each year, in addition to the many volunteers who went to such lengths to proudly share their culture with others.

In front of each tent there was frequently a stage, which was used for traditional dances from each country, and sometimes live music, each stage operating alternately so that all performances could be truly enjoyed.

Of course, Canada was represented as well, with First Nations drum circles, dances, and more, often featuring our friend of many years Amanda Lamothe, who draws especially the young with her haunting music and storytelling.

The huge outdoor covered amphitheatre, which we have used for the Earth Day Festival, has over 1,100 permanent seats, plus hundreds more can be seated on the grass, and we have done a Klondike set, a Jazz set, or an uptempo Irish party set on different occasions, with extra musicians when needed.

Aside note: While writing on festivals, I must acknowledge the efforts of Brian Calnan and later Ted Greer, in co-ordinating and liaising with performers for the Edmonton Klondike Days Association. Both seasoned performers themselves, Brian subsequently went on to

Lake Havasu, in Arizona, now the location of the rebuilt London Bridge, over which I used to walk, in its original site, when I first left school all those years ago. Brian performed as Brian O'Callaghan in the replica English pub next to the bridge and remained there for some time. Ted Greer, who had earlier led the popular band "Shaken, not Stirred", (reminiscent of James Bond), did gargantuan work for the Association, seemingly appearing simultaneously at every venue to ascertain that all was well.

"A Taste of Edmonton" was no less tirelessly booked and stage managed by Wanda Feland, herself a fine blues singer, who seemed to be by the stage 24 hours a day; while Michael Kurylo, of FM sound, organized and ran the Heritage Festival mainstage. He was on the organizing team of all three major festivals, helped over the festival weekend in later years by Janice Boudreau, (now Wilson), when they were both with Earth Day.

FORT EDMONTON PARK

*I*n addition to our extensive touring, the area positively exploded for us over the next few years. We were already appearing at special events for Fort Edmonton Park, both on stage and in a "strolling" capacity, where we would appear in appropriate period costumes to fit different sections of the park, and play music to suit the time depicted. It was, of course, fine to play anything older, but we were always very careful not to play a piece that hadn't been written yet! Sometimes we'd go on the train and do a short performance of 3 or 4 songs, starting off by ourselves, but with everybody singing and clapping when we reached the Fort itself, all ready for their day back in time. We'd be on the streetcar too, usually with Judy Garland's "Trolley Song", amongst others, and loved helping to build the ambience of the park, often telling participants the background to pieces being played, which they loved.

An example of this would be the story of an aspiring English songwriter, Harry Dacre, in the early 1890's. Charles K. Harris in New York had just sold a million sheet music copies of his song "After the Ball", the first popular song writer to achieve this, so Harry thought that if he were to be successful, he should emigrate. Which he did, taking his bicycle with him, for use in his new home. He was going through the Customs and Immigration line up in New York and was told he would have to pay a small duty on the bike, at which point the person in the line behind him said, "You're lucky it isn't a bicycle built for two". That night, Harry wrote the song.

The season started properly on the Victoria Day long weekend, with a three-day event, hopefully telling everyone that winter was truly over. We would usually be strolling on 1905 and 1920 streets for this occasion, with the "Banjo Busters" on the station platform, and Jay Kuchinsky in the Fort itself, sometimes with daughter Georgia, playing old time fiddle tunes. Capital Brass would be at the Firehall, and possibly somebody on 1885 street too, so there was music everywhere, with our friend John Spearn as well near the ice cream parlour, in more recent years. One year we were asked to do only Victorian music, so we did just that, performing songs that were all composed during her reign - which was long, so a huge choice of material. We'd already had a taste of the season over the Easter weekend, when there was a special event called "Sweet Treats", with the inevitable Easter Egg hunt. Also, there was "Hats off to Dad", on Fathers Day, plus Dominion Day, with its big parade, as there frequently was on Victoria Day. If we came in for Dominion Day, we always did a stage show, including Bob Shortt, (banjo & mandolin), and sometimes Cynthia Horton, (string bass). In the earlier and later parts of the season there could be some colder days, when we'd be trying to play stringed instruments out of doors in temperatures a little below freezing. Eventually, we worked out that the trick was to play two songs indoors, rush out and play one, or possibly two, very short pieces, then quickly back inside to adjust tuning and restore circulation.

We wrote several songs about the park. "Sweet Treats", for Easter, had an 1890s waltz feel to it, "Fort Edmonton Park" we generally only did on stage, unless requested, as an audio system was needed. This piece told visitors all about the park, and what they might see, being included on our "Flying high for Kids" C.D., as was "Things that go bump in the night", written for a Halloween playlet that we wrote and performed for "Spooktacular". This had no less than 72 performances over 2 days one year, with spooky lighting, a witch, plus a dragon blowing smoke to revive a body, (me), that had been asleep for 1,000 years, and definitely didn't look too good!

One "Spooktacular" we went in as the "Lost Souls Blues Band", with appropriate lighting and dry ice effects. We, of course, were not of this world, and told audience members that they were welcome to join us, but the gig would never, ever end. One boy of about 12 or 13 really wanted to join in; we repeated the fact that he would never return to his normal life - to which he said, "I don't care, I just want to join....".

Every year there was a storytelling festival, where we came up with the idea of doing songs with stories -ours and others - and set up in Kelly's Saloon on 1885 street, which we loved; being able to share the story behind each song and present the whole in an almost folk club atmosphere.

There was a Children's Day, Harvest weekend, Free Access Day, and often private events, some huge, where we would be asked to provide music and ambience. Celtic weekend, again with appropriate music, often saw Mary out with her Scottish vent. figure "Martha McHaggis", having fun with all and sundry. There were highland games to go with this, plus of course a pipe band, and I remember Mary, (except it was

1905 Street – photo Tracy Grabowski

Mary with one of George Formby's first Ukulele banjos

Martha talking really), on CBC radio telling everyone to come down quickly and see all the burly men, especially their knees!

In 2001, no, we didn't meet up with HAL - you must have seen the movie, which sowed the seed for David Bowie's "Space Oddity", and was shown in London's West End on the vast "Cinerama" screen, blowing us all away – no, this was another event, where we played at the Fort to celebrate the 8th IAAF World Championships in Athletics, an occasion only fractionally less than the Olympics, and with many of the same athletes. Prince Edward, together with his wife Sophie, were in attendance to open the games, and we were all at Fort Edmonton for a huge informal get-together, with barbeque and everyone mixing freely. "MeMe", Mary's alter ego ventriloquist puppet, who knows nothing about protocol, was totally smitten by Edward, even stealing a kiss, to Sophie's great amusement, and they seemed like a truly special couple.

We were in one of our period costumes, I don't remember which, but our next Royal event was to be in 2005, when Her Majesty the Queen and Prince Philip, Edward's parents, came into Clarke Stadium for the City's centennial. This time we had special 1905 costumes designed, as we were to play the Royal visitors into the stadium with appropriate music, and it was such a privilege to be involved. Our costumes, created by Kathleen Mulder, were amazing, and we use them at Fort Edmonton Park, to this day.

"Christmas Reflections" was magic. The shops would be decorated in true Dickensian style, with a choir in one of the churches, and sleigh rides along the snow-covered streets. Somewhere, there'd be a fire burning, with the smell of hot chestnuts attracting visitors to stop for a chat. We'd be in the Masonic Hall, which, while still a period building, was not "time sensitive", as it was used in season for a food concession. We would set up and do a proper Christmas show for all ages, especially having great fun with the kids, and looked forward to these performances in such a special atmosphere, for the whole year.

1919 Baldwin Locomotive 107 at Fort Edmonton Park

Christmas at The Fort

LET'S TAKE IT FROM THE TOP

Aside note: We have made so many friends at Fort Edmonton Park that this book would need a supplement to list them all, but I absolutely must acknowledge Leslie Fulks, with whom we worked for so many years, and Tannia Dowler, (now Franke), whom we first met at Fort Edmonton Park, and who, together with her family, has become such a significant part of our lives.

Some park events, especially in summertime, would immediately follow a Sunday lunchtime session on the "Edmonton Queen" sternwheeler, which has already been mentioned. We wrote an uptempo 20s-style song about that as well, which is featured in many of our performances, especially for a seniors' audience. We had it down to a fine art, getting from the boat to the park, knowing every kink in the road and where to change lanes, so that we never, ever, arrived late.

So many things. We took our environmental show "Planet Kindness" into the Valley Zoo, (also to Calgary Zoo, and to Phoenix Zoo in Arizona, several times), in addition to doing strolling sets every Easter, and being involved, amongst other things, with "Dream night at the Zoo", a special event where those children that were able were brought in from the Stollery children's hospital, by ambulance if necessary, and would have a never to be forgotten evening seeing all the animals, and being entertained by professional performers, which was a privilege for all involved. A huge undertaking to coordinate, and we especially remember the efforts of Jasmine Hestad and Tyler Pollock, in addition to several others.

Sometimes we'd take a trip north, to Fort McMurray, in the Oil Sands area, where we once used to play the big hotels, and there would be a special kids' day for one of the oil giants, Suncor, Syncrude, or Albian Sands. Or south for one of many Arts Council shows, booked from our booth at Showcase, with theatre and other appearances throughout western Canada, and so many kind letters from presenters following our performances, which are treasured to this day.

UKRAINIAN CULTURAL HERITAGE VILLAGE

The Ukrainian Village, close to Elk Island National Park, became a regular venue, with annual appearances at schools' outings immediately before and after Father's Day. These shows for the children were amazing. There would be around 2,000 students daily, plus teachers, and of course some members of the general public. I would bring in a couple of other children's performers as well: Mugsy the Clown, time traveller Phileas Flash, or Kip, the Court Jester, who would go in a different area to us, and run their day as they wished, interacting with each other or doing separate spots. We were set up in the grassy main courtyard, with an open-sided tent to protect us, equipment, and instruments from possible showers. It being June, we always carried large garbage bags to cover the main speakers if needed. We would be in nice and early for setup, sound checks etc. before the children arrived, also bring a plethora of patch cords, as we alternated with one or two members of a Ukrainian dance troupe, who taught some basic steps, to the delight of the children, and we never knew what we were going to have to try and connect to our system. One thing we always knew, was that the dancers would be of top quality. The strong Ukrainian heritage on the Alberta, Saskatchewan, and Manitoba prairies means that dance troupes, such as Shumka and Cheremosh, are among the world's finest, who frequently perform in the country of their ancestors, to great acclaim.

We would each do five shows daily, plus I would of course monitor sound for the dancers as needed. Our show would be a mix; we would usually start with a high energy instrumental piece to bring people over, if the benches were not already full. Then the show got going big time, with all kinds of interactive music, magic, ventriloquist puppets, hula hoops, dances, jug bands, whatever suited each group. There was an original song "Kindness", from our children's C.D., very Caribbean in style, with the sound of steel drums wafting over the courtyard. This taught, "Kindness to the planet, Kindness to each other, and Kindness to oneself", always so popular with students and teachers alike.

By mid-afternoon, the buses headed back to their respective schools, and we could pack up and load, followed by a big communal buffet dinner, for staff, volunteers, and performers, when we were able to discuss the day and relax, looking forward to the following Monday, when we would do it all again.

I must acknowledge the friendship and hospitality we have always received, especially from Pamela Trischuk and Karen Johnsrud, plus of course Arnold Grandt and David Makowsky, consecutively at the helm since our first appearance in 2007. The Ukrainian village is very different, depicting the rural lives of settlers from just before 1900 onwards. Interpreters live the part, speaking as though one had truly travelled back through time, with the exception of those in the churches. To me, the "burdei", a shelter dug from the ground, and often one's only home for possibly years, is a sight well worth the trip out from Edmonton, with the many other sights: churches, houses, businesses, and all the animals, as a huge bonus. Fort Edmonton Park shows the growth of the city from the days of the Hudson's Bay Fort to the arrival of the railroad, followed by streetcar and automobile, while the

Ukrainian village shows a different culture, yet with similarities, in a partially parallel time frame, and we have been so fortunate to perform for them both over the years.

Often in the summertime we'd be running through the Rockies for B.C. gigs, especially in Harrison Hot Springs, or Fairmont, in the Columbia Valley. The town of Revelstoke, en route to Harrison, has a beautiful downtown plaza, with a large bandstand, which booked music throughout the season, to packed crowds of locals and tourists alike. Tables and chairs were put out, and there were many restaurants and coffee shops eager to add to the ambience. It was very much an evening gathering place, such as one might see in Europe, and, in fact, we always had to do our few Italian songs, and often one in Greek, French, or Spanish, which would have several of the residents joining in with gusto. The music was organized by Vern Enyedy, who, with his wife Gwen, owned the "Piano Keep" B & B, with an amazing collection of about 70 fully restored pianos, plus many more that were kept for parts. Vern was a piano repairer and restorer par excellence, and musicians from all over the world knew of his work. We would always come in for at least one three- day run each summer, often two, both for the joy of playing to the plaza crowds, and to catch up with Vern and Gwen.

The "Piano Keep", a large house, was built in 1905, for the expensive price in those days, of $10,000. Originally it had wood-burning fireplaces throughout, but, after around ten years, radiators were installed, which are amazingly still in use today. Vern restored just about any high-end piano or harpsichord, but had 2 or 3 Broadwood Grands, that were by far his favourites, for their warm, rounded tone. There was a railroad track close behind the bandstand, and we could almost guarantee the blast of a train whistle should we decide to do a quiet ballad, but all was taken in good humour, and it was part of the atmosphere of a very special place.

FORT CALGARY

Our Canada day show took us to many venues, large and small. For two or three years we appeared at Fort Calgary, where a huge marquee would be erected. There was going to be a big show, with us doing two sets, Mary emceeing the whole event, and dance groups, plus other musical acts as well. Not only that, but I was operating our sound system, somewhat boosted, for the day, and had recorded music ready, should there be any "dead air". There was to be a large stage, very wide, which I suggested should be made into two, with the gap of a couple of feet between. This way, one stage could be set up with several mics., monitors, and plug-ins for musical instruments, while the other just had one mic. for possible introduction to dance items, otherwise plenty of space, and no cords or speakers in the way. The stages would run alternately, with only one lit at a time, the other being unobtrusively set for the next act, plus one could move through the gap between the two unnoticed.

There were Citizenship ceremonies, and many new Canadians were welcomed by the thousands attending. Mary emceed perfectly, and the recorded music was never used, as the two stage system worked so smoothly, without a hitch. We had our trailer, and Meggie behind the stage, so I could set up the day before, with some measure of security, and we had access to food, drink, and sleep, throughout, and after, a hugely busy day.

TELETHONS

*I*n addition to the several fundraisers we have put on over the years for the work of the Canadian Hunger Foundation globally, we have also been privileged to be involved in Telethons for various children's charities closer to home. This included the Children's Miracle Network, for whom we have done televised live shows from the Stollery Children's Hospital, for patients and staff alike, also "Telerama", which was a 20-hour live transmission to raise funds for children with mobility issues, either since birth, or from subsequent disabilities. The goal was usually to raise $1 million, which I am pleased to say was always exceeded, sometimes by a considerable amount.

"Telerama" was held in the Mayfield Inn, where we had done residencies some years before. Each act was given a room for changing, quiet time, and possibly a couple of hours sleep, should the opportunity arise. We had a great cast, which included Lucille Starr, who had the first female million seller in Canada, with a gentle ballad "The French Song", produced by Herb Alpert back in 1964, when much of the world was listening primarily to sounds of the Beatles. Also, we had the Good Brothers, Ronnie Prophet with wife Glory- Anne Carrière, Paul Hann, ourselves, and others. We were all trying to do things, backstage and in the 'Green' room, to keep each other awake. There were sandwiches and fresh vegetable plates to keep us going, the latter decorated with sprigs of purple cabbage. Lucille was just about to go on camera, having put on a matching purple dress and shoes for the occasion, when she realized she had forgotten her earrings. She quickly grabbed two small bits of purple cabbage, putting one in each ear, and rushed out to do her next song. We were all laughing our heads off in the 'Green' room, and at the end of the song, Ronnie and one of the Goods walked out and said, "Great song Lucille", then "Nice earrings too", each grabbing a bit of purple cabbage from her ear, eating it, and walking off stage, leaving Lucille in fits of laughter to go into her next song. Lucille, you will always be remembered, but a small group of us have an extra special memory that is truly priceless.

Not all of life was easy. We were doing a tour in Saskatchewan for the Saskatchewan Arts Councils and were booked into Wadena for a concert. This turned out to be in a gymnasium, but with a properly equipped stage at one end. We were due to set up in the afternoon, the seating had yet to be arranged, when suddenly a basketball game erupted in the inevitably echoey building. The noise was horrendous, the game was not going to stop, and we had no choice but to continue our work. By the time we got out, our heads and ears were bursting, totally useless for the performance to follow. There was no improvement when we had a sound check just before the audience came in, but we did the very best show we could under the circumstances, and made sure this never, ever, happened again.

The millennium celebrations were huge all over the globe. We were performing at the Lake Louise Inn, in the pristine snow-covered ambience of the Rocky Mountains, where we had our dog, Meggie, with us, who was going to be left in our room for her first time ever while we worked. However, we checked with the desk, and they promised to see that all was well. After a mammoth evening, working two huge banqueting rooms with all the attendant New Year's hoopla, we rested, then went down to breakfast. There was a Japanese lady, very proud that she had just invented a joke, going to each table to share it. "So, no problem with Y2K, except in Japan, one lady, camera not work!" A special weekend; we were kindly invited to stay over, which we did, taking quiet walks with Meggie on a peaceful New Year's Day.

In our earlier days together, before we had a fully developed stage show, we used to play service clubs for listening and dancing, as we sometimes did later in the resorts. One night, we were playing at the Montgomery Legion, in Edmonton. It was a good evening, and the floor was full. On a break, I was approached by an older gentleman, who, very pleasantly, said, "Last song, a bit slow". I made the normal placatory comments, and was heading off to get my coffee, when a lady of similar age called me over and said, "Last song, a bit too fast!". This was something that I don't think had ever happened before, but the punch line, as I was to find in the next set, was that they were husband and wife!

Incidentally, talking of tempos, while playing in the Rockies resorts, or in the dance crazy Kensington Legion in Calgary, we had a few couples who always came to see us, because our music was in strict tempo, unlike many acts of the time. One couple, Jim and Carol Gow, were positively brilliant dancers, and guaranteed to be given the entire floor. They used to follow us, because we could give them the exact timing they needed for their complicated footwork, and we became good friends over the years.

We stopped doing dance venues when our stage show was ready, with loads of spare material to fit any possible audience. On one occasion, we were doing a dinner show in Cranbrook, B.C. The audience was a perfect fit for both our music and comedy, so this was destined to be a very special night. Everybody was laughing at one bit of "business",

OUR THREE DOGS - Ben, Meggie and Jenny

"Nice Pussycat!"

including ourselves, when Mary let out a loud snort! That truly did it, within no time at all the entire room was snorting, or laughing, totally unable to stop. It was one of those nights where one can do no wrong, we could have read an extract from the Yellow Pages to thunderous applause; a night never to be forgotten.

While reminiscing on earlier days, there was a time back in New Brunswick when we had been booked, probably as a fill-in, at a restaurant/bar by the docks in Saint John, which turned out to be a great week, with sailors in from all over the globe. There was a big cargo ship in from India, and one night we were sitting with some of the senior officers on a break. Knowing by the accent that we were from the U.K., one of them asked if we liked curry. The fish and chip era had possibly dwindled somewhat, and there were not yet take out Chinese food places everywhere, but curry was huge in Britain, especially around Newcastle and South Shields, where I recall seeing eight curry houses in one street. So, we, of course, replied yes, and were invited to lunch on board the next day, showing up dressed for the occasion. We were escorted up the gangway, and to the smart Officers' Dining Room, with white tablecloths, gleaming silverware, and the officers dressed in their finest.

We were probably there for three hours at least, maybe more, enjoying our meal and the company of these beautiful people, punctuated by copious amounts of export Heineken, which was never seen in any store.

It was time to leave, and probably take a bit of a rest before preparing for the evening, so we headed back towards the gangway. However, Saint John is on the Bay of Fundy, where the incoming tide is pushed up by the waters behind, with the difference between high and low tide of up to 56 feet, one of the biggest in the world. The ship was now high in the water, the gangway gone, and a rope ladder, with wooden "steps", hanging, not even vertically, but back towards the hull, and the dock, so far below. Possibly without the Heineken we might have made it, but I doubt it. Mary was wearing a dress, I had a jacket, tie and blazer, and, no, it was not going to happen. The captain called somebody, and a huge solid gangway on wheels, such as might be used for a cruise ship, was brought over with some difficulty. I think everybody on the docks thought we were at least royalty, but all went well.

Talking of gangways on wheels, there was yet another time when a similar thing happened, which might not happen today. We were flying from Heathrow, (London), to Halifax, Nova Scotia. Mary's brother, John, was driving us up from the West Country, as he kindly always did, when we blew a tyre. Suffice to say, that by the time we reached

Heathrow, time was a little tight. We checked in and ran as fast as we could through what seemed like miles of corridor, to the gate assigned. By the time we got there, a different gate was showing on the board, and this gate was empty. We were so lucky to see a friendly Air Canada lady, who had a radio, and made several calls to fix the problem. Firstly, she got patched through to the pilot of the aircraft, via the control tower, who by now had left the gate where boarding had actually taken place and told him of the situation. Then she called a van to come and pick us up, which was a long way from the aircraft, followed by a call to get a flight of steps taken to where it had stopped. Then she was back on to the pilot, (maybe they knew each other?), and talked about his wife and family, the dog, anything she could think of, while we sped across the tarmac to the distant aircraft, with her chatting all the time so that he wouldn't move. We boarded, and the plane took off, again with others wondering who we were, and us a little red-faced. An amazing thing to happen in one of the world's busiest airports, and this lady, together with the pilot, certainly go on my list of people I would like to thank again.

I have always felt that one of the most important things I can do in life is make somebody laugh, and, if it is a complete stranger, so much the better. If one is fortunate enough to live in a democracy, it is really worthwhile to be involved in an election, at least once, for the sense of connectedness you will feel as a part of what is happening. Coincidentally, I have been involved in three: one federal, one provincial, and one civic. One night, on voting day, it was getting near time for the booths to close, when a middle-aged man in a Superman T-shirt came over to the table where I was checking in voters. I hunted through the voters list and said, "Kent, Kent? no, I can't see you anywhere!" He said that had made his day.

There have been so many thousands of performances over our career that it is only practical to mention a few, when maybe something different or laughable happened; possibly a venue where we have appeared regularly over the years, and it has become an "anchor", around which I have been able to arrange other non-conflicting events. This last is important. In a small town, such as Jasper, where we had a local following, I would only ever book one establishment. When playing at the "Athabasca" hotel, you would never see us at the "Marmot" lodge, until we moved there as our only stop. Then we moved solely into Jasper Park Lodge, for up to three months of the year, although we did come in for the Canada games at one time when invited. In a city such as Edmonton, with over a million residents, and several towns adjacent, there are many events all year, which are not in conflict with each other. We could appear for Family Day at City Hall, possibly with a seniors' lodge or school the next day. Maybe a show at Griesbach Officers' Club, or the N.C.O. club at Lancaster Park military base. I recall a staff dinner at the Alberta Legislature one year, also a party for the Members of the Legislative Assembly. A "Robbie Burns" night was possible, usually complete with pipe band, for which we had the music of Kenneth McKellar and Andy Stewart wafting through the house for around two weeks to brush up on the accent!

There would be a special show created for the "Summer Reading Programme", which we took to library performances for children over large swaths of the Prairies, customizing the show each year to fit a nationally designated theme. One year we did a tour of over 40 towns, with Meggie and our trailer. We did the show, but Meggie was the star, who lay quietly beside us on stage, and nearly always left at the end with yet another cuddly toy.

MUTTART CONSERVATORY

There were several City of Edmonton venues where we would appear two or three times per year, in the vast City Hall on Canada Day, or outside on a packed Churchill Square. Often, we'd be there for the Christmas "Lights up", or "First Night" celebrations, with around 13,000 in attendance, and I recall one very memorable Christmas season when Edmonton Transit had special buses running people all around to see the Christmas lights, ending up with a City Hall show from us, complete with hot chocolate and gingerbread. Perfect!

Another venue was the Muttart Conservatory, down near the river. Four huge glass pyramids showcased the trees and flora of different parts of the world, connected by a central area in which we would perform. One pyramid depicted the local scene, (except that it didn't rain or snow on you), one was tropical, and one depicted the Sonoran Desert of Arizona. The final pyramid had regularly changing spectacular floral displays of various kinds, as needed.

We played all sorts of music there: jazz, country, folk, blues, 60s, multi-lingual and more, but our very favourite was the children's shows we would do on a New Year's Eve afternoon. We instigated the idea of a "count down" every hour, at which point there would be a "Happy New Year", everyone would go nuts, and we would tell them where in the world it was now New Year's Day. Then we would stop, grab a coffee or pop, reset the stage, and do it all again. Our very special friends Iain and Val Little, who are mentioned earlier in the book as "Mother Nature", and "Captain Zero", were frequently involved in this event, as they were on so many other occasions. Iain was, and is, a costumier par excellence, producing costumes from "Star Wars", through "Alice in Wonderland", and many more, of very high quality, especially possibly those with a Dickensian background. As performers they have produced

"Murder Mysteries" at Fort Edmonton Park and other places for years, all of which they have written themselves, plus we have also seen them singing and dancing with leading roles onstage, in period musicals such as Noël Gay's "Me and My Girl".

On one occasion Mary's brother John and his wife Liz were over from the U.K. for a special visit, along with daughter Kaye and husband Jonathan. There was to be a surprise party; I was showing them around Fort Edmonton Park, assisted by our friend Geri, whilst final touches were put to the party. I returned, followed later by Geri, bringing the 4 of them at a pre-arranged time. Iain answered the door, dressed and made up as a VERY old retainer, asked for their invitations, which of course they didn't have, and said he would "fetch Madam", insisting fiercely that everyone huddle tightly on the small doormat, in no way touching the highly polished floor. Then Mary appeared, followed by Val, as an elderly Victorian parlour maid, complete with little white cap and frilly apron. John and Liz were treated as guests of honour, with complete disdain for the other 50 or so people present. Iain and Val remained in character for a considerable time, which is so typical of their talents, and there are many other stories one could recount. Once they were doing a "Raggedy Ann & Andy" piece, where Iain had created a background, transportable, of a large storybook with turning pages, and had doors and windows that were actually usable on each page.

They also had an agency, named "Clown Cartel", for children's performers, corporate adult game shows, and "fun" casinos, a specialized market in which their office continues to excel. Performers we would occasionally see included "Kip, the Court Jester", "Choo Choo the Clown", and children's magician Dave Wilson, who had created the very likeable character of "Cornelius Copperpot", guaranteed to keep the kids riveted.

Dave sometime later married Janice Boudreau, who had taken my place at the helm of Earth Day, and they had a memorable wedding, where everyone came in a costume of the past or future, and instead of formal speeches, there was an open mic., which everybody loved.

All of our performances at Muttart have been special, with songs from "Easter Parade", (my dad's favourite), to Jazz, to Folk, to our own songs, for children and adults. It is definitely included amongst our favourite venues, and we must thank Alex Hamilton, Crystal Jones, and Neil Cramer, as well as, of course, Leslie Fulks and Tannia Franke, for their ongoing warmth and friendship.

There is a perception that, in Canada, with the exception of First Nations or Inuit peoples, who of course have many languages of their own, that everybody in Quebec speaks French, and everybody else speaks English. In fact, there are French speaking communities dotted all over the country, and most of the larger Quebec cities have English speaking areas. Bilingualism is normal in these communities, whilst the only officially bilingual province in the country is that of New Brunswick, where we had our first home together, near Fredericton, for five years.

Beaumont, just south of Edmonton, was totally French until recent times, as was Morinville, just north of us in St. Albert, and we have been to Morinville on more than one occasion for St. Jean Baptiste day, the only time in our entire career when we have done performances with all our audience "patter" in both official languages. There have been several events in this community, for children and families, plus a big seniors' dinner theatre, and we've always worked together with Melonie Dziwenka, (now Lubensky), whom we have got to know so well over the years, and are pleased to have kept in touch.

Mentioning First Nations and Inuit peoples, the more we travel and learn about this world, the more aware we become of the horrors of colonialism, which were definitely pushed under the carpet in my childhood years. So many of those that we were brought up to revere as heroes at that time were also in fact inflicting appalling atrocities on the indigenous peoples of other parts of the world, with the impression being given in Britain or Europe, as that of a benign grandfather travelling the world to make everything better for the "primitive people" of each country. Nothing could be further from the truth. In Alberta, where we currently live, all indigenous children were forcibly taken, often as far from their parents as possible, to residential schools, where they were abused physically and mentally, for even speaking one word in their own language, and semi-starved, over a period of up to nine years. The numbers vary across the country and in other "colonized" countries, but, in Alberta, nearly 50% of the children died. The purpose of this book is not to write a treatise on colonialism, but it is autobiographical, and this needs to be mentioned. In the "suggested reading", at the end, are one or two titles, relating to this issue, in different parts of the world.

Many years ago, when "My Fair Lady", the musical version of George Bernard Shaw's play "Pygmalion", opened in London's West End, following a hugely successful run on Broadway, something happened that would be inconceivable nowadays. No radio or T.V. station would, by mutual agreement, play any of the music from the show until the moment that the curtain was lowered at the end of the first night's performance. The build-up was phenomenal, and in those days, there was not the technology available in the average household to tune into a transatlantic station. The musical was, justifiably, a colossal success, and many stories abound.

One of these concerned pianist Stan Tracey, (who did the classic "Under Milk Wood", jazz suite). The story goes that Stan was playing a room, either in the Dorchester or Savoy, where many of the diners couldn't see the band. The version I heard had Jack Fallon, who was to book us in to "Remzi's" in Oxford so many years later, on bass, and Phil Seaman, Britain's finest jazz drummer, to round out the trio, about whom there are enough stories to fill another book. As with all stories, it may be told with different names, or it may evolve in another direction over time. However, as it started, the trio was playing, and couldn't see any of the diners in this "L" shaped room. They played a good set, with the odd couple dancing, and Stan said he was going to grab some coffee. Jack & Phil said they'd keep things going, which they did, both being highly inventive in their playing. After a few minutes, Stan had not returned, and Jack said he was going to find him and maybe they should take a break. Phil, the drummer, was playing away, somewhat oblivious to the world, and kept going on his own. A couple came around the corner to dance, so Phil did some fancy work and a big finish. The two of them then approached the stage and said, "Can you play something from "My Fair Lady?", to which Phil's reply was "What the .... do you think I've been doing for the last ten minutes??".

Some years later, when the movie of "My Fair Lady" was being envisioned, I don't know if the role of Eliza was offered to Julie Andrews, who had of course played on stage to such acclaim in both New York and London; maybe the studio wanted to reprise the combination of Cary Grant and Audrey Hepburn, that had been so successful in "Roman Holiday". I know the role of Professor Higgins was offered to Cary Grant, who turned it down, and basically said, "If you do not give it to Rex,

(Harrison), I shall not only not go to see it, I shall tell my friends to do likewise". Whether this made the studio think, we shall never know, but Rex brilliantly portrayed Higgins, and Stanley Holloway also reprised the part of Eliza's father, roles that both had played on Broadway and in the West End. Audrey was an excellent Eliza, but, even though she had sung previously on film, the studio rightly thought that the music in "My Fair Lady" was too important to be handled by anyone but the very best. Rex's part was semi-spoken, and nobody could have done it better, but Audrey's singing needed dubbing for the musical to work.

There was a classically trained singer in Hollywood at the time named Marni Nixon, who, in addition to her other busy work, could be called upon to dub female voices in films. Highly talented, she used to say that she "got inside the head" of the actress for whom she was doing the overdub and would sing in "what appeared to be their natural voice". The absolute classic of her work was probably the "King and I", where she reproduced Deborah Kerr's voice so immaculately, was paid $420, and had to sign a document that she would never tell. For this movie, Marni and Deborah sang all the songs together, on separate tracks, which were then edited skilfully to create one solo voice. Marni, who became known as "Hollywood's worst kept secret", appeared on the soundtrack of over 50 films, sometimes for a single note. In "Gentlemen prefer blondes", she dubbed one line for Marilyn Monroe on "Diamonds are a girl's best friend", with Marilyn singing the rest. She sang for Sophia Loren in "Boy on a dolphin", she dubbed Jeanne Crain in "Cheaper by the dozen", Ida Lupino in "Jennifer", and Janet Leigh in "Pepe". Of the really huge musicals, she not only dubbed Deborah Kerr, she also dubbed Natalie Wood in "West Side Story", together with the voice of Rita Moreno on the quintet version of "Tonight"; plus of course, Audrey Hepburn in "My Fair Lady". She did a national tour of the pieces she had overdubbed in later life, as well as appearing on stage as Eliza in the New York 1964 revival, and playing a nun in the movie version of "The Sound of Music".

Marni also had a huge classical career, singing with virtually every major conductor and composer on both sides of the Atlantic. As a coloratura soprano, she appeared many times in front of the world's leading orchestras, from the Hollywood Bowl to the Royal Albert Hall. She sang for a while with Liberace, then Victor Borge, doing both classical and Broadway material, and even sang for 3 cockney geese in the movie "Mary Poppins".

When Alan Jay Lerner, "My Fair Lady" composer, passed in 1986, there was a big memorial at the Shubert theatre. Instead of a clip of the Broadway production with Julie Andrews, a clip of the movie was shown by mistake, thus showing Audrey Hepburn, with of course Marni's voice. Then a spotlight picked up Julie Andrews, who had to think fast, and said "Hello, everyone, I'm Marni Nixon". Needless to say, the house, all pros., went wild, and the media loved it. Marni's contribution to music and the theatre was colossal, yet some do not know of her, which I try to rectify, whenever I can.

Of course, in current times it seems to often to be the case in a musical where the voice of a brilliant actor or actress, who is not a singer, is left on the track during musical numbers, with no subsequent overdubs, to disastrous effect. Pitch correction technology may help in fixing a note, but the subtle nuances that make a great singer are woefully missing. Some otherwise good productions have managed to destroy the music that could make the movie into a classic, and I, plus many other musicians, simply don't get why they would do this.

One time, back in the 80s, we were doing a run at Edmonton's Mayfield Inn, where we have known so many "name" actors in the past, who were working at the "Stage West" dinner theatre. We were performing in the hotel's main dining room "The Captain's Table". It was late, on a quieter night, and one couple kept asking for requests, of mostly 60s and some 50s material, much of which we knew. We sat with them on a break, and they introduced themselves as Bob and Pat Nagel, who owned a busy tour bus company, running throughout Canada and the U.S. We hit it off with them immediately, and they were very interested in Mary possibly hosting tours for them as a tour director, if there was ever room in our busy musical schedule.

We kept in touch with each other over the years, both at social gatherings, and having visits to their reservation office, where Bob was based, with Pat, a one-time music teacher, managing the company from the planning office in a different location. Bob organized the "Alberta All-Girls Drum and Bugle Band", which was so popular in parades throughout the province, as well as at events across Canada, the U.S., and Europe. They sadly disbanded during the 80s, but had appeared during the previous decade at the lighting of the flame for the Munich Olympics in '72, at the final game of the World Cup in Germany, '74, also a concert for Pope Paul VI at his summer residence in Castel Gandolfo, Italy, in 1977, as well as many other events. There were two groups of 125 girls each, in addition to other marching bands in earlier years. Bob was always interested in our musical activities and there was many a good "catch-up" together.

Coincidentally, our friend Nina, from Bermuda days, had left the music profession, qualifying in tourism, and was now working for the same company, both in reservations, and also as senior tour director, which she did for a considerable time. So, if in town, we would stop by for a visit with Bob, and a lunch break with Nina.

But it wasn't until 2005 that our paths, and those of Nagel Tours, finally intersected professionally, with, for Mary, the perfect tour. This was to be a "fly-in" tour, arriving in Halifax, Nova Scotia, travelling throughout Atlantic Canada, and flying out of St. John's, Newfoundland 15 days later, all areas that were so very familiar from our extensive musical travels.

There were, of course, many highlights throughout this first tour, one of which was meeting our old neighbours from just outside Fredericton,

Fred and Jan, who, being Maritimers, and therefore some of the friendliest people in the world, came on the bus to welcome everybody, after which we had a special couple of hours together before Mary had to catch up with the inevitable calls and paperwork, before the next busy day. However, Murphy's Law also kicked in on this tour, and yes, if it could go wrong, it probably did. But ultimately the passengers had both a great and a memorable time, giving Mary an extended standing ovation on the final night, for the way in which she had handled seemingly impossible odds. She was to host the Atlantic Canada tour several times more, in addition to tours in the British Columbia interior, up the Inside Passage, also to the huge Scandinavian "Hostfest" in Minot, North Dakota, with its many "star" acts, which she did frequently. I rode along as "shotgun", (back seat), on a few of these, when I could be away from our office and Meggie was in safe, familiar hands, fielding questions, and acting as Mary's "Ambassador" when needed. Sometimes I'd do a mini comedy set if Mary was busy on the phone, and on some tours, she would bring out her ventriloquist figure "Martha McHaggis", to the delight of all present, and adding an extra spark to their holiday.

Of course, once we were based in Alberta, rather than just coming through on tour, we joined the local branch of the American Federation of Musicians. It would be impossible to overstress the importance of joining the appropriate professional organization, if you plan to make a living in the Arts. Equity for an actor or other stage artists, the A.F. of M. for a musician, or other societies depending on your direction. Sometimes there can be a few hoops to jump through for full membership; fine, jump through them. In the case of the Musicians' Union, there is always friendly advice, access to a legal department in the case of contractual difficulties, a pension fund which classes as an employer's contribution, (think about that!), and more. Most of all, in the Edmonton local, we have found that all musicians are on the same page, regardless of musical genre, and we all support each other in any way we can, thanks to the leadership of Eddy Bayens, assisted by Edith Stacey, whom we are proud to think of as friends. Maybe the fact that they both play the same instrument, (bassoon), is why everything blends and runs so smoothly, with a good and caring executive board for backup. I also remember well one-time President of the local, Hank Smith, born in Garmish-Partenkirchen, Germany, where I once played with the "Zephyrs", back in '68. Hank was founding President of what was to become the Canadian Country Music Association, and was awarded the Order of Canada in 1994, in addition to becoming a member of the Country Music Hall of Fame that same year.

We did most of our own booking once we had a home this side of the country, having pretty much finished with the hotel and lounge market, and moving on to other things. However, we still did quite a few functions, mostly corporate, for Margie Zahn, or Wanda Feland, in many parts of the province, with a huge variety of events.

Sometimes we'd work Arts Council shows through Maureen Saumer, who, with the aid of her husband Paul, ran Guildhall Productions. With her English background, we connected on many levels, and could talk about things theatrical on both sides of the pond. Maureen and Paul were such special people, missed by all who knew them, and never to be replaced. If there were several phone calls to be made, and one was to Maureen, the lesson was soon learned to leave that one until last, as Maureen had this uncanny knack of mixing so many subjects in her long conversations, that the original reason for the call was soon lost, and more often than not, completely forgotten, until the next time.

However, I am sure that every one of us would love to have a call from her right now, which would ensure laughter for a very long time. When Maureen passed, we kept in touch with Paul, having phone calls and an occasional lunch together, which remain as very singular memories.

Other events in our area included various church concerts, including our own. Sometimes there would be a church fund raiser, sometimes a regular concert. Often, we did fund-raisers for the Canadian Hunger Foundation and their overseas work, always telling the congregation where the money was going, which we also did when selling crafts for the work of Wanjiku, in Nairobi. On occasion we'd be a part of the service itself, sometimes writing a special piece to fit the day's theme.

There are many children's events that we have done for years, some already mentioned. The Christmas season is always an opportunity to connect with younger children, which is very special to us. There are performances in various city locations, shows to welcome Santa in one of the leading shopping centres - we always do two of these a year - or corporate events, the very favourite being at the Glendale Golf and Country Club, which, at the time of writing, we have done over 19 seasons, for the membership and their children, with 2 separate events each Christmas. We have watched many children grow there and look forward to the day when one of these brings in a child of their own to meet us for the first time, as has happened so often at Fort Edmonton Park over the years.

Corporate Christmas shows could be a challenge. On one occasion we were performing a huge children's event for an oil company, and actually playing Santa's entry music, when one of the organizers came over to me and said, "Have you got a beard?", to which my response was, "Yes, but it's growing"! It was a Sunday afternoon, as these events usually are, and we had to keep the kids 'pumped' until a beard of sorts was found at a dollar store some 45 minutes later. Another time we were confronted with the prospect of an unbearded Santa, Mary asked him to pull his hat down and the top of his coat up over his mouth, saying it was so cold on the run from the North Pole that he had to keep his face partially covered to try and keep warm. Fortunately, the kids bought it, and all went well. Having now had this happen twice, I went and bought a Santa beard, which still reposes in its sealed packet, but means we can sleep at night.

Before moving on to other things, we'll leave you with a taste of our children's Christmas show. It usually starts with a high energy version of "We need a little Christmas", with a big sound from keyboards and guitar, then straight into a banjo/guitar version of "Sleigh Ride", having kids all along the front playing sleigh bells, and cameras flashing everywhere. There will be magic tricks interspersed throughout, but the next major item will be Mary's magic drawing board, where a face, partly drawn by a child from the audience, comes alive, to colossal response. "Feliz Navidad" is an excuse for hula hoops and skipping, (when there is space), then it's off to Australia for "Six White Boomers", where the children all become jumping kangaroos. They'll of course sing "Rudolph" together, having at least one go on the mic. each, plus "Dexter", the smoke-blowing dragon will appear, much to the children's amazement. There will be a huge jug band, plus other things, before the lights go down, and we start the buildup to the arrival of Santa himself, who often comes across the snow-covered golf course to the Clubhouse on a horse drawn sleigh, festooned with lights. Magic!!

VENTRILOQUISM & LAUGHTER

By the time we did the first of so many winter tours in the Southern U.S., in 2005, Mary had been attending the Vegas Ventriloquist Convention since 1997, whenever possible. We had made our first Vegas trip at the beginning of that February, during which time Mary met up with a top ventriloquist from the U.K., Valentine Vox, now resident in Las Vegas, and operating the "Magic and Movie Hall of Fame", a museum which had original figures from the world's leading ventriloquists, in addition to a live theatre which operated daily. Valentine was also running the convention at the end of May, and so rightly advised Mary to attend if at all interested in the art form, which she clearly was, as many of the world's "greats" would be there, on a one-to-one basis, in addition to doing performances, making this a life-altering experience.

Which it was. Imagine a Las Vegas showroom, with around 200 ventriloquists, (plus their figures, making this 400), many of them old style vaudevillians, and a warmth and camaraderie that would be impossible to top. Workshops, demonstrations, and the western world's leading puppet makers on hand with their latest creations, plus advice wherever and whenever needed.

We met with so many top vents. over the years, but I especially remember Mary talking with Paul Winchell, now an older man, who had a hugely popular U.S. television show for many years, with his figure "Jerry Mahoney". Paul was qualified in medicine, and, amongst other things, had created the world's first artificial heart, to great acclaim. Paul's response was, "I don't know why they're making such a fuss, I've been making little people for years, and this is only one part!" Such a nice man; it was a privilege for us both to have met him. There was Jay Johnson, whose Broadway production "The Two and Only" made him the first ventriloquist to ever receive a Tony Award, plus Sammy King, with "Francisco", again so warm, with a career of over 26,000 performances. Incidentally, Sammy talked of the huge difference in having a live band, which responds to the varying energy of each audience, unlike a recorded background. We've maybe used a self-made track for one specific piece very occasionally, adding our playing on top, but the energy that flows between performers, band if any, and audience, is what keeps us all alive, and is never the same twice.

We appeared with an extract from our own show twice at the Convention in later years, the focus of course being on Mary's ventriloquism, once at the "Imperial Palace", and once at "Harrah's". In 2003, Mary was to attend on her own, to emcee the International Stage of ventriloquists from different parts of the world, including our friend "Stevo" Shuling, from Germany, plus several members of the always large Japanese contingent, where ventriloquism is so popular. This was also the year that Valentine was to marry Eyvonne Carter on live T.V., each with their figures taking the vows. Over 200 ventriloquists, including Mary, were invited, each, of course, with their "alter ego". It was shown on more than 60 news outlets throughout the world, in addition to "Jimmy Kimmel Live", the "Rita Rudner Show", "Live with Regis & Kelly", and the "Tonight Show", with Jay Leno, all from Las Vegas.

Mary is a lover of physical comedy with her various vent. figures, and this is a key part of our performances, inspired by the truly amazing work of Dan Horn, who we have met many times.

One year, we met Candice Bergen, daughter of the great Edgar Bergen, (Charlie McCarthy), who was doing a special for NBC, on which Mary appeared. Also, there were appearances in the movie "I'm no Dummy", starring Jeff Dunham, Jay Johnson, and Lynn Trefzger, filmed both in Vegas, and at Fort Mitchell, Kentucky, home of the "Vent Haven" museum. This was the world's largest, so ably run at the time by Lisa Sweasy and Annie Roberts. Plus, there was a huge annual convention in

Fort Mitchell, organized by children's ventriloquist Mark Wade, which attracted vents. from all over the world.

Because of the demise of the "Ed Sullivan Show" in the U.S., which featured vents Edgar Bergen, Seňor Wences, and Ricky Layne , (with whom we had a memorable breakfast at around three o'clock one morning, full of laughter, and quite the single funniest performer I have ever met - who had no less than 48 appearances); plus the almost simultaneous drop of T.V. variety in the U.K., therefore less visibility for Peter Brough, Arthur Worsley, Ray Alan, Terry Hall etc., the public at large might be excused for believing that ventriloquism is a dying art. One only has to walk into a large showroom, containing over 500 ventriloquists from many parts of the world, all with figures, to realize that nothing could be further from the truth.

Again, so many people to recall. There was Jimmy Nelson, (Danny O'Day), with his wife Betty, lovely people, Jimmy being remembered especially for his Nestlé's drinking chocolate commercials over the years with "Farfel" the dog, also Terry Fator, now virtually a fixture at the Las Vegas "Mirage", who won "America's Got Talent" in 2007, and whom we used to meet at the "Rocky Mountain Assn. of Fairs" convention in previous years. When working the fairs, there would often be three shows daily. The evening one would be packed, the afternoon one usually good, but if there was an earlier one, it would be soul destroying, with a few people looking at 'phones, or half asleep. Terry used to say that he had to make it big, or quit, and we're so glad the former happened. He is a fine singer, then the remainder of the show is the cream on top, with his success richly deserved.

The biggest name of all is of course, Jeff Dunham, noted for his just-on-the-edge, "Achmed the Dead Terrorist", plus "Walter", beloved by late-night talk shows, "Peanut", and "Josè", the talking jalapeño. Jeff knew at age 8 what he was going to do, and rarely misses a convention of like-minded performers.

Who else? Mallory Lewis, daughter of Shari, who used to be involved in production of her mother's T.V. shows, and occasionally appears with "Lamb Chop", plus so many other friends: Wendy Morgan, from the U.K., with whom Mary always keeps in touch, Bob Rumba, Nancy Roth, who does mainly cruise work, as does master ventriloquist Ronn Lucas. Willie Tyler, so technically brilliant, another U.K. vent. Nina Conti, daughter of actor Tom, who landed herself a U.S. television sitcom with her naughty "Monkey", as had Jay Johnson with "Bob", on "Soap", many years before. Don Bryan, (Noseworthy), Bob Isaacson, Pete Michaels, Dale Brown, Liz von Seggen, Al Getler, Tom Ladshaw, Carol Greene, Buddy Big Mountain, and our special friend Carla Rhodes, who had a puppet of Dave (Bowie), with whom she was in touch over the years, custom made for her by Verna Finley and which, now that Dave is gone, must surely be a prized possession.

To end this section, we move to 2017, and a very young girl named Darci Lynne, again on "America's Got Talent", and heading towards the finals. The Vent Haven ConVENTion was on prior to this, and Darci attended. Just about every major ventriloquist on the planet, especially Gary Owen, sat down with her with so many tips, and, as we all know, she won.

The great thing about ventriloquism, is that it is, more than anything else, a community of like-minded performers, who love what they are doing, and want the art form to stay alive and well, for all the years to come.

SOUTHERN TOURS: ARIZONA, CALIFORNIA, AND LAS VEGAS

*I*t was early January, and the day we had scheduled to head south for our first ever California/Arizona tour, to which we had been looking forward for so long. Some nearby friends, Tim and Vi, were coming in convoy with us, and volunteered to help with equipment whenever needed.

Our trailer was initially only a nineteen-footer, medium weight, and held the road well, plus we had a 4-wheel drive. Theirs was somewhat longer, with only a 2-wheel drive, so Tim had to be careful in heavy cross winds. It was probably around - 20 °c, and the roads needed to be treated with respect, as there was much ice and compacted snow. We set off excitedly, but with a degree of trepidation, as this was a 3,000 km. (2,000 mile) trip to our first show, in the depth of winter, with 3 major mountain passes to be navigated en route, and both pulling trailers, plus our truck was loaded with instruments, lights, and 2 sound systems, one for concert size venues, and one for smaller.

After a couple of hours, we stopped for gas and coffee, when it was announced that the road was closed both north and south, so we were not going anywhere. Not a good start, plus we were still very close to home, but we managed to find somewhere to stay, pulling out later the next morning when all the big trucks had left, and roads were somewhat clearer. We made it to Lethbridge that day, about an hour from the border, again with poor conditions, a distance from home that would normally be done easily in a day, even with a late start. The region from Lethbridge south to well past Great Falls in Montana is noted for high cross winds, with many stories told over the years – "If the winds stop, all the cows will fall over", or, "It was so windy that one little brown hen laid the same egg three times!"

We of course had passports and work permits all in order and knew there would be a stop for a while at the Canada/U.S. border while this was all processed. For those who don't know, when applying for a P2 U.S. work visa, it is necessary to include the date that you plan to cross the border. You can arrive later, but never early. However, you must be performing within five days of the date you *intended* to cross, so it is essential to be vigilant of upcoming weather and road conditions, and we were constantly on the 'phone, also checking with other drivers any time we stopped for gas, which is frequent when pulling a trailer with a full truckload of equipment; of course, not forgetting Meggie, who needed her breaks too!

The border was reached, paperwork handed in, and we settled down patiently to wait. Some years before, we had been coming in to do some summer fairs in Montana and Idaho, when we were advised that there was a delay in permits, and one would not be issued, "Unless you've got a U.S. Senator in your back pocket". Which of course we didn't have, but we had a friend who ran the D.A.R.E. programme, as a volunteer, for the whole of the United States. A quick 'phone call, and twenty minutes later we had a call from the office of a very popular Senator, which meant an endorsement of our application, plus permit issued immediately, which we collected from a hotel en route to the border. The endorsement from this kind Senator's office of course went on to our file, and I think certainly did no harm in many border crossings over the years.

Once the paperwork was complete, we headed south through Montana and Idaho, with the often challenging high Monida and Malad passes, about which we shall hear more later. Conditions remained poor until we were in Utah, and had reached Salt Lake City, home of the Mormon Church, where we knew from once visiting the Cardston Temple in southern Alberta that it was not permissible to go into any of their huge buildings. Snow had given way to rain, and we had a short drive around, getting a feel for the place, before heading on down the highway. After the Fremont pass, usually somewhat easier than the first two, we started the gradual descent from Cedar City to St. George, (no connection with Bermuda or Grenada), after which the road dropped steeply through a cut in the amazing red rocks into a corner of Arizona, and a totally different climate. Then we reached the Nevada border, with the town of Mesquite, and several large casino hotels. We were now in beautiful warm weather, which one could already taste when arriving in St. George. Palm trees abounded in the immaculate gardens surrounding the major casinos, and it felt like a different world. We have often stopped here in later years to de-winterize the trailer and prepare it for use, but this year we headed straight on to Las Vegas, where we booked into the RV park next to Sam's Town, a huge hotel/casino with a magnificent indoor atrium, on the Boulder Highway. We were a little concerned by the razor wire on top of the RV park walls, but anyway headed into Sam's Town for a good meal, having of course given Meggie a walk plus her supper first, and so relieved that the hard, possibly dangerous, part of the journey was over. We spent a couple of nights in Las Vegas, de-winterizing, and checking that all was good in both trailers, (heat, air conditioning, hot water, stove, microwave, etc.), as well as having a walk on the Strip, and a little "down" time, which was needed by all five of us after such a challenging drive. Then it was time for the final leg to Mesa, east of Phoenix, which was uneventful, apart from hitting the freeway at the busiest time of day, which I don't believe we ever did again.

As we headed South-east from Las Vegas, we started to pass the occasional Joshua tree, so very different with their waxy, spiny leaves; standing like cheerleaders with pom-poms raised high. Then we came into the Sonoran Desert itself, with giant Saguaro cacti that grow up to 50 feet tall, and can live for over 200 years, stretching their arms skyward; always such a welcoming sight after days of ice and snow covered highway. Of course, some of them eventually fall, and there are several postcards available of totally flattened vehicles, with an 8-ton Saguaro on top!

We pulled into Mesa Dunes, one of the many parks on the east side of Mesa, that had been recommended by our friend Bernie, of "Bernie & Red", that we first knew from "Widgeon's", in Calgary. This was a place where many entertainers stopped when on tour in the area, and we had arranged a site on a come-and-go basis, as needed. "Bernie & Red" were one of the very first acts on the southern circuit, and had built up a big following with their somewhat edgy onstage banter, Bernie's comedy lyrics to established songs, Red's "big ballads", and their general rapport with the audience.

Equally popular were two other U.S. acts, Dave & Daphne, and Keith Longbotham. Dave Salyer and Keith originally had a duo together, which evolved into separate acts over time. Dave had been Barbara Mandrell's lead player, and also played regularly in Bluegrass shows at the Grand Ole Opry, with his uncle, Jesse McReynolds, plus Vince Gill, all three superb musicians. Daphne Anderson had many awards for her Country Gospel work, and Keith now had a no less impressive trio.

We were so grateful to Bernie for his help when we planned to come south, as we were to Sharon Pippin, an Edmonton-based mostly country music agent that we had known for some years, who booked her then husband Rick Morgenstern on the same circuit and toured with him during the winter season.

A plus at the time with Mesa Dunes was that laundry facilities were available 24 hrs. per day, as was the swimming pool, so long as one was quiet, and clothes could be hung out to dry in a special area, (excepting Sunday), all three things unusual, and very helpful to busy musicians who are on the road at all times, and sometimes need a laundry after returning from a show, when everyone else is asleep.

We slowly assimilated into what was, for us, a very different market. Some of the venues were large, and high end, some smaller, and more down to earth. Some had a fully equipped theatre stage, complete with lighting crew at the rear of the hall, in others, you might be trying to move a huge pile of paraphernalia to one side of the stage so that you could find room to set up. One or two acts carried a backcloth, and you could quite see why. Some parks were filled with permanent residents, some catered to the winter "Snowbird" market with their RVs or Park Models, but in almost all of them, shows were open to the public.

One thing we learned to do quite fast in what came to be our annual southern tour over a 14-year period, was to always find out the home locations of audience members. Somebody from Saskatchewan might be laughing uproariously at a piece of comedy that a group from Minnesota, with their Scandinavian origins, wouldn't see as funny at all. Or vice versa. We had several bits of "business" to suit different backgrounds, and, once we knew the audience demographics, we knew how to work the evening, which applied to our music as well, with several extra languages available as needed to create a different colour.

Every day, Monday to Friday, unless there was a show, would be spent calling or visiting Activity directors in the literally hundreds of venues to secure dates for the following year, which was very competitive. Of course, if you had a really good night, you would usually be re-booked before leaving the building, or, at worst, by the next day. Some places had a policy of missing a year, but most were happy to have you back, especially if much of the show was going to be different to the one they had just seen.

Smaller parks, if they had a show at all, it could be once a month, every two weeks, or weekly. A great deal depended on local community spirit, plus promotion by the Activity director. Some medium-sized venues would be constantly packed, some huge places virtually empty, but after a season or two, we had a good idea of places that were a "fit" and looked forward to our return. One Park used to book around three or four acts a week, which was fine if you marketed the event via newspapers or other media, but somewhat erratic otherwise. Strange things could, and did, happen.

Posters left our office months before they were needed, then there would be a 'phone call to make sure they had arrived, with another follow-up two or three weeks before the event, to remind the Activity office that the posters needed putting on the noticeboards! We arrived at one park to see no posters, so I went to the Activity office to check, when I was told that they hadn't arrived. Since I could actually see them sitting on the desk, I queried this, and the somewhat embarrassed Activity director spent the rest of the day making sure that residents knew of the show. Amazingly, we became friends. At another park, the Activity director got in his golf cart with a bullhorn, when posters had again somehow disappeared, and there was an almost full house that night.

To be fair to Activity directors, many of whom are volunteers with little or no experience, the job can be difficult and time-consuming. In the larger parks there is usually a full-time Activity director who is skilled and on salary, but in the smaller parks the maximum they receive is a free trailer site, if anything at all. So, it is up to the performers to make sure Activity directors have the tools needed to do their part of the job, and with a few notable exceptions, they are personable, and do things well.

At the time of writing, we no longer perform on the southern Arizona/California circuit, but occasionally the phone still rings with a special call from one of the parks, or an ex-Activity director, just to see how we are, which I, of course, reciprocate.

Life in Mesa Dunes as a "home" base was good. First and foremost, there were five acts coming and going, so we could all compare notes and share laughs from time to time. There was Rebecca Dawn, from

Heading South

"Goldfield Ghost Town" Arizona

Branson, Missouri, who had a high energy show, with her husband Joe operating tracks as needed, and doing the occasional fill-in when Rebecca needed a costume change. Also, Jerry Huck, from close to Edmonton, who had worked as a single in the Mayfield Inn, plus ourselves. A little later in the season would see the arrival of our friends Bernie & Red, plus Freddie & Sheila, a popular traditional roots/country act from Saskatchewan, both acts having worked the Texas circuit before coming west to Arizona each year. Freddie Pelletier is a whiz of a guitar player, as is his son Clint, while Sheila does more than competent rhythm and vocals, and we were always pleased to see Freddie & Sheila back in Mesa Dunes. We also encountered another fine Edmonton act "Six Feet Up", who had a permanent home in Phoenix, and produced a satisfactory wall of brass, unlike other acts on the circuit.

The weather in January, even in southern Arizona, can be erratic. There was once an ice storm the day of our show at Mesa Dunes, and a snow dust on the Superstition Mountains is not unusual, but most days are between 50 and 70°F. in the day, occasionally dropping to below freezing at night. In which case, the trick is to leave taps dripping to avoid a freeze-up, especially in Tucson, which is higher, and can have very cold snaps even into February. But mostly it's a very positive place to be, and Mary, Meggie, and I loved it, after the cold winter blanketing most of the U.S. and Canada. Especially if we had a free day on the weekend, when we would visit the Superstition Mountain Museum on the Apache Trail and their bookshop, probably the best on Arizona history and lore. We'd have a stroll around the desert garden, or head to the walkway at Weavers Needle Vista, which leads for 4 miles into the incredible beauty of the Sonoran Desert, quite unlike any other place in the world.

There was also "Filly's Pub", with an outdoor stage, and very high-quality older country or Eagles-style musicians, who had obviously been around the block several times, and knew exactly what they were doing. Many of the guests, especially on a weekend, came on horseback in full Western attire, regardless of what they wore Monday to Friday. There was a hitching rail, and water for the horses, making us aware that we were truly in the West, even if the Wild part was no longer here.

Sometimes we'd pop into Goldfield Ghost Town, a bit kitschy but still the real thing, where the "McNastys" entertained in the dining area of the old Mammoth" Saloon, and mock gunfights would erupt at scheduled times in the dusty main street; at which point one of us would make sure that Meggie was away from the noise and crowds. Or we might head up the road to the once stagecoach stop of Tortilla Flat. Most importantly, we would take Meggie to Canyon Lake, where she was able to swim to her heart's content; making this day out such a break for all three of us, after a busy week performing and marketing for the following year.

Our very first show was at a smaller park in Apache Junction, where the Activity director, Reba Platz, became a friend over the years, and we kept in touch year round. One time, we were in our trailer at Mesa Dunes, and there was a call from Reba inviting us to join her for a special park pot luck lunch on the following day. We went out, and the three of us were sitting together chatting, when pretty much everybody except us left the hall and went outside, yet there were still piles of food left. This seemed odd to us, but Reba said, "Oh, they all go out to break wind!" I'm still laughing at that one many years later.

Sometimes we'd park at a casino for a day or two between shows, where they had huge spaces for trailers. We had by now graduated to a 27' model, well equipped, but trailers of any size were always welcome, in that they provided extra security, as well as extra custom. Or, we'd

Magnificent Saguaro Cacti

Relaxing at Saguaro Lake with Jenny

stop in the desert and wake to peace, silence, and total freedom, temporarily disconnected from the world....

Hundreds of parks. Desert Trails in Tucson was a favourite, where we would base for several days. The owner, Pericles Plantagenet Wyatt, descended in a direct line from Henry II, ran the park with his wife and daughter as though everyone was family. The only venue in my entire career where I've done a "pass the hat", but Pericles knew what he was doing. There would always be an acceptable guaranteed fee; the hat would be considerably more than this, and the hall would be packed solid, ensuring a great evening, of course making certain that much of our material was fresh each visit.

Desert Trails was literally that, surrounded by Saguaro, Organ Pipe, Agave, Beehive, Barrel Cactus, Prickly Pear, Cholla, and so much more, just a few yards from the trailer. Once it gets hotter, at the end of February, and certainly by March, it is prudent to watch for Diamond-backed Rattlesnakes, and also Gila Monsters, the latter of which you are unlikely to see, as they are chiefly nocturnal.

I remember a presentation once at the amazing Sonoran Desert Museum, with its popular Javelina Peccaries running around part of the grounds, when an audience member asked what the bite of a Gila Monster was like, to which the response was, "Have you ever given birth?". When the reply was "yes", the presenter said, "That was nothing!"

Scorpions are also something to avoid, especially in summer. Chiefly nocturnal, there is the Giant Hairy Scorpion, 4 inches long, which stings, also the small Bark Scorpion, 1 1/2 inches long, whose sting can be life-threatening to young children.

Incidentally, while on the subject of Tuscon, I should mention "Old Tucson", which is a huge mostly outdoor movie studio, where so many notable Westerns have been made, and is still in use on occasion today. It is a full day visit, as a company of talented performers gradually rotates around the site, doing many different things, including a production with some pretty serious "stunt" work later in the day.

We of course had our first show "ready to go" when we headed south, which was tweaked as needed. Gradually we built a formula for a 2-hour concert, including intermission, which we use to this day, and is modified if there's only to be one set. For example, a typical first set would start with a short, high energy instrumental piece, followed by the opening song. Then a bit of patter, after which there would be an uptempo banjo/vocal, partly instrumental, for a colour change, or a slower vocal, as a "settling down" song, these two being sometimes reversed if needed. For a senior audience there would be a Big Band piece, if not it was straight into a comedy routine, often with audience participation. After which, a slower guitar piece, a big ballad such as "Smoke gets in your eyes", "Over the Rainbow", "Georgia", something fairly jazzy.

Which would set the stage for Mary to introduce a vent. puppet, or do a more involved magic piece. Maybe a more uptempo Gospelly song, such as "Lord of the Dance", then either an old-time Country medley, or a fast 12 string guitar instrumental polka, to create the energy needed prior to an intermission. This would all be interspersed with comedy, chat, and general fun for the audience, including at least one song in another language, should we have audience members from different parts of the world.

Not all of our Down South performances were concerts, by any means. We frequently visited the Phoenix Zoo, where we did a modified version of our "Planet Kindness" schools' show, or, if in Tucson, there was a magnificent museum, just for kids. One of our very favourite venues was Golden Village Palms, the largest park in California, at a little town called Hemet, where we would have a packed children's show at the library every time we were in the area. Yuma, on the California/Arizona border, is the largest winter producer of lettuce in North

America, and we would often perform on an outdoor stage for the huge three day "Lettuce Festival", as well as strolling through the crowds, for fun, with banjo and guitar to add ambience. Not only that, but we did schools' performances in Yuma too, as it was so important for us to remain connected with the children's market whilst on tour, and we were grateful to have the opportunity.

Golden Village Palms was a year-round luxury resort, in a perfect location, being a short distance from both the California coast and Palm Springs. There were permanent residents, plus winter visitors from mid-October to mid-April. It had a large main showroom for cabaret-style performances, which could also be arranged into theatre seating, or for dances, all of which were well attended. We started off with our usual shows, but soon saw that the energy level of the audience was such that we felt we should bring in our "British Pub Night", which had been performed so successfully for Arts Councils across Canada, and this would be a whole new slant for the Southern market. Most of the acts at this resort were high-end tribute bands out of Los Angeles, or sometimes the real thing, but there had never been an audience participation show such as we were offering before, and both events co-ordinator Tracie Rodgers, a friend since our first tour, plus ourselves, were certain it would work. Audience members love to see their compatriots doing silly things on stage, and this, together with all our bits of "business" - sing along, comedy, magic, and Mary's ventriloquism, made the night a success to be repeated every year.

Many other venues were also interested, and in a very short space of time we were doing as many, or more "British Pub Nights" as we were our regular shows, and repeating different versions of this annually.

Close to our "home" base of Mesa Dunes, was the large, mostly residential park of Fountain of the Sun", with Activity director Heather Roberts, with whom we keep in touch. It was the same there, with happy crowds every time we brought in the show, and our "British Pub Night" soon went annually to resorts and parks all across southern Arizona and California, so many places, again and again.

We put together a special St. Patrick's Day show, totally Irish, and did 3 or 4 performances of that each year. Mary had a new hard ventriloquist figure of a leprechaun, christened "Sheamus Shenanigan Michael O' Flanagan" that was a hit, plus we were able to feature high energy party songs, a different version of "Danny Boy", and of course Billy O'Brien's "Wi' me shillelagh under me arm", Bill with whom I had worked at Filey, Yorkshire, in earlier days. Plus, the inevitable Irish comedy, beloved by all, and a big finish. Again, many venues over the years. Some resorts insisted on very high-end motorhomes, $300,000 and up, and one St. Patrick's Day show we did in Indio, California, had many motorhomes costing in excess of $1 million to be seen in the sumptuous park.

Before going into Irish shows close to the end of the tour, we would sometimes take a 3 or 4 day break in San Diego, on the California coast, always staying at "Campland on the Bay", right on Mission Bay waterfront. This was a family resort for all ages, unlike the parks in which we had been working, which were mostly 55 +, and it prepared us again for family audiences when we returned to our regular Easter Weekend engagements back in Canada.

It would be early March in San Diego, therefore springlike weather, and we loved being in our favourite waterfront city. We'd visit the quayside, and the "Star of India", the world's oldest operational square-rigger, which I had visited when it was in Bermuda. Also, we toured the vast aircraft carrier "Midway", and so much more, including an unbelievably cramped B-39 Soviet submarine, where one felt so much sympathy for the sailors living under such conditions. There would be a visit to Old Town, with al fresco dining under myriads of lights at Casa de Reyes, plus Mariachi concerts under the stars, daily visits to Dog Beach with Meggie, or maybe a run up the coast to Del Mar for a different atmosphere.

Balboa Park was a must, with its operational Globe Theatre replica, and the huge Spreckels Organ, 5017 pipes in 80 ranks, making it the world's largest outdoor musical instrument, with free concerts regularly. On the occasions we were there, we would listen to and chat with Carol Williams, a brilliant Welsh musician, who was Balboa Park's resident organist for 16 years.

There were several waterfront restaurants, on the quay, at Seaport Village, and also at Pacific Beach, where we had a truly memorable lunch at "The Green Flash", with special friends from Edmonton, Phil and Glynis. We also used to run over to the "Hotel Del Coronado", opened in 1888, and one of the very few remaining wooden resort hotels, with its amazing ambience. Another, but newer, (1927), is the "Prince of Wales", in Waterton, Alberta, by the U.S. border. There are incredible winds in Waterton, and this large hotel is actually anchored to the ground by a huge chain, as it has been known to move.

Incidentally, yes, I have seen the "Green Flash"; not in Canada or the United States, but on a week's break in Puerto Vallarta, Mexico. I had heard of it for many years, especially from sailing friends, and was fortunate to see it from the waterfront, on a perfectly clear, calm day.

Our small break in San Diego would come to an end, and it was time to head back over the mountains into Arizona, where one learns to be careful, especially with a loaded truck and trailer, not to overheat in the hot weather, but mid-March is usually not a problem.

Mary had started off on the southern circuit with a puppet of herself, "MeMe" as her main figure, made for her by Verna Finley, but soon added "Martha McHaggis", crafted by Mary Ann Taylor, who had worked with Verna, and subsequently took Verna's art to a whole new level. Mary Ann gave Mary all kinds of facial features from which to select, and we came up with the absolutely perfect figure of a little old Scottish lady, to be instantly loved by all.

Back at Mesa Dunes, we'd go into our Irish shows, plus a few others, before the long drive home. Our friends Bernie and Red would usually have been based in the park for a while by now, and there would have been many get-togethers after shows, sometimes meeting for supper out, sometimes in one of our trailers, often until 3:00 a.m., mostly talking about music and show-biz. Conversations to which others might not relate, but for those in our walk of life, they mean almost as much as breathing, making these get-togethers among the most memorable parts of every tour.

On our first year in Mesa Dunes, Meggie had met a Bichon Frise, named Ben, who was living a few trailers away, and they became huge buddies. Some months later, we were in our trailer at Pembina Park, about an hour from our home in Alberta, and 2000 miles from Mesa Dunes, when they met up again, with great excitement, and we discovered that Ben's people, Garry and Sophie, with whom we of course became friends, lived only a couple of streets away from us. It truly is a small world, and it often seems that the further you are from home, the more likely you are to meet someone you know, or with whom you might have a connection.

Mesa had several things that, to me, were very special. Firstly, there was my favourite second-hand bookshop on Planet Earth. Large, meticulously arranged, it was possible to think of a subject and walk straight to several books from which to choose. There was a huge section on music, another on performance arts, another on artists, plus excellent biographies, and it was impossible to walk in without coming out clutching a new treasure.

Sometimes we'd go into the old part of Scottsdale, with its amazing bronzes of horses running, at which I could look for ages. We would have an explore around the old wooden storefronts, hear country music coming from the saloon, or just sit on the grass with Meggie, or Jenny in later years, maybe outside at a favourite restaurant, soaking up the ambience.

There was an exceptional pizza place in Mesa that had a huge organ, which came up from under the stage slowly revolving, so that one could see the entire console with its Art Deco styling. Originally built as a theatre organ for the town of Denver in 1927, it was a four manual Wurlitzer, with over 1700 pipes. Not only that, but it was also connected to both a grand and a honky-tonk piano, in addition to drums and a plethora of other instruments, spread over two floors. American and Canadian flags could be lowered from the ceiling, and there was even a little stage recessed into the wall, with some dancing cat puppets. The "house" organists, who could also control the instruments around the room, were highly skilled, and a visit to this, called "OrganStop Pizza", was an absolute must, together with a walk around the outside of the building to view the huge pipes. And yes, they sold pizza and other things, all at reasonable prices. Needless to say, the place was always packed, and it was prudent to avoid the busiest times.

Two acts on the circuit that absolutely need mentioning are "The Calhouns", and "Laughing Bird". I already mentioned Jim Calhoun as being a part of the Rocky Mountain Assn. of Fairs jam sessions, also, along with his wife Chris, being with us at the Texas Fairs Convention in Houston. Jim is a fine guitarist/vocalist from Nebraska, who lives for the music of the 50s and 60s and reproduces them impeccably on an old Harmony Sovereign guitar, with a wall of original audio equipment to produce the authentic sound. He worked for many years with Chris, then with another keyboardist Charlene Cusilito for a couple of years before joining with Melanie Thompson, with whom he performs to this day, and they have all been good friends.

For many years, Jim has been operating a radio station, named "Thunderbolt Radio", which is on the Internet and therefore global in its reach. It has a different "feel" to commercial stations, is well worth a listen, and they have been very supportive of our music, for which we are always grateful.

"Laughing Bird", out of Wyoming, were another talented and very different act. A mix of Folk, Roots Country, and Bluegrass, on many instruments, their act was one of energy and warmth, with the bulk of their music being original compositions about their own lives. Interspersed with much comedy - Janey Wing Kenyon was a prolific spoons player, and her red dress held enough props to fill a small house - we didn't cross paths as much as we would have liked. Tupelo Kenyon, her husband, a fine musician, passed recently, and this book would be sadly lacking were his name not mentioned.

Palm Springs we loved; in fact we love the whole Coachella Valley. We would base in Desert Hot Springs, at Catalina Spa, and do several performances in the area, tailored to fit the varying clientele. If we had some free time, we'd sit outside our favourite coffee bar on Palm Canyon Drive, along with Meggie, or later Jenny, and people watch, or should I say dog watch, as Palm Canyon Drive must be one of the most dog oriented streets on Earth, with water bowls outside most shops and restaurants, and we met many nice folks, with and without dogs, who would stop for a visit.

We'd have a lunch at "Lulu's", where we loved their Vichyssoise, or supper at "Ruby's" 50s diner, with its ubiquitous model railway running around at almost ceiling level, where Dads couldn't get at it! We'd sit outside, especially for the Thursday VillageFest, when stalls were being put up for a memorable evening out. All on the same street, and all dog friendly.

Our base at Catalina Spa was north of the I-10 freeway, and there were several parks and country clubs, golf clubs etc. in the vicinity, many of which we worked. There were some amazing desert hikes in the area - at 1,000 Palms Oasis, also the Agua Caliente Indian Reservation, with its 15-mile Palm Canyon. It was possible to take a day trip to Disneyland from here or from Hemet, which we did once, but preferred to wait until we had the chance to base closer, in Anaheim for a few days, and pick a time when "The Happiest place on Earth" was a little less busy.

We of course would visit Riff Markowitz' "Palm Springs Follies", which ran for 23 seasons until 2014. This amazing production, different each year, featured top-class dancers and other performers, aged between 54 and 84, in a high energy revue, with varying guest stars for a month or two at a time, usually names from the 50s. Riff was a master of Jewish-styled comedy, and frequently left the stage to work the floor in front, to the delight of the mostly senior audience. Ventriloquist Sammy King, with "Francisco", was often in for the season, and we would be so pleased to see him in one of his favourite venues, a theatre always being preferable to a cabaret room.

In some towns, there might be a large, very upmarket park, that would only book you provided you did no other venues in the area. If there was extensive media promotion, either by the park or yourself, this could be worthwhile - or not. We played many big venues, but were also happy to visit a few others, if confronted with this stipulation from an uppity park Activity director.

Depending on the ever-changing date of Easter, our tour would somewhat regretfully, wind down, and we would say goodbye to the beautifully heated swimming pools, the magnificent Sonoran Desert, our many friends, and prepare for the drive home, leaving either from Mesa Dunes, or from Catalina Spa. Our first stop from Mesa was always

"Arizona Charlie's", on the Boulder Highway, close to "Sam's Town" in Las Vegas, that we had discovered after our first season. There was a large casino at "Arizona Charlie's" with showroom, hotel, several restaurants, and a big RV park with, amazingly, private bathrooms, that were a treat after using the trailer, or possibly challenging park facilities, for 3 months. If heading north, we would often winterize here, but sometimes it could wait until we got home. If heading south, we always de-winterized, and checked that all appliances in the trailer were in order.

The long drive North would start generally with great weather, and we of course had favourite stopping-off places and restaurants, as do all of us who spend much of our lives travelling, and need to maintain our sanity. Once past Utah, the weather could change. One time it was mid to late March, on a beautifully sunny day, as most of them are. We had gone over Malad without even noticing, and were heading for the Continental Divide at the top of the long Monida Pass. It was still bright sunshine when we reached the top, but there was suddenly a gentle crosswind blowing over the big snowbanks that appeared by the side of the road, and visibility dropped down to virtually zero. One could just about make out the now oh-so-slow-moving rear lights in front, and hoped the person behind could see yours. It was impossible to stop, as one would be instantly rear-ended, as would also happen if you were to pull onto the hard shoulder.

The Monida Pass in those conditions seems to go on forever, then the highway comes down into the small community of Lima, where there is a popular restaurant, and there were several of us sitting shaking, with much coffee before we could continue our journey. Sometimes the pass is closed, and on more than one occasion heading either way we have had to wait for the signal to leave. There is a motel at Lima, with a campground behind, and I recall the owner coming out to clear us a site with his snowplough, so we could plug in and get some heat. If the pass closes, the people of Lima are amazing. The school gym is opened, and the residents appear with mattresses, blankets, pillows, tea, coffee, anything to make stranded travellers comfortable, or frequently take them into their own homes.

The remainder of the journey was usually uneventful. We would hand in our U.S. work documents at the Canadian border, and continue to Lethbridge, where we would stop in a sometimes snowy campground for the night. Then it was the last leg home, where our welcoming house seemed huge after another long tour.

At the "Winspear" – Patricia Gavreau deLisle, Us, Cynthia Horton

Headlining the British Pavilion at Northlands, Edmonton

"Klondike Days" - Rex Moore, Kennedy Jenson, Us.

FULL CIRCLE

Every few years, we would take a trip back to Britain to catch up with family and friends, intentionally visiting different people each time, apart from a few close family members that we always saw if possible.

It was the year 2017. We went first to Maidstone, where I had lived from age five up to around twenty-two. Just by the bottom of the road where I had once lived there were three houses that had been some time ago joined together and made into a hotel. We'd stayed there before, and it had all the amenities needed, plus good food, and right on my old stomping grounds. A restful sleep was necessary before we got into our various plans, which included showing Mary not only "Kitscot", home of "KPT Productions" when I was little, but also where I had lived in an apartment up the road some years later, plus the walk up "Scrubbs Lane" (which Martin & I called "The Walls"), to my prep. school, and more.

Things could not have been timed better. At the bottom of Bower Mount Road was the Methodist Church Hall in which the "Cherrypips" had played, but on the other side of the main road was a much larger church, St. Michael's, a fairly "high" Anglican Church, with which our family when I was a child had not been connected, mostly because of the incense used, to which we had all seemed to be allergic. (Mary and I went to the Sunday morning service before leaving Maidstone, and I had to leave, for the same reason.) Every Church in Christendom has a different sounding peal of bells, and we arrived from Heathrow airport on a Wednesday evening, when practice was on. In my primary school days, St. Michael's bell practice always seemed to coincide with warm summer evenings, open windows, and Geography homework, which was one of my favourite subjects. I looked at the house where I had once lived, with its much-altered garden, but nothing in my entire life has made me feel that I had come home more than did the sound of those instantly recognisable bells, which I had not heard for so long.

We met up with Cynthia Robertson, as we had on our previous U.K. visit, the three of us having a memorable day at Leeds Castle, where the "Jazz Gentlemen" and also the "Downtown Jazzmen" had played on occasion for Lady Baillie in years gone by. We discussed life in general, especially the era of "Band Seven" and the "Manish Boys", when Cynthia had run the fan club, along with her friend Pam. We talked about the original band members, including Davy Jones, who joined a bit later, and we re-christened David Bowie. Incidentally, the inevitable question that comes to mind is, "Did I in later years ever feel envious of Dave and his successes?", to which the answer is, of course not. His direction was so different to mine; he was determined to be Britain's answer to Elvis Presley, but in my mind, he became much more, in that he created, brilliantly, almost all of his own music, in addition to a spectacular show. I never wanted to be a solo artist, preferring instead to share the stage, and life, with creative equals, playing many styles, in addition to my own. My one and only regret regarding David is that he was taken from us far too soon, and I would like to have known him again in his later years.

As well on this trip, we had the pleasure of staying with Philip and Beryl Charlton; Philip of course being the "Pip" of the "Cherrypips", on tea-chest bass, in that first skiffle group. We were welcomed so very warmly, and not only that, the four of us also had a truly amazing evening visiting Martin and Christine Sharp, yes, the boy on the bike, who had been co-performer and co-producer of all those early shows, as well as being one half of "The Magicalis". This was the first time that Philip, Martin, and I had been together since leaving Hill Place primary school, all those years ago, at the age of twelve.

Then we headed off westwards along the south coast, via Brighton, where the "Jazz Gentlemen" had played at the once sumptuous Royal

Pavilion, built as a seaside pleasure palace for King George IV, and nicknamed the "Onion Palace" for its 19th century Indo-Saracenic style domes. My brother-in-law, Roy, was older, and had some health issues, so we wanted to spend the bulk of our time at the family's Devonshire farm on this trip.

One Sunday, my sister was doing what many families do, and her three children, now grown and with their own families, came for Sunday lunch. One family member was not staying for the meal, so we had a good catch up first, then the rest of us sat down to the table. At one point of the meal, Mary made the comment that this would be the last time that we would all be sitting around the table together, which was so true, as two of the family would be missing in a very short space of time, making the moment very poignant for both of us.

Which seems to me to be as good a place as any to end this story for now, with us, plus my sister, brother-in-law and their extended family, all seated around the big dining table, the same table that had been the one under which my mother, sister, and myself as a tiny baby, would have been "in bed", should my father be called out as part of the local Civil Defence unit, to assist any who might need help during an air raid, in the latter part of World War II. This was also the same huge oak table that had been the stage for "Kitscot Private Theatre", until it had been time to move to larger stages, and audiences. I had truly come Full Circle, in the words of T.S. Eliot, "and known the place for the first time". Mary and I were performing regularly, as much as we wished, doing what we loved. Many of the places we worked were places where we had appeared for fifteen or more years, in one case over twenty-five, (Fort Edmonton Park). They were special places to us, our health was reasonably good, and nothing was likely to slow us down, except maybe a global pandemic, about which so much had been written, both in science fiction and in other articles. It was obviously going to come one day, but whether it would come in our lifetimes, we had no idea.......

"Peter & Mary" with Martha McHaggis – photo Tracy Grabowski, ventriloquist figure by Mary Ann Taylor, M A T Puppets, Virginia.

EPILOGUE

Random thoughts

Selected writings, poetry, and song lyrics

Acknowledgements

Suggested reading

RANDOM THOUGHTS

Notes on the text

I have attempted to write this book using the English and spelling which I knew when young, bearing in mind differences between the spoken and written word, which are so often ignored today. I have hopefully avoided the cardinal sins "can't" or "a lot of", or ending a sentence with a preposition, unless for a very specific reason, such as a quotation. Having said this, I have picked up many expressions through encountering different versions of the English language in various countries over the years, and these have inevitably slipped onto the pages, regardless of traditional grammar, for they are who I am, or have become. I have used exclamation marks, with apologies to F. Scott Fitzgerald, who hated them, for they suited my purpose at the time. As a musician, the sounds of words are frequently more important to me than an exact interpretation, and this may have been found on occasion. My main purpose has been to paint a picture of an era, and I hope this has been partially successful, and enjoyable.

Accolades

I have been often asked what was the greatest accolade I have ever received. There have been several. It could be one of the environmental awards on the mantelpiece, or framed on a wall, it could be in the acknowledgement of a life's work from one's peers, or in the many letters from presenters and audience members over time, most of which

I still have. It could be in a standing ovation mid-performance, but for me, the ultimate was when a young boy, bursting from within, came up to the stage and said to someone more than 60 years older than himself "You Rock!"

Memory

"It was a long time ago, yet it seems like yesterday". Sometimes the brain shuffles the deck of memories and brings a different one to the fore, to be polished and re-evaluated from current perspectives, so very altered from when the memory was actually created, because it is now viewed through the lens of thousands of subsequent experiences. That may have happened with this book.

Reactive or Proactive?

It seems that the human species tends to be reactive rather than proactive, which is why so many issues are not properly faced until after the event, even though we can all see them coming. Climate Change is a classic example, which the human race absolutely refuses to face square on, even though huge differences could be made. I am not one of those who believes that Climate Change is solely the result of human action, but do believe that it is a large contributing factor. Another thing that has that has always concerned me, is that humans mostly believe that Planet Earth exists solely for their purposes, and that everything else, all other species, are to be manipulated at will, instead of thinking of themselves as part of a cohesive whole, where everything interacts in rhythm, and all species are equal, to be treated with respect, no matter where they lie on the evolving ladder of life.

Out of the mouths of babes.....

There was one time when we were driving along the south coast of England and stopped for the night in Bournemouth, where we saw that the brilliant songwriter/actor Kris Kristofferson was doing a rare one man show, which was of course sold out. Two weeks later, we were in Minot, North Dakota, in the U.S., where Mary was tour directing one of three full buses from Edmonton to visit the huge Scandinavian "Hostfest". Amazingly, Kris was on again at this event, so I quickly grabbed a ticket, as I especially wanted to see him work his own songs, just with guitar, as originally written. At the end of the performance, he was chatting about one occasion where he hadn't done his music for a while, and was practising "The Silver-tongued Devil and I", when his young son said, "Dad, that's not a very good song". A little surprised, Kris asked why his son had said that, and the reply was "Because you're blaming someone else for all the things you did wrong!" Kris said he thought about that one for a long time.....

SELECTED WRITINGS
BY PETER

A Summer's Night In Filey

Soft, shimmering night,
Soft and warm.
Myriads of gulls rest o'er the distant sea
Like a carpet of narcissus on a summer's night,
While sleepy crabs shift lazily through
Silent rivulets of sand,
Watching and waiting
For the waves to return and encompass them.

Fishing boats lie idle now,
Dark against the shining sands
Creaking softly to each other of
Times far off – and times to come.

One by one the lights go out
As seabirds snuggle in their nests,
Then, gurgling gently o'er the rocks,
Chattering through the hollowed pools,
Chasing itself, then chuckling quietly in retreat,

Comes the sea
1966

Genesis - Revelation

And so,
From its Mother Earth, came the stream,
Chattering and gurgling
In its new found freedom.
It paused, as if to view its world, then
Rushed
Heedlessly on down the steep valleys,
Collecting branches, twigs and grasses
On its way.

It collided recklessly
With huge boulders;
Laughed,
And plunged on into the Ravine.

Time passed, it grew
And soon was a mighty, rushing torrent,
Tearing down trees;
Ripping apart the rocks;
And carrying its load to cascade
Over the Thundering falls . . .

But it weakened
And grew old;
It moved sluggishly now,
Collecting the silt and mud of time,
Through drowsy marshland
It slowed, and paused;
As though awaiting death;
Then suddenly it was

Huge; engulfed in a
Mesmeric vastness
Of Kaleidoscopic blues and greens;
Twisting and tumbling through its own self
In a sea of ecstasy.

1967

The Soul of the Sixties

Did you go to Haight Ashbury with flowers in your hair?
Can you still hear Woodstock on the sweet morning air?
Did you walk the canals down in Old Amsterdam?
And was Gandalf your hero above every man?

Did you gaze upon Everest from Kathmandu?
Did the peace of the mountains get right inside you?
Did you hear Maharishi? He had something to say
Well, the Soul of the Sixties is reborn today

Were you spellbound by Dylan's Rolling Thunder Revue?
With Baez, The Band, and some other folks too
The Beatles and Donovan had the same thing to say
Well, the Soul of the Sixties is reborn today

(CHORUS)
Well the Soul of the Sixties is reborn today
And we've got a debt that we all must repay
So let's get together and learn how to sing
With the souls of Mahatma and Martin Luther King

Right now this world's hurting like never before
And each day we hurt her just a little bit more
You had some ideals then; now the best you can do
Is all get together and help her pull through

Well I know many folks can't remember that day
So the music's come back just to show you the way
Well there's lots of folks out there tryin' to help her I'm sure
But no matter how old you can do a bit more

(CHORUS)

We've got to clean up the air – and clean up the land
Clean up the oceans; the rocks and the sand
Clean up the rivers, but don't hesitate
For if you start it tomorrow you may be too late

Remember those days; how everyone cared?
How we loved each other, and everything shared?
Remember the peace and the seed that was sown
To respect every life as if it were your own

(CHORUS x 2) + tag

Composed for the first International
Earth Day 1990

People and Species (Reggae)

Ever since this world began
Way before the dawn of man
Dinosaurs all ruled the earth
But they were not the very first
For one hundred million years
Imagine that if you can
Trilobites swam in the seas
No plants, no life on the earth to see

(Chorus) x 2
People and species come and go
What comes next, we'll never know
Everything changing very fast
What we have now won't be the last

Man began in Africa
That's not back so very far
One hundred thousand years is all
And they were not so very tall
They moved around the earth
Establishing their worth
To Australia they went we know
Sixty thousand years ago
(Chorus x 2)
The Mayans are no more
The Incas lost to war
The Roman Empire with its might
Crumbled slowly out of sight
The Phoenicians travelled far

Navigating by a star
The powerful Persian Empire too
And many more gone out of view **(Chorus x 2)**

Our native peoples here
Have seen the north frontier
From Siberia they crossed the snow
Fifty thousand years ago
Itinerant people first
They loved their Mother Earth
But their way of life is going fast
We must preserve their sacred past **(Chorus x 2)**

Now man destroys this Earth
The place that gave us birth
There's greed and pollution everywhere
And mankind doesn't seem to care
See another species go
Every hour, don't you know
Maybe we won't hear the call
Maybe we won't be here at all **(Chorus x 2)**

(The last verse is not included in a children's performance)

Schooldays

At sunup many years ago
Police and Churchmen came
They took the children screaming,
but their screams were all in vain

To residential schools they went
for many lonely years
and none of us could help them
as they dragged them off in tears

That generation's mostly gone
but the wounds still make us ill
They talk of trying to heal us,
but I doubt they ever will

The white man isn't known for truth
we learned that long ago
and the screams of all our children
lie buried in the snow

What did we ever do to them
apart from give our trust?
Now every pointless treaty
lies buried in the dust

They pushed us from our tribal homes
and to our lands laid claim

assimilate, exterminate...
the words sound just the same

Nine agonizing years was spent
away from all we knew;
disease and malnutrition
was the norm for but a few

Eleven cents a day was spent
to keep a child just fed
Our languages were never heard
and half of us lay dead

Don't know if there's an answer
so many years have passed
We try for a solution
perhaps we'll share at last

We try for a solution
with every passing day
but the screams of all the children
will never fade away....

Peter Jansen 2016

LIFE

Life is caring

That's it

Nothing else

Caring about the planet

Caring about all life, not just one species

Caring about one's friends

Caring about those who are not one's friends

No provisos

If you reach the word But, put a full stop before it and erase the word But

Nothing else

So very simple.

Time to think

Love is different.

It is invisible, yet you can see it.

If you are very lucky, you will see it at the moment of your birth.

Or you may give it to another at the moment of their birth.

It weighs nothing, so it is easy to carry in large amounts; in fact it lightens the load of other things you may have to carry through life.

It is the only thing in life that, if you give it away, there will be more of It left than when you started, and it will grow every time you give.

Yet, if you do not give of it, be careful, for what you have could shrink, and one day be very hard to find at all.

Fortunately, this probably will never happen, for it is given to you in so many ways – a lovingly prepared plate of food, a beautiful poem, the smile of a complete stranger, the lick from a new puppy, a piece of music, or the gift of a cool drink on a hot day.

Read this, and you are being given some, even now …

We're all the same

We are all the same
Black or White or Brown
We all can feel the pain
When others put us down
If only we could make them see
The way we are is meant to be
We all need treating equally
We're all the same

We are all the same
No matter how we speak
Be it Inuit or Blackfoot
Be it Japanese or Greek
If only we could learn to see
The way we are is meant to be
We all need treating equally
We're all the same
(Jazz Solo)

We are all the same
No matter whom we love
We're all part of the tapestry
That's sent from up above
A rich mosaic of people
of which each of us is one
We all need treating equally
Forgetting none

We are all the same
Be it young or be it old
If we listen to each other
What stories can unfold
If each of us could learn to see
The way we are was meant to be
And treat each other equally
We're all the same

Music by Peter Jansen

Evening Thoughts

What did I do today to serve a purpose?
Did I help another soul along the way?
Was I kind in all I said?
Or did I complain instead?
Did I bring a smile to anybody's day?

Did I write some words to try and make a difference?
Did I try to tread more gently on the Earth?
Did I create a song
That you might sing along?
Did I make another roll around in mirth?

Did I do anything to help my neighbour?
Did I greet a stranger with a warm hello?
Did I console a friend?
Or a caring hand extend?
Did I call someone from many years ago?

Did I show respect to every living creature?
Did I give only love and never pain?
If I didn't, I must do it all tomorrow,
If I did, then I must do it all again

Music and lyrics by Peter Jansen

ACKNOWLEDGEMENTS

To write an autobiography it is necessary to relive the life in question, and I have done just that. Mary and I have spent many hundreds of hours talking about our amazing career together, and checking thousands of contracts to make sure that facts were straight, for which I shall be eternally grateful. Many people have been mentioned in the book, but I must acknowledge the efforts of Sandi Sawchyn, who has spent so much time typing, and re-typing, when I felt things were not coming off the page as intended. Also, to jazz singer Cindy McLeod, who has helped administer our website over many years, thank you again. Not mentioned in the book are others who also made a difference:

Tim Marriott, Sophia Maher, Joan Fitzpatrick, Shawn Buchanan, Jaclyn Landry, Charlene Roche, Teresa Ryan, Maura Penn, Lacey Huculak, and Janet Tryhuba (all from Fort Edmonton Park), Dean Tichel (from the Valley Zoo), Ellen Finn, Barry Sawchuk, Laine Lunde, Shelley Cornfield, (from the City of Edmonton), and Gord Ganser (from Edmonton Transit). Many media people, especially Eve Noga, from Global T.V., who was so supportive during our Earth Day years; plus, in addition Floyd Murphy, (Edmonton Queen), and Joe Nugent, whose help and friendship in our early Maritime years was invaluable. I am also of course grateful to the many musical friends and associates who have encouraged me along the way with the writing of this book, especially Robert and Leah Toma, plus Jim and Donna Poirier. Acknowledgement must as well go to Peter Heyes, who 'proofed' the book concurrently with me, along with others mentioned earlier.

Last, but by no means least, I must mention our three dogs, firstly Ben, then Meggie, and currently Jenny, who have kept Mary and I sane during many thousands of miles of touring, as well as when at home, filling our lives with unconditional love, as we have hopefully done for them.

SUGGESTED READING

British Popular Music, Musicals, and Jazz

Eddie Rogers. *Tin Pan Alley*. Robert Hale.
George Melly. *Owning Up*. Penguin.
Ian Whitcomb. *After The Ball*. Simon and Schuster.
Ken Colyer. *When Dreams are in the Dust*. Ken Colyer Trust.
Kitty Grime. *Jazz at Ronnie Scott's*. Robert Hale.
    (Reference book, quotes from everybody)
Many Contributors, *The Entertainers*. Pitman House.
    (Mostly U.K. reference book)
Patrick Humphries. *Lonnie Donegan and the birth of British Rock 'n' Roll*. Robson
Brian Bird. *Skiffle*. Robert Hale
    Various groups
Simon Philo. *British Invasion*. Rowman & Littlefield
Alison Pressley. *The 50s & 60s (The best of times)*. Michael O'Mara Books Ltd.
Cole Lesley. *Remembered Laughter (Biography of Noel Coward)*. Knopf

American Popular Music, Musicals, and Jazz

Thomas Brothers. *Louis Armstrong's New Orleans*. W.W. Norton
Ted Antony. *Chasing the Rising Sun*. Simon and Schuster
Douglas B. Green. *Country Roots*. Hawthorn
David Leopold. *Irving Berlin's Show Business*. Harry W. Abrams Inc.
Alan Jay Lerner. *The Musical Theatre*. Collins
Marni Nixon. *I Could Have Sung all Night*. Billboard Books
Kent Hartman. *The Wrecking Crew*. Thomas Dunne

Colonialism

(Canada and U.S.A.)
Thomas King. *The Inconvenient Indian*. Penguin Random House
Geronimo. *Geronimo – My Life*. Dover
(Kenya)
Caroline Elkins. *Imperial Reckoning (Pulitzer Prize)*. Henry Holt and Co. New York
(Australia)
Robert Hughes. *The Fatal Shore*. Vintage Books (Random House)

Show-Biz Fiction

J. B. Priestley, *The Good Companions*. William Heinemann
J.B. Priestley, *Lost Empires*. Grafton
Marina Endicott, *The Little Shadows*. Doubleday Canada
Elizabeth Renzetti, *Based on a true story*, Anansi

Life after Death

John G. Fuller. *The Airmen who would not die*. Souvenir Press

Other

Dylan Thomas. *Collected Stories*. Everyman
Andrew Sinclair. *Dylan Thomas (No man more magical)*. Holt, Rinehart, Winston

*Some of these are out of print, but still available on E-bay

RECORDINGS

THE JAZZ GENTLEMEN
(No longer available) Swingin' the Blues; Marching through Georgia; St. Louis Blues; Trouble in mind; All of me/Who's sorry now?; Charleston; St. James Infirmary; I can't give you anything but love; When you're smiling; Mamma don't allow.

BAND SEVEN
(No longer available) Shishkebab; Manhattan Spiritual; Some other guy; Where have all the flowers gone?

PETER, JAN & JON
Mountain Boy (HMV); I'm lookin' out (HMV); There's a new land coming (no longer available); Wabash Cannonball (no longer available);

PETER & ELISABETH
I like the Wintertime (no longer available)

LONDON COUNTRY
(no longer available) Wreck of the Old '97; If I were a carpenter; Cryin' time; John B.; The three bells; Green, green

TWO SIDES OF PETER JANSEN
(Sam Cat records, not available at present) Top of the World; Me and Bobby McGee; Kentucky Woman; For the good times; Early morning rain; Take me home, Country roads; Bermuda is another World; Yellow Bird; I like the Wintertime; You are the sunshine of my life; Delta Dawn

PETER & MARY and friends
(Sam Cat records, not available at present) Turn on the Sun; Walk on out of my mind; Wild mountain thyme; Russian medley; My elusive dreams; Listen to the rain; Shake the dust; Fernando; Back in Bermuda; You needed me; Lord of the Dance

SWEET ROCKY MOUNTAINS

(Sam cat records, available on CD and reissued on vinyl). Sweet Rocky Mountains; Old age pensioner; Twelve bar blues; Yesterday the leaves began to fall; Here's to the flyers; Dedicatio; Willie's song; Payin' our dues; Goin' back to Jasper (6060); Sadie; I need a lady; Milenna de San Christobel; If you got the food (an' I got the beer)

OVER 'OME

(Sam cat records, not available at present) Over 'Ome; Bye Bye Blackbird; Whispering; A Nightingale sang in Berkley Square; When I'm cleaning windows/Leaning on a lampost; I'm gonna sit right down and write myself a letter; The Marrow Song; Bye Bye Blues; Danny Boy; White Cliffs of Dover/We'll meet again

FLYING HIGH FOR KIDS

Kindness (for you and me); Animals in the City; Make every day Earth Day; Reduce, Reuse, Recycle; Jambo, Jambo, Jambo; Fort Edmonton Park; Nature Sings; Flyin' in my rocket; Tread a little lighter; Things that go bump in the night

REFLECTIONS

(Sam cat records, available on CD) Lord of the Dance; Turn on the Sun; A Nightingale sang in Berkley Square; Early morning rain; Bye, Bye Blackbird; Whispering; Me and Bobbie McGee; You needed me; Bye Bye Blues; Kentucky Woman; Wild Mountain Tyme; back in Bermuda; Russian medley; Listen to the Rain; For the good times.

The End

Photo: Tracy Grabowski

PageMaster Store
https://pagemasterpublishing.ca/by/peter-jansen/

To order more copies of this book, find books by other
Canadian authors, or make inquiries about publishing
your own book, contact PageMaster at:

PageMaster Publication Services Inc.
11340-120 Street, Edmonton, AB T5G 0W5, Canada
books@pagemaster.ca
780-425-9303

catalogue and e-commerce store
PageMasterPublishing.ca/Shop

www.ingramcontent.com/pod-product-compliance
Lightning Source LLC
Chambersburg PA
CBHW071655170426
43195CB00039B/2201